Coaching
BASKETBALL

Jerry Krause, Editor

MASTERS PRESS

A Division of Howard W. Sams & Company

Published by Masters Press
(A Division of Howard W. Sams & Company)
2647 Waterfront Pkwy. E. Drive, Suite 100
Indianapolis, IN 46214

© 1994 Masters Press

Published 1994

97 98 99   10 9 8 7 6

Printed in the United States of America

Library of Congress Cataloging-in-Publication Data

Coaching Basketball: the complete coaching guide of the National Association of Basketball Coaches / edited by Jerry Krause. -- [2nd ed.]
      p.   cm.
    Includes bibliographical references.
    ISBN: 0-940279-86-X
    1. Basketball -- Coaching -- United States. 2. National Association of Basketball Coaches of the United States. I. Krause, Jerry. II. National Association of Basketball Coaches of the United States.

Credits:
Cover design by Sara Wright
Cover photos by Brian Spurlock
Diagrams by Julie Biddle
Edited by Jon Glesing, Holly Kondras and Mark Montieth

TABLE OF CONTENTS

CONTRIBUTORS

Forrest C. "Phog" Allen: An influential basketball figure, Allen was co-founder of the NABC and its first president. He is considered the first great basketball coach. His teams at the University of Kansas won three national titles and 771 games.

Sonny Allen: Allen popularized the modern numbered fast break system while at Old Dominion, Southern Methodist, and Nevada–Reno. His team won the Division II national title in 1975, and he was named National Coach of the Year.

Tom Barrise: Barrise has been an assistant coach at East Carolina University since 1986, with previous experience at Jacksonville, William Patterson, and Fairleigh Dickinson.

Clair Bee: A Hall of Fame member, Bee wrote children's fiction as well as technical basketball books. He coached for 29 years at Rider College and Long Island University. Bee originated the three-second rule and the 1-3-1 zone defense.

John Beecroft: Beecroft formerly coached at the University of Delaware.

Jim Brandenburg: Brandenburg won conference championships at Montana and Wyoming and coached the Gold Medal West team in the 1982-83 U.S. Sports Festival. Jim's teams were noted for their aggressiveness, strong inside play, and zone offensive play.

Steve Brennan: A former high school and college coach in Nebraska, Steve directs his own sports psychology consulting firm, Peak Performance, Inc. in Omaha. Steve is also co-author of The Basketball Resource Guide.

Charles Brock: Brock is the successful head coach at Trinity (Texas) College.

Bob Broeg: A longtime sportswriter, Broeg was highly respected in his profession.

Dale Brown: In his 21 seasons at Louisiana State University, Brown has taken the Tigers to 15 consecutive non-losing seasons, 14 straight post-season tournament bids, and two Final Four appearances (1981 and 1986). He has won many coaching honors, and no coach in LSU history has coached more consecutive games — more than 600.

Hubie Brown: Brown coached the Kentucky Colonels to the ABA championship in 1975 and later coached the Atlanta Hawks and New York Knicks in the NBA. He is respected for his intensity and strategic knowledge.

Larry Brown: Brown played on the 1964 U.S. Olympic gold medal team, and distinguished himself as a professional player. He has coached six pro teams and at two colleges, enjoying great success at each stop. His UCLA team reached the Final Four in 1980 and his University of Kansas team won the national title in 1988. He now coaches the Indiana Pacers of the NBA.

John Bunn: Basketball Hall of Famer John Bunn began his coaching career as an assistant to Forrest C. "Phog" Allen at Kansas. He had a 25-year career at Stanford, Springfield, and Colorado State College. The author of numerous books on basketball, Bunn was rules interpreter for eight years (1959-1967), and became the first executive director of the Basketball Federation in 1965.

Bradley Cardinal: Formerly the fitness center director at Eastern Washington University, Cardinal has extensive experience developing conditioning programs for athletes.

H.C. "Doc" Carlson: Carlson is a Hall of Fame member who coached at Pittsburgh for 31 years. Known for his invention of the "figure 8" offense, he led Pittsburgh teams to national championships in 1928 (undefeated) and 1930. Carlson held an M.D. degree and served as NABC president in 1937.

Lou Carnesecca: Carnesecca coached at the high school, college, and pro levels for more than 40 years and won more than 800 games. He was head coach of the St. John's Redmen for 24 years, compiling more than 500 wins. Carnesecca took all 24 of his St. John's teams to post-season play, and his 1985 team advanced to the Final Four.

Jim Casciano: Casciano coaches at Radford University.

Don Casey: Temple University coach for nine seasons before becoming a pro assistant, Casey is a zone defensive specialist.

Jim Conn: Conn coached high school basketball in the state of Washington as well as at Eastern Washington University, and became a prolific writer and sports law expert.

Bobby Cremins: Cremins has been named National Coach of the Year twice at Georgia Tech, where he made nine straight NCAA appearances and reached the Final Four in 1990. Previously, he won three titles at Appalachian. His teams are known for their exciting, uptempo brand of play.

Denny Crum: Crum has coached at Louisville since 1971 and directed the 1980 and 1986 teams to the NCAA championship. Before going to Louisville, he played and coached at UCLA under John Wooden. Crum is noted for his calm game demeanor and his team's uptempo style of play.

Chuck Daly: Formerly the coach of the two-time NBA champion Detroit Pistons and now coach of the New Jersey Nets, Daly also was a long-time coach at the University of Pennsylvania, where his teams won four Ivy League titles and three Big Five championships. He also coached at Boston College and was assistant coach at Duke University. He is well known for his organizational skills and his ability to relate well to players. Chuck coached the "Dream Team" to the 1992 Olympic title.

Everett Dean: Dean is a Basketball Hall of Famer who played and coached at Indiana University (15 years) as well as Carleton College (one year) and Stanford (18 years). His Stanford team won the NCAA title in 1942. Dean, who passed away in 1993, was known as one of the finest gentlemen in the coaching ranks.

Bruce Drake: This Oklahoma Sooner coach spent 16 years at his alma mater while winning six titles. He created the "Drake Shuffle" offense and led rules makers to establish goaltending while serving as chairman of the National Rules Committee from 1951 to 1955. He is a member of the Basketball Hall of Fame.

Don Eddy: Eddy's 20-year college coaching career included eight trips to the NCAA Division II national playoffs. He was best known for his teaching ability as he carried out coaching tours at Eastern Illinois, East Tennessee, and Texas-San Antonio.

George Edwards: Edwards is a former basketball coach at the University of Missouri and one of the founding members of the National Association of Basketball Coaches.

Dave Farrar: This national junior college NCAA champion coach at Hutchinson Community College, Kansas, is well known for his strong mental approach to the game.

Steve Fisher: Fisher led the University of Michigan to its first-ever national title in 1989 after taking over as interim head coach two days before the first-round game in the NCAA tournament. A week after winning the tournament, Fisher was named head coach. Before taking over the head coaching job, Fisher was an assistant at Michigan and at Western Michigan University.

Bill Foster: Foster's last coaching posts were at Clemson and Miami (Florida). He developed a "delay" offense called the "Tiger Pause."

Don Frank: Frank coaches at Rancho Santiago High School in California.

Clarence 'Big House" Gaines: America's winningest all-time coach with more than 800 wins, Gaines's Winston-Salem team won the NCAA College Division title in 1967. "Big House" was elected to the Hall of Fame in 1981 and was NABC president in 1989.

Mike Gentry: Gentry has been the director of East Carolina University's strength and conditioning program for eight years.

Bill Green: A legend in Indiana high school basketball, Green's state champion Marion teams have built their success around the match-up zone defense.

C. Eric Gronbech: Gronbech is a professor at Chicago State University.

Joe B. Hall: Hall won the national title at Kentucky in 1978 when he was National Coach of the Year. Hall also coached in high school and at Regis and Central Missouri and was one of the early proponents of strength conditioning and "big men" development.

Bob Hallberg: A native Chicagoan, Bob has been a championship coach at the high school and collegiate levels. He has completed 17 seasons at the University of Illinois–Chicago.

Marv Harshman: Harshman's 40-year coaching career includes 642 victories at Pacific Lutheran, Washington State, and Washington. He was voted 1985 Coach of the Year and was NABC president before being inducted into the Hall of Fame in 1984. Harshman's teams were known for their team offense.

Jack Hartman: Hartman was head coach at Kansas State University from 1971 to 1986 and before that at Southern Illinois. Known as a developer of underdog teams, this 1981 National Coach of the Year coached for 37 years. He coached Coffeyville, Kansas, to the national title in 1962 with a 32-0 record. He won the NIT at Southern Illinois, led Kansas State to three Big Eight championships, and won the Pan American gold medal in 1983.

Don Haskins: The 1993-94 season marks Don Haskins' 33rd year as head coach at the University of Texas at El Paso (UTEP). In 1966, his team finished the year with a 28-1 record and won the NCAA championship by beating Kentucky.

Dan Hayes: This championship coach has spent most of his career in New Mexico and Oklahoma, but served two years at Eastern Washington. An excellent teacher of fundamentals, especially shooting, Hays now coaches at Oklahoma Christian University.

Jerry Healy: Healy is the publicity director for the Naismith Basketball Hall of Fame.

Jud Heathcote: Heathcote has been the head coach at Michigan State University since 1976. His teams won the NCAA championship in 1979 and Big Ten titles in 1978, 1979, and 1990. Heathcote, the winningest coach at MSU, was selected National Coach of the Year in 1979. He also won conference championships at Montana and coached at Washington State University. Heathcote's teams feature a running attack, disciplined offense, and his popular match-up defense.

E.S. "Eddie" Hickey: A member of the Hall of Fame, Hickey had a 35-year coaching career at Creighton, St. Louis, and Marquette. Hickey was a prolific writer and contributed to basketball through research and clinics. His teams won seven Missouri Valley titles and were NIT champions in 1948.

Ed Hickox: Hickox coached for 40 years. He was the first executive secretary of the NABC, was its president for two years, was a member of the rules committee, and was its historian for 20 years. He served as the first executive secretary of the Naismith Memorial Basketball Hall of Fame.

Nat Holman: A Hall of Famer and a member of the Original Celtics, Holman coached his entire career at City College of New York (41 years), where his team won both the NIT and NCAA titles in 1950.

Bailey Howell: A legendary collegiate player at Mississippi State in the late 1950s, Howell had a long professional playing career at Boston and Philadelphia. A forward, Bailey was noted for his rebounding.

George Ireland: Ireland coached at Loyola of Chicago for 24 years. His 1963 team won the national championship, winning its five tournament games by an average of 23 points, the second-largest average victory margin of all NCAA champions.

Bill Jones: Jones was the head coach at the University of North Alabama from 1975 to 1988 and compiled a 259-141 record that included six NCAA tourney appearances, four Final Fours, and a Division II national title in 1979. He served on the Basketball Rules Committee from 1984 to 1990. He is now the athletic director at North Alabama.

Alvin "Doggie" Julian: A Hall-of-Fame member and former NABC President, Julian coached for 41 years. His Holy Cross team won the NCAA Tournament in 1947. He later coached the Boston Celtics for two seasons before returning to the college ranks with Dartmouth, where he coached from 1951-'67.

Yvan Kelly: Kelly is a former assistant at Auburn University.

John Kimble: Kimble coaches at Crestview High School in Florida.

Bob Knight: Knight has been a head coach for 29 seasons, the last 22 at Indiana University. He has won 11 Big Ten titles, three NCAA championships, and an NIT title. The Big Ten's winningest coach, he led U.S. teams to Pan Am gold in 1979 and an Olympic gold medal in 1984.

Jerry Krause: Krause has a 34-year coaching career at elementary, secondary, college, and Olympic development levels. Krause has served for 26 years as research chairman of the NABC. He also has served as president of the NAIA Basketball Coaches Association and on the Board of Directors of the NABC. He is a past member (for 10 years) and chairman of the NCAA Basketball Rules Committee.

Mike Krzyzewski: One of the most respected men in the profession, Kyzyzewski got his start as the head coach at Army. He took over at Duke in 1980 and guided the Blue Devils to the Final Four six times in seven years from 1986-'92, and won national championships in 1991 and '92.

Mike Kunstadt: Kunstadt coaches at Irving High School in Dallas, Texas.

Harry Larrabee: Currently coaching at the University of Alaska, Anchorage, Larrabee has coached two league champion teams. His 17-year tenure also includes a stop at Southwest Texas.

Bill Leatherman: Leatherman has been a successful coach at Bridgewater (Mass.) for six years, where his teams are noted for rebounding and defense. His 25-year career includes an NCAA tournament team in 1988.

Rick Majerus: One of the nation's most successful college coaches, Majerus now works at the University of Utah. He was a long-time assistant and head coach at Marquette and led Ball State to a Mid-American Conference title and NCAA berth.

Greg Marshall: Marshall has coached 13 seasons at Christ College in Irvine, Calif.

Rollie Massimino: This emotional coach gained renown at Villanova when his 1985 team played the "perfect game" to upset Georgetown and win the national title. Massimino coached high school (13 years) and college (21 years) basketball at SUNY-Stony Brook, Pennsylvania, and Villanova before moving to UNLV in 1992.

Branch McCracken: Elected as a college player to the Hall of Fame, McCracken went on to become a great coach at Indiana, winning four Big Ten titles and two NCAA championships, in 1940 and 1953.

Al McGuire: McGuire coached at Marquette University from 1964 to 1977, winning the national title in his final season and finishing with a 295-80 record. He also won the NIT in 1970 and was a two-time national Coach of the Year. The New York city native also coached at Belmont Abbey College, compiling a 109-64 record. A popular TV analyst. McGuire played at St. John's University and in the NBA with the Knicks (1951-52) and the Baltimore Bullets (1954).

Frank McGuire: A Hall of Famer, McGuire is the only coach to win 100 games at three colleges: St. John's, North Carolina, and South Carolina. His 1957 North Carolina national champions went undefeated. He was named National Coach of the Year three times.

John McLendon, Jr.: Elected to the Hall of Fame as a contributor, McClendon coached college, AAU, and professional teams. His many coaching stops included Tennessee State, where his teams won three consecutive NAIA national titles. He was known as a disciplined, fast-break coach.

Don Meyer: NAIA national champion coach in 1985-86 at David Lipscomb University (Tennessee), Don is renowned for his disciplined, team-oriented approach to basketball. Lipscomb has averaged more than 20 wins per season and set the national record for most wins in a season (38 in 1989-90) during Meyer's 18-year tenure.

Ray Meyer: Elected to the Hall of Fame in 1978, this former Notre Dame player became DePaul's coach in 1942 and won 724 games in 42 years. His team won the NIT in 1943 and he was named Coach of the Year in 1978. He coached one of the first great centers in the game, George Mikan.

Vinnie Mili: Mili serves as high school coach at Cambridge and Latin in Massachusetts.

Ralph Miller: Miller was the winningest NCAA Division I coach with 674 victories when he retired in 1989. This Hall of Fame member coached 38 years at Wichita State, Iowa, and Oregon State (19 years), winning conference championships in three leagues.

James Naismith: Dr. Naismith invented the game of basketball in 1891 in Springfield, Massachusetts. Dr. Naismith was a minister, doctor, educator, physical education teacher, and basketball coach.

Pete Newell: A Hall of Famer, Newell was the first coach to win the "triple crown" of coaching: the NIT, NCAA, and the Olympics. Newell won the NIT with San Francisco and the NCAA with California, and an Olympic gold medal in 1960. He also has won wide respect as an administrator and teacher.

C.M. Newton: Active and respected in collegiate basketball circles, Newton coached at Transylvania, the University of Alabama, and Vanderbilt University. He retired from coaching to become athletic director at his alma mater, the University of Kentucky. Newton currently heads USA Basketball.

Robert J. Nichols: Nichols was a long-time coach at Toledo University, where his teams were known for their sound fundamentals and team play.

Joe O'Brien: The present executive director of the Naismith Basketball Hall of Fame, O'Brien had outstanding teams at NCAA Division II Assumption College. He also served as NABC president.

Lute Olson: The coach at Arizona since 1984, Olson also built two other programs – Long Beach and Iowa – into national powers. Olson also coached high school basketball for 11 years and led Long Beach City College to the 1971 state juco crown. His 34-year career includes 1980 and 1988 selections as National Coach of the Year.

Chip Parsley: Parsley coaches at Tarkio College (Missouri), after coming from St. Paul's College (Missouri), where he earned four consecutive conference titles. At Tarkio, his teams have posted consecutive District Playoff appearances.

Tom Penders: Penders played baseball and basketball at the University of Connecticut and led the basketball team to NCAA Tournament berths in 1965 and 1967 and the baseball team to the 1965 College World Series. Before entering coaching, he was a third baseman in the Cleveland Indians' farm system. He coached at Tufts (1971-74), Columbia (1974-78), Fordham (1978-86), and Rhode Island (1986-88) before taking over at the University of Texas in 1988.

Garland Pinholster: This long-time Oglethorpe coach popularized the "wheel" offense and wrote many basketball books and articles.

Rick Pitino: Pitino has made a career of rebuilding basketball programs, both at the collegiate and professional levels. He served as an assistant coach at both Syracuse and Hawaii before taking over Boston University's program in 1978, at the age of 25. He was an assistant coach for the New York Knicks under Hubie Brown for two seasons (1983-

85), became head coach at Providence College in 1985, head coach of the New York Knicks in 1987, and head coach at the University of Kentucky in 1989.

Bud Presley: This legendary California coach won a state juco championship at Menlo, and has coached at Gonzaga, Santa Anna, and UNLV. His teams played a disciplined style with pressure man-to-man defense.

George Raveling: Raveling has been the head coach at Washington State, Iowa, and the University of Southern California. Considered an outstanding recruiter, he is renowned for his promotional skills and is a leader in collegiate basketball circles, serving on the NABC Board of Directors.

Adolph Rupp: The famous "man in the brown suit" played on the 1924 NCAA champion Kansas team and won four NCAA titles and one NIT title whle coaching at the University of Kentucky. Rupp is the winningest college coach of all time with 875 victories.

Dr. Alvin A. Saake: Formerly a coach at the University of Hawaii, Saake has been a productive contributor to the NABC Bulletin.

George Sage: Sage coached at Pomona College (California) and the University of Northern Colorado. He was NABC Research Committee chairman from 1964 to 1967 and retired to become a writer in the area of the psychosocial foundations of coaching.

J. Dallas Shirley: One of two basketball referees elected to the Hall of Fame, Shirley has devoted a lifetime to officiating and the development of rules.

Kevin Sivils: Sivils is head coach at Runnels High School in Louisiana.

Dean Smith: A Hall of Fame coach, Smith played for Forrest Allen at Kansas and coached at the Air Force Academy and North Carolina. Smith has won the NIT (1979) and NCAA tournaments (1982 and '93), as well as the Olympics (1976). He served as NABC President in 1981-82 and is highly respected for his integrity.

Sonny Smith: Smith has coached at Auburn and Virginia Commonwealth.

Norm Stewart: Another Hank Iba disciple, Stewart's 27 years at Missouri have made him the winningest coach in school history. His team won the conference championship with an undefeated record in 1994. Stewart also has coached at Northern Iowa.

Ken Swalgin: Coach at Penn State University–York, Ken has been active in NABC research.

Jerry Tarkanian: Tarkanian coached UNLV from 1973 to 1992 and led his team to the NCAA championship in 1990. Tarkanian also coached at Long Beach State from 1968 to 1973. He compiled a .823 winning percentage as a college coach.

Dick Tarrant: Formerly the head coach at the University of Richmond, Tarrant began his collegiate coaching career at Fordham University, his alma mater, where he served as assistant coach from 1965 to 1969. Taking over Richmond's program in 1981, his teams appeared in four NCAA Tournaments and three NIT Tournaments. They upset Syracuse and Indiana in the NCAA Tournament.

Fred Taylor: Elected as a Hall of Fame coach in 1986, Taylor played and coached at Ohio State. His 18 years as head coach there included an NCAA title in 1960. He was twice named Coach of the Year, and also served as NABC President.

John Thompson: Thompson was named head coach at Georgetown in 1972 and established a modern juggernaut. He has led his team to a national championship, three Final Four appearances, six Big East Tournament championships, four Big East conference regular season championships, and 13 NCAA Tournament appearances. His teams are noted for their full-court defense and up-tempo play.

Jim Valvano: This passionate coach won a national championship at North Carolina State in 1983 after taking Iona College to the NCAAs prior to that. He was a television sports commentator before losing a courageous battle with cancer in 1993.

Jim Wasem: A longtime basketball coach and baseball coach at Monmouth, Northwest Missouri, and Eastern Washington, Wasem is a recognized expert in sports law.

Jerry Welsh: Welsh's teams at Potsdam State College (N.Y.) were renowned at the NCAA Division III level, where they won three NCAA championships. Now the coach at Iona College, his teams feature multiple pressing defenses and the fast break.

Paul Westhead: Westhead coached the Los Angeles Lakers to the NBA championship in 1980. He also coached the Denver Nuggets in the NBA, and gained fame as the coach at Loyola-Marymount, where his teams led the nation in scoring. He is now the coach at George Mason. His background is the Philadelphia basketball hotbed.

Dennis Wills: Wills is the assistant athletic director and athletic academic advisor at Chicago State University.

Fred "Tex" Winter: Winter was head coach at Kansas State from 1954 to 1968. His teams made six trips to the NCAA Tournament, and two teams made it to the Final Four. Winter also has coached at the University of Washington, the NBA's Houston Rockets, Long Beach State, and Louisiana State. He's now an assistant with the Chicago Bulls.

Hal Wissel: Wissel has coached college and professional basketball, where he is known for his strong emphasis on basketball basics.

John Wooden: Wooden achieved rare Hall of Fame election as both a player and coach. A three-time All-American at Purdue University, he coached high school teams in Dayton, Ky. and South Bend, Ind. before taking over at Indiana State University. He became head coach at UCLA in 1948 and built the most dominant program in the history of college basketball. His teams won 10 NCAA Tournament titles, seven of them in a row, and also won 88 consecutive games.

Phil Woolpert: Woolpert, a pioneer in recruiting black players to mainstream colleges, coached the University of San Francisco to national championships in 1955 and '56. He later served as athletic director and basketball coach at the University of San Diego from 1963 to 1972.

Morgan Wootten: Another legendary high school championship coach, Wootten has spent his career at DeMatha High School in Maryland. His teams are noteworthy for their fundamentals and balance, while his program has become a veritable college player pipeline.

PREFACE
....

"A promise kept, a dream come true."

The National Association of Basketball Coaches (NABC), as the leading professional organization for basketball coaches at all levels in the United States, is charged with promoting and improving the sport of basketball. One tool used in that process was the Basketball Bulletin, the quarterly publication of the NABC. This professional magazine has been in existence continually since May 1933, over 60 years.

Even though the Bulletin is distributed worldwide, its audience consists primarily of NABC member coaches. Contributing authors range from beginning coaches to the legends of the game, members of the Basketball Hall of Fame. Up to this time, this information has been unavailable to all basketball coaches. No more!

As research chairman for the NABC for the past 26 years, I have gained the unique perspective of viewing a truly American team sport that has gained worldwide acceptance. As we passed the 100th anniversary of basketball in 1991, it seemed especially important to commemorate that occasion with a basketball coaching book representing the game at all levels and with the best of the coaching articles from the NABC Bulletin.

In the summer of 1989, the NABC Board of Directors commissioned me to undertake this enormous task and develop a 100th anniversary coaching edition.

James Naismith, the inventor of basketball, said, "I seek to leave the world a little better than I found it." As editor, I picked up this basketball torch to keep the Naismith promise to make the basketball world a little better with this coaching compilation.

This "dream come true" for me was carried out around the theme of championship coaches. I was able to compile a comprehensive basketball coaching book using the concepts and ideas from the total spectrum of coaching. Most of the NCAA Division I champion coaches are represented, from the "Tall Timbers" Oregon coach Howard Hobson in 1939 to Cinderella coach Steve Fisher of Michigan (1989) and current championship coach Dean Smith. Champion coaches are represented as well from the Olympic, professional, NCAA Division II and Division III, NAIA, community college, and high school ranks. In addition, more than 30 Basketball Hall of Fame members contributed articles. Finally, as editor I have filled in the gaps and completed the roster with personal articles or outstanding works from other coaches who might be relative unknowns or future legends. A truth I have found is that the seed of a great idea may spring forth anywhere.

For me, this indeed was a "dream come true." To bring together this collection of basketball coaching concepts has been another opportunity to give something back to the sport that has meant so much to me. I am pleased with the results – it was a unique contribution to the celebrations of basketball "breaking 100." More than 50 years of contributions from NABC coaches were, for the first time, organized into a comprehensive coaching book that promises to be a classic. I hope you find it as valuable in your coaching career as I found the process of poring through the 57 years of materials. What a trip!

The 100th Anniversary edition of *Coaching Basketball* was an unqualified success, with a first edition sellout. As a comprehensive coaching reference from a historical perspective, it developed a huge following from basketball coaches, young and old. In fact, it has become the "gold standard" for basketball coaching textbooks in colleges and universities. What better reference than one that covers all aspects of coaching from many masters of the game?

The second edition of *Coaching Basketball* has been improved in many areas: Some of the articles with less practical application have been deleted, but many have been added — including an original article one by Duke Coach Mike Krzyzewski — to provide a more well-rounded reference book.

In addition, all the diagrams have been redrawn by another expert, coach John Kimble, who is a coaching diagram perfectionist.

This re-visitation to *Coaching Basketball* is an opportunity to reaffirm, evaluate, replace, and expand upon the first edition. Whether you are a beginning coach or an experienced veteran, I believe you will enjoy this revised and improved version of a classis. Come with me to visit basketball history with the coaches who made that history.

JERRY KRAUSE,
Cheney, Washington

ACKNOWLEDGEMENTS

This book is dedicated to those who have influenced my basketball life:

♦ George Sage, my teaching and coaching mentor who provided the direction and inspiration.

♦ Dan Hays, one of my many fellow/assistant coaches who counseled and taught me.

♦ Don Meyer, one of my many players who were the reason for my coaching career.

♦ Credit for this project goes primarily to the National Association of Basketball Coaches (NABC) Board of Directors, which authorized the concept, and to Joe Vancisin, former NABC executive director, who provided the assistance to bring it to reality.

♦ Thanks to Joe O'Brien, executive director of the Naismith Basketball Hall of Fame and the director of research, Wayne Patterson. They provided access to their basketball library and helped me with the needed research. Wayne's assistance was critical to carrying out the project.

♦ John Kimble, basketball coach at Crestview High School, Florida, who translated all the diagrams into coaching works of art.

This book is also dedicated to those who have influenced my personal life:

♦ Christy, my wife, who gave me the support and understanding that allowed me to complete this dream of a lifetime.

♦ Harold Meili, my longtime friend, who has always been there when needed, for his creative ideas and his ideas for the original book cover design.

Jerry Krause
Cheney, Washington
December, 1993

Part I COACHING FUNDAMENTALS

KEY TO DIAGRAMS

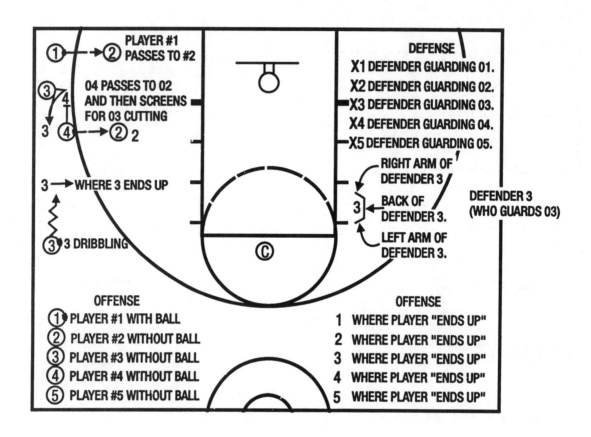

PLAYER #1 PASSES TO #2

04 PASSES TO 02 AND THEN SCREENS FOR 03 CUTTING

3 → WHERE 3 ENDS UP

3 DRIBBLING

DEFENSE
X1 DEFENDER GUARDING 01.
X2 DEFENDER GUARDING 02.
X3 DEFENDER GUARDING 03.
X4 DEFENDER GUARDING 04.
X5 DEFENDER GUARDING 05.

RIGHT ARM OF DEFENDER 3
BACK OF DEFENDER 3.
LEFT ARM OF DEFENDER 3.

DEFENDER 3 (WHO GUARDS 03)

OFFENSE
① PLAYER #1 WITH BALL
② PLAYER #2 WITHOUT BALL
③ PLAYER #3 WITHOUT BALL
④ PLAYER #4 WITHOUT BALL
⑤ PLAYER #5 WITHOUT BALL

OFFENSE
1 WHERE PLAYER "ENDS UP"
2 WHERE PLAYER "ENDS UP"
3 WHERE PLAYER "ENDS UP"
4 WHERE PLAYER "ENDS UP"
5 WHERE PLAYER "ENDS UP"

Success is peace of mind which is a direct result of self-satisfaction in knowing you did your best to become the best that you are capable of becoming.

John R. Wooden

Our coaching skills and abilities are built upon our personal and professional foundations. A knowledge of basketball history can provide perspective for you and your players as you teach them to learn to love and appreciate the sport as you do. This section provides a background for the sport of basketball, the NABC and *The Basketball Bulletin*, the primary source for this publication. Good luck in gaining an appreciation of basketball and its premier coaching organization, the National Association of Basketball Coaches.

BASKETBALL: A NEW GAME
Springfield College

This advertisement appeared in *The Triangle*, Volume 1 Number 7, September 1892, the official publication of Springfield College, Springfield, Massachusetts.

BASKETBALL

A New and Popular Game

Instead of KICKING the Ball Toss It

Instead of KICKING a Goal, THROW It

Instead of "DOWNS" Keep the Ball Up

Like Football it requires "Team-play," "Tackling," "Blocking," and "Passing." BASKETBALL can be played Out-doors or In-doors by small or large teams. It is interesting to players and spectators. Send ten cents for descriptive pamphlet containing rules, etc., to THE TRIANGLE PUBLISHING CO., Springfield, Mass.

"Basketball is a game easy to play and difficult to master."

James Naismith

BASKETBALL: THE BIRTH OF THE GAME

James Naismith

We present to our readers a new game of ball, which seems to have those elements in it which ought to make it popular among the Associations. It fills the same place in the gymnasium that football does in the athletic field. Any number of men may play at it, and each one gets plenty of exercise; at the same time it calls for physical judgment, and co-ordination of every muscle, and gives all-around development. It can be played by teams from different Associations, and combines skill with courage and agility so that the better team wins.

The ground is the gymnasium floor cleared of apparatus (it may be shoved behind the sidelines), though it could be played in the open air, at a picnic, etc. When there is running track around the gymnasium, the ground might be marked out just under the track, and the baskets hung up, one at each end on the railing. All outside of this line is then out of bounds. When there is no running track, the ends may be cleared of apparatus, and the goals fixed on the wall, then a line may be drawn along the sides of the gymnasium about six feet from the walls, or enough to clear the apparatus. Across these lines would be out of bounds.

The goals are a couple of baskets or boxes about 15 inches in diameter across the opening, and about 15 inches deep. These are to be suspended, one at each end of the grounds, about 10 feet from the floor. The object of the game is to put the ball into your opponents' goal. This may be done by throwing the ball from any part of the grounds, with one or both hands, under the following conditions and rules:

1. The ball may be thrown in any direction with one or both hands.

2. The ball may be batted in any direction with one or both hands.

3. A player cannot run with the ball. The player must throw it from the spot on which he catches it, allowance to be made for a man who catches the ball when running at a good speed if he tries to stop.

4. The ball must be held in or between the hands, the arms or body must not be used for holding.

5. No shouldering, holding, pushing, tripping, or striking in any way the person of an opponent shall be allowed; the first infringement of this rule by any player shall count as a foul, the second shall disqualify him until the next goal is made, or, if there was evident intent to injure the person, for the whole of the game, no substitute allowed.

6. A foul is striking at the ball with the fist, violation of rules 3, 4, and such as described in rule 5.

7. If either side makes three consecutive fouls, it shall count a goal for the opponents (consecutive means without the opponents in the meantime making a foul).

8. A goal shall be made when the ball is thrown or batted from the grounds into the basket and stays there, providing those defending the goal do not touch or disturb the goal. If the ball rests on the edges, and the opponent moves the basket, it shall count as a goal.

9. When the ball goes out of bounds, it shall be thrown into the field of play by the person first touching it. In case of a dispute, the umpire shall throw it straight into the field. The thrower in is allowed five seconds, if he holds it longer, it shall go to the opponent. If any side persists in delaying the game, the umpire shall call a foul on that side.

10. The umpire shall be judge of the men and shall note the fouls and notify the referee when three consecutive fouls have been made. He shall have power to disqualify men according to rule five.

11. The referee shall be judge of the ball and shall decide when the ball is in play, in bounds, to which side it belongs, and shall keep the time. He shall decide when a goal has been made, and keep account of the goals with any other duties that are usually performed by a referee.

12. The time shall be two 15 minute halves, with a five minute rest between.

13. The side making the most goals in that time shall be declared the winner. In case of a draw, the game may, by agreement of the captains, be continued until another goal is made.

This game is interesting to spectators as well as to the players, and may be made quite scientific by good judgment combined with good coordination. Several good points have been scored by two or three players working together. The number composing a team depends largely on the size of the floor space, but it may range from three on a side to forty. The fewer players down to three, the more scientific it may be made, but the more players the more fun, and the more exercise for quick judgment.

The men may be arranged according to the idea of the captain, but it has been found advantageous to have a goalkeeper, two guards, three center men, two wings, and a home man stationed in the above order from the goal.

It shall be the duty of the goalkeeper and the two guards to prevent the opponents from scoring. The duty of the wing man and the home man is to put the ball into the opponents' goal, and the center men shall feed the ball forward to the man who has the best opportunity, thus nine men make the best number for a team.

It is well suited for boys. Director Finch has introduced it in his boys' classes with apparent success. We wish that the physical directors would try the game, and report any points that might be amended.

It is intended that this game should be free from much of the reputed roughness of Rugby, and in the framing of rules this has been kept strictly in view. If some of the rules seem unnecessarily severe, it will be remembered that the time to stop roughness is before it begins.

A gymnasium is bounded by hard walls, and has a pretty solid floor, and for that reason, any shoving that would injure a person must be stopped, e.g., when a man raises his arms to throw the ball, another might give him the shoulder, and disable him, but if this is stopped there will be an understanding that it is not allowed. It is for the benefit of a physical director that no man be hurt in his gymnasium, so that any director who tries it should make every man conform to the rules, strictly at first, and then he would soon get accustomed to playing ball instead of trying to injure his neighbor, when it is nothing but a friendly tussle in which they are taking part.

The very men who are rough in playing will be the very first ones to oppose the game on this account, for there is that in man's nature which will retaliate, and the rough player generally gets the worst of the roughness. If there is need for such a game, let it be played as any other game of science and skill, then men will value it. But there is neither science nor skill, in taking a man unawares, and shoving him, or catching his arm and pulling him away, when he is about to catch the ball. A dog could do as much as that.

There seemed to be no way of compensating the opponents for a foul made. A free throw was thought of but after a little practice, a good thrower could convert it into a goal almost every time, because of the limits of the ordinary gymnasium. Then the idea was that three fouls would count as goal, and would be deterrent to the making of them. This is true for when a team finds that another foul would count a goal against them, the extra foul is hardly ever made, showing that it is possible to play the game without making fouls.

If men will not be gentlemanly in their play, it is our place to encourage them to games that may be played by gentlemen in a mannerly way, and show them that science is superior to brute force with a disregard for the feelings of others. The umpire will thus be responsible for much of the roughness if he lets it go unchecked, but if he is firm and impartial in his ruling he will gain respect even of those who suffer at the time.

We would advise the director to keep a good firm grasp on the ruling for a while at first.

THE BASKETBALL MAN

Bob Broeg

A short, stocky old man with a bristling mustache and a thick, powerful neck that belied his age wandered into a gymnasium some years ago. He was asked by one young chap to referee an impromptu basketball game.

Another youth interrupted and said in a semi-whisper, "Oh, you're wasting your breath. That old guy can't know anything about basketball."

John Naismith, the man who invented the game, told me that one about himself. When I repeat it, people think I'm so old I must have been the official scorer when Naismith came up with the greatest invention since indoor plumbing.

Truth is, though basketball now ranks internationally behind only soccer as a team sport, the great American game – invented by a Canadian with a Scottish accent – really isn't that old, but neither was Doc Naismith when he devised it nor was I when he talked to me about it two years before he died.

As a sophomore at the University of Missouri, I visited the University of Kansas at Lawrence on Thanksgiving 1937 for the annual football game between the oldest rivals west of the Mississippi. At my social fraternity's KU chapter house, I met with delight the professor emeritus. A widower, Dr. James Naismith was wooing the chapter housemother, who would become his wife a few months before his death two years later at 78.

With a twinkle in blue eyes framed by severe gold-rimmed glasses, Naismith told about meeting the kid who hadn't thought "that old guy" knew enough about basketball to referee a game. Naismith told me he'd been the featured speaker that night on the young man's campus. The "old guy" noticed the younger man in the audience and gave the red-faced kid a good-natured ribbing.

I found the inventor grumpy about the only two changes made in the 13 rules he had set down for the game in 1891. Five years earlier, in 1932, the rules committee had instituted the rule giving the offensive team ten seconds to move the ball beyond midcourt. Now, in 1937, they were eliminating the center jump after each score.

"They've spoiled it," Naismith said, a bit peevishly, yet with a pretty sound argument. Naismith recognized that the 1932 ten-second rule had been installed primarily to keep a team from playing patty-cake with a ball in its half of the court. But elimination of the center jump, he felt, created a disadvantage to the team that had scored.

But, Doc, weren't they trying to speed up the game, increase the score, and make basketball more interesting?

"But have they?" Naismith asked rhetorically. "They've cut the court in half, requiring ten men to play in it, but they still haven't eliminated the stall, which they tried to do. A player scored against now has five seconds to throw the ball in and ten seconds more to take it over the center line. With the center jump after each basket, it took only an average of four seconds to take the ball to midcourt and toss it up.

"Spectators don't like the stall, I don't, and I believe most coaches don't. I saw one game where one side passed the ball 343 times, and a great referee, Ernie Quigley, stood there 12 minutes watching them. I still say that eliminating the center jump penalized the team that has scored."

Naismith talked about time, i.e., the modern shot clock, and about bonus points for outside shooting, both of which came long after he was gone. "Scoring is important," he said, "but not all-consuming. I think speed is. Speed, passing, and the unexpected. To curb the stall, I'd put in a time limit on the team with the ball. To make the defense come out, I'd score from 30 feet out."

Naismith's suggestion became pro basketball's 24-second clock nearly a quarter-century later and more recently the 45-second-shot requirement in college ball. Even more prescient was his proposal to double the point value for a shot from nearly ten feet farther out than the current distance for three-point shots.

Born in Almonte, Ontario, in 1861, James Naismith was a son of Scot immigrants. Orphaned at 9, he was reared by an uncle and an older sister. Rugged both physically and in spirit, James was interested in hunting and the outdoors. He was a high-school dropout. To envision his becoming an honorary doctor of divinity, a medical doctor, and an honorary master of physical education would have been difficult—as difficult as suggesting that a person who reveled in Rugby, soccer, lacrosse, and wrestling would devise the scientific poetry of motion that is basketball.

The young Jim Naismith suddenly saw the spiritual light. He went back to school and graduated in theology from McGill University at 26 in 1887. He didn't smoke or drink and he rarely swore. In fact, he had a purity of heart that made him the counterpart of college football's Amos Alonzo Stagg in St. Louis.

Mrs. Dodd, one of Doc's five children, was named Hellen "with two l's," she quipped, so her father could say, "'Hellen blazes,' his only curse word."

Naismith began teaching at the YMCA's training school at Springfield, Massachusetts. The head of the physical-training department, Dr. Luther H. Gulick, told Naismith he wanted a winter activity that would keep budding young physical culturists in shape for spring. Something that could be played on the gym floor, Jim.

Naismith studied and borrowed from various games. Duck on a rock suggested the use of a ball tossed in an arc rather than hurled. Lacrosse contributed the arrangement of players. Rugby furnished a hint of putting the ball in play, and soccer—well, association football, as they called soccer then, offered a ready-made ball.

A goal on the floor, as in hockey, wouldn't do because it would be too easy to defend, especially if Naismith were trying to accommodate Dr. Gulick's 18 students. So, Jim got himself a peach basket and a ladder. He installed the peach basket at a height the Y's gymnasium floor would permit—nine feet from the floor. He began the game with nine players on a side, tossed the ball, and—as prescribed by Naismith to keep the game from becoming indoor football—a player was required to dribble the ball and to take only a stride before passing the ball to a teammate.

Because the court was only 35 feet by 45 feet, Naismith reduced the number of players from nine to seven, and then to the current five. Where permitted, he elevated the basket to 10 feet, still the current height (even though Naismith's prized product at Kansas, the coaching legend Forrest C. ["Phog"] Allen, later urged an increase that today would negate dunking—12 feet!). I wish I'd asked Doc Naismith about that one in our meeting 51 years ago.

Even though Rugby still bore the name of where the sport began at a British school in 1823—a guy named Ellis picked up a soccer ball in frustration and ran with it—Naismith declined to have his new game named for him. So heck, since they were using peach baskets, why not call it "basket" ball?

Peach baskets weren't always easy to find, and after a score, using a rod to poke the ball out—or, even worse, a stepladder—was troublesome too. So a carpenter's aid made the game more sophisticated and, at least temporarily, seemed to make rule No. 8 laughable. In part, the rule stated: "If the ball rests on the edge of the basket and the opponent moves the basket, it shall count as a goal."

Even in our own era of height matched only by agility, or vice-versa, it's still a two-point no-no to goaltend against a ball in downward flight in the basket's perimeter and, just as Doc wrote in 1891, two points if a defensive hand disturbs the basket.

By 1893, at which time Yale had already become one of the first colleges to adopt the game, a carpenter devised a wire cylinder to replace the original peach basket. At first, chicken-wire netting under the cylinder kept the ball from swishing through the nets as it does now.

By '94, also, the first basketball had replaced the soccer ball's size and weight; a 30-inch circumference limited the size of the ball to 20 to 22 ounces. Over the years, smart-alecs like me have called the game "roundball" because in early days of rubberized inflation the ball often became a tad lopsided. Yet it wasn't until 1938, the year after I met Naismith and shortly before his death, that the rules were amended to state that a spherical basketball not vary more than a quarter of an inch in diameter.

To Oklahoma State's "Iron Duke," Henry Iba, like Phog Allen an early-day legend, "true bounce" has always been the gentle synonym for the game he loves dearly (in effect, if you will, a dig at what Iba calls "bad bounce," i.e., the crazy caprice of a football).

Over the years, added safeguards made Naismith's game as good as Doc wanted. To keep spectators in shoebox gyms from deflecting shots, backboards were devised—wood, at first, then glass. Ultimately, played on stage auditorium floors, basketball required a net to keep the ball from bounding away—which generated the term still seen in an occasional newspaper headline: "cagers."

Jim Naismith next left for the foothills of the Rockies. There, at the present-day University of Colorado, he studied to become an M.D. because, as his daughter Hellen Dodd explained, he felt he could better direct young men's physical activities if he knew as much about the body as. . . well, yes, a physician.

Over the years, as an intellectual roughneck, an academician with muscles, Naismith lived with a head-in-the-sky attitude toward such mundane things as money. For instance, he twice lost homes to a foreclosure gavel. Even though he might have earned much from the game he invented, the royalties he received belatedly from a basketball named for him didn't cover what he had spent.

Naismith was interested in body and soul; ergo, what better job than to serve as the director of chapel and physical education? Naismith moved to the University of Kansas in 1898. He was 36 then, already burning the candle at both ends, in the nicest sense, Hellen recalled. Not only was he supporting a family, but he was studying and teaching, as well as working.

One night he didn't come home. The family was alarmed, as were the faculty and the university kids. An alarm was sounded. Finally, searchers found him, asleep on a park bench. "Like Rip Van Winkle, utterly exhausted, he'd sat down and fallen fast asleep," his daughter remembered fondly.

Kind, soft-hearted, and considerate—that's the way they remembered him at Kansas, where he lived out his last 41 years. Loosely coaching KU's first eight basketball teams through 1908, he was barely a break-even coach, yet he helped establish a tradition. The defending NCAA champion Jayhawks have more basketball victories than all universities except Kentucky, North Carolina, and St. John's. KU became NCAA champions in the tournament's 50th year, 1988. Kentucky's long-time coach, Adolph Rupp, was a Kansas man, and North Carolina's famed current coach, Dean Smith, also played under Phog Allen.

Allen, an osteopath who played under Naismith, coached Kansas 38 years through 1956 and achieved a .729 record (590-219). The university's field house is named for him, but it also contains a handsome painted portrait of that stocky, thick-necked little man who began it all, James Naismith.

Allen maintained constant affection for Naismith. When basketball first became an Olympic sport in 1936—imagine how far, fast, and strongly it has come in the quadrennial games since then—Phog Allen practically horsewhipped the NCAA to send Naismith to Berlin for the ceremonies.

Doc came back as exhilarated as when he had been stationed on the Mexican border in the U.S. Army in 1916 or served as a Y representative in Europe in World War I, as happy as when he worked on a road gang with one of his sons "just for the fun of it."

He'd seen basketball go from narrow, low-ceilinged gyms and parish basements to dance halls and haylofts, then ultimately to giant field houses and arenas. The year he died, 1939, the NCAA began its annual postseason tournament that now, through its Final Four, rivals the Super Bowl and the World Series.

Naismith said on his return from Berlin that basketball had "grown tremendously [overseas], and I think it will continue to grow, perhaps not in this country, but in foreign countries."

Jim Naismith was both right and wrong. The roundball, not the snowball, is the symbol of winter now, and really, winter hasn't been the same since 1891. But then, the master of the game always thought there was too much ado about his sport. Like the time early in the century when Baker University near Lawrence wrote him to inquire about hiring a young KU athlete as a part-time basketball coach. Naismith called in young Phog Allen to announce the news.

"I've got a joke on you, you bloody beggar," Doc Naismith said with a laugh. "They want you to coach basketball down at Baker."

Phog bristled. "What's so funny about that?"

"Why, Forrest," explained the man who invented the game to one of the greatest who would ever coach it, "you don't 'coach' basketball. You just play it!"

TEN THINGS YOU NEVER KNEW ABOUT JAMES NAISMITH

1. James Naismith was born in Canada.

2. He was an ordained Presbyterian minister who never preached, preferring a career in physical education.

3. An assistant physical education director, Naismith invented basketball at the YMCA gymnasium in Springfield, Massachusetts, in 1891, but only played the game twice.

4. He nailed vegetable baskets—not peach baskets, as is commonly thought—to an elevated running track circling the gymnasium. The height of the track was 10 feet, an arbitrary choice.

5. At the Springfield YMCA, Naismith worked with Amos Alonzo Stagg, later a legendary football coach, in creating the first football helmet. It resembled a cotton stocking cap with a strap under the chin. Years later, Stagg credited basketball with the development of the forward pass in football.

6. Naismith's interest in basketball waned as the game's popularity grew. "Basketball is just a game to play," he said often. "It doesn't need a coach." Nonetheless, he became basketball coach at Kansas University and lost his first intercollegiate game, 48-8, to Nebraska.

7. One of Naismith's favorite sports was fencing. He trained regularly and was regarded as one of the best fencers west of the Mississippi.

8. Naismith earned a medical degree, but chose not to practice medicine, instead becoming head of the Kansas physical education department.

9. The first golf course in Kansas is attributed to Naismith's meticulous design.

10. Naismith profited little from his invention. Even though lawyers encouraged him to seek a patent on the game, he strongly opposed the suggestion. His personal finances dipped so low at one point that he had his house repossessed by a bank in Kansas.

BASKETBALL HISTORY

Jerry Healy

Before his death in Lawrence, Kansas, November 28, 1939, Dr. James Naismith, the founder of basketball, experienced the thrill of seeing "his" game become truly an international sport.

One of the underlying themes of the Naismith Memorial Basketball Hall of Fame in Springfield, Massachusetts, is "The American Game Played Worldwide."

From its humble beginnings in December, 1891, at the School for Christian Workers, the International YMCA Training School, (now known as Springfield College), basketball — in less than three decades — was played in all corners of the world.

The game was "carried" throughout the world by alumni of Springfield College through their work in and with the YMCA program.

In his lifetime, the native of Almonte, Ontario, personally saw basketball attain many "firsts."

Certainly the most significant "first" occurred in 1936 when basketball was played for the first time as an Olympic Sport in Berlin when USA defeated Canada 19-8 for the gold medal. It's strange to note that up until that time basketball was primarily an indoor sport. The 1936 Olympic gold medal game was played outside, in the mud and rain, on a tennis court!

Basketball historians are quick to point out that "The American Game," when it was in its 13th year, was an exhibition sport in the 1904 Olympiad in St. Louis. Five of the top basketball teams in the nation played a round robin tournament in an exhibition series with the Buffalo German YMCA claiming a "world title" after defeating the Chicago Central YMCA, 39-28.

The AAU, an organization which pioneered tournament competition for men in 1897, and women in 1926, attempted to get the Naismith game as an official team sport for the 1932 Los Angeles Olympics. The International Olympic Committee turned down the request.

By 1932 more than 18 million people in more than 50 different countries were playing basketball.

On June 18, 1932, at the First International Basketball Conference at the International YMCA School of Physical Education in Geneva, the International Amateur Basketball Federation (FIBA) was created. This established basketball as a worldwide game.

Chaired by Dr. Elmer Berry of Springfield College, the Geneva conference adopted a unified set of international rules. The first president was Leon Bouffard of Switzerland, and the first secretary-general was R. William Jones of Rome, Italy, a Springfield College alumnus. The late Mr. Jones introduced basketball in Switzerland. During his four-decade career with FIBA he helped spread basketball to 130 nations. It is currently played in over 160 different nations throughout the world.

ABAUSA is the United States governing body for amateur basketball and is the FIBA representative in this country.

Dr. Naismith was 30 years old when he invented basketball. During the next 48 years of his life, here are a few of the thrills he must have experienced besides the Olympic competition and spread of the game throughout the world.

The first public game was played March 11, 1892, at the Armory Hill YMCA. It attracted a crowd of 200 as the students defeated the teachers 5-1. Football immortal Amos Alonzo Stagg scored the only point for the faculty.

On March 22, 1893, his game was first played by women at Smith College in Northampton, Massachusetts, where it was introduced by Senda Berenson Abbott, a native of Lithuania. Mrs. Abbott is one of three women enshrined in the Basketball Hall of Fame. The others are Coach L. Margaret Wade of Delta State and Bertha F. Teague of Ada, Oklahoma. They were elected in 1984 and enshrined July 1, 1985, when the new Basketball Hall of Fame was opened.

On February 9, 1895, the Minnesota State School of Agriculture defeated Hamline 9-3 in the first game played between two college teams. In April, 1895, one of the first intercollegiate women's games was played between California and Stanford.

On January 16, 1896, the University of Chicago, where Amos Alonzo Stagg was athletic director, and the University of Iowa met in Iowa City to play the first college game with five players on a side. Chicago won 15-12 and neither team substituted.

In 1896, in the Masonic Temple Auditorium in Trenton, New Jersey, professional basketball came into existence.

The first professional league was established in 1898 and was known as the National Basketball League. The league operated for five seasons. Teams were from Trenton, Millville, Camden, Philadelphia, Chester, Burlington, Conshohocken, and Wilmington. After the turn of the century other professional leagues were formed, such as Philadelphia League, Hudson River League, Eastern League, New York State League, Western Pennsylvania League, Pennsylvania State League, Inter-State League, Metropolitan League, American League.

In 1897, in New York City, the 23rd Street YMCA won the first AAU National Championship on their home court. The AAU basketball championship for women was started in Pasadena, California, in 1926.

During the Summer of 1901, at the Pan-American Exposition in Buffalo, New York, high school basketball came into its own. Holyoke (Massachusetts) High School defeated Mt. Vernon (New York) High and Pratt Institute in what was billed as a "national" high school basketball tournament.

In 1900 Dr. Naismith became the first basketball coach at the University of Kansas. (In 1907-08 he stepped down for the legendary "Phog" Allen.)

In 1901-02 the first collegiate conferences were formed. The Triangular League included Yale, Trinity, and Wesleyan; followed by the New England League with Amherst, Williams, Dartmouth, Trinity, and Holy Cross; and then the Ivy League.

In St. Louis at the 1904 Olympics, the committee staged a national college tournament outdoors as a basketball exhibition. Hiram College defeated Wheaton 25-20 and Latter Day Saints University (now Brigham Young) 25-18. Wheaton took second place with a 40-35 win over the Utah collegians.

Wisconsin claims credit for the first state high school tournament in 1905 at Lawrence College which was won by Fond du Lac.

It was 12 years later, 1917, when high school basketball attracted national attention. Amos Alonzo Stagg started the University of Chicago Interscholastic Basketball Tournament.

The first organized professional basketball league was formed in 1925 as the American Basketball League. The ABL included teams from Washington, Trenton, Philadelphia, New York, Cleveland, Fort Wayne, Detroit, and Chicago.

Dr. Naismith, along with Gen. John Pershing, was on hand to present the first international tournament championship trophy to a United States team in Paris, France. It was the Inter-Allied Games and played by servicemen who were still in Europe after World War I.

On January 7, 1927, the Harlem Globetrotters, organized by Hall of Famer Abe Saperstein, played their first game in Hinckley, Illinois. The Trotters are the ambassadors of basketball since they have appeared all over the world and play "The American Game" in front of countless millions of people – including a crowd of 75,000 in Berlin in 1951!

On March 12, 1937, Dr. Naismith had the honor of presenting the first national collegiate basketball tournament championship trophy to Warrensburg (now Central Missouri). The national championship is now conducted by the National Association of Intercollegiate Athletics. The trophy – also on display in the Basketball Hall of Fame – was named in honor of Dr. Naismith's wife.

Dr. Naismith's game – basketball – celebrated its Golden Anniversary. The 100th anniversary was observed in 1991 all over the world. Several special events were being planned at all levels of play — amateur, scholastic, collegiate, and professional — to salute "The American Game Played Worldwide."

THE NATIONAL ASSOCIATION OF BASKETBALL COACHES (NABC)

Ed Hickox

The National Association of Basketball Coaches was born out of necessity, sired by courage, and fostered by far-sighted confidence in the basic greatness of this game of basketball. We are fortunate today that forward-looking basketball coaches had the courage and willingness to take responsibility, the energy and interest to give it expression, the optimism and confidence to implement it, and the continued forcefulness to carry on in the face of the seeming indifference of some of their colleagues.

The Joint Basketball Rules Committee in its meeting of April 9, 1927, voted unanimously to limit the dribble to a single bounce. This decision was so suddenly arrived at, so decisive, so unexpected that it startled the whole basketball world and immediately aroused a storm of protest.

One of the most vocal of the opponents of the change was Dr. F.C. Allen, highly successful coach at the University of Kansas. His opposition was voiced in an attack on the changed rule itself, on the committee for an ill-considered premature action, and on the committee's failure to consult the basketball people the country over. He became the leader and mouthpiece for those opposed to the one-dribble rule. On April 15, 1927, less than a week after the announcement of the committee action, Dr. Allen appeared before the American Physical Education Association in convention at Des Moines, Iowa.

In his address Dr. Allen called on all the antagonists of the new rule to express this opposition to the rules committee. He also called on the coaches to come to the meeting in Des Moines at the time of the Drake Relays, April 29, 1927. In the meantime, he urged them that they poll their own areas as to the sentiment concerning the committee action and that they bring or send to the April 29 meeting at Des Moines their own thinking and the results of their opinion polls.

The attendance at the first meeting was discouragingly small but encouragingly serious and enthusiastic. Some basketball coaches actually at the relays were also track coaches, hence unable to attend the basketball meeting. However, letters and telegrams had come in, representing more that 50 coaches and as many others interested in this protest meeting. Dr. Allen as temporary chairman called on A.A. Schabinger of Creighton University to act as temporary Secretary and the first meeting of the NABC became a reality. The men attending this historic get-together were: F.C. Allen, University of Kansas, A.A. Schabinger, Creighton University, J. Craig Ruby, University of Illinois; Don S. White, Washington University; H.W. Hargiss, University of Kansas; and Geo. R. Edwards, University of Missouri.

These six men decided that only through organized effort could the coaches have any voice in the making of basketball rules (in 1927 on the national rules committee of 20 members, there were only two who were actively coaching the game). These six men proceeded to organize, elect officers, discuss policies, and vote a later meeting for Chicago in June, 1927, and a National Convention for the year ahead. Dr. Allen was elected president and Schabinger secretary-

treasurer. The two "were instructed by those present to proceed with the organization. We needed stationery, stamps, secretarial help, and many other items. We had a lot of ambition but no money" (extract from secretarial minutes).

Only Dr. Allen and Craig Ruby of the six men at the Des Moines meeting were able to be present at the Chicago meeting, but a larger and more representative group of other coaches did attend. Among these were: Price of University of California, Edmundson of University of Washington, Stewart of University of Montana, Mc Millen of University of Minnesota, and Lew Andreas of Syracuse University. Since the records of that meeting have been lost, the present writer can only conjecture that several more from the Chicago area must have been present, and later correspondence available seems to indicate that. Thus new members and new strength were added to the movement with encouragement to the organizers to proceed. Discussions of purpose and procedures helped clarify the problems and helped suggest the personnel for the Executive Staff and for the various committees. Allen in a letter to Wachter of Harvard in January, 1928, wrote: "The National Organization of Basketball Coaches which was formed last year in Chicago." This would indicate the importance of the Chicago meeting as he saw it.

It developed on the two officers to find the finances, to carry forward the organizational activities, and to write the literally hundreds of letters thus necessitated. The effectiveness of their efforts is fully indicated by the results. Before college opened in September, 1927, "The National Association of the Basketball Coaches of the United States" had become a reality with a full complement of officers and committees, with a constitution, with a monogram, and with letterhead stationery.

The constitution included: "The purpose of this association shall be:

1. To dignify the basketball Coaching Profession.

2. To elevate the game to its proper plane in the scheme of education.

3. To foster and encourage a better understanding between basketball coaches of the various sections of the United States.

4. To maintain even to a greater degree the standards of sportsmanship as outlined in the basketball code."

Dues were set at $2.00, and the campaign for membership moved forward.

The first National Convention, held at Hotel Windermere, Chicago, Illinois, April 5 and 6, 1928 showed the results of the immense amount of work done by the organizers that first year. There was a paid-up membership of 96, of whom 54 were in attendance at this meeting from all over the United States. Also present were 14 interested guests who were persons influential in the field of athletics.

The first morning session was taken up with addresses by President Allen, Honorary President James Naismith, Mr. W.L. St. John, and Major John L. Griffith. The afternoon session was given to reports of the various committees and to discussion. The second day, Friday, April 6, 1928, the morning session was held in Gage Park Field House. There for the first time in history a basketball rules clinic and an interpretation meeting were held on a national scale. More than 50 coaches from New England, New York City, South East Atlantic, Texas, California, Washington, Missouri Valley, Utah, and the states of the Big Ten Conference altogether discussed, interpreted, and suggested, and finally approached some sort of common agreement which could be forwarded to the Joint Rules Committee as the voice of the men who teach this game.

For a quarter of a century now this organization has been the greatest single influence in guiding the discussions and the decisions of the National Rules body. Today one-half the members of the present rules body are themselves actively engaged in coaching the game. Today the National Association of Basketball Coaches (NABC), The National Association of Intercollegiate Basketball (NAIB), and the National High School Federation furnish the experienced leadership, the research technicians, the experimental opportunities, and the considered judgments that influence most strongly the changes in rules. They have much to do with the standards of behavior, types of play, techniques of coaching, direction of tournaments, emphasis or overemphasis, sanity or insanity, and the place of the game in our scheme of education.

What a quarter of a century for "Phog" Allen: The 1927 organizer of the NABC! The 1952 Coach of the World's intercollegiate championship basketball team and the Co-coach of the world's champion Olympic basketball team!

Pleased with the fine work done by their officers that first year, the coaches attending the 1928 convention reelected these men to office for another year, certain the organization was off to a good start, then went home convinced that soon the association would reach a membership of 500. It has failed to reach that total even yet. But by 1929, the membership did hit 123, then began to fall off for some years. Not until 1940 did the active membership finally pass the 200 mark. The various fluctuations were traceable more directly to the effectiveness of the membership committees than to any other single influence. The active membership reached 170 in 1939 with the present writer as membership chairman, passed 200 with Gullion as chairman, went to 260 with Hobson, 364 with Karl Lawrence, and finally topped 400 with Everett Shelton in 1950-51.

Possibly the greatest single factor retarding the growth of the association was the lack of a publicity medium. Only once a year did the membership receive news of the activities of the association. After the printed report of the 1928 convention gotten out by Secretary Schabinger, succeeding reports were published for five years in the Athletic Journal, then for a further five years in the Scholastic Coach. Hence only by letters could direct contact be made between officers and the membership except through attendance at the convention itself. The files of the association correspondence show a great volume of personal letters and give a clue to the reason for the early vigor of the movement and a possible reason for decline after new regimes took office.

Lack of funds was a constant handicap to the association activities. The convention of 1932 voted an increase from $2.00 to $5.00 for annual dues. This new rate was in force for five years, but like many other taxing schemes the higher rates tended to reduce the number of members. In 1938 the present scheme of $2.00 membership and $3.00 convention fees was voted in. This has remained a satisfactory arrangement because other sources became available to the association. These will be noted later.

During the year 1933-34, Dr. H.C. Carlson of Pittsburgh, then secretary, put out the first *Trial Bulletin* which he fondly hoped would pay for itself on the basis of sales. But he found, as did his successors, that an organization magazine is not self-supporting in groups of rather limited size. However, he had started something that was badly needed, and the following year, Secretary George Edwards issued five bulletins using his college facilities, his own typewriter, and his own family as aids to establish solidly our policy of a NABC Bulletin. So well did he do that he was made Bulletin Editor for the following two years, when he asked to be relieved.

However, by now the desirability and value of an association bulletin was firmly established. At the 1937 convention, Frank Kearney of Rhode Island State was appointed editor and bore the burden for five years. Then followed a period of no bulletin until 1947, when F.C. Cappon began the present line of editors to be followed by E.S. Hickey and now Clifford Wells. Another potent influence on membership and attendance at conventions has been the opportunity to see teams in tournament action. At the 1934 convention, Atlanta, Georgia, President Mundorff arranged for four college teams to play on two successive evenings for demonstration and interest. These teams cooperated to a great extent even to paying part of their own expenses – University of Pittsburgh, Illinois Wesleyan, DeKalb Teacher, and South Carolina. This was the real beginning of what has turned into an important and immensely popular educational feature of our convention programs.

The 1936 convention was held in New York, where the coaches had opportunity to see the Olympic tryouts including the best collegiate and best AAU teams.

In 1938 the Metropolitan Basketball Writers Association started the National Invitational Tournament at Madison Square Garden. By courtesy of the management these have been free to the active members of our association in attendance at our New York conventions. In 1939 the NCAA Tournament was started largely through efforts of the Coaches Association, and the first final was part of the Chicago Convention program of that year. At the 1940 convention in Kansas City, that final was the high point of the program.

So valuable have the coaches felt the tournaments to be that the location of the tournament now determines the location of the convention. Not all the coaches feel this to be an unmixed blessing, however, as they think of the tournament as taking away from the importance of the proceedings of the convention proper.

The tournament as an educational as well as a competitive activity, however, has strong support amongst the college coaches. Many tournaments of many types are annual affairs, many of them widely intersectional in makeup. This leads to the spread of common types of play and, better yet, to common types of officiating and interpreting the rules.

In this year of Olympic Basketball competition we should be reminded that the NABC perhaps more than any other group of men urged and worked for the inclusion of the game in the Olympic program. Also we raised the funds that sent to the 1936 games Dr. Naismith, inventor and patron saint of basketball, who was so warmly received and spontaneously acclaimed by the officials and players of many nations that we were proud indeed of him and of that for which he stood.

Other phases of the work of the NABC cannot be developed in an article of this length and should be outlined at a later date. The most important phase of all perhaps is that of rules consideration, and this could be a lengthy article. Finances also deserve discussion because we have been blessed in later years with generous friends ready to help us in our service study and research. The Metropolitan Basketball Association of New York City and the NCAA have each aided us materially, and the Ned Irish organization has been both thoughtful and generous.

The logical climax for this particular article is undoubtedly a short statement relative to the high point of our history — the establishment of a Hall of Fame for Basketball to enshrine its inventor, to honor its great men, to commemorate their glorious deeds, and to provide a museum and library where may be kept in perpetuity the memorabilia and history of the great moments and great achievements of basketball.

THE HISTORY OF THE NABC BULLETIN

E. S. Hickey

The National Association of Basketball Coaches of the United States was organized in 1927. As a medium of contact for its members, a trial bulletin was prepared and distributed by Dr. H.C. Carlson (Pittsburgh), Secretary-Treasurer of the Association, during his term of office in the 1933-34 school year. At the time of the preceding Convention held at the McAlpin Hotel, New York City, April 6-8, 1933, a motion from the floor was unanimously passed which initiated the requirement for the newly elected Secretary-Treasurer to mail information regularly to the Association membership. Thus six full years after the inauguration of the Association steps were taken which were destined to lead to the eventual publication of an official organ of The National Association of Basketball Coaches of the United States to be known as *The Bulletin*. Dr. Carlson's trial bulletin – making a strong plea for information material, diagraming "the Pitt offensive system for 1933," listing the new rule changes as edited by Oswald Tower and encouraging attendance at "the annual National Convention to be held at Atlanta, Georgia, March 29-31, 1934" was the first tangible progress toward *The Bulletin*.

Prior to the trial bulletin there was no medium of contact other than the usual correspondence between members, the officers, and the board of directors. Just as the publication of the Trial Bulletin had been assigned as an added duty for the Association's duly elected Secretary-Treasurer, so too had the previously elected Secretary-Treasurers assumed the responsibility of publishing a full report of the proceedings of each of the annual National Conventions of the Association. While these publications were not referred to as bulletins, they contributed greatly in emphasizing the eventual need for some publication as a more frequent contact between the Association's membership.

A.A. Schabinger (Creighton), the first Association Secretary-Treasurer, printed and distributed the first formal report following the Chicago Convention April 5-6, 1928. Actually, this was the second annual meeting of the newly organized Basketball Coaches Association. No general report or publication had been made of the proceedings of the first meeting.

The report of the proceedings of the Second Annual Convention prepared by Mr. Schabinger was a neat printed folder that concisely told the story of the Convention meeting. It carried a roll of members, the new officers and various committees and printed in formal fashion for the first time the Constitution of the Association. This report did much to enliven the thinking that was eventually to bring about the

Secretary-Treasurer	Convention Date and Place	Publication
H.G. Olson (Ohio State)	April 35, 1930 Hotel Windemere Chicago	May, *Athletic Journal*
H.B. Ortner (Cornell)	March 27-28, 1931 Hotel Astor New York City	May, *Athletic Jounal*
A.C. Lonborg (Northwestern)	Mar. 31-Apr.1,1932 Hotel Shoreland Chicago	June, *Athletic Journal*
H.C. Beresford (Colorado)	April 6-8, 1933 McAlpin Hotel New York City	June, *Athletic Journal*
George R. Edwards (Missouri)	April 3-5, 1935 Hotel Sovereign Chicago	May, *Scholastic Coach*
W.S. Chandler (Marquette)	April 2-4, 1936 Hotel Pennsylvania New York City	May, *Scholastic Coach*

Table 1.1

preparation and distribution of the *NABC Bulletin*.

In the early years of the Association that followed the report of the Second Annual Convention, the Secretary-Treasurer made a full report of the annual convention proceedings. At the invitation of John L. Griffith, (deceased) founder and Editor of the Athletic Journal, the report of A.A. Schabinger (Creighton), serving an additional term as Secretary-Treasurer, 1928-29, was published for the first time in the June issue of the Athletic Journal for 1929. This report carried the proceedings of the Convention of April 4-6, 1929, Hotel Windemere, Chicago.

Up to the time the Association's own *Bulletin* fully carried the annual Convention proceedings, these succeeding reports of the Secretary-Treasurer and their medium of publication were as shown in Table 1.1.

At the time of the 1933-34 Annual Convention (March 29-31, 1934) held at the headquarters of the Atlanta Athletic Association, Atlanta, Georgia, George R. Edwards (Missouri) was elected Secretary-Treasurer. The pioneering era for *The Bulletin* was at this time greatly strengthened. Whereas the first issue by Dr. H.C. Carlson (Pittsburgh) had been described as a trial bulletin, the new Secretary-Treasurer forged ahead enthusiastically with his first issue in November, 1934, entitled *Bulletin*. It was a mimeographed copy consisting of five pages filled with important data concerning rules, experimentation in rules, problems dealing with the "deeply retreated defenses," a plea for *Bulletin* information, and a promise to publish a

Membership Directory in the next issue. Of interest in this first *Bulletin* was the announcement of a planned experiment between the University of Kansas and Kansas State College wherein it was agreed "The goal shall be TWELVE FEET high and the backboard shall be placed six feet from the endline."

THE BULLETIN'S BEGINNINGS

H. C. "Doc" Carlson

The following is from the first NABC Bulletin *published May 1, 1933.*

The National Basket Ball Coaches Association is considering a medium of contact with its membership. This bulletin is a personal effort to elicit opinons. It is being sent to every member. The Bulletin should be procurable at all clinics or from the Secretary. The members are requested to send in suggestions and contributions. The High School coaches are invited to send in specific requests for articles, and incidently a small contribution to defray increased expenses. The response to this bulletin will determine the future policy in regard to similar efforts.

A method of contact has received extensive discussion at the last two annual meetings. A number of contributions were made to the Athletic Journal last year under this guise. Some of the members felt that a direct communication would be more efficacious. But printing and mailing costs come high. This bulletin is intended to soften up your bill. You have received something as a member, and so you can conscientiously send in a check for your dues. We plan to have some of these bulletins on hand. They will be free to members. To non-members, the cost will be a dime and a stamped addressed envelope, or fifteen cents. If the income does not justify other bulletins, we must seek other means of contact with our members. President Mundorf has pending an arrangement with the Associated Press. Of course, this bulletin involved some expense, so everybody should pay up. This matter merits the personal efforts of every coach. It must be realized that these papers will not spring up spontaneously. There must be suggestions, contributions, and correlation in getting the papers printed and distributed in a most efficient manner. Every member has some obligation to express himself positively or negatively. This paper carries a challenge to every coach. Do you want a bulletin of this kind issued at frequent intervals? Are you willing to make contributions and to help in distribution? Are you sufficiently interested to sit down and send in your opinion today? The Association wants to know.

The 1934 annual meeting of the National Basket Ball Coaches Association will be held in Atlanta, Georgia, March 29-30-31. This is immediately before Easter, and conforms in most cases to the Easter holidays. The time also brings the advantage of holiday rates on railroads. The headquarters will be at the Atlanta Athletic Association. President Mundorf is arranging for an edifying and enjoyable three days, with meetings in the mornings and the evenings, and recreation in the afternoons. He will have Bobby Jones in on one of the meetings and one of Bobby's golf courses will be available for play. One of the proposed innovations of this year's meeting will be some games. Official permission has already been granted to the Pitt team to make this holiday jaunt. Anyone who has never attended an annual meeting should plan to attend this meeting.

Atlanta presents the first departation from the alternate New York and Chicago meetings. There was a wholesome effort to bring next year's meeting to Pittsburgh, but promises for the following year caused a graceful pass.

In the summer of 1992, the National Association of Basketball Coaches appointed a new Executive Director, Jim Haney, and moved their corporate offices to Overland Park, Kansas. By November, 1992, the official publication of the NABC was changed from the Basketball Bulletin to the NABC Courtside.

This publication is a coaching resource that offers features and interviews with the top names in basketball. Each issue also contains game strategies, coaching tips, pertinent rule reviews and college reports. It provides a unique view of the game — from the college ranks to prep hoops.

COACHES' CODE
George Edwards

This code was adopted by the Association at the Chicago meeting of 1932.

I believe that basketball has an important place in the general educational scheme and pledge myself to cooperate with others in the field of education to so administer it that its value never will be questioned.

I believe that other coaches of this sport are as earnest in its protection as I am, and I will do all in my power to further their endeavors.

I believe that my own actions should be so regulated at all times that I will be a credit to the profession.

I believe that the members of the National Basketball Rules Committee are capably expressing the rules of the game, and I will abide by these rules in both spirit and letter.

I believe in the exercise of all the patience, tolerance, and diplomacy at my command in my relationships with all players, co-workers, game officials, and spectators.

I believe that the proper administration of this sport offers an effective laboratory method to develop, in its adherents, high ideals of sportsmanship; qualities of self-control; desires for clean, healthful living; and respect for wise discipline and authority.

I believe that these admirable characteristics, properly instilled in me through teaching and demonstration, will have a long carryover and will aid each one connected with the sport to become a better citizen.

I believe in and will support all reasonable moves to improve athletic conditions, to provide for adequate equipment, and to promote the welfare of an increased number of participants.

Chapter 2 — DEVELOPING YOUR PHILOSOPHY

Philosophy has been described as the general principles or laws of a field of knowledge or activity. To me, it is the written or unwritten basis for your coaching. An almost universal question in coaching job interviews is to identify and describe your coaching philophy. Make it a solid foundation that will help you develop each of your players and teams as they reach toward their full potential.

MY PHILOSOPHY OF LIFE

Dr. Alvin C. Saake

What I believe:
  That in this world of things and people it is a
      privilege to be alive—
  To feel, to think, to watch, to listen—mostly
      to listen—to the great undertones of
      beauty surging about us.
That's a great privilege.

  I believe that living is the hardest thing any of us
      has to do
          Living "beautifully" that is.
I believe that in all of us there is something divine—
    Something which is always reaching for the ideal.
      It's the striving that's glorious.

  I believe in democracy because my needs must
      have freedom and choice
        Realizing at the same time that it
        demands a contribution from me.
I accept that responsibility.
      My contribution is to keep alive the tenets
      of democracy.

  I see advancement for the world only as we and
our children are attuned to social progress
      for the whole world.
      Therefore I must teach: Life as I know it—
      Life as I know it should be.

THE WIZARD'S PHILOSOPHY

Jerry Krause

"They asked me why I teach. Where else could I find such splendid company?". . . "Talent is God-given, be humble; fame is man-given, be thankful; conceit is self-given, be careful". . . In his autobiography, John Wooden sums it up best himself. "Honors are fleeting, just as fame is; I cherish friendship more." He is the only man to make basketball's Hall of Fame as both a player and a coach. . . . Wooden: "I didn't get there alone. Every man who has been with me from my grammar school days on a dirt court in Centerton, or in Martinsville, Purdue, Dayton, South Bend, Indiana State or UCLA holds a share of the honors. Their contribution reminds me of these words: Kindness in words creates confidence, kindness in thinking creates profoundness, kindness in giving creates love. I hope that in some way each of my players, whether he may now be 50 or just 18, will understand somewhat why I do things the way I do."

TEACHING

Clair Bee

Objective Conditions

Teaching is conditioned by numerous factors over which the coach has no control and others which are directly his responsibility. Such matters as practice hours, class responsibilities, ventilation, lighting, equipment, practice programs, and discipline are subject in most cases to his supervision.

Methods

Teaching methods may include illustration, exposition, reflective thinking, inductive and deductive methods, or a combination of all. Deductive teaching starts with a principle and works down to particulars. It assumes certain principles apply in particular instances. In practice this may not be true and therein lies the danger. This method possesses little value in securing emotional or drill outcomes and, in addition, encourages guessing.

Reflective thinking is an excellent teaching medium. How did Luisetti use the one-hand shot? How did Southern California beat us? This method sets up a situation, analyzes, verifies, and then seeks a solution. In midseason the method is excellent in maintaining the interest of the players.

Drill work will involve several problems. Do certain players need the work, or is it applicable to the whole squad? Will repetitive methods be sufficient to hold the attention of the squad during a period of sufficient length to establish the principles? The solution to these problems is in the hands of the coach.

A number of devices may be used in drill work: competition (opposing one player against another in a shooting drill), emulation (comparing the shooting of Beenders with Lobello), time limit (how many passes can be made in three minutes), problems (how would you solve a three-two zone), and rhythm (counting as players shoot or using music while teaching footwork).

The use of psychology in the drill is important. The drill should be fun, short, and snappy. Game situations should be used as much as possible. The fatigue point must not be approached. Staleness results from monotony; it is mental rather than physical. Repetition is the secret of all knowledge, but invites disinterest. Individuality should be recognized (the best shot, dribbler, passer, feeder, scorer, cutter, guard, rebound worker).

Teaching by movies, discussions, skull practices, illustrations, examples, and exposition is excellent. Probably the best method of all is the use of induction principles. Here the problem is attacked from the bottom and the system is built up. It is a sure way to teach because it connects each step and develops from a good foundation up and through the application of the practice material to the game. Several steps may be followed in this development:

1. Recall information players already have so that the starting point can be determined.

2. Assign players to collect the material. Draw up the plays or arrange the defense under consideration.

3. Ask players to compare and draw out the points which seem most effective and applicable to the styles decided upon.

4. Require players to work out their own plays, attacks, and defenses.

5. After reviewing the above, determining form and practicability, select the final plan of offense and defense and practice it.

Results

Good coaching is not defined by the number of games which have been won or lost. Victory has no place in the definition of a good coach. Those with inferior material may be great in every sense of the word. Coaches with fine material may be inferior with respect to knowledge and the ability to teach, yet they may have a fine victory record. There are many factors which influence coaching success. First, if the material is poor, a great team is too much to expect. Should the squad be fairly strong but the competition weak, victories will not determine coaching ability. When the opposition is particularly strong, good players may be matched by opponents and the record may not be on the victory side even with expert coaching.

Good coaching may be defined as the developing of character, personality, and habits of players, plus the efficient teaching of fundamentals and team play. The development of harmonious teamwork, a spirit of fair play, and an aggressive spirit are just as much a part of the definition of good coaching as an undefeated season. To play to win, to observe the rules, and to act like gentlemen are other factors.

Results are measured in terms of drill benefits, the degree of emotional control, and the application of coaching methods and tactics to games.

A COACHING PHILOSOPHY

John Bunn

Webster defines philosophy as "A systematic body of general conceptions or principles ordinarily with implications of their practical application." Everyone has a philosophy. Every basketball coach has a basketball philosophy. That philosophy reflects his attitude toward boys and toward the sport, and it dictates the kind of game he will coach.

The purpose of this article is to present a philosophy of coaching which relates sports to education and life and forms the only justifiable basis for including sports in an educational program. Implicit in this philosophy is the thesis that sports provide the only practical laboratory for all aspects of education and life. And, since sports are so dynamic and challenging, they reveal the individual participant in his true light.

Sports – An Integral Part of Education

In the first place, sports (in this instance basketball), if they are to be included in the school program, should be an integral part of the total educational program; they should receive neither more nor less support than any other area of the curriculum. Teams should be made up of students who, on their own initiative, desire to participate. There should be no more solicitation of athletes than of any other students, nor should there be any inducements or awards other than those available to other students. Sports should be conducted for the benefit of and in the interests of the students and not at their expense or for their exploitation. The sports program should be financed and administered in the same way as other aspects of the educational institution program. In short, a sports program in an educational institution is difficult to justify when conducted on any basis other than as an integral part of the educational

program. Unfortunately, too many sports programs would not be recognized by these characteristics. But, there are many institutions which operate according to the above plan; and most secondary schools have a truly educational program.

The methods practiced in interschool sports provide the pattern upon which the total program for physical education should be based. In an age of soft living, the vigorous, intense nature of interschool sports is the only sound basis upon which to build the physical education program for the total student body. Fitness for emergencies, for survival, and for healthful living cannot be attained by other methods, certainly not by passive activities.

The Influence of the Coach

The coach is the key to the benefits that will accrue to the players as a result of their participation in the sport. He wields a powerful influence over his players. In order to get to play, they will submit to almost any demand he may make of them. They reflect their coach regardless of his principles, and the institution is measured by the kind of man he is.

Recently, one of the most admirable leaders in basketball resigned his coaching job in one of our great universities under the pressure of not having won a championship. Yet, the constructive and positive influence which he has had on his boys is worth more than a hundred championships. The respect and esteem with which he is held by his colleagues has reflected his institution in a most favorable light. His successor may win more games with his teams, but the institution which places winning ahead of constructive leadership is bound to suffer in retrospect.

Be Yourself

A coach, to do his best job, must be himself. He cannot be a shadow of another. Personalities and backgrounds are never the same. They may be antithetic. One person is phlegmatic, another high-strung; one is mild-mannered, another hard-driving and demanding; one may be kind and personal, another cruel, even brutal; one may be encouraging and complimentary, another discouragingly critical. A coach may have a basketball hero (his old coach, for instance) whom he idealizes, but he should not try to mimic him. A coach should study the performance (which is the implementation of a philosophy) of all his colleagues and predecessors. From such a study, he may find valuable and useful ideas which he can incorporate into his own philosophy. He should, however, pick and choose on the basis of whether or not the principles of others fit his own to help make a more effective and harmonious whole. To sum up, "To thine own self be true" – be yourself.

Coach-Player Relationships

Coach-player relationships should be such that a lasting, wholesome influence is created. A coach may be stern, dignified, and formal; he may be cordial, personal, and informal as befits his own characteristics. But if his relationship with his players is to be worthwhile, he must command their respect not only at the time they are playing, but more particularly after 10 years have elapsed. This should be true in defeat as well as in victory. They should respect him as a man as well as a coach.

To earn this kind of relationship, the coach must be a person of high standards. He must be a desirable example for his boys. He must be ready to defend them when they are maligned. He must demand of them the highest integrity and not be reluctant to discipline them when such methods are indicated. And yet, he must have a forgiving heart without being weak and vacillating. He must recognize that he is being entrusted with boys who are growing to be men; boys who, in the process, are often groping and need a friendly guiding hand of one who is a bit farther along the road.

The Game Should Be Fun

Basketball should be fun for those who play and for those who coach the game. This does not mean there is no hard work to gain perfection, no strenuous effort to attain top condition, or no self-denial in the interests of the team. In the last analysis, these help to make the game more enjoyable. Even these arduous preparatory tactics can be great fun if an enthusiastic attitude is created toward them. I actually believe there is more enthusiastic spirit generated for the very intense conditioning exercises which my teams go through each pre-season than there is for any other stage of our practice. The players have learned that gaining top condition permits them to play with zest throughout a game and throughout the season, so they make fun of what could be drudgery. There is more bantering, kidding, and whooping-it-up than at any other time during practice.

Every red-blooded American plays hard to win. But, when players are sorry to see a strenuous season come to a close whether they have been winning or losing, it is a sure sign that they have been having fun. The coach, by his attitude and his emphasis, can help build this kind of spirit within his squad.

To have fun does not imply a lack of serious effort. It does, however, indicate a lack of tenseness. It indicates a state of relaxation which is necessary to the best in basketball performance, because a tense, worried, harried team is not likely to perform at its best. The author has worried more when his team appeared too tense. He has resorted to more tactics to produce relaxation than to create a serious attitude.

Often, incidental acts create the desired mental poise when planned tactics are ineffective. The first championship playoff in which the author's team, a sophomore group, participated is a case in point.

Before the game, the squad was too serious and so tense and irritable that it was not pleasant to be around. Planned attempts to change the atmosphere were futile. But a chance prank turned the trick and sent a carefree squad on the floor to win easily over a team which had soundly defeated it twice, earlier in the season.

The first appearance of the author's squad in Madison Square Garden was another example. The team started the game under great tension and was not playing up to its ability. Midway during the first half a player in control of the ball fell at the free-throw line. As he fell he tossed the ball back over his head. By some stroke of luck, the ball went through the basket in a perfect arc. The player who tossed the ball stood in amazement when told by his teammates that he had scored a goal. This crazy incident caused the whole squad to break into uproarious laughter. What was previously a nip-and-tuck game turned into a rout of the top team of the East and created the moniker of "the laughing boys" for the team.

These illustrations can be multiplied. These two, however, are sufficient to emphasize the fact that for the best interests of the boys and the best results, one should play to win, but have fun doing it.

Practice Democracy

Democratic policies should be practiced with the squad. Democracy implies leading and following. It also means that all should have a voice in making decisions. It is recognized that the coach has certain definite responsibilities thrust upon him; however, much value can come out of sharing with the players. Plans of play strategies can be presented and the opinion of the squad secured. Many times, excellent suggestions come from squad members; when they are brought into the picture in this manner, players feel as though they have a more important part to play and it builds greater unity in the squad.

To permit the squad to select its own captain, or floor leader, is more democratic than for the coach to appoint him. This is another means of building greater unity in a squad – permitting the boys to exercise their own choice. One need not fear clique action if the coach has established desirable coach-player relations. The boys usually give stronger support to their own leader than they are likely to give to a leader imposed upon them. In most instances, the players choose the boy with the best leadership qualities. They sense who the leaders are. Unfortunately, the social trend in America has been to stifle democratic principles. In sport, we should do everything possible to nurture them.

Encourage Freedom and Initiative

Akin to democratic action is the encouragement of freedom and initiative in play. Play should not be so mechanized in its organization that no freedom of choice is left to the players. Basketball action changes so much during the progress of a game that it is detrimental for a team to be too stereotyped in its play. It is impossible for the coach to plan every move in advance; therefore, practice and organization of play should be set up so that the players are encouraged to think and are given an opportunity to use their own initiative. A team organized on this plan is always more resourceful. When unusual situations arise, they are usually able to cope with them successfully.

The author has always developed a general plan of offensive movement for his team with the definite provision that the player with the ball is free to do whatever seems best to him under the circumstances at that moment. On defense the primary goal is to get the ball. The players are free to use any tactics which they feel will help them to get the ball. What better method is there to develop freedom and initiative in American youth?

Encourage Fast and Aggressive Play

A fast and aggressive game should be taught. Contrary to the opinion of many coaches, there is as much plan and organization in a fast-break, passing type of game as there is in a conservative, ball-control game. The fast, aggressive game is more difficult to learn, but there are several reasons for advocating this type of play. It permits greater freedom and more initiative. It is more fun. Players generally like a fast, aggressive style of play. It is consistent with the foregoing phases of our philosophy. In addition, it is better strategy to prepare a team to play fast. A fast team can play a slow game, but a slow team has great difficulty adjusting to a fast game.

Bob Richards, the great Olympic pole vaulter, has said that sports symbolize life situations. The important thing is to provide an atmosphere in which, by the way boys react to the challenges they receive in sports, they are strengthened for their role as responsible citizens. The coaching philosophy which has just been described is directed toward that goal. It is the author's philosophy.

THOUGHTS ON COACHING

Al McGuire

I am going to cover a variety of things to give you some idea of what makes a guy tick. The thing I am most proud of in my 20 years in the coaching profession is that I think I started a little more love between the coaches. I remember going to a major conference tournament and all the big-name coaches refused to associate with each other. This has been changing and in the last seven or eight years we've seen coaches showing much more consideration for each other. So stay together in your profession, because it's certain that none of your superiors will help you. No one can help you but yourself. You are born alone and you die alone. The moment will come when you have to gently pack coaching away – everyone else had to do it so why not you? Don't try to climb over anybody trying to get a better position. Do the best you possibly can with the material you have and without any fear.

When I come onto a court, the first thing I do is look at the top seats to see if they are filled. There are four seats in each corner of the Milwaukee arena where we play our home games. I look up there and see if they are filled. If they are filled, I feel good. Then I walk up the court and shake hands with the two officials. I don't like it when they call me Mr. McGuire. I tell the officials, if the other team wants more time fine. I tell them to do the best job possible and that I am coming at them.

I've always coached the same. I've never changed. In 12 years I have never blown a whistle. I have never worked from a blackboard and never watched a film. I have never asked for an official, blackballed an official, or rated an official. I have never filled out a card on an official. Any official that gets to that point is good, and you don't do the game any good rating them.

When the National Anthem is played, I talk to myself and say, "Keep it simple, stupid." Don't get complicated. You forget the obvious when you try to force knowledge into young people who can't absorb our knowledge. You must only give them what they can absorb.

As a coach, you must have no indecision–none! I have missed practices because I think people get tired of your voice. During practice I go up and down the court working a practice and I yell as I go up and down the court, "Hey, move up on that peg, will you?" He will say, "I did." I will say, "You're nuts." That's the way I operate. I have no problem knowing who the boss is. I know I am the boss. I am not trying to prove to anyone that I am running the show. I know when the score is 62-62 everybody will be quiet and I will make the decision on what to do.

One thing you must remember about the carnival atmosphere around Marquette University and around me is that it is created, because I feel you are out for a certain percentage of the entertainment dollar. You people in your towns and hamlets, you too are out to get a certain percentage of the entertainment dollar. You have to produce a certain number of dollars. You have to make basketball an attractive thing.

It is my obligation to take care of my team. It is your obligation to take care of your people and not to be frightened by board members and other outsiders. We take care of our players. We allow them a place in our plans and that's why there is no more disciplined team in the United States than the University of Marquette.

Don't make the game of basketball your mistress. We all want to improve on our station in life. We keep trying to advance and sometimes find ourselves running toward an impossible goal. I did it myself 19 years ago. I'm not saying everyone else is wrong. I was wrong. Moving my family down to North Carolina — why? I was running toward my mistress. Basketball was my mistress. Basketball was my world. Be careful. It is a beautiful thing you are building as a coach, but don't get it all mixed up. You have to take care of your home first.

The only reason I yell at a player is because he has talent. If I didn't think he had talent, I would not yell at him. It would be a mortal sin if I didn't get the talent out of a person. I have a player who is the nicest young man that I have ever met in my life. I have to hurt him. I have to hurt the guy because the guy plays without knowing the score. To him everything is beautiful. He's so nice that all he wants to do is play. This is all right if a guy doesn't have talent, but when a guy has talent I have a marvelous obligation to get him to produce. Talent is rare and you have to get it to produce. Just because you have ability doesn't mean that you are going to produce or reach a certain level. You must study your players to know what is the best for each particular person so that you can get the most out of his talent.

Sometimes you have a situation on your team in which one guy constantly throws the ball to a buddy. They come to practice together and leave together like a husband and wife. You must break up the husband and wife act on your team. All teams have these husband and wife acts and you must watch them closely. A lot of times this happens subconsciously. I don't care. They have to knock it off. If they don't break up this act, I let one go early or rearrange the locker room. Don't allow your lockers to sit there for the school year with the same guy going to the same spot. This is how cliques form. It's up to you to watch these things and to take care of them.

Most people in our profession are afraid they might be wrong. I can understand this. I'm wrong too, almost all the time. But I can't wait until the fifth time out to make a correction. I can't wait until they chart it or take a picture of it. When a coach sees something, he can't hold anything back. Don't be embarrassed. Don't be afraid to be wrong. You are a coach, not a spectator. You're not out there to please anyone. You're not an executive who can post-date a memo. What you do as a coach is out there in the open. There is no equity in your profession. You have to accept that. It's a very, very manly type of pressure. When you win a national championship or a state championship in high school, you have got one year equity. You have one year of grace, you can't let it pass by.

You have to eliminate jealousy on your team. I try to teach players in a rough way to avoid jealousy. You have to make them work together and the only way to have teamwork is to eliminate jealousy. Eliminating jealousy is the answer, it's the key to the game, so you've got to work on it. All I really do is work on

the minds of the young guys and hope that we can succeed together. If we can all go uptown together, it will all be worthwhile.

WHAT I'D DO DIFFERENTLY, THE SECOND TIME AROUND

Everett Dean

The coaching profession is unique among professions. We are not only building teams and programs, but we are, more importantly, building men and women and at the same time developing a great winning spirit, a will to win which permeates other fields and professions, and this contribution enhances our profession. Today and tomorrow our country needs this desire, this winning spirit.

Having been out of basketball coaching for 28 years, I will not discuss X's and O's. Whatever I say in my second time around reflects my philosophy of coaching, teaching, and living. Keep in mind that the following suggestions and principles are things I think I would do!

First, I would get organized by establishing my goals, giving much thought to my priorities. As a coach, I must have something to offer, to give, such as leadership, dedication, purpose, motivation, enthusiasm, and much more.

I would owe something to the game for what it has given me. I would also owe much to my players, the students, and the university that prepared me for my profession. I would also owe much to NABC for what it has done for me.

If I were to start over again, I think I would major in business. In this new world it is imperative to have business acumen for obvious reasons. I would get a Masters degree in education because the most important fundamental in coaching should be the fine art of communication.

Some Coaching Suggestions

1. I think the art of communication is a must when working with people. It comes naturally for some and difficultly for others.

2. I would master the fundamentals of the English language by taking all the basic English courses possible. I would try to be articulate in expressing myself while coaching and at other times.

3. I would try to be an avid reader of good material, thus keeping my mind alert and making myself a broader person.

4. I would work for good relationships with the athletic department, the administration, the

students, and the alumni.

5. A fine example of good public relations would be the day when the university administration asks me to be the honorary chairperson for a national fund drive to build a new building on the campus. This kind of service helps our profession.

6. It is good public relations to join your faculty club. Many faculty members are red-hot basketball fans and want to meet the coach.

7. There are many examples of good public relations within the community, and I would take public speaking courses to help my public relations.

8. I would take courses in counseling and guidance because they would be valuable in coaching and in other ways.

9. I would be interested in boys' and girls' summer camps, because they hold great possibilities for coaches.

Some Principles to Follow

1. A meaningful sign for the players' locker room: "With every right there must be a positive responsibility." If that statement could be activated, think what this old, old rule could do for our teams, our schools, and our dear country.

2. I would try to learn the great art of "giving" before "getting." This is a tried-and-true formula which pays off ten-fold.

3. To have friends, we must be a friend. Coaches need friends when they aren't winning.

4. To develop my philosophy, I would want to be for something, to have a conviction on the big issues of today – to have *ABSOLUTES* sufficient to guard against my colors running together into the gray causing me to be unable to distinguish between right and wrong.

5. I would consider it a must to provide good leadership and sound and sensible discipline for my players.

In closing, I remember years ago when the Fellowship of Christian Athletes breakfast was started at the Basketball Coaches Convention. It was a new thing to hear a coach talk about his religion and what he believes. It is different now. To be a Christian one must be dedicated. A basketball coach who is not dedicated to his coaching cannot be a successful coach over the long haul. I have found it is easier to win basketball games in a tough conference than it is to be a Christian.

PLAYING HARD THROUGH TEAM ATTITUDE
Don Meyer

There seems to be a similarity between outstanding basketball programs and outstanding organizations in business and other competitive fields. The outstanding organization seems to have one overriding purpose that is brought to the forefront of that organization and kept as a focal point for everyone involved in a cooperative effort. We have decided that in order to play championship basketball and develop players in all areas of life we must emphasize a team attitude. We have taken each of the letters of attitude to develop an acrostic to help teach our players what we think are the essential qualities that a solid team attitude contains.

AWARENESS AND COMMUNICATION. In order to be a successful player in a championship program, you must be aware of what is happening on the floor and off the floor as it relates to your team's success and your success. Awareness involves a perception of how you are really doing in classes, your relationships with other people, and your ability to perform on the basketball floor. Once you are aware of aspects that will influence the success or failure of the basketball team and your teammates it is essential that you communicate with teammates and coaches at every opportunity. The team that communicates on and off the floor is the team that most often shows the maturity and discipline necessary to do the right thing in games and more importantly in life.

TEACHABLE. This is probably one of the most important factors that we evaluate in determining who will be our top recruits. There are so many players with great talent that never become great team players because they do not have a teachable attitude. Many of us are limited in physical ability but our desire to continue to study and learn more about the game and our abilities within the game can keep them operating at their highest level of excellence.

TENACITY. This is the ability to stick with things when the newness and the novelty of it all has worn thin. We tell our players that most people would rather be bitten by a French poodle than by a bulldog. Bulldogs attack with great fury and they have the ability to maintain the attack. This is the illustration we use with our team relative to the concept of tenacity.

INTENSITY. We believe intensity is best defined as singleness of purpose, devotion to a cause, and a focus on a goal. We try to tell our players that it seems foolish to wash your car by just letting the water run out of the hose. We all know that by putting our thumb on the hose we increase the speed and the force of the water and with this concentrated focus it becomes more effective. We like our players to have this same type of intensity and concentration on their goals both on the floor and off.

TECHNIQUE. You can have all the intensity of a mad dog in a meathouse, but you will end up eventually running into a bullet if you do not learn proper technique. Technique is a responsibility of the coach and his teaching during practices and is the responsibility of the player through his ability to learn as much as possible about the game and execution in game situations. This is why teams with lesser levels of physical ability are able to win important games. We try to stress to our players that they need to be a practice player first and learn to properly and quickly execute the fundamentals of the game for the welfare of the team. This "practice player first" approach really puts an emphasis on technique.

UNSELFISH. The ability to display unselfishness is probably one of the last traits that we develop as human beings. It certainly shows a great deal of maturity and self-esteem when it is exhibited by either an individual or a team. The best way to obtain unselfishness in your program is to first of all, exhibit it as a coaching staff and secondly, reward it when it is displayed by your players.

DISCIPLINE. We define discipline as doing what you have to do, doing it as well as you possibly can, and doing it that way all the time. This is not a matter of saluting or dressing the same, but making the proper choices for the welfare of the team. We try to explain to our players that they need to try to do the next right thing, and they will be close to perfect as any human being can be.

EXECUTION. If you have the above mentioned qualities, then you will have the mental toughness which is necessary to execute in pressure situations. All the aforementioned attributes will help you make winning decisions and execute.

If there is a choice between the individual or the program we try to make sure that our players understand that choice has already been made. We feel that by stressing a cause over self, our players will always try to do the right things for the right reasons. We try to keep this idea of having something more important than yourself in your life by having our practice gear, on a nameplate, on our camp basketball, and stationary that they might use.

INTERNAL LEADERSHIP. We stress a great deal of senior responsibility and ask that they help in teaching the team concept to younger players in the program. We try to avoid the dreaded "pecking order syndrome" by emphasizing that each player is his own captain. We feel that we must be able to deal with our best players and our leaders in a little tougher fashion than we would players with lesser ability and leadership opportunity or we really don't have a team. We like our players to be aware of what we stand for and what we are about so that they will understand how to make decisions. We try to stress the idea that on a good team you have players that do the dirty jobs but on a great team everyone does the dirty jobs.

STAFF LEADERSHIP. We really try to stress a servant-leadership concept for our staff from the head coach on down to all of our student offices. We really believe that the players must have a respect for coaches and that will give much greater degree of team attitude than a fear of the coaches. We would suggest the following books to help get this concept of servant-leadership into your mind and hopefully exhibited to your players in your relationships with them.

- *Improving your Serve - The art of Unselfish Serving* by Charles Swindoll
- *Bringing Out the Best in People* by Alan Loy McGinnis
- *The Jesus Style* by Gayle D. Erwin
- *The Greatest Salesman In the World* by Og Mandino
- *The Art of War* translated by Samuel Griffith

Many coaches stress the concept of team attitude but their only real purpose for doing this is to elevate themselves to their next job because of their successful team. That is something that we all have to search in our hearts individually and determine why we are coaching. We really believe players know whether or not their coach expects greatness from them for the right reasons. Usually it's not what you have that determine what your attitude is but what has you.

BELIEF. This probably is the most critical factor for a coach and his program. We feel that the two most important aspects of belief are a strong feeling that you have done everything possible within your power to be the best you can be, and that because of this work you deserve to win more than your opponent. The teams that have this type of attitude feel that they determine the outcome of the game. We try to stress to our players that the team that wins games is the team that should have. In our program the concept of belief includes the stressing of relationships, because they are what kids remember most about their athletic career. We really try to stress the concept of not letting your buddy down.

AN O-F-F-I-C-I-A-L

J. Dallas Shirley

Why would a man of outstanding character want to subject himself to all the abuses heaped upon his shoulders by becoming an official? This and other questions regarding the men in the striped shirt have often been asked by many.

In order to get a clear answer to these questions we need to look deeper into the personality and background of these men who are so *important* to me success of Intercollegiate and Interscholastic Sports.

Who is this strange creature who enjoys blowing a whistle and imposing penalties for infractions of the rules? He may be a rich man, a poor man, a doctor, a lawyer, an Indian chief, or the butcher, the baker, the candlestick maker. More often than not however, this gentleman may be your next door neighbor, your acquaintance at the grocery store, barber shop or gas station, the man you sit next to in church on Sundays, the leader of your boy's Scout Troop, or the active worker in your community affairs. In other words, he is "Mr. Average Joe" coming from all walks of life including the professions, business, trades and industry. An everyday American citizen just like *you*. He, like all your friends, enjoys playing with his kids, attending church, engaging in wholesome activities and social events, attempting to make his community a better place in which to live, being proud of his wife and her accomplishments, etc. All too often, when the official is observed from the stands the qualities of the man are forgotten or overlooked. The next time you are inclined to cast reflections on the official's reputation, honesty, or birthright it may be fair to stop and reflect on "Who is this man?"

A recent survey revealed that the average collegiate basketball official is:

- ♦ 39 years of age
- ♦ 6 feet in height
- ♦ 182 pounds
- ♦ married with three children
- ♦ 14 years of high school officiating
- ♦ 8 years at the college level

The majority played varsity basketball in high school and a large percent in college.

It is reasonable to assume that basically the same figures would hold true of officials in other major team sports.

To understand further and possibly appreciate the official it may be interesting to know a little about the background of "Mr. Average Official." Most of the time he is a college graduate with one or more degrees in many different fields. Generally, he has played, with varying success, in the sport in which he is officiating. It is likely that he has had somewhere in the back of his head, since high school days, that when his playing days were over he would like to "blow the whistle." This individual is usually the one who has volunteered during his playing career to referee the scrimmages or fill in if an official fails to show up for an assignment.

Once he has cast his lot and really becomes serious about his ambition to become an official he must now start an intensive program of preparation. In most cases, this means filing an application with a photo and his birth certificate. Then it is the long hours of study of the rules and the manual of officiating. All this is preliminary to taking a written examination in both of these areas. This is really only a screening process since if one is successful with these examinations he must now take and pass a series of practical floor or field tests where he shows his ability to officiate under game conditions. Having met with success here he starts in the lower caliber games and after several years experience works his way up to varsity high school contests and then if he shows outstanding ability he will then move on to collegiate assignments.

At this point, many will say he is real lucky, he has made it, now all he has to do is sit back and wait for the assignments to come in each season. Nothing could be farther from the truth. This is only the beginning for now he has to constantly prove himself in each game he officiates. His yearly preparation to perform satisfactorily includes pre-season clinics. Clinics he is required to attend, often many miles from his home, usually at his own expense.

Further preparation includes the taking of examinations on the rules of the game and the mechanics of officiating, physical fitness tests, viewing of films, slides and transparencies, constant study of the rules, interpretations' notes and bulletins. This is hard road and while many travel the road, only a few reach the end.

While it may appear that it takes a long time to reach the collegiate level, it depends upon what is a long time. If the average man gets into officiating by the time is 25 years of age he should be in the collegiate ranks within five to seven years if he really has it. In fact, many conferences are not interested in taking on an official after he has reached his thirty-fifth birthday. Retirement is set at about age fifty and thus this allows a maximum of fifteen years to the conference.

So it is easy to see that "Mr. Average Official" did not just decide to put a whistle around his neck, pull on a striped shirt and go on the field or court to make a few bucks. These men are well trained, certified, supervised and dedicated officials.

Now the question in minds of many, why would a man as described above seek and desire to enter into such an avocation? If there is a need for additional money, surely there must be an easier and less hectic way of supplementing one's income. This may be true, but there are several important reasons why these men are willing to subject themselves, yes, sometimes their families, to such abuse and public criticism. First, the man must love the game and want to continue to be part of it. He has generally been connected with the game for many years of his younger life and wants to stay with it. He loves being around athletics and real men. Sports has been a part of his life and it now has become a way of life to him. He gets a thrill out of his associations.

Secondly, he finds that he can maintain good physical condition by officiating. The official must be in as good physical condition as the players. This means that well in advance of the season he starts a vigorous physical fitness program which he must maintain throughout the season. He has also learned that during the off-season he cannot allow himself to get too far out of shape for each succeeding year of life it is more difficult to return to good physical condition. Therefore, he has found that he must engage in a year round program of physical activity. This in itself means better over-all health.

Next, it is true that officiating does supplement the income. It provides those little extras, often the difference between just living and enjoying a few luxuries of life. However, it must be remembered that when one breaks down the fees received for collegiate officiating, which range from $35.00 to $200.00 per game, the hourly rate is quite low. In the minds of many, not connected with officiating, they think the official makes big money and can get rich off blowing the whistle. Yes, a few even say officials are overpaid. But a study reveals this is far from the fact.

Regardless of the fee paid, each official sincerely believes that the game he is officiating is the most important game being played on that date. To the players this is so true and the official feels the same way.

Last, many men are so dedicated to athletics that they feel this is one way they can pay back the sport that has been so kind to them. It has provided an education for many. In fact many would officiate a limited schedule even if there were no pay, just in order to assist athletics. These same men are all interested in perpetuating the history of their sports and are actively engaged in promoting the great Halls of Fame erected as shrines to their game.

Having read this article it is the hope of the author that "Mr. Average Fan" will have had answered for him many questions which he has often asked. Also, that he will learn to have a greater appreciation and respect for the men who officiate games from border to border and coast to coast.

The official is *not* a necessary evil, he is a most vital and important part of the game. He is the guardian of the game. Without him we have no contest. God bless him and long may he live.

NATIONAL ASSOCIATION OF BASKETBALL COACHES CODE OF ETHICS
Jerry Krause and George Sage

This code of ethics was adopted in 1987 in New Orleans, Louisiana.

The National Association of Basketball Coaches (NABC), the professional organization for coaches of men's basketball teams in the United States, is taking a strong leadership position at this time to develop a code of ethical conduct. This is especially appropriate as the sport of basketball nears its 100th anniversary. Moreover, the immense popularity of basketball, advanced levels of competition, and the public pressure on both coaches and athletes suggest quite clearly the need and importance of an ethical code. A Code of Ethics can act as a professional guideline in gaining and maintaining the respect and confidence of athletes, other coaches, and the public, as well as providing each basketball coach with the incentive to conduct himself in a highly ethical manner. A Code of Ethics has the potential to serve the following functions:

1. Allow basketball coaches to maintain autonomy and establish guidelines for the profession of coaching.

2. Further the development of basketball coaching as a profession.

3. Ensure that coaching will be carried out with the highest possible standards.

4. Inform member coaches of acceptable behavior in order to provide self-regulation of conduct.

5. Reassure the public that basketball coaches are deserving of public trust, confidence, and support.

Preamble

The Code of Ethics of the basketball coaching profession sets forth the principles and standards of basketball coaching and represents the aspirations of all members of the NABC. Ethics are defined as principles for right action. These principles are not laws but standards and are intended to guide basketball coaches individually and collectively in maintaining the highest professional level of ethical conduct.

Principles

1. Coaches are accountable to the highest standards of honesty and integrity. All practices should be consistent with the rules of the game and the educational purposes of the institution.

2. Coaches are responsible for assisting athletes in acquiring the necessary knowledge and skills of basketball as well as promoting desirable personal and social traits in athletes under their direction.

3. Coaches treat all persons with dignity and respect providing a model of fair play and sportsmanship.

4. Coaches observe the letter and intent of the rules of the sport and insist that athletes and teams under their direction do the same.

5. Coaches clarify in advance and act in full accordance with institutional, conference, and national governing body rules while avoiding actions that may violate the legal and/or civil rights of others.

6. Coaches have a primary concern for the health, safety, and personal welfare of each athlete. The athlete's education is also held foremost.

7. Coaches perform their duties on the basis of careful preparation, ensuring that their instruction is current and accurate. They use practices for which they are qualified and continually acquire new knowledge and skills.

8. Coaches accurately represent the competence, training, and experience of themselves and their colleagues.

9. Coaches honor all professional relationships with athletes, colleagues, officials, media, and the public. They avoid conflicts of interest and exploitation of those relationships, especially by outside parties.

10. Coaches have an obligation to respect the confidentiality of information obtained from persons in the course of their work.

11. Coaches take an active role in the prevention and treatment of drug, alcohol, and tobacco abuse.

12. Coaches carry out all obligations of employment contracts, unless released from those obligations by mutual agreement. When considering interruption or termination of service, appropriate notice is given.

Implementation

The Code of Ethics will be used as a condition of membership in the National Association of Basketball Coaches. All members will be provided a copy of the Code as a part of the membership application. To qualify for membership, an applicant must sign a statement acknowledging having read the Code and subscribing to the principles of the Code.

Enforcement

The coaches of the colleges, universities, and institutions that are members of the NABC are also members of governing organizations for those schools (NF, NJCAA, NAIA, and NCAA). The enforcement of a violation of the Code of Ethics will be executed by the rules, regulations, and procedures of the appropriate governing organization.

Chapter 3   PLANNING YOUR PROGRAM

BUILDING A PROGRAM

C. M. Newton

When I'm talking about building a basketball program, I'm talking about specific situations I've been in, hoping that you can get an idea that will help you in your own situations. I would like to suggest to you that if you get the opportunity to go in and build a basketball program, you jump at that opportunity. I'd also like to suggest to you that you change some of your own thinking.

I had two unique opportunities to build a basketball program in 23 years of college coaching. One was in a small college situation in Kentucky where there was really no hope – no subsidy, no scholarships. I just had to go ahead from scratch and build something. And then I had the opportunity some years ago to go to the University of Alabama where, as all of you know, a great football tradition exists, but no basketball tradition. And I had an opportunity to build a program there.

Before you accept a "construction" job, you need to evaluate certain things. First, you must have a commitment to a basketball program. What do you expect and what will be expected of you?

Second, you need strong administrative support for the program. Without that support you'll run into problems, such as budget considerations. Third, you must be given time. It cannot be done quickly, at any level.

The next step in building a program is to consider some immediate critical needs. First, evaluate the players there, both returnees and the new ones you are going to get. They should be those that can be developed.

The second immediate need is staff. What I wanted in my building program when I hired an assistant coach was *loyalty*, first and foremost. Technical competence was assumed. Loyalty is critical in a building program. Furthermore, there must be compatibility among the coaches and love for the sport.

The last and most difficult need to overcome is the development of good work habits and a positive attitude. You've got to change attitudes and become success-oriented. There probably is no winning tradition, and you must help generate one.

I believe the three steps to a winning program are these:

1. Define your goals.

2. Devise a plan to achieve your goals.

3. Execute the plan.

And finally, a successful program must have the following six vital ingredients:

1. **Talent.** This involves recruiting, and recruiting to me is selecting people who in turn select you and your program. Talent is where you start.

2. **Organization.** This is the ability to organize talent so it plays as closely as possible to potential. This is the coaches' job – what you and I get paid for. We should communicate success to the player and educate him. This process involves practice plans, utilization of assistant coaches, and participation in actual teaching situations.

3. **Team concept.** This is, I think, the hardest thing to achieve. First of all, we achieve it at Alabama by talking about it as a team. We discuss the importance of the word "team." We change the word "I" to "we"; we eliminate "I" from our vocabulary. Third, we carry it over in practice, such as we always acknowledge a good pass or assist.

4. **Discipline.** This we try to do by minimizing rules and maximizing guidelines. We only have three rules: (a) You must go to class; (b) No drugs allowed, *period*; (c) You must be on time to all basketball-related events. By having guidelines, we try to instill discipline rather than impose it.

5. **Winning attitude.** A positive attitude is needed to build a program.

6. **Leadership.** We must allow youngsters to experience leadership for it to develop. The point I want to make is this: Don't strictly gear yourself to thinking, "Will I go to a Kentucky, a North Carolina, or a UCLA or whatever?" Think in terms, rather, of that opportunity to build a program. To me, that's one of the real unique and exciting coaching opportunities.

PROMOTING YOUR PROGRAM
George H. Raveling

Objectives

1. Raise money.

2. Improve the existing facilities.

3. Visibility — create a greater awareness of the program in the community and nation.

4. Create enthusiasm, pride, and a winner's attitude.

Individuals Involved in Promotional Program

1. Coaches, players, parents (be certain to involve women)

2. Faculty (important to include people like janitors and secretaries)

3. Students (fraternities, sororities, cheerleaders, campus leaders)

4. Community (find good artists, good writers)
   a. Civic groups
   b. School interest groups (alumni)
   c. Athletic interest groups

5. News media (start with your sports information director; have personal meetings with him)

Plan of Operation

1. List your program's goals in order of importance (how much money is needed).
   a. Long-range goals
   b. Short-range goals
   c. Create a slogan for the year

2. Assign individual areas of responsibility.
   a. Schedule periodical meetings with group leaders
   b. Encourage creative and new ideas

3. Establish an operational schedule.
   a. Weekly objectives
   b. Monthly objectives
   c. Keep accurate records

4. Devise imaginative point of sale materials.
   a. The more controversial, the better
   b. Distribution of materials is important; have mass exposure

5. Implement your plan.

Review of Year's Efforts

1. Review promotions.

2. Discuss methods for improvement.

3. Discontinue promotions that were not effective.

4. Consider new ideas.

5. Be certain to praise and thank all individuals concerned.

6. Don't overwork an idea – leave them hungry.

Money-Raising Promotions

1. Sell placemats.

2. Sell T-shirts.

3. Calendar ads.

4. Coaching clinic.

5. Games around the state (exhibition).

6. Sell pressbooks.

7. Sell bumper stickers.

8. Raffle ball at booster meetings.

9. Hoop Club group (newsletter, parking, weekly meetings).

10. Fundamentals notebook.

11. Make the team clinic.

Game Promotions

Identify games that are likely to have poor attendance in advance. The following are ideas for special promotions:

1. Homecoming.

2. Dad's weekend.

3. Mother's weekend.

4. Bus trips (two-hour radius of school).

5. Free tickets to radio station for giveaway.

6. Supermarkets.

7. Wrestling bear.

8. Alumni game.

9. Pie-throwing contest

10. $100 pick-up

11. Poster night.

12. Game program with lucky number.

13. Sign night.

14. Date night.

15. Sox night.

16. Foul shot night.

17. Band day and cheerleader day.

18. Invite area teams to play preliminary game.

Team Promotions

1. Team awards.

2. Basketball banquet.

3. Autograph and picture day at shopping center.

4. Fan club.

5. Pressbook.

6. Pre-season flyer.

7. Clippings sent to parents and coach.

8. Picture of player to his high school.

9. Foreign trip.

10. Highlight film.

Program Promotions

1. Summer camp.

2. Basketball clinics.

3. TV show.

4. Radio show.

5. Faculty meeting (once a month) welcome faculty to practice, let them sit on bench, and so on.

6. Sponsor's Player of the Game.

7. Visiting locker room.

8. Academic booklet.

9. Visit children's hospitals and old-age homes on trips.

10. Speaking engagements.

11. Telephone call in hook-up (for writers and fans to call in on).

12. Weekly radio tapes and TV tapes.

Facilities that are Important to Improve

1. Office.

2. Dressing room.

3. Press room.

4. Visiting locker room.

5. Film room.

6. Weight room.

7. Hallways.

8. Basketball court.

9. Billboards

Groups to Create

1. Sign makers.
2. Visiting team greeters.
3. Noisemakers at games.
4. Office helpers (volunteer).
5. People to fix up motel rooms of visiting team.
6. Managers to host visiting team.

DAILY PRACTICE

John Wooden

It is quite probable that the success or failure of most coaches is in direct proportion to their ability to devise practice drills to meet their particular needs, and then properly coordinate them into the daily practice program. A tremendous knowledge of the game is wasted if the coach cannot pass along his ideas to the players.

Each practice should be carefully planned and organized to prevent waste of time. There must be a specific purpose for every drill, and every drill must be placed in the most advantageous time during the practice period. A drill used at an improper time is about as useless as a drill that has no concrete purpose at all.

The daily practice program should never be planned in a hurry, but at a time when the coach and his assistants can consider all relevant factors and then develop the program for the day. Both the past and the future must be taken into consideration as well as personnel, physical condition, morale, available facilities, and many other things.

I keep a record of all of our practice sessions from year to year, and keep the record of the two previous years at my fingertips for reference when planning our practice for the day. Comments are made in regard to each drill after each practice and then written at the side of the record that I keep. This serves as a very valuable reference.

Here are a few of the things I believe I must be aware of:

1. After practice starts, the program must be followed to the letter. If not enough time was allowed for a drill, you must not continue it past the designated time. This would mean that you would either have to eliminate something else that you had felt was important or you would have to run overtime. Neither would be advisable.

It is all right to add something when it turns out you have allowed too much time for a specific drill, or you might replace a drill with another if the player around whom the drill was designed is absent.

2. Be certain to start each practice with warm-up drills that are specifically devised to loosen up players well. Stretching, bending, and jumping drills should be used as well as running and should be progressively more intense.

3. Drills must be varied from day to day to prevent monotony, although it is possible that some will be used every day. This should be true of warm-up drills just the same as shooting, rebounding, defensive or any other drills.

4. If the purpose of every drill is explained before it is used the first time, the players generally respond better.

5. The same drill should not be continued for too long. It is better to have more drills for the same purpose.

6. Physically difficult drills should be followed by more pleasurable drills and vice-versa.

7. Drills should be as competitive as possible and should simulate game conditions whenever possible.

8. New drills should always be presented early in the practice period before the players become too tired and their learning processes slowed down. I believe that it is not wise to try to practice a new drill the first time it is presented; it is better to come back with it the next day and start practicing it.

9. Every effort should be made to condition the players for game competition, and the drills should be devised and used to best advantage for that purpose.

10. More time for team drills must be allowed as the season progresses. Never forget, overlook, or neglect the individual fundamentals that should take up at least 50 percent of the practice time.

11. Analyze each day's practice while it is still fresh in your mind. I like to discuss the practice with my assistant before leaving the dressing room and make notes that will be taken into consideration when planning the practice for the next day.

12. Combine as many fundamentals as possible in your drills, although your emphasis may be on one only. Do not permit a player to develop a bad habit in one fundamental merely because your emphasis is on another.

13. Use small, carefully-organized groups of from three to five players for teaching fundamentals. At times you will have all your guards, forwards, and post men in their own specific groups. However, you must remember that each player doesn't need the same amount of time on each fundamental.

14. Although it is almost impossible to work on one without the other, offense and defense should be emphasized on alternate days.

The top six, seven, or eight players should be on offense during the time permitted for the development of team play on an offensive day and on a defensive day.

15. Close each practice with a drill that leaves both players and coaches in a pleasant, optimistic frame of mind. This is good for everyone, including the coach's wife and children.

Condition players before this last drill, as you do not want them to leave the floor feeling punished.

FINDING ADDITIONAL PRACTICE TIME

Jim Casciano

Our practice session is one of the most important areas in our basketball program. Practice time is precious, so we spend a great deal of time planning each session. We have a master, weekly, and daily practice plan that enables us to use our time more effectively and better prepare our team.

We were able to find additional practice time without actually extending the length of each practice. By taking a careful look at our practices, we found the following three areas to be lacking in both organization and purpose:

1. The time before the start of actual practice.

2. The time immediately after practice.

3. The time during practice when our players were not involved in on-the-court instruction.

In an attempt to make better use of our practice time, we decided to utilize these periods. We began by simply defining each area in the following manner:

Pre-Practice — the time spent working on a given area before the start of actual practice.
Post-Practice — the time spent working on a game area after actual practice.
Side-Work — work to be done by each player when not involved in on-the-court instruction.

Through simple definition, we gave an organized approach to our total practice time while selling our players on the importance of each practice session. We look upon these times as a supplement to what we cover during practice, and generally the time is spent working on both individual and team-related fundamentals. It also enables us to concentrate on fundamentals during the course of the year when most coaches are inclined to move on to more team-oriented areas.

We feel the following principles should be present during each of the defined practice times:

1. Sell the importance of each area to your players.

2. Each area should be supervised by a coach.

3. Coaches must be involved and enthusiastic.

4. Insist upon intense concentrated effort – no room for poor execution.

5. Utilize teaching aides such as toss-backs, rebounding machines, and mini-leapers whenever possible.

6. Drills must be quick and game-related – we are looking for a carryover as much as possible.

7. Drills should be changed weekly to prevent monotony and boredom.

8. Read the situation and be flexible. For example, you might need to include more "fun" drills during pre-practice or have no post-practice session when you sense an air of staleness.

9. Remember that the pre- and post-practice are a supplement to actual practice and will set the tone for each practice.

10. Remember that the pre- and post-practice are actually done on your players' time, so each should be treated more informally without sacrificing execution. Make the most of each available minute!

Because most players become psychologically conditioned to a set amount of time for practice, it is important that the pre- and post-practice not be handled in the same manner as the actual practice. Otherwise, your players might view it as nothing but a longer practice and develop negative attitudes – not only toward the work before and after practice, but more importantly toward the actual practice. By being more informal and by keeping the drills short and quick, you can create a positive attitude toward practice.

Two other areas that help us create a positive situation at Washington and Lee are the following:

1. The pre-, post- and side-work areas are the sole responsibility of the assistant coach(es). This enables him (or them) to become more involved with the players and create an identity.

2. This in turn enables the head coach to communicate informally with the players, especially the eleventh and twelfth man who normally do not have much contact with the head coach during practice.

(Do not underestimate the importance of these two intangible areas within your program).

Pre-Practice

How many of you have had players casually stroll onto the practice floor with no idea of what to work on?

We have solved that problem by demanding that all players must jog five laps to warm up, followed up by a series of stretching exercises, as soon as they hit the floor. It is then time for pre-practice. Our players work in pairs on some area of their game. There is no room for "social shooting" within our program.

Our pre-practice begins 20 minutes before the start of our actual practice. The following outline should help you understand our objectives for this period:

1. Each player has the responsibility of knowing when pre-practice begins and what areas to work on. This eliminates valuable time being wasted.

EARLY SEASON ASSIGNMENTS		
Time	Group A	Group B
6 mins. (3 minutes each group then rotate) 5 minutes	Ballhandling (6 drills, 30 sec/each) Ex: figure 8 w/wo dribbling the ball	Quickness - Reaction (6 drills,, 30 sec/each) Ex: speed jump rope consecutive jumps
Dribbling	(both groups) 1-on-1 half court then half court 1-on-1 chaser drill	
5 minutes	Passing - (3 man groups) work on G to F pass with defense on guard work on F to post pass with defense on forward.	
4 minutes	Shooting - (3 man groups) need passer and defense 30 seconds from foul lane intersection to intersection, total of 2 minutes per player	

Table 3.1

2. Schedules for the pre-, post-, and side-work are posted in the locker room as well as on the practice floor.

3. During pre-practice, we concentrate on individual fundamentals (ballhandling, passing, dribbling, and shooting), a breakdown of our offense, a breakdown by position, and also individually assigned weakness work.

4. All work is done in groups of two or three players, with each group being changed on a weekly basis. There will be exceptions to this; for example: the Blue Team (our first team) working together on our passing game.

Time	Assignment - Blue Team And White Team
7 minutes	4-man breakdown of early offense
7 minutes	3-man breakdown of plays #2 and #4
6 minutes	Shooting: (30 seconds at a time - 2 minutes per player) 1. Transition shots - #2,, #3 men (45 degrees 16 feet off the glass) 2. Penetration and pullup for jump shot #1 man (10 to 12 feet in blue) 3. Low post shot - #5 man (turn around off glass from block and baby hook) 4. Dribble to baseline for jump shot - #4 man (15 foot corner shot)

Table 3.2

Post-Practice

The following outlines our post-practice routine:

1. The post-practice must be kept short - about five minutes. It should not be viewed as punishment.

2. Work can be assigned in the following ways:
   a. By position.
   b. According to individual weaknesses. For example, player Smith working on defensive rebounds and outlet passes.
   c. As a result of poor individual and/or team execution. For example, a unit working on proper execution of the passing game, with concentration on proper cuts.
   d. To allow extra game-situation and free throw shooting. For example, four sets of 30-second shooting or 10 free throws – two at a time.

3. Not all players need be required to work each day. For example: Monday – only #2 and #3 men work on transition jump shots.

4. Remember, the post-practice session sets the tone for practice the next day.

5. Read the situation; a cancelled post-practice session, when it is deserved, does wonders for mental well-being.

Side-Work

Because only 10 players can play at a time, what are the two or four players on the sidelines doing during a scrimmage or halfcourt drill? Are they permitted to do anything they want, or are they instructed to work on some specific area?

Each player should be kept busy during the entire length of practice – not with busy work just to fill time, but as an opportunity to work on fundamentals.

The following outline explains our philosophy on side-work:

1. The actual time spent by each player on side-work drills varies because of the amount of practice time each player receives.

2. Each player is expected to complete the assigned side-work during practice, but flexibility is necessary because of point number one.

3. Free throws must be shot each day, with the results recorded.

4. During side-work we concentrate on game-like shooting and free throws, rebounding, and quickness/reaction drills.

5. All work should be done in pairs to ensure competition. Here are two examples of our side-work sessions:

I

20 free throws – five at a time with a two-way sprint between each set.

40 shots by position (20 each side of floor).
> #1 men – intersections of foul line.
> #2,3 men – 45-degree angle, 16 feet, off glass.
> #4,5 men – turnaround jumper from the block, off glass.

Tap drill – 20 each hand.

Repetition layup drill – use toss-back; two sets of 30 seconds each hand.

II

20 free throws – similate one-and-one opportunities, running a one-way sprint for each shot missed.

Repetition shooting – four at 30 seconds; 45-degree angle off of toss-back.

Rebound and outlet – two at 30 seconds off of toss-back.

Offensive rebound and outlet – 20 each side.

As you can see, many things must be considered to get the maximum results from each area of practice. You not only should be well-organized, you should believe strongly in the objectives that you have given to your pre-, post-, and side-work sessions. Your players are a reflection of you and your philosophy and will respond to the examples you set.

The way you utilize these times and your objectives should be consistent with the philosophy of your program. Every minute can be a timely investment in your program and in what every coach is looking to achieve: success.

ORGANIZATION OF PRACTICE AND SEASON
Chuck Daly

I would like to discuss a variety of topics that relate to coaching.

When I was at Duke University, where I was an assistant for six years, we started something that is not done much in basketball, but is done in football: going to watch other people's practices. In football they exchange films and do some other things that we don't do. I have kept up that practice since then at every school where I have been.

I know many fantastic egos inhabit the coaching world, and people tend to believe that whatever they do is best. My feeling, however, is that there are a number of ways to skin a cat. I will relate two recent incidents that show why I think this.

I was in San Diego at the Final Four in 1975. I watched all four teams work out and I was very impressed with the ideas from their practice. And the other day I was involved in an All-Star Game in which Lefty Dreisell was working with a group of players. He did a little something with his group. I picked up a drill that I thought was fantastic for working against zones.

I think John Wooden, at the conclusion of a game, made a statement to the effect that it would be a shame if brute force won out over mobility and finesse, and I think he is right. Unfortunately, I think that we are going in the other direction on the collegiate level. Because of the scholarship rule and the freshman rule, it is of concern to me. As you go along I think that you have to start talking about philosophies and decide what you are trying to accomplish.

I think that the whole idea of practice and pre-practice planning is really what it's all about in terms of your year. If you make incorrect decisions and you can't do anything about your plan to make your kids happy, you will be very limited in what you are doing. You will spend the year defending things or making changes in your offense or defense and that won't bring success.

The other thing that I have noticed about college coaching is that the people who are succeeding are the ones who have an unbelievable intensity about the game. They have a real basic philosophy about the game and the intensity and basic approach go hand-in-hand. I think they are right. They are a little bit like Vince Lombardi in their approach. The more intellectual you get about the game, the more problems you develop for yourself, because you start to change up and get away from your basic philosophy.

The two steps to success are:

1. Know where you are going.

2. Know how you are going to get there.

This again goes back to intensity and the success of that basic philosophy. I am going to touch on some of these areas.

One thing that you should be concerned about is the place in which you play. I know many coaches have no control over where they play and their situation. It is very definitely a problem. You must decide what you can do to make your facility a better place in which to operate. First of all, what kind of floor do you have? I am not talking about the surface, I want to know if it is dirty. I have a fetish about that. I was not a great player, but when I played it really bothered me to have dirt on the ball when I was practicing shooting. Our managers must sweep the floor before we start. It is a small thing, but it is important. How about lighting? Can you do anything about the lighting? How about the temperature of your building? Does that have any effect on your program? I think that it does. We play in a place called Palestra. We have a horrible time in there many times because of the temperature. What kind of equipment do you have? Do you have old balls that are scuffed up and dirty? I think the managers ought to keep them clean. I think that this is important. I don't think that the managers should sit around and become the best shooters on the team. I think they should be willing to clean the balls. If you ever get them dirty, forget it, you will never get that ball to come back. They should be cleaned every 10 to 15 days. The atmosphere of the place where you practice should be as pleasant as you can make it. I know you have heard about cluttered locker rooms, but it is true that you must do anything that you can for your players. Some of you don't have this problem, because you have a new facility or a more than adequate building for your program.

Developing the Support Staff

Now, let's go on to people. You must decide where and how your assistant coaches and other associates will fit into your program. I think it can vary in certain situations. In a high school program you might not have very much control over this. If you don't, I don't believe you can have a very good program. The only way you can succeed at the high school level is if you have control over your assistants, all the way down to the beginning levels of your school. Whatever you are trying to do in your program, you must teach those who are helping you what you want accomplished. If you do not play a zone defense, your lower-level coaches should not be teaching their players how to play a zone.

Managers are very important in any program. You must decide what you want them to do and assign them duties. They can get to the point where they are almost assistant coaches. They can really be a help in statistics, for example. I believe that one of the least-kept statistics in basketball is in blocking out for rebounding position. I used to have my managers keep a daily chart and indicate when a player missed a check-off. They can get pretty good at it.

The administration is important to us all, and like the media you must work on a close basis with them. You have to know the people you are dealing with and be able to present your thinking to them on many topics. They must back you and supply the things you need to get where you are going. You must recognize their role, but you must also be your own man.

I don't know how you feel about it, but I think that it is pretty well established that we all want our players to be on time for practice. This could be a rather tough situation in some schools and it is something that has to be sold to the kids. You must remember that our situation is different because we don't offer a grant-in-aid. Our players are there in a situation that is based on financial need. I think that everything we do has to be more saleable. Things in coaching have changed in recent years. We are wanting discipline, but that discipline must be sold to the players because of a changing philosophy of discipline and the more intellectual kids we deal with. I believe that players must be on time, but in our situation, because of the academic demands, we have a problem getting all of our players at the same time. We have no control over the academic situation. Some of the players come for an hour or an hour and 15 minutes. This is a problem for us.

The coaches and players should dress well. I think this is a pride factor and creates a positive approach. The practice uniforms should all be alike. We get our players a shooting shirt with their nickname on the back.

Organizing Practices

Now, let's get into the actual planning of the workout sessions. It is kind of interesting, but I believe that planning never really stops. We think every day about what we can do to help our program. It is a constant thing that might not be written down, but is considered each day. We as coaches are constantly planning what we will do next year. You do not wait until September to do your planning, even though much of your planning occurs at that time for the coming season. Your planning for next year should start right after your last game this year.

There are a number of things that we try to do in organizing our practices and other phases of our program. On game day, our players know exactly what they are to do, as do our coaches. It is important that everyone know what to do and when they are to do it. I think that you must utilize all of your players and coaches to the best of their abilities.

We practice for two hours, or two-and-one-half hours in the pre-season. In December we go to two hours. After we get to January, if we stay longer than an hour-and-a-half we feel we are belaboring the situation. I think you have to think about your kids mentally at that stage of the season. You have to be very careful about the length of practice in terms of keeping your players alive and keeping people involved. Again, I go back to using the people you have with you. I think that the kids get very tired of hearing the same guy over a period of five or six months. He hears you say the same thing in the same tone of voice over and over again.

Let's talk about the post-mortems of practice. I think a lot of people practice, walk to the locker room, shower, and they're gone. I think that it is important to have what I call a post mortem. You have 12 guys on your club; we all talk about doing as much with the twelfth guy on our club as the first, but that is an out-and-out lie. If you are doing it, you are super, because I think that it is very, very difficult. No matter what anyone says, we all get involved with the players that produce for us. I think that it is very hard to keep that twelfth guy interested.

I think that you can do a lot in evaluating your players by sitting down after practice and talking about each player and deciding what they need to keep their interest. I don't like guys to get disinterested. Those people are the basis of your program. We all agree that your first group is only going to be as good as the group they are going against. The more you can get the substitutes to put out on a day-to-day basis, the better club you are going to have. I believe that you can do something about that through the post mortem situation. After practice you can say, "What happened today? How involved were we?" You then can get a better idea if you accomplished what you wanted from your workout.

We start out every day with a meeting, whether it is five minutes or ten minutes. I believe that it is a good way of getting into practice, and you establish a rapport with the players. We do calisthenics, and I am a firm believer that different players warm up to different degrees. It takes some players longer to warm up than others. We have a warm-up aspect where we try to get everyone ready, then really get into practice. Our post portem is spent with the coaches for the most part, but we will work with players after practice on things we feel they need work on.

Everything we do is timed, and we try to stay within the framework of our practice schedule. I do not do a good job of coaching unless I can stay on a daily schedule. But, we work so hard at planning our practices that we usually do not make a mistake in doing what we want to do in the certain time limit.

FORMULATING A GAME PLAN
Bob Knight

The game plan for any given game begins with your first day of practice. I cannot get ready for an opponent in a week or a few days. Things that happen all come about because of organization and planning.

The following areas are crucial in formulating a game plan:

1. Practice schedule

2. Competition

3. Conversion

4. Individual work

5. Team work

The practice schedule is the most important area. You must be dedicated and ready for hard work as of the first day of practice. We believe that our practices must be similar to a game in time, length, and in everything that we do. We spend no more than five minutes per drill. I feel that various practice areas should be spread out. We don't like to spend 40 minutes on defense at one time. We would rather have four 10-minute sessions on defense. It is my job to get the team ready to play and I set the tone in practice. For example, I will call out "two-ball passing" and they know that I want a two-minute drill on peripheral passing. (Refer to Figure 3.1.)

1. Players spaced 12 to 15 feet apart.

2. Random passes.

3. You cannot pass to the man next to you. The ball always goes back to the middle man and the two end men are a full step behind the central feeder.

4. The rotation is clockwise and goes every 15 seconds.

We want to get from one drill to another as quickly as possible. This is where many coaches waste time.

Every drill needs to incorporate quickness, motion, and movement. We will change a drill right in the middle of it by making a "call." This is to get the players to think. I call the instructions one time only. We chart all drills and keep track of errors. They have to run laps for various mistakes. This causes peer pressure and competition, both individual and team.

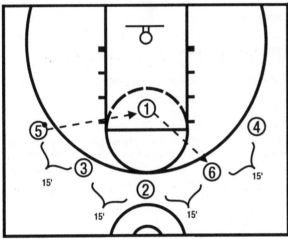

Figure 3.1

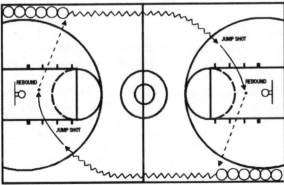

Figure 3.2

We work our five-ball passing drill for 60 seconds. The group that scores the most baskets wins. This is called out and the kids know what to do. Refer to Figure 3.2.

1. We like to start practice with this.

2. Drive to free throw line extended and shoot a jumper.

3. This is both individual and team competition, and also good for ending practice.

Competition is very important in your daily practices. We will set up "Partner shooting, three games to 10, losers run." This is the actual call and we will go right into the drill. In any learning situation, reinforcement is necessary to ensure that learning actually takes place. Reinforcement of winning is vital.

Conversion from offense to defense is more important than offense and defense themselves. We work on this every day when we are working five-on-five. I will have a ball at midcourt and I will throw it on the floor or to another defensive man and call "white ball going the other way." The red must change from offense to defense and get back to stop the break. I will change the drill and call "white ball going the other way." The red must change from offense to defense and get back to stop the break. I will change the drill and call "white going the other way, change men," so we can make conversion as hard as we would like.

Individual work each night is essential in developing an offensive or defensive system. Fundamentals are important and we work on them after our players warm up. We begin warm-up at 2:50, and when we finish with that we begin our individual fundamentals, as follows:

1. Screening

2. Defensive stance

3. F denial (take away the lead)

4. Block out

5. Shooting
   a. paired
   b. set up man, cut, and shoot

In between each shooting drill we shoot free throws. We even incorporate working on passing and faking during this time.

   c. free throws (one to two minutes) are charted and even made into games
   d. slide to open spots and shoot, individuals work as to where they will get shots against a zone
   e. pressured shooting, five shots at a time in a paired situation

We will work on a combination of skills during individual work as well.

6. Defensing the flash pivot (offensive and defensive)

7. Screening and cutting (offensive and defensive)

Team work is the last of the five areas I mentioned that we work on daily to help formulate our game plan. Many of our drills use all five people. We strive to always work under game-type conditions. When working in a five-on-five situation, we vary our point of pick-up and change possession on a call. For example, we will be playing five-on-five and red will have the ball. I will call "white ball three-on-three with post man and block out." Refer to Figure 3.3.

When working in this setup, we might try to give a lot of perimeter pressure.

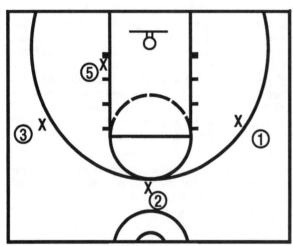

Figure 3.3

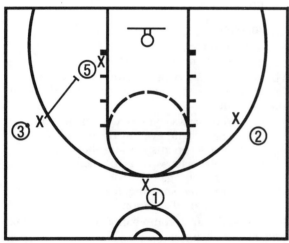

Figure 3.4

We could pressure the passer, and if the ball goes inside we will help out with our outside defenders. If we are defending a wing passer and the ball goes into the post, the outside defender collapses *now*, face-to-face on the post man. Also, when we are in this three-on-three with a post, the outside offensive people can't post up (see Figure 3.4).

We also play four against five with pressure on the most logical people and try to get in the passing lanes. We leave the man farthest from the basket open.

On any kind of ball movement we must constantly be changing men and making "game decisions."

Another audible call is "defensive break" — a coach passes the ball to a defender and the offense must put down the ball and break back with the change of possession. We will call out "five man change – switch men."

Now our players have to communicate, change ends of the floor, and prevent the basket too. Sometimes we will do this and not change ends of the floor.

I mentioned before that it is a game of quickness, change, and adjustment. Our drills emphasize change. We work on possession change every day in practice. All of the above really are focused on the defense.

We can now change gears and work on our offense and its related drills of change. You must be able to change with the defense. Again, our ability to react with quickness under stress is the key to finalizing any game plan. You can go back through the above drills and simply stress offense instead of defense. Whenever we work against the press, we automatically use six men against five. This puts pressure on the offense and makes them think and execute.

I am going to cover some other important areas in regard to practice and its planning. A head coach must be able to utilize his assistant coaches fully. We will have a coach assigned to watch a particular thing during a segment of practice, such as watching for block-out. He will usually work at one end of the floor or follow the flow of the action. I have the luxury of using two or three coaches.

We change players every 20 minutes. We will break at this point to shoot free throws for two or three minutes and make the changes. Some players may never change, but your sure-fire first group must get practice time with the backup people.

After we get into the season, we enter our second area of concern. We use each game as a guidepost. We go over the game film and check all areas. As soon as one game is over we begin planning for the next one. First of all, we make verbal and working changes in our new game plan. We get the opponents' basic set and check out what is involved in beating them and if they have any similarities to the last game we played. If there are any new ideas for our players to have or any major changes, then they have that knowledge before the next morning.

Scouting reports are very important; we want to know the following things:

1. Defensive match-ups and the alternative, if any.

2. The offensive percentage breakdown as to what they do best and what they do most often.

3. What they do that we can get into drill form and do in practice.

4. Where we can get help from on offense and defense. Sometimes if you have a poor scorer you can put him down.

5. How far out we can pick them up (contrast in speeds).

6. Out-of-bounds setup from under and sideline.

7. What defense they run and what we will do against it.

8. The strength of their defensive players and their speed, foul problems, and anything they do that is unusual. If they like to run and have an outlet man, he will be made to play post defense.

We then give the information on the other team to our players in practice and team meetings. They are given this information in a precise, condensed form, none of which is written. If we have back-to-back games, we will go over the new opponent at a morning walk-through and team meeting. All of the above information is listed in order of importance. We don't like to tell a player to do something in a game that we have never done before. If I have to do that, I feel as if I have made a coaching error. Most of the previously mentioned scouting information is individual. From a team standpoint we work on changing tempo and we also like to walk through our opponent's offense.

At our pre-game meal we will go over everything again and make any changes that we have to make.

We make a lot of use out of visual aids. I subscribe to the newspaper in the town of every team we play and also to the school paper. I read them all myself. They will give you enough information to make it well worth your while. I don't allow any telephone calls to the players and no interviews unless they are conducted in the sports information director's office, and those are by appointment only. Take the information gathered from the papers and set up individual or team challenges, such as a point total or a field goal percentage.

Reorientation of purpose is very important in basketball. We put an important point on each player's plate and on the blackboard as soon as one game is over. Forget the last game and go on to the next. Football is the easiest game in the world to coach. They have six days before every game and about 40

seconds between each play. A play only takes an average of about six seconds in basketball.

We make out grade sheets for the players and then before each opponent we will set individual and team goals. We see how many of these goals we can attain. If we achieve the right six we can beat most people; eight is the highest we have ever made and that was during our championship year in 1976. If you reach all 11 goals, you could beat the NBA champions. Here are the goals – four defensive, three offensive, and four combination points:

Defensive Goals
♦ Give up x number of points each game
♦ Opponents' turnovers — (use a percentage of possessions)
♦ Opponents' field goal percentage (42%)
♦ No opponent scores 20 points

Offensive Goals
♦ Your field goal percentage (52%)
♦ Your free throw percentage
♦ Turnovers — (use a percentage of possessions)

Combination Points
♦ Percentage of rebounds we get
♦ X number of shots more than opponents
♦ Number of personal fouls we make
♦ Score first each half

You set your own standards and work from there. When we won the national championship in 1976, we averaged 4.9 in attainment of goals. The field goal shooting percentages I have recommended are two things I have always maintained as constants.

The other things that I have told you are things that work for me. Some of these things might help you. If they all help you, your program is in a lot of trouble. I hope that you will disagree with some of the things I have mentioned.

I think the greatest statement about the game I ever heard was made by Pete Newell, who in my opinion is one of the two or three greatest coaches ever. He said, "You've got to get better shots than your opponents, and that describes your offense. And you've got to get more of them (shots) and that describes your defense."

HIGH SCHOOL ORGANIZATION AND EVALUATION

Morgan Wootten

The most important factor is the relationship between the coach and his individual players. To develop a good relationship, a year-end evaluation meeting is held with the coach and the individual player. At this meeting the player's strengths and weaknesses are discussed. Players are informed of exactly where they stand and what they need to work on over the summer. I have found the players to be much happier and willing to work much harder after these meetings, because they know that the coaches care.

The evaluation sheet is also reviewed with the players when they return to school in the fall. It is also important for the coach to keep in contact with his players in the summer. One-on-one talks with players are also most important during the season.

A master plan for the coming year, a monthly plan, a weekly plan and a daily plan are essential for the good organization. All old plans and reports are filed and kept so they may be referred to. Assistant coaches are assigned specific areas. Plans are changed from year to year to fit the personnel.

Dematha High School Master Plan Sheet

I. Offense
  A. Team
    1. Against man-to-man
    2. Against zone
    3. Against combination
    4. Against pressure
  B. Individual
    1. Without the ball
    2. With the ball

II. Defense
  A. Team
    1. Man-to-man
    2. Zone
    3. Combination
    4. Press
  B. Individual
    1. On the ball
    2. Away from the ball
    3. Pivot or post area

III. Conditioning
  A. Physiological
  B. Psychological

IV. Fundamentals
  A. Footwork
  B. Passing
  C. Shooting
  D. Dribbling

V. Rebounding
  A. Offensive
  B. Defensive

VI. Conversions
  A. Offense to defense
  B. Defense to offense

VII. Free throw situations
  A. Offensive alignment
  B. Defensive alignment

VIII. Jump ball situations
  A. Offensive circle
  B. Midcourt circle
  C. Defensive circle

IX. Out-of-bounds situations
  A. Defensive end
  B. Sideline
  C. Offensive end

X. Time and score situations
  A. Delay game for lead protection
  B. Special blitz offense when trailing
  C. Special plays

XI. Player and team evaluation
  A. Dematha
    1. Charts and statistics
    2. Scouting reports
    3. Film
  B. Opponents
    1. Statistics
    2. Scouting reports
    3. Film

XII. Rules

XIII. Game organization
  A. Pre-game
  B. Strategy
    1. Game play
    2. Bench
    3. Timeouts
    4. Half-time
  C. Post game

XIV. Trip organization
  A. Schedule
  B. Players
    1. Rules
    2. Dress code
    3. Curfew
  C. Staff
  D. Guests
  E. Transportation
  F. Lodging
  G. Meals

XV. Public relations
  A. Faculty
  B. Students
  C. Parents
  D. Community
  E. News media
  F. College coaches

Dematha High School Evaluation Sheet

Name_____ Age_____

Hgt._____ Wgt. _____ Reach _____

Vertical Jump_____ Scoring Avg. _____ Rebound Avg. _____

F. G. % _____ F. T. % _____

#1 Excellent #2 Good #3 Average #4 Poor #5 Start from Scratch

Defense Ability

1. Stance

2. Contest passing lane

3. Hedging

4. Helpside defense

5. Ballside defense

6. Full-court defense

7. Taking offensive charge

8. Anticipation of next pass

Ballhandling

1. Passing

2. Dribbling

3. Seeing and hitting open man

4. Use of opposite hand

5. Moves on the move

6. Pressure situation

Shooting (minimum of 500 shots a day)

1. Release

2. Rotation

3. Follow-through

4. Shoulder square to basket

5. Jump shot

6. Foul shot

7. Hook shot

8. Drives

9. Power shots

10. Baseline shots

11. Shot selection

Offensive Moves

1. Triple threat

2. Stationary moves
   a. six-inch jab step – take the jump shot
   b. strong-side drive
   c. strong-side jump shot
   d. crossover drive
   e. crossover jump shot
   f. frog move

3. Moving without the ball

4. Moves with back to basket

Rebounding

1. Blocking out

2. Ddefensive rebounding

3. Offensive rebounding

4. Anticipating the shot

5. Aggressiveness

6. Outlet pass
   a. baseball
   b. overhead

Physical Ability

1. Work on weight machine

2. Jumping ability

3. Strength

4. Aggressiveness

5. Speed and quickness

Dematha High School
Game Plan ————————————————————

Opponent_____ Date_____
At_____ Time_____

   A. Offense   G. Match-ups

           1. man-to-man   _____ vs. _____

           2. zone   _____ vs. _____

           3. pressure   _____ vs. _____

   B. Defense   _____ vs. _____

   C. Jump balls   _____ vs. _____

   D. Out of bounds   _____ vs. _____

   E. Free throws   H. Game captains

   F. Time and score

EVALUATING A COLLEGE PROGRAM

Yvan Kelly

All collegiate basketball programs want to develop athletic excellence in their players that leads to their success and a winning record.

Here is a subjective self-evaluation form for a collegiate program that can help you identify strengths and weaknesses. It is divided into two areas, administration and practice. Rate yourself and base it on a scale of 100. You might want to try to evaluate other teams in your conference to see how you stack up.

ADMINISTRATION

Graduation Rate

Regard student-athletes as students first and athletes second. Be committed to your players' academic progress and timely graduation.

Sportsmanship

This refers to the moral development of the players, making them both quality players and quality people and allowing them to derive the idealistic values associated with sports.

Team Interactions

This is the social development the players need, just as any young person does. Players' communication skills can be developed through contact with the media, receptions, and banquets. Also, drug education should not be ignored by the athletic department.

Use of Statistics

Beyond the box score several methods of statistical evaluation are available: computer indexing of positive and negative points, the offensive efficiency rating, running game summaries. Whether computer-assisted or not, these methods help you to form an objective evaluation of individual and team play.

System for Film Evaluation

Allow players and coaches to get the most out of their viewing. Be selective with what you show players, and help identify strengths and weaknesses.

Game Objectives

Based on the scouting reports, a game plan is developed in relation to the effect it will have on your team.

Graduation Rotation

Avoid having to recruit six players in one year and having to rebuild every two seasons. Two players graduate and two are brought in, or three go out and three come in.

Style Matched to Talent

Try to recruit players to the style or make adjustments for each individual. The players should feel confident in the style of play and confident that the style is capable of winning.

Budget

Have a budget large enough for recruiting, for hiring quality assistants, for team travel, and for guarantees to play an attractive schedule. This is a very important item.

Commitment from Externals

Have several people involved in the program. Contributions and fan support might have to be solicited. The athletic department has to be committed to having a successful basketball program.

Organization

Delegate your duties to take advantage of the specific strengths of your staff.

Visibility

Increase the profile of your program through visibility. Nationally televised games, and national awards and recognition aid in promoting a program.

PRACTICE

Mental Preparation

Some players motivate themselves, others need assistance. Of two equal teams, the one best mentally prepared will win.

Stretching-Flexibility

Begin practice with stretching and end practice with stretching.

Fundamentals

Spend sufficient time on passing, catching, dribbling, shooting, and individual work. Use drills that simulate game conditions.

Team Concepts

Plays and patterns vary from coach to coach, but they ought to be taught in a progressive order and with enough time spent on them so the players will be able to master the system.

Teaching Aids

There are lots of devices on the market. Use practical ones that can aid in precision or can overcome previous incorrect learning of fundamental skills.

Endurance

Don't lose games because your players are not in good enough shape to play hard late in the game. Develop their oxygen transport system using both aerobic and anaerobic running. The pre-season is a great time to develop their aerobic (distance)

Strength Development

Performed outside of practice time, this is an important area. A stronger athlete is less susceptible to injury as well as being able to run faster and jump higher. Full range of motion should be used as it allows the player to sustain his level of performance longer. Use weights three times a week before the season and twice a week during the season, exercising the larger muscle groups first. Only one set of 8 to 12 repetitions is needed with the appropriate amount of weight.

College Basketball Program
Evaluation Form

Instructions: The maximum point value for each item is next to the item in parenthesis. Fill in a number from zero to that maximum point value for each item. Total the two columns for the final rating score.

Administration

1. Graduation rate (4) _____
2. Sportsmanship (3) _____
3. Team interactions
   (social development) (3) _____
4. Use of statistics (3) _____
5. System for film evaluation (2) _____
6. Game objectives
   (scouting) (2) _____
7. Graduation rotation (1) _____
8. Style matched to talent (2) _____
9. Budget (recruiting) (4) _____
10. Commitment from
    externals (4) _____
11. Organization (delegation) (3) _____
12. Visibility (2) _____
Process subtotal (33) _____

Practice

1. Mental preparation (9) _____
2. Stretching-flexibility (10) _____
3. Fundamentals (13) _____
4. Team concepts (11) _____
5. Teaching aids (2) _____
6. Endurance
   (cardiorespiratory) (13) _____
7. Strength development
   (weights) (9) _____

Product subtotal (67)_____
Total Program (100)_____

The evaluation form on the preceding page does not evaluate every aspect of a program, but it does center around the areas you have the most control over. We as coaches need to make periodic evaluations of ourselves in order to optimize our efforts and benefit our programs by making gains in the areas we need to develop.

THE BASKETBALL EVALUATION SYSTEM: A SCIENTIFIC APPROACH TO PLAYER EVALUATION

Ken Swalgin

Basketball is one of the most intricate and fast-paced games in sports. From a coaching standpoint, it takes a trained eye and years of experience to understand exactly what is going on at any given time during a game. The coach, who is a manager of players as well as game strategy, is required to make many decisions that might affect the outcome of a game.

One of the most critical decisions all coaches must make is to determine the amount of playing time for each player, because this decision most directly influences a team's performance. To determine playing time for players, the coach needs to evaluate individual performance in practice and under game conditions. This evaluation process is a task that is normally based on the coach's knowledge, experience and ability to accurately measure individual performance under game conditions. Many attempts have been made to evaluate basketball skills in an attempt to project game performance. But it is obvious that a player will not perform the same in a practice or scrimmage as he will in a game.

Evaluating players in the context of an emotionally charged game situation is a difficult task. This is largely due to the fact that so much is going on in a game that the coach cannot possibly receive and process enough objective information on players to make rational decisions concerning their performance. Therefore, a more true and complete evaluation in most cases is only feasible after the game when coaches have access to complete game statistics and videotape.

I have found game statistics to be somewhat limited. This is largely because standards of measuring successful or unsuccessful play do not exist, which means it is difficult to accurately interpret game statistics. If, for example, a player scores 20 points in a game but shoots only 30 percent from the field and 50 percent from the line, the 20 points would give the appearance of successful play. However, the player's shooting percentages lead to a much different evaluation.

From this example, it is apparent that the interpretation of game statistics is more important than the raw numbers compiled. Here, the accurate interpretation of game statistics leads to an accurate interpretation of player performance.

To determine successful or unsuccessful performance, I developed The Basketball Evaluation System, based on a scientific approach to evaluate player performance under game conditions. The Basketball Evaluation System is based on three scientific measurement concepts developed from an understanding and evaluation of the structure of the game. The first concept deals with a common set of objective performance criteria to evaluate player performance, the second measurement concept develops a context to measure the performance criteria, and the third concept was developed to increase the accuracy of the evaluation process.

Performance Criteria

To measure successful or unsuccessful play, performance factors that could be objectively measured must be developed. Fortunately, these criteria or performance factors have been established within the NCAA box score. The factors include: field goal percentage (FG%), free throw percentage (FT%), rebounds (REB), personal fouls (PF), turnovers (TO), assists (AST), blocked shots (BKS) and steals (STL).

Performance Context

To give meaning to the above performance criteria, a context to evaluate each performance factor must be developed. Looking again at the structure of play in games, it is clear that the roles of players in today's game have become more specialized. An example of this specialization can be seen when attempting to evaluate the role of a point guard as opposed to the role of a center. Both players shoot, rebound, and pass, but in terms of judging performance, each performance factor evaluated for a point guard certainly needs to be judged on a different scale from those of the center. It is clear then that the context to measure a player in relationship to the performance criteria becomes "position of play."

To formulate this context, a national survey to establish "norms" by position of play was conducted for Men's Division I college basketball over a three-year period. Standards or norms were established for the following positions: point guard (PG), off guard (OG), small forward (SF), power forward (PF), and center (C). Norms were also established for "swingmen" as follows: PG-OG, OG-SF, SF-PF and PF-C.

With this performance context established, each performance factor could now be measured by position of play. Point guards could now be measured on norms established for point guards and centers could be evaluated against national norms for centers.

Accurate Evaluation

Another important factor that must be addressed is the relationship of "time played" in a game to performance. To make an evaluation system as accurate as possible, as well as fair, "time played" must be considered. Here, each player's performance is graded in relationship to the number of minutes played in a game as opposed to the current method of "games played."

To illustrate the flaw in the "games played" method, evaluate the rebound effectiveness of two players. Player A plays 20 minutes in a game and is credited with six rebounds. Player B is also credited with six rebounds but plays a total of 30 minutes. In judging the rebounding performance of the two players, it is clear that Player A's performance was better than Player B's performance. Yet in the "games played" measurement system, both players would be perceived to have performed equally after one game.

Obviously, an evaluation of the number of minutes played in a game increases the accuracy of the evaluation. Six of the eight performance factors in The Basketball Evaluation System are graded in relationship to minutes played (REB, PF, AST, TO BKS and STL). Field goal percentage and free throw percentage are not graded in relationship to time.

The Basketball Evaluation System is based on a common set of objective performance criteria – an evaluation context to measure the criteria based on national norms, and on an accurate means to measure performance in relationship to position of play and time played.

With this framework established, a statistical evaluation model based on Normal Probability Theory or a "bell shaped curve" was developed. As one of the goals of the system is to find a means to measure successful or unsuccessful performance, the evaluation model accomplishes this by qualitative measuring each performance factor in relationship to the national norms developed. Each performance factor is measured on a scale ranging from 0-4, much like the college grade point system.

Due to the large number of mathematical calculations and data access requirements of the evaluation model, a computer program was written to make the system functional. The program was written in dBASE III and is IBM-compatible. Built into the software are a number of features that allow the user a degree of flexibility and also increase the validity of the evaluation process.

First, the user has the option to change a player's position of play designation, and therefore the norms on which he is evaluated. Another option enables the user to eliminate the performance factor of blocked shots for guards if the coach feels that is not relevant to the player's evaluation. Still another feature in the computer program increases the accuracy of the evaluation process by not grading a performance factor until a "time threshold" has been agreed upon. These time thresholds vary in relationship to the performance factor evaluated and by position of play.

For example, in the case of rebounding, a point guard's time threshold is five minutes, whereas a center's time threshold is two minutes. All performance factors, however, are graded despite reaching time thresholds if the player records a score greater than zero for the factor.

After grading each individual performance factor, which are collectively called "Scaled Performance Scores" (SPS), the system then calculates an overall grade for the game called the "Graded Performance Score" (GPS). The GPS is determined by comparing a Cumulative-Scaled Performance Score (CUM-SPS) to a CUM-SPS National Norm for the position. The system also prints out a seasonal grade for each SPS and GPS after each game.

In Figure 3.5, the evaluation of a power forward is illustrated. The illustration is a "snapshot" of the computer screen after game statistics have been entered and each performance factor has been evaluated. Note that field goal and free throw percentages are indicated with the scaled performance scores (SPS) they represent. The remaining scores indicate scaled performance scores only.

SINGLE GAME EVALUATION
INDIVIDUAL GAME STATISTICS DISPLAY

FIRST NAME: Pat   **LAST NAME:** Henry
POSITION: PF

GAME DATE: 12-01-90
OPPONENT: Penn State/Altogoma   **SCORE:** 64-63

Minutes Played	35	
Field Goals Made	2	FG - 50.0%
Field Goals Attempted	4	2.175
		GPS - 2.651
Free Throws Made	3	FT - 60.0%
Free Throws Attempted	5	1.560
Rebounds	5	RB - 1.589
Personal Fouls	1	PF - 3.220
Assists	0	AS - 0.000
Turnovers	0	TO - 4.000
Blocked Shots	2	BS - 3.231
Interceptions/Steals	1	IS - 1.952

Figure 3.5

The Basketball Evaluation System also can generate printed reports for each player evaluated. Figure 3.6 illustrates the printed report for the power forward evaluated in Figure 3.5. The first line shows an evaluation of each performance factor as well as an overall Graded Performance Score (GPS) for the game. The second line gives season-to-season averages for each performance factor and the seasonal GPS.

The Basketball Evaluation System also can evaluate players on a seasonal basis. Figure 3.7 shows the seasonal evaluation of Bo Kimble for his senior season at Loyola-Marymount. Kimble was the most highly-graded player named to the 1989-90 Associated Press College Basketball All-America Team. The evaluations of the entire team(s) named is illustrated in Table 3.3. Note that NG represents "no grade" and indicates that the performance factor was not evaluated or the "time threshold" for the factor was not surpassed. Because this is a seasonal report, the NG indicates that the factor was not evaluated.

Many factors influence the overall performance of players. Many of these factors cannot be easily measured. Hustle, court sense and the ability to perform in pressure situations are a few examples of the intangible factors that contribute to successful play. The Basketball Evaluation System makes no claim to measure the intangible aspects of the game. These aspects are best left to the coach's knowledge, judgment and intuition.

The Basketball Evaluation System does, however, give coaches an accurate, reliable, valid, and functional means to evaluate performance that can be measured objectively. The system can show the strengths and weaknesses of each player in relationship to position. It helps motivate players to improve by showing the relationship between statistics and successful performance. It puts a greater premium on all performance factors, not just scoring. And, finally, The Basketball Evaluation System is a statistical game performance data base to judge the progress of each player and the team.

The research for The Basketball Evaluation System was partially sponsored by a grant from the National Association of Basketball Coaches (NABC). To learn more about The Basketball Evaluation System or to have your team evaluated, feel free to write or call Dr. Ken Swalgin, Assistant Professor of Exercise and Sport Science, Men's Basketball coach, Penn State University-York Campus, York, PA, 17403. Telephone: (717) 771-4037.

GAME AND SEASONAL REPORT

PLAYER NAME	POSITION	MIN	FG%	FG	FT%	FT	REB	PF	ASST	TO	BLK	STEALS	GPS
Pat Henry	PF	35.0	50.0	2.2	60.0	2.0	1.6	13.2	0.0	4.0	3.2	2.0	2.651
Season to date average:		33.8	46.7	1.5	61.1	2.1	1.5	3.0	2.3	2.9	2.3	2.2	2.547

Figure 3.6

B E S ALL-AMERICA 1989-90 GAME STATISTICAL SUMMARY REPORT

PLAYER NAME	POSITION	MIN	FG%	FG	FT%	FT	REB	PF	ASST	TO	BLK	STEALS	GPS
Bo Kimble (LMU)	OG	32.9	52.9	3.3	86.2	3.5	3.5	1.9	1.6	2.0	3.6	3.4	3.689
Derrick Coleman (SYR)	C	35.3	55.1	3.0	71.5	3.0	2.7	2.4	3.3	1.7	2.6	3.1	3.606
Larry Johnson (UNLV)	PF	31.2	62.4	3.8	76.7	3.3	3.1	2.0	2.6	1.3	2.9	2.8	3.577
Kenny Anderson (GT)	PG	37.7	51.5	3.2	73.3	2.6	3.2	2.7	2.8	2.2	NG	2.3	3.483
Lionel Simmons (LASAL)	PF	38.1	51.3	2.4	66.1	2.5	2.6	2.8	3.2	1.8	3.1	2.7	3.457
Kendall Gill (ILL)	OG	34.5	50.0	2.9	77.7	2.9	2.5	2.4	2.2	2.0	3.3	2.8	3.403
Gary Payton (OSU)	PG	36.5	50.4	3.1	69.0	2.1	2.9	1.6	2.8	1.7	3.8	3.2	3.375
Doug Smith (MISSOURI)	SF	29.4	56.3	3.4	71.4	2.6	3.2	1.8	2.2	1.4	2.8	2.6	3.242
Alonzo Mourning (GTown)	PF-C	30.2	52.5	3.0	78.3	3.4	2.5	1.9	2.1	1.2	3.8	1.7	3.198
Steve Smith (MSU)	OG	34.9	52.6	3.3	69.5	2.1	3.2	2.2	2.8	1.4	3.3	1.3	3.141
Hank Gathers (LMU)	PF	30.2	59.5	3.6	56.8	1.7	3.0	2.6	2.2	1.4	2.4	2.9	3.106
Steve Scheffler (PUR)	C	33.1	72.7	4.0	82.1	3.7	1.7	2.7	2.0	2.0	1.3	1.3	2.196
Dennis Scott (GT)	SF	39.1	46.5	2.0	79.3	3.3	2.1	2.7	1.9	1.8	2.6	2.5	2.876
Rumeal Robinson (MICH)	PG	34.0	49.0	2.9	67.6	1.9	2.8	1.7	2.4	1.4	3.8	1.8	2.835
Chris Jackson (LSU)	PG	37.6	46.1	2.4	91.0	3.8	1.8	2.6	1.5	1.7	NG	1.9	2.592

Table 3.3

SEASONAL EVALUATION

SEASON TO DATE STATISTICS DISPLAY

FIRST NAME: Bo **LAST NAME:** Kimble (LMU)
POSITION: OG

GAME DATE: 12-01-90 **OPPONENT:** All
SCORE: 0-0

Minutes Played	32.9	
Field Goals Made	404	FG - 52.9%
Field Goals Attempted	763	3.336
		GPS 3.689
Free Throws Made	231	FT - 86.2%
Free Throws Attempted	268	3.500
Rebounds	7.71	RB - 3.466
Personal Fouls	3	PF - 1.872
Assists	1.9	AS - 1.636
Turnovers	2.4	TO - 2.000
Blocked Shots	.65	BS - 3.555
Inteceptions/Steals	2.9	IS - 3.356

Figure 3.7

THE SUE SYNDROME

Jerry Krause and Jim Wasem

In an age filled with frivolous litigation, it is critical for physical educators and coaches to be aware of the knowledge required to lessen the likelihood of being involved in a financially devastating lawsuit. It is tremendously important to stay abreast of critical issues and professional problems to circumvent or prevent this "sue syndrome."

This article presents several alternatives that reasonable and prudent teachers and coaches can utilize that enable them to be more effective and efficient in becoming aware of and performing their duties and responsibilities.

We in sport and education can expect more frivolous lawsuits in the future with the concept of "joint and several" liability becoming more prominent (1). This type of liability found all parties involved in the litigious activity being sued, partly due to the "deep pockets" moneyed philosophy, and partly due to a "shotgunning" effort – shoot (sue) and hope you hit something (collect damages).

We recommend several excellent readings, principle among them Borowski's "Avoiding the Gavel," (2) in which 69 allegations of negligence as part of a legal action against an educational agency are itemized; Koehler's "Sport Activity and Risk Management," (3) a book concerned with critical issues in sports activity,

and The American Effectiveness Programs, Level 2, Sport Law Course (4), a volume written to illustrate to coaches and athletic directors how to reduce the likelihood of a lawsuit occurring in their program.

All of these readings have a great deal to offer the fledgling educational "legal beagle," but the large amount of information mandates that the authors compile a brief, workable list of duties, insights, understandings, and devices that might help educators understand, cope with, and win the battle with the judicial system's legal "treasure hunt."

We all need to be reminded that a "negligence" lawsuit requires the presence of four factors to have a legitimate chance of success, although one can never guess what a jury composed of 12 citizens will decide. Those four factors are as follows:

1. Actual harm or loss must result due to a neglect of duty.

2. The teacher/coach owes a legal duty to perform for the injured party.

3. A breach of that duty owed did in fact occur. (You failed to do what you should have done, or carried out the duty incorrectly, under the "prudent person" doctrine.)

4. The establishment of that breach was the principle factor or the primary cause of the harm.

Because all of these factors deal directly with the concept of "legal duties," educators should be knowledgeable about the following legal duties required of teachers and coaches:

Nine Legal Duties in Education

1. **Duty to warn.** Physical educators, coaches, and athletic personnel must warn participants of the inherent dangers of an activity. They should itemize what disasters might befall the participant for failure to follow fundamental form.

2. **Duty to properly instruct.** This includes formulating and following a properly constructed lesson or practice plan from inception to closure. Proper learning theory progression must be utilized, and any variance from the plan should be done for a valid reason.

3. **Duty to properly supervise.** This depends to a great extent on the severity, complexity, or danger of the activity. In general, the more dangerous the activity, the more specific the supervision must become.

4. **Duty to provide a safe environment.** As an educator in charge of physical activity, you have the responsibility of thoroughly and regularly inspecting the facilities, equipment,

and/or playing fields for unsafe situations. (And you must rectify those situations, if they are found to be unsafe.)

5. **Duty to match or equate students.** Athletes and physical education students must be matched not only by their skill and experience, but by age, height, weight and maturity as well.

6. **Duty to provide temporary care and to evaluate injury or incapacitation.** An injured student is entitled to immediate and temporary care until a physician can be summoned, and after having had that care administered, is entitled to have that injury or incapacitation evaluated properly before being returned to any activity.

7. **Duty to provide proper and adquate equipment.** The philosophy that "it's good enough for the J.V. team" is gone forever. If equipment is damaged or unsafe, it must be discarded or rehabilitated by an approved vendor.

8. **Duty to know and apply emergency treatment and first aid.** All educators should stay abreast of new developments in emergency treatment and first aid. All physical educators and athletic coaches should carry a first aid card, and be certified in CPR as a minimal requirement.

9. **Duty to compile, maintain, and keep accurate records.** While some teachers and coaches are relatively delinquent in this area, it is absolutely essential that pertinent data about all phases of an activity be kept sacrosanct in a well-documented, easily accessed filing system. Records of instructional plans, accident reports, and equipment inventories are examples of needed records. These records should be kept on file until the statute of limitations has expired (generally three to seven years).

To further insulate or "bulletproof" ourselves in the "land of litigation," we might all benefit from following these guidelines:

1. Develop a wellness approach to our legal duties by preventing problems before they happen.

2. Know, understand, and carry out our legal duties.

3. Show caring, professional behavior (parents might hesitate to sue if they respect your teaching/coaching behaviors).

4. Be aware of the following suggested additional defenses in case of litigation:
   a. The alleged negligence was not the "proximate cause" (there was an intervening cause for the injury).
   b. The plaintiff had an "assumption of risk."
   c. "Contributory negligence" was present; a portion of the accident could be attributed to the plaintiff. (This defense is outdated, and the courts are adopting the doctrine of "comparative negligence." In other words, the fault of the injury should be pro-rated.
   d. There was unforeseeable harm – the accident was unavoidable. (Some people insist that an "unavoidable accident" does not exist, that all accidents are foreseeable and therefore preventable.
   e. There was an "act of God."
   f. There was "volentia non fit injurie" (another assumes the responsibility for the injured).

Conclusion

By being aware of the various nuances and intricacies of legal liability, we have a much greater chance to be an effective teaching/coaching professional. Only by becoming such an effective educator can we hope to escape from the "sue syndrome" we face in sports and education today.

References:

1. Adams, Samuel, "Current Trends in Sport Law Litigation," WAHPERD conference, Pasco, WA., October, 16, 1993
2. Borowski, Richard, "Avoiding the Gavel," *Athletic Management*, Oct./Nov., pp 22-24.
3. Koehler, Robert, *Law: Sport Activity and Risk Management*, Stipes Pub. Co., 1991.
4. Martens, Rainer, et al, *Coaching Young Athletes*, Human Kinetics Press, 1988.

Chapter 4

PSYCHOSOCIAL SPORT SCIENCES

CONCERN FOR PLAYERS

Mike Krzyzewski

Certainly it is an understatement that coaches are concerned about their players. Coaches want their players to do well and to be at their best. In this regard, I've found that talking to your players while they are competing, giving them emotional support, is essential. It is extremely important, however, that we as coaches show interest in what our players do off the court and during the offseason.

Probably the most important area in which we should show concern is academics. What type of concern do you show for your players' academics? Do you have a way of monitoring their progress during the school year? What do you do for them academically during the summer? If you are a college coach, do you know your players' academic majors and what classes they are taking? If you are a high school coach, what classes do your players take and how are they doing? What are their goals? Do they want to go to college, and if so, do they know how to get there? What schools are they considering and how can you help them? If you try to find out the answers to these questions, you are showing a player that you are concerned about what he or she is doing. You are treating them like people, and they really believe that you are on their side.

I keep close track of what my players are doing academically. During summer school, I will have meetings with my team as a whole and individual meetings with my players to discuss what they are doing academically. We work very closely with our academic support personnel to ensure that our players are getting all the assistance they need. If I feel that a player is not responding well academically, I will call his parents or guardians to make sure that everyone on the player's team will help motivate him to do a better job.

During one of my early years at Duke, I had a player who was struggling academically. He wasn't ineligible to play, but he needed help. Our coaches and academic people all agreed that he would be better served by not playing basketball during the spring semester. I called his mother and talked it over with her and she agreed. When the player came to see me and I told him he needed to sit out the semester to concentrate on his academics, one of his initial fears was how he was going to tell his mother that he had been suspended from the basketball team. Then I told him that I'd already talked to his mother and enlisted her support, and he began to realize that all of us were on the same team – his team. He began to put more work into his academics and eventually graduated on time with his class.

In our locker room, we post academic as well as athletic accomplishments. During the spring semester of 1993, our team had a grade point average of 2.7. I considered this an excellent achievement because our spring semester ends in April and it is also the semester that is the busiest, basketball-wise, for our players. If an individual player does well, I will bring this up in front of the team, and privately, to tell him what a good job he is doing.

In following a player's academic progress, you become aware of when papers are due or when major tests will be given. You understand better what is going on with him off the court. He may be a bit more tired or more easily distracted on certain days. If you know the reason for this is that he has a big test coming up, you can work with him in budgeting his time or maybe use a better motivational method to get him to perform at his highest level.

I hear too many coaches complain that they would have won if their players hadn't had so many papers due in the past week. Unfortunately, most coaches do not know about these things until after the fact. You will be a better coach if you make it a point to know what is going on in your players' lives.

I believe that it is very important to get your team involved in outside activities during the year. Some of our players are involved in a reading program we started in our community. Our players go out to third- and fourth-grade classes in the city of Durham and read to them. They tell the kids about their experiences of reading and try to get youngsters to start reading more. There are incentives in the program for youngsters who actually do read more.

This kind of program requires some administrative or clerical support to implement and schedule, but from the player's standpoint it is relatively simple and enjoyable.

He simply has to go to an elementary school an hour or so a month and read to the kids. It's simple, but the community interest that is fostered develops the player's self-worth to a much higher level. It also makes the player realize that he is quite fortunate to be in his present position, and he should share what he has accomplished with those less fortunate.

There are many, many avenues to getting your players involved in extracurricular activities. We have our players visit the Duke Children's Hospital and take part on an individual and team basis with activities there. Many players enjoy the chance to champion causes or interests that mean a lot to them personally. Just about every year one or more of our players perform public service announcements about staying in school, using the library or staying away from drugs. One of our players served as the chairman and promoter for the local alcohol-free citywide high school graduation party because he believed it was important for young people to know what kind of alternative celebration was available. Another of our players donated his time and celebrity to the Mothers Against Drunk Driving (MADD) program, primarily because his mother had been injured in a car accident caused by a drunk driver. The point here is that there are limitless opportunities for your players. Why not help them get involved in community action? A team can benefit greatly from these experiences.

Another area in which you as the coach can tangibly demonstrate true concern for your players is the importance you place on their basketball experiences during the offseason. I love to have my players involved in summer competition, whether it is our own team going on some type of foreign tour or individuals participating for USA Basketball. This can require quite a commitment from the player, but the experience of traveling with another team, learning from other coaches and representing yourself or your country is absolutely the best.

During one of my early years at Duke we had an extremely young team of talented players who had not yet enjoyed much success at the college level. As a mater of fact, we had an 11-17 record with this freshman-dominated group. Before the next season we were able to take a trip to France, where we spent a lot of time together and played several club teams. Traveling abroad, getting to know one another better, experiencing some success after a disastrous season, all of this helped the players gain confidence and enabled them to mature. The next year it was obvious to me that the trip had been very beneficial to our program, and it helped build the foundation for our first trip of another kind - to the NCAA Final Four when those freshmen had become seniors.

During the summer I also recommend that our players work at camps where they are the teachers. If I were a high school coach I would want my players to go to summer camps. Many coaches want their players to only go to team camps so that they can develop their own team. While I am obviously a strong proponent of building team chemistry, I think it is more important for the development of a high school player if he or she uses the summer to go to camps where individual learning and improvement can take place.

The summer is a great time for a player, whether in high school or college, to experience self-discovery. When a player constantly stays in the role expected of him or her in the school program, the role becomes confining. The player begins to accept a certain set of limitations and expectations, when in reality he or she might be capable of much more when given the chance to experience other circumstances and other coaching philosophies.

The case of Cherokee Parks comes immediately to mind. As a freshman he was in a reserve role on our front line, playing in the shadow of senior Christian Laettner. The summer before his sophomore year, Cherokee played for an Atlantic Coast Conference team that toured Europe. With that team, he took more shots, got more rebounds, played better defense and became a key player. He used the experience to get ready for the new role that was waiting for him after Christian's departure. I always enjoy seeing the level of play of each one of my players when they come back for practice in the fall.

Players will appreciate your help in getting them set up for a good summer program and in getting them involved outside your program. As coaches, we should not assume that they are able to do all this on their own. If we do all we can in showing concern for our players, we will be rewarded by seeing our players develop as people while they are developing as players.

TEACHING-LEARNING PRINCIPLES

Jerry Krause

I have found a number of guidelines to be helpful in teaching basketball skills. Coaches always should be alert for teaching principles for players that speed the learning process.

1. Practice makes permanent, which may improve or worsen the present skill level of your players. Instead, have your players understand that only perfect practice makes perfect.

2. Continuous learning and progress depends primarily on each player's interest, motivation, and attitude.

3. Practice mistakes are necessary for learning to occur. Your player's mistakes should be used as feedback or status reports, because success comes through being aware of and learning from mistakes. Work to reduce the number of similar mistakes. Also teach players to forget mistakes and not let them affect the next play.

4. Problems are opportunities and challenges to meet. Successfully meeting challenges can result in your players becoming better people and players.

5. Teammates should be encouraged. Your players should inform each other when outstanding team plays are made — pass assists, screen assists, rebounds, and defensive plays, for example. Have them let a teammate know verbally and physically when they have done well.

6. Develop balance and emotional control. Basketball is a game of finesse and reasoning, so players need to be taught to be spirited without being temperamental.

7. Motivation is possibly the most important factor in determining learning speed. Players should take the primary responsibility for their motivational levels. A coach serves as only one resource to improve motivation.

8. Feedback is necessary for effective learning. Each player should develop many channels of feedback concerning both effort and performance of fundamental skills. Coaches should make every effort to provide feedback about what is being done right as well as what is being done wrong. Give them information, not just emotion.

9. Practice must be active and purposeful for maximum learning to occur. After a skill has been learned correctly, players should practice game moves at game speeds. Players should be constantly reminded to do it right, and then do it quickly.

10. Mental practice can be as effective as physical practice for learning fundamental skills. The subconscious can't tell the difference between a real experience and a vividly imagined experience. The skill must be heard, felt, and seen. To paint complete mental pictures, players should shut out all mistakes and concentrate on seeing perfect performances in their mind.

11. A final note is directed to both players and coaches. Players should expect constructive criticism from coaches and should make every effort to accept and learn from such feedback. Both groups can expect both justified and unjustified criticism and should develop the mental toughness to accept and learn from the best and worst of experiences. As Parkenham Beatty wrote:

> *By your own soul learn to live*
> *And if men thwart you, take no heed*
> *If men hate you, have no care*
> *Sing your song, dream your dream*
> *Hope your hope and pray your prayer.*

PLAYER-COACH RELATIONS

John Thompson

The first statement that I want to make is, "You can communicate without motivating, but it is impossible to motivate without communication."

To properly communicate with players, a coach must fully explain his or her terminology. Often the player isn't executing properly simply because he doesn't have a clear understanding of what his coach is talking about. That was one of the initial things I had to do when I started coaching at the college level. At the very beginning, I had to sit down with my players and explain to them exactly what I was talking about.

Sometimes I think college coaches try to be too smart and sophisticated for their own good. You need to know what you want to accomplish and your players need to be able to understand you. A player might not be simply lazy or slow; he just might be confused as to what is expected from him. This is why I believe there's a distinct difference between communication and motivation. In order for a player to move, he at least has to understand where you want him to go. However, it doesn't necessarily mean that because he understands what you're saying he's going to do it. We have to stay away from the point that when we talk to people, we become so clinical and coach-oriented that we lose track of simplicity. Establish a basic level of understanding and keep it simple.

I disagree with coaches who say, "I treat every one of my players equally." I think this is impossible to do because each player is different and has a different level of understanding. Coaches possess varying degrees of strengths and weaknesses in regard to communication. As a coach you need to be totally honest with yourself and evaluate your strengths and weaknesses.

We can communicate with players and create atmospheres that help form an understanding with those players in many ways. Some of the methods that I use to communicate follow:

Voice Inflection

Some coaches like to shout and yell, while others are more comfortable with their regular tone of voice. As a coach, you must know what is effective with each of your players. You have to realize when to talk softly and when to raise your voice. It's extremely important that you know the emotional reaction of each player to what you are saying. Once again, this concept reinforces my thoughts on treating your players as separate individuals. Two players might make the same mistake and one will need criticism while the other one needs encouragement. The very next day the roles may be reversed.

Involvement

There are no secret formulas in the area of player relationships. One thing you need to do is be sensitive enough to try to find out who is inside each one of those uniforms. You have to realize that he's a person and not an "x" or an "o." As a coach you need to become acquainted with your players and find out what makes them tick. Whenever possible you should involve the player in what you're doing.

Flexibility

This is really important because you'll never have the same 12 or 15 players, and every year each player changes. After people started to deny penetrating passes, we gave players the opportunity to pass and pick away or go through. We must have the ability to change with the times. You need to be able to see that players are not receiving what you're teaching and you must know how to change or make corrections.

Atmosphere

I feel this is essential because I personally get bored very easily. We try to change our practice sites every two or three weeks just to break up the monotony. The environment must be such that it is conducive to learning. There shouldn't be a lot of distraction for you to compete with while teaching.

Simplicity

I remember this area by the acronym KISS: "Keep it Simple, Stupid." I'm not interested in trying to prove to you or my players that I'm a genius. Before you put in a complex offense, you have to know the learning capabilities of your players. We like to start and stay with an easy, simple approach to basketball. Don't get complicated, because eventually you'll lose some of your players.

Illustration and Demonstration

A coach must be able to explain and show the players what he wants. If you're unable to demonstrate a skill correctly, don't try to select a different method of illustration such as using a player and talking him through the fundamental. There's no easier way to lose a group of kids than to perform a basic skill incorrectly.

Props

There are numerous teaching methods available to help convey your thoughts to the players. However, you must realize that what is effective for me might not be effective for you. It's good to experiment with different ideas and drills, but don't initiate something into your program simply because another successful coach does it.

Fluency

English and grammar competence are necessary, as well as an ability to talk to a group. From time to time ask your players to explain what you're saying. If they're honest, you'll find out how well you're communicating.

Before the season begins, I sit down with each player and go over expectations that I have for him and the team. You need to talk with each player and let him know how you feel about the upcoming season. A player must be coachable, and by that I mean he needs to be able to accept suggestions made by all coaches. A player who decides to assume the attitude of "doing his own thing" is not worth having on the squad. As a coach, you must decide what you want to teach and be entirely sold on those ideas. Then you need to have the ability to sell them to your players. A good coach is able to adjust to change and newness. You don't have to be indecisive, but you also can't live in the past.

I feel that it's important that you understand why you feel the way you do about the game of basketball. Equally important is that both you and your players understand why they feel the way they do about basketball.

Coaches and players develop their attitude toward the game because of a few basic reasons. The first area involves heredity, which will greatly influence a player's degree of success in playing the game. When I speak of heredity, I am talking about the physical and psychological makeup of the individual. I feel it's important that you measure a person's speed, strength, jumping ability, and intelligence as well as his height and weight. Often when we're afraid we're not motivating or communicating, we're actually asking the player to do things he's not physically capable of doing. The mental frame of mind is also important and must be kept in proper perspective. Coaches have an obligation to be honest and sincere with the player in regard to his ability. This, it is hoped, will help each player recognize his own physical limitations.

Another area of importance is the player's environment when he was acquiring his basketball background. As soon as you meet a player, find out about his background. His basketball background will include C.Y.O. and playground experience, grade school and junior high coaches, the senior high school coach, and his immediate family. You need to understand the basic basketball influences that have gone into making up each athlete. You might have a player performing a skill entirely different than what you've been teaching simply because he learned the skill another way at an early age. Coaches need to realize that time builds habits, both good and bad. After you find out what type of exposure a player has been subject to, it is much easier to understand the steps for attacking those bad habits.

Sincerity is the key to motivation. If you want to talk to someone, do just that. Talk to them honestly! If you happen to make a mistake, say you're sorry and try something else. I feel that it's extremely important that we find out something about each player. Know about their physical abilities, where they get their thoughts, and how they formed their habits.

I think many coaches feel something is wrong if they have a problem. I try to plan for various conflicts because I know they're going to occur. I spend a lot of time before the season begins going over possible conflicts that may occur with each player. I'm not going to go over each one, but the following list probably includes most of the reasons problems occur.

1. Pro ball
2. Coaches
3. Black and white
4. Playing time
5. Recognition
6. Girls
7. School
8. Opinions
9. Parents
10. Car
11. Time
12. Friends
13. Self
14. Scholarship
15. Personal goals

Pro ball is one of the biggest deterrents today to our programs. Every player on a college campus thinks he's going to be a professional athlete. I have to talk to each player realistically about his future and personal goals. Parents are extremely important. You need to try to get to know all of the parents. Do not think you can ignore them. Coaches who try it often run themselves right out of a job.

If you have a black player and a white player, sit down and talk to both of them. Do you know the best way to communicate with kids, black or white? Try the English language. Don't let anyone try to give you a formula for dealing with kids. The best thing for you to do is to be yourself and to be as honest as possible.

The last area I want to talk about involves motivation of the coach. We can't assume that the coach is always going to be motivated. Some of the very same things that are necessary to motivate players are also necessary to motivate coaches. The difference is that a coach can identify when a player is not motivated. Therefore, the coach must know himself and be able to move himself. Socrates said, "In order to move the world, one must first move himself." Methods of motivating the coach include the following:

1. Sometimes it is necessary for a coach to relax before going into practice, if only for 10 minutes.

2. Positive-minded, enthusiastic assistant coaches at points when the head coach is flat.

3. Don't stay on a negative point, or player. Back off and return to the matter later.

4. Change of atmosphere is just as important for the coach as for the player.

5. Learn to communicate through others (staff) to your players, rather than harping on one player with whom you are having a problem.

6. Reading and music can serve as motivators while one is relaxing.

7. In selecting a team it is good to have one player who, through his attitude and enthusiasm, can lift you and your team up. This player is usually not a starter.

8. Manager's enthusiasm, alertness, and attitude can often lift the coach and players.

9. Good planning keeps your level of enthusiasm up because it gives you a sense of accomplishment. This plan should be one that the coach finds to be comfortable.

In summary, I want to say that it's necessary to become involved, to try to know your players, and to do it your way. You have to feel comfortable coaching the way you coach. Any player that you make a mistake with should be dealt with in the same manner. Go to him and say "I'm sorry," if you are truly sorry. If he doesn't understand that, then the two of you must part company because he no longer respects you.

MOTIVATING YOUR PLAYERS

Dale Brown

I would like to quote the introduction to Bill Libby's book, *The Coaches*:

He's called a coach, and it's a different job. There is no clear way to succeed. One cannot copy another who's a winner, for there seems to be some subtle secret chemistry of personality that enables a person to lead successfully and no one really knows what it is. Those who have succeeded and those who have failed represent all kinds. They are young, old, experienced, and inexperienced. They are soft, tough, gentle, good-natured, foul tempered, proud, and profane. They are articulate and even inarticulate. Some are dedicated and some casual. Some are even more dedicated than others and just wanting to win is not enough. Losers almost always get fired but winners get fired also. He is out in the open being judged publicly for six or seven months out of the year by those who may or may not be qualified to judge him. Every victory and every defeat is recorded constantly in print. The coach, this strange breed, has no place to hide. He cannot just let the job go for awhile or do a bad job and hope no one will notice as most of us can. He cannot satisfy everyone, seldom can he even satisfy very many, and rarely does he even satisfy himself. If he wins once, he must win the next time also. They plot victories, they suffer defeats; they endure criticism from within and from without; they neglect their families, they travel endlessly and they live alone in the spotlight surrounded by others. Theirs may be the worst profession in the world. It's unreasonably demanding, poor pay, insecure, full of unrelenting pressures, and I ask myself: Why do coaches put up with it? Why do they do it? I've seen them fired and hailed as genius at gaudy press-like parties. I've seen them fired with pat phrases such as, "Fool," "Incompetent," or "He couldn't get the job done." I've wondered about that, having seen them exalted by victory and depressed by defeat. I've sympathized with them, having seen some broken by the job and others die from it. One is moved to admire them and hope that someday the world will understand them, this strange breed they call coach.

What does it take to become successful? I think it comes down to six basic steps.

1. Be yourself. Don't imitate anyone regardless of their success. The two most successful basketball coaches in the history of college coaching have completely opposite personalities: John Wooden and Adolph Rupp. You must coach within your own makeup. You have to be flexible in your personality, but you must coach with your personality and not someone else's.

2. You must have confidence in your own technical ability, and you've got to experiment. Just because you're not at some high-powered college doesn't mean you can't coach. Let your own abilities show through your team.

3. Keep it simple. The first and last law of learning is repetition. Eighty-five percent of what you obtain today will be forgotten within 48 hours. You will retain almost 70 percent of what you listen to if you listen to it six times or more. Don't overcoach or make it complicated. Keep it simple, as there are no secrets. You must convince your players to play certain roles: lead guard, shooting guard, rebounding forward, and so on.

4. Discipline. You've got to have several forms of discipline. I'm not talking about suppression or whipping, but teamwork. It's not just enough to talk about it, you've got to implement it on the floor. You've got to put the team above yourself. Every time I see something in the newspaper or magazine about teamwork, I put it up in our locker room, to keep emphasizing teamwork. I'll also bring in as many outstanding athletes as I can during the season to talk about teamwork.

Another form of discipline you must have is good shot selection. C.M. Newton does this and to assure good shot selection he has different colored dotted lines on the floor for guards and forwards, to remind them that they shouldn't shoot beyond these lines. Another form of discipline is team defense. We can no longer just play individual defense, so you've got to stress team defense. The last form of discipline is superb physical condition. You have to find out what this is for your team and apply it.

5. Be firm and consistent. You must coach with a positive attitude and be a problem-solver. To be firm is to not have two sets of rules. If you say something, you must follow through with it. Otherwise the players will lose respect for your authority.

   A coach also must show love for his players and be positive. The only lasting form of discipline is self-imposed discipline. I do not want to dehumanize my players. A coach must be a problem-solver, as athletics is a constant daily crisis and those of us who handle it the best are the most successful.

   How would you like to have Kareem Abdul-Jabbar criticize you in the *Los Angeles Times* for being too conservative and not knowing what's going on? Or read *Sports Illustrated* and see Greg Lee say that you are losing your touch and that he should be starting? Or have Mike Lynn get picked up for forged credit cards in Covina, California? Or have Lucius Allen twice picked up for possession of marijuana? Or have Edgar Lacey blast you in the Houston paper? Or have a senior at your basketball banquet get up and say you are a hypocrite, that you have two styles of discipline and that he's glad his four years are over?

   Those were problems, but John Wooden was a problem-solver and he solved them all. Everyone has problems; the big as well as the small schools. You've just got to be a problem-solver.

6. Expect and learn to accept criticism. You will not be free from criticism regardless of your success or effort. You must have confidence in yourself and stand by your philosophy. It's your FQ (Failure Quotient) in life that makes you successful. In John Wooden's last coaching game of his career, his UCLA team had just defeated Kentucky for the national championship, and he went over to shake Joe B. Hall's hand. One of John's best supporters came over and hugged him in glee and said, "John, congratulations! You had us all worried. We thought you were going to blow it like you did last year." You must expect criticism at any time, and don't let it get to you.

With those six things I think we're ready to motivate ourselves and our players. No one has ever been successful without motivation, and I don't mean the false kind, like "Win one for the Gipper." With genuine motivation you can work wonders. You cannot motivate your players if you yourself are not motivated.

You do not have to be dynamic to motivate. Tell yourself and your players that you are competing in a race and you have four hurdles to clear: peace, love, happiness, and success. Everyone must learn how to run their own race and overcome these obstacles.

Four things must be done to motivate people. Number one is to teach them to get over the hurdle of "I can't." Remove that phrase from their vocabulary. Number two is to teach them not to be afraid to fail. You cannot be afraid to fail to be a success. Number three is to eliminate the excuse of handicaps. "My father left home." "My mom's on welfare." "I come from a poor family." Although obstacles, they can be used as excuses for failure. Number four is to help people know themselves. Who am I, and where am I going?

In an independent study, 12 runners ran a race. Six of the runners were allowed to do anything they wanted to before the race. The other six were told repeatedly they wouldn't become tired during the race. Those six finished the race in the top six positions. You can do things that you don't think you can, if you believe.

You can't be afraid to fail, as your failures will lead to success. When Babe Ruth retired, he had hit more home runs than anyone in baseball. He also had struck out the most. Both Albert Einstein and Leonardo da Vinci said that 90 percent of their solutions were incorrect. Yet they persisted. You cannot be afraid to fail.

You cannot allow handicaps to hold you back. If you want it badly enough, you can get it done.

You must know yourself. Buddha said in his teachings that before man can ever find happiness, he must know himself. You can fake it, but deep down you really know if you are comfortable with yourself. If not, you'll fall along the way.

What motivates successful people? Many of them say the same thing: The thing that drove them over the top was wanting to do something besides be great, and make the world a better place to live.

I'm convinced that you can motivate your athletes. You have to be reasonable, but they can do more than they know, and all of us can go to the top.

Man can fly faster and higher than any bird in the history of the world. He can dig deeper and longer into the earth than any burrowing animal in the history of the world. The only thing that man hasn't learned to do is walk on earth like a man.

CREATING AN ATTITUDE

David Farrar

Creating an attitude that relates to the way we play and playing offense against pressure defense — both subjects are the basis of our program.

In Hutchinson last year our kids played in front of 150,000 people. We average about 5,000 people per game; we play a lot of home games because I would rather stay in the area and play in front of 5,000 people than drive all night, miss class, and play in front of 200.

We have to play certain ways to take advantage of the skill levels of our players. Teddy Roosevelt once said, "Do what you can, with what you have, where you are." As I move in to try to create a style of play and an attitude with our players, that has some meaning for me; I want to do something with our kids to create an environment of success.

After we won the national championship, we took our kids to a number of schools to speak. During one speech, one of our kids said, "I happen to play for a guy who thinks that you can train to be successful, that it's a learned process, that you can be around people who will help you learn skills to be successful. As an example, he makes us sit in the first two rows of every classroom we are in. We have to sit in the front one-third of the seat, lean forward, and make eye contact with the professor." I liked his comments and believe them. I think you can train kids to be successful. We think we can get you to think about some things, about your receptiveness, your practice habits, practicing so you can get into the game so you might be able to make your team a better team.

We let almost anybody speak to our team. Last year 11 people spoke. Junior college rules allow us to start practice the first day of school if we want to. Last year we played 39 games – half a pro season – and three scrimmages, and the season lasts seven months. This with freshman kids who have been used to playing 20 games and practicing one and one-half weeks before the first game. So in September we condition three days a week. Two days a week we come in split groups of eight apiece, with two coaches, and we work on offense, passing and releasing for defense, getting lift into our jump shots, trying to raise their work level through offense.

After we start on October 1, defense takes so much of a priority that I think we don't give enough attention to individual offense. In that time period, we bring in 11 guest speakers – faculty, people in different walks of life – to speak about time management, budget, listening skills, study skills.

I took my kids to prison last month. If you want an education, check it out. Why did I take them? After we left the prison, I said to my kids, "Hey, I don't think any of you are going to be in there, but I want you to think about it. Think about the fact that there is a whole group of people who thought there was something for nothing, who thought they were smarter than everybody else, who thought working for $4 to $5 an hour was chump change." I want them to visually think about these things.

Something else we do along that line. We have what we call the "Wall of Shame" in our locker room. I have them bring anything that is negative about an athlete, coach, or administrator, a comment, getting in trouble. My point is, we want them to think about it; we want them to look at it. We want them to see what the media can do with a comment. We videotape our kids in the fall. I don't like to not practice anything that can have an effect on me, on the team, or the community. We give them some tough situations to try to answer, then we come back and look at them. The greatest kids in the world are going to think about short cuts, about making a phone call home and charging it to someone else. At least I am going to make an attempt to get them to understand something and think about the ramifications of little things. Is a coach good because of what he teaches? I don't think so. Certain coaches can take your team and beat people; they can take my team and beat people; they can take their teams and beat people. Why? Because of their enthusiasm, their attention to little things, their attitude, the attitude they create with their players. What we need to learn from people, more than what they are teaching, is how and why they are teaching it.

I think I have the best assistant coach in America in Steve McClain. I say that because of his work habits, his enthusiasm, the little things he does and the things he does for me that I don't have to do. I am at the point right now in the season that all I have to do is concentrate on coaching the basketball team and getting myself ready to be difficult with 15 kids for two hours. He takes care of so many other things. Basketball, to me, is a game of distractions. If practices don't reflect the distractions that occur during the game, I don't think you have any chance of getting that into the game.

Game slippage - what does it mean? A term originated by Bob Boyd, it means the difference between what you practice on the practice floor and what you actually get in a game. You're distracted by the crowd. We're practicing in there every day, but there aren't 5,000 people in there. You're distracted by fatigue, which I think is probably the greatest distraction. Fatigue wears everybody down. It changes everybody's attitude. I am going to try to practice to fatigue. The distractions of ego, talent, officials, crowd, and coach. If you practice one way and coach another, that is a distraction. If you ask more in a game than you do in practice, that is a distraction. I think we have to find a way of practicing to those things.

If you think your warm-up is important, then you should practice it. We film our warm-up and we film our bench. In our warm-up, we do a little bit of everything we expect to do in the game. I think this: If you are concentrating on passing, cutting, and catching 30 minutes before the game, you have a better chance of getting that into the game than someone who is out there performing. You practice loosely in the warm-up, you can expect to play loosely. I value the ball, so I am going to start it in warm-up.

I don't want my kids being embarrassed when they enter or leave a game. How can you hold them accountable if you don't tell them what you expect? I tell them: "You come sit by me when I put you in a game. We are going to talk about the offensive set. Then get to the scorer's table quickly with your little white towel. I want you to sprint onto the floor. I want you to find that guy and I want you to communicate." Tell him, "I've got 45, and you're out. And when it's your turn to come out, I want you to sprint and come sit next to me. I don't care if you just made five baskets, I don't care if you missed five baskets, you come sit next to me, lean forward, and act like you are interested in the game." Why? Because I don't want to have to discipline a guy who comes out, takes a towel, throws it down, and goes to the end of the bench. The number one job we have as educators, in the classroom, on the court, or anywhere else, is being problem-solvers. We want to eliminate as many problems as we can, and that's one of my goals in doing something like this.

Along the same line, the practice environment is for creating an attitude about what you expect from your team. We videotape our practices. You can make your players much more receptive to learning in that setting. We start every practice with the ropes. To me it establishes the importance of the comfort zone. Everybody likes to play in the comfort zone. I think you have to practice being uncomfortable. We do the ropes three times from one to one and one-half minutes. I expect them to have all the other stretching done before that time. You raise people's performance by raising their work level in small doses.

Passing

If you are going to pay me a compliment, one of the things I would like to have you say is, "Man, your team really releases from the defense, and passes and catches and gets good shots better than any team I have seen play." How do you build those skills? The thing we do that builds those skills most effectively is the "five-man weave." Running, communicating, passing, cutting, and having to make a basket. Every time you make a pass to your inside person, you have to go around two at full speed. I never take a ball and throw it to a player in practice; every ball I give to a person, I pass to them. I put backspin on it, and I make it as hard as I can and still make it catchable. I expect them to do the same thing. In this setting, I expect them to make lead passes and go around two. They are going to make four trips this time of year; the fourth trip has to be perfect - the ball can't touch the ground at any point. They have to make the layup at both ends, and they have to call out the name of the person they are giving it to.

I never do for a kid what he can do for himself. This is a self-help program. In the practice setting, I see too many drills where we've done all the work for them. I'm not going to pair them up, I'm not going to decide the five, I'm not going to decide who the rebounder is. I expect them to take care of the indecisions by communicating. That's what the game is all about.

We do a number of 30-second to two-minute drills. We value the ball highly; we don't want turnovers. We don't want a player who makes five great passes, then makes five turnovers. That doesn't balance out. Pair up, and don't walk to a drill. You can't shoot if you can't catch, and you can't make baskets if you can't keep from walking. Enforce it from that point of view.

Chapter 5

PHYSIOLOGICAL SPORT SCIENCES

Inside Shot

Flexibility
Charles Brock

Strength and Conditioning
Tom Barrise and Mike Gentry

Endurance
Bradley Cardinal

Coach-Conditioning
Jerry Krause

FLEXIBILITY

Charles Brock

We believe that our flexibility exercises at Drew University are a big reason our team has a history of very few injuries. In my three years at Drew, I have lost only one player to an injury. It is helpful to organize the exercises in such a way that players can remember the sequence, and also not waste time. We do each exercise twice and stress improvement each day. Our practice begins with these exercises, which take 15 minutes. This may seem like quite a bit of time, but it's worth it!

I.   Jog around the court for two and one-half minutes. This increases the viscosity of the muscles and tendons, which is what we are working on. It also allows the players to "shoot the breeze," which we don't allow while stretching.

II. Sit in four lines, with the captains facing the group.
   1. Hamstrings: Legs straight and together, knees locked, toes pointed to forehead.
      a. Reach down and grab leg or foot as far as possible and hold for five seconds. Repeat.
      b. Isolate. Spread legs apart and reach right hand to left leg, hold for five seconds. Left to right, hold for five seconds. Repeat.
   2. Groin: "Butterflies." Put soles of feet together, pull in to body with hands, and push down on knee or calves with elbows.
   3. Gluteals: "Butt." Bend left knee and cross over right knee, pull knee to the chest, hold for five seconds. Cross right over left and pull in and hold for five seconds. Repeat.
   4. Lower back: Pull knees to chest. Roll back and forth, arching back.
   5. Upper back and neck: Raise feet overhead and touch ground behind head. Expel air from lungs. Bring legs back and hold six inches off the ground for 15 to 20 seconds; legs straight.
   6. Abdominal: Roll over on stomach and push up with arms, arching back, twist side to side.

7. Quadriceps: Kneel and lean back and try to touch the head to the ground. Always support with hands behind.

III. Standing.

1. Groin: (Note: We work on this area of the body twice). Legs spread wide, point left foot to the left; lean in that direction, right leg should be straight and right foot perpendicular to left. Reverse and repeat.
2. Sides: Latissimus dorsi. Interlock fingers and reach straight up (palms facing up). Bend side to side.
3. Ankle walks: Walk the length of the floor, up and back. Stretch ankle ligaments.
   a. 1/2 length: heel to tips of toes
   b. 1/2 length: tips of toes to heel
   c. 1/2 length: outside of foot, roll in
   d. 1/2 length: inside of foot, roll out

IV. Against the wall.

1. Quadriceps. (Note: We also work on this area twice). Grab the instep of the foot and pull to butt. Pull back with upper body upright, support with the other hand on the wall.
2. Achilles: Lean straight against the wall on both hands. Push back one foot at a time; foot must be pointed straight ahead, heel down on floor. Stretch with knees straight and bent slightly.

V. Four lines.

1. Easy jog up and back.
2. Trotter step: Up and back, push off back foot and stretch out, at a slow to medium pace.
3. Strider step: Up and back, push off back foot and stretch out, at a slow to medium pace.
4. Sprint: Up and back twice. All-out sprint.

These exercises have never taken longer than 15 minutes. The players are physically and mentally prepared to work.

Editor's Note: Recent research indicates that stretching *after* practices or games is more important than stretching *before* workouts.

STRENGTH AND CONDITIONING

Tom Barrise and Mike Gentry

We have three "seasons" or cycles of strength training for our basketball team. These cycles are designated as follows: off-season, immediately following the season until September 1; pre-season, September 1 until the start of official practice; in-season, which lasts throughout the competitive season.

During all of these cycles, flexibility training is emphasized. Each individual stretches immediately following the strength workouts during the off-season and pre-season. After the flexibility program, the players are encouraged to go to the gym and shoot.

During the off-season, the primary goal of the strength program is to increase the muscular size and body weight of the players and to develop a good overall strength level. Secondary goals include development of intensity, pride, and fostering a sense of team unity by working hard for common goals. We train four days a week during the off-season and train each body part twice a week. We use a light-heavy system, with one day a week being heavy with the big compound lifts, going all out for sets of five reps. The next time these big lifts are trained we do sets of light reps with approximately 15 percent less weight than was used for the heavy day. The weight is increased each set on both days. Assistance lifts are generally kept at six to eight repetitions both days.

No formal running program is implemented during the off-season, but the players are encouraged to continue playing basketball in their free time.

We strength train three days a week during the pre-season cycle. We also cardiovascularly condition the team three days a week during this time. The strength goals at this time include more emphasis on the development of explosive power. We are hoping to be able to develop this explosive power on the strength base we developed in the off-season. The goal of the running/ability program is to condition the players so they will be prepared for the onset of practice. The players still shoot after going through the flexibility program after lifting.

With the onset of the competitive season and organized practice, the strength program is reduced to twice per week and the conditioning and flexibility program is handled by the basketball staff. During each strength workout the total body is trained. The goal is maintenance of strength and power developed during the previous training cycles.

Description of Exercises

Bench press: Use a shoulder-width grip. Lie down on your back on a flat bench. Lower the weight slowly until the bar touches the middle of the chest and drive the bar upward. Keep the feet flat against the floor and the buttocks on the bench at all times. Use a spotter. This exercise works the chest, shoulders, and triceps.

Incline bench press: Use a 45-degree incline bench and a shoulder-width grip. Bring the bar down until it touches the upper chest near the neck and drive it back up toward the rack. Stay in control of the weight at all times. Always keep the back flat against the bench and the buttocks on the bench throughout the lift. Use a spotter. This exercise works the upper chest, shoulders, and triceps.

Close grip bench press: Use the same technique as the regular bench press, except move the grip in to approximately 12 to 14 inches apart. Use a spotter. This exercise primarily works the triceps, shoulders and chest.

Fly: This exercise is done lying on a flat bench. Take two dumbbells and extend to full extension over the face. Then bend the elbows slightly and slowly lower the dumbbells down away from the body. Get a good stretch. Bring the dumbbells up with the same plane of motion. This exercise works the chest.

Hang clean: This exercise is a variation of the power clean. It incorporates the explosive rotary hip drive of a power clean and is much easier to teach. Take the weight off of blocks about 2 1/2 inches high or out of a power rack set at knee level. Stand erect, then bend the knees slightly and let the bar dip about 5 inches with the shoulders over the bar. From this position, jump and shrug the shoulders hard. Keep the weight over the wrist during the pull. Rack the weight on the shoulders then repeat the movement. Feet should be shoulder-width apart. Hand spacing should be directly outside the thighs. This is a quick, explosive movement. This exercise primarily works the hips, legs, and back.

Shrug: This is an assistance movement for the hang clean. Don't pull the weight all the way up or rack it on the shoulder; instead, stop the movement after the powerful shrugging of the shoulders. Keep the elbow locked throughout the movement. Still use the hips in an explosive manner. Use a lot of weight in this exercise. This exercise works on the trapezius, upper back, hips, and legs.

Power pull: This is a great assistance exercise for the hang clean. Everything is done the same way as in the hang clean except the weight is not racked on the shoulders at the completion of the upward pull. At the end of the pull, the elbows should be up, over the wrist. The bar should be pulled to at least chest level. Remember to use the hips and legs in the exercise. Be explosive. This exercise works the hips, legs and upper back.

Pullup: We do our pullups with a medium grip about shoulder-width apart so that we get a fuller range of motion. We alternate underhand and overhand grips. Make sure to go all the way down on each repetition and get the chin over the bar. This exercise stretches the lower back and works the lats.

Bent-over row: Place the barbell on the floor, bend over at the waist with the knees slightly bent, and take a medium grip on the bar about shoulder width. Pull the weight off the floor while maintaining the same body position and make the bar touch the abdominal area. Lower the weight under control until the plates almost touch the floor and repeat. Remember to get a good stretch. This exercise adds back strength and thickness.

Pullover: Lie down on your back on a flat bench with your head at the end opposite the standards. Have your partner hand you a curl bar or straight bar so that you may take a close grip approximately 8 to 10 inches apart. With the elbows bent, slowly lower the bar back over the head until the plates almost touch the floor. Then pull the bar back over the head to your chest. Keep the elbows bent, then repeat. Remember to exhale as you pull the weight up. This exercise primarily works the lats and chest.

Back squats: This is one of the best exercises known to man. Rest the bar on the back of the groove between the deltoid and trapezius, keep the lower back arched and the weight over the hips at all times. The feet should be slightly wider than shoulder width and the toes pointed out slightly. Use a rack and spotters.

Go down slowly and under control until the bottom of the thigh is parallel to the floor. Keep the head up and eyes fixed on an object straight ahead. Drive up quickly. Do not bounce at the bottom of the lift. Keep the knees over the feet at all times. This exercise works the hips, legs, and lower back and stimulates overall body growth and strength.

Nautilus leg curl: Lie face down on the machine, place the feet under the roller pads, and place your knees slightly off the edge of the bench. Grasp the handles and flex the knees until the pads almost touch the buttocks. Pause at the point of maximum contraction. Lower the weight slowly until the weights touch. Keep the toes close flexed throughout the movement. This exercise works the hamstrings and is very important in the prevention of hamstring pulls.

Calf raise: This exercise can be done on a variety of machines, with a barbell or with partners. Regardless of which method is chosen, you should lock the knees and concentrate on getting a full range of motion with the ankles and put the pressure over the big toe. This exercise works the calves.

Bench jump: This is a basic plyometric exercise. We stand on the floor and leap up on a box varying from 24 to 36 inches high. This exercise develops explosive power.

Seated behind-neck press: Use a behind-the-neck bench or sit on a regular flat bench facing the standards. If using a regular flat bench, lean forward and take the weight out of the rack, placing the bar behind the neck. Have a partner sit with his back against yours to act as a brace. Press the weight to full arm extension and lower the weight slowly. Get a full range of motion and try to keep the back straight. This exercise primarily works the shoulders.

Bent-over lateral: Take two dumbbells and bend over at the waist with the knees slightly bent. Perform a reverse fly movement, a semicircle away from the body. Try to get the dumbbells out and up away from the body. Stay in control of the weight at all times. This exercise works the rear deltoids.

Lying tricep extension: This exercise is done lying on a flat bench, with the head away from the standards. Use a curl bar with an inside grip. Extend the arms fully and slowly lower the forearms until the bar is almost touching the forehead. Don't let the elbows move while extending. Then extend back to the starting position. Keep the back and hips on the bench throughout the movement. This is an excellent strength and size builder for the triceps.

Tricep pushdown: Use a lat pulldown machine for this exercise. Stand erect facing the machine and grasp the bar with a close overhand grip approximately four to six inches apart. Keep the elbows close to the body and stationary throughout the exercise. Extend the arms down to full extension and repeat. This exercise works the triceps.

Barbell curl: Use either a straight bar or curl bar. We do a method called 6-6-6. It is an old bodybuilding method and demands high intensity. You go through half of a full curl for six reps, bringing the bar to waist level and returning to the starting position. Then immediately do the top half of the range of motion going from the finish position of the curl and lowering the weight halfway and returning to the top for six reps. Then immediately do six reps throughout the full range of motion for six reps. This is one set. Avoid excessive back swing. This exercise works the biceps; it is a screamer.

Hammer curl: We do this exercise seated on a flat bench with two dumbbells. Alternately curl each dumbbell with this variation: Keep the ends of the dumbbell perpendicular to the floor at all times. Don't swing the weight. This exercise works the forearms and biceps.

MEN'S BASKETBALL OFF-SEASON STRENGTH PROGRAM				
MONDAY	**TUESDAY**	**WEDNESDAY**	**THURSDAY**	**FRIDAY**
Chest, Shoulders, Arms	*Legs, Back*	*Rest*	*Chest, Shoulders, Arms*	*Back, Legs*
Bench Press 5-5	Back Squats 5-5		Bench Press 4-8	Hang Cleans 5-5
Close Grip Bench 3-6	Leg Extension 3-8		Incline Bench 3-8	Bent-Over Rows 3-6
Flies 3-8	Leg Curls 3-8		Flies 3-8	Pullups 3-10
Behind-Neck Press 3-6	Calf Raises 3-10		Behind-Neck Press 3-8	Pullovers 3-8
Bent-Over Laterals 3-8	Shrugs 3-6		Bent-Over Lats 3-8	Back Squats 4-8
Lying Tricep Ext. 3-6	Power Pulls 3-6		Lying Tricep Ext. 3-8	Leg Ext. 2-10
Tricep Pushdowns 3-8	Bent-Over Rows 3-6		Tricep Pushdowns 3-8	Leg Curls 2-10
Curls 3 Sets 6-6-6	Pullovers 3-8		Curls 3 Sets 6-6-6	Calf Raises 3-10
Hammer Curls 3-8	Situps 2-30		Hammer Curls 3-8	Bench Jumps 2-10
Situps 2-30	Bench Jumps 2-10		Situps 2-30	Situps 2-30
Flexibility Program	Flexibility Program		Flexibility Program	Flexibility Program

Table 5.1

MEN'S BASKETBALL IN-SEASON STRENGTH PROGRAM			
FIRST SESSION — TOTAL BODY		**SECOND SESSION — TOTAL BODY**	
Bench Press 4-5	Lying Tricep Ext. 3-8	Hang Cleans 4-5	Tricep Pushdowns 3-8
Back Squat 4-5	Leg Extensions 2-10	Pullups 2-10	Leg Extensions 2-10
Shrugs 3-6	Leg Curls 2-10	Bench Press 3-8	Leg Curls 2-10
Power Pulls 3-6	Situps 1-50	Back Squats 3-8	Situps 1-50
Pullups 2-10			

Table 5.2

Situp: Abdominal training shouldn't be overlooked. Not only will the athlete have stronger abs, but lower back problems can be avoided. Do bent knee sit-ups on the floor and hook the feet under anything or have someone hold the feet. The feet should be flat on the floor and close to the body. Keep the hands and arms in front of the body with the hands on the shoulders and the arms tucked into the side. Go all the way up and lower the body until the lower back touches and repeat. Two to three sets of 25 to 30 reps should be enough.

Editor's note: One set of 8-12 reps (60-80% of TRM) will give baseline results.

ENDURANCE

Bradley J. Cardinal

"You get in shape to play sports, you don't play sports to get in shape."

John Wooden, in his "Pyramid of Success," lists conditioning on the same level as "skill" and "team spirit" in terms of its importance in making a successful athlete; although this is a debatable issue, it ought to demonstrate the important role of conditioning in basketball.

The major components of a conditioning program are: flexibility, strength, and endurance. Each one is important and must be developed along with

MEN'S BASKETBALL PRE-SEASON STRENGTH PROGRAM				
MONDAY	**TUESDAY**	**WEDNESDAY**	**THURSDAY**	**FRIDAY**
Flexibility Program	*Back, Legs*	*Chest, Arms*	*Flexibility Program*	*Total Body Workout*

Sprint Conditioning Sample Workout
 	
Set 1:
  4-220's at
  34 sec. ea.
  1 min. 30 sec.
  rest
  between 220's
Set 2:
  8-110's at
  17 sec. ea.
  45 sec. rest
  between 110's
Set 3:
  8-55's at
  9 sec ea.
  24 sec rest
  between 55's
	Back Squat 5-5
	Leg Ext. 3-8
	Leg Curls 3-8
	Calf Raises 3-10
	Shrugs 3-6
	Power Pulls 3-6
	Pullups 3-10
	Bench Jumps 2-10
	Situps 1-50
	Flexibility Program
		Bench Press 5-5
		Incline Bench 3-6
		Flies 3-8
		Lying Tricep Exts. 3-8
		Tricep Pushdowns 3-8
		Curls 3 sets 6-6-6
		Hammer Curls 3-8
		Situps 1-50
		Flexibility Program
		Jump Rope Routine
		Agility Program
		Cone Drills —
		sample workout
		     3 each
		4-way Box Drill
		run, shuffle,
		backpedal, shuffle
		     3 each
		Fig. 8 Box Drill 3 ea
		Lateral Shuffle Shuttle
		Drill, 30 sec. 2 ea.
		Up & Back Shuffle
		Drill - 30 sec., 2 ea.
			Cardiovascular Conditioning
			1 mile for time -
			gradually decreasing
			the time each week
				Hang Cleans 5-5
				Pull-Ups 3-10
				Back Squats 4-8
				Leg Extensions 2-10
				Leg Curls 2-10
				Calf Raises 3-10
				Bench Press 4-8
				Flies 3-8
				Tricep Pushdowns 3-8
				Curls 3 sets 6-6-6
				Bench Jumps 2-10
				Situps 1-50

Table 5.3

Basketball's Daily Eleven Flexibility Program
Ankle Rolls
Calf Stretch
Hamstring Stretch
Double Leg Stretch
Quadricep Stretch
Groin Stretch
Lower Back Stretch
Side Bends
Shoulder Stretch
Chest Stretch
Fingers and Wrist Stretch
Note: When appropriate, perform exercises on both sides of the body.

Table 5.4

basketball skills. Well-conditioned teams play aggressively, rebound ferociously, and have enhanced confidence, particularly in the final minutes of a close game.

Flexibility

Flexibility exercises are often brushed over by coaches in an effort to get on with skill development. Some coaches all but neglect it by stating to their players (at some point before, during, or after practice), "Don't forget to stretch." Failing to emphasize flexibility exercises denies athletes the benefits of a comprehensive flexibility program. Flexibility exercises improve a player's power by increasing range of motion at a given joint. They also decrease the likelihood of injury, promote circulation, develop a sense of body awareness, and relax the body and mind.

A sound flexibility program for basketball involves exercises for the entire body (ankles, knees, hips, trunk, shoulders, elbows, and wrists) with a special focus on the ankles, knees, and shoulders; these joints are particularly vulnerable to injury (see Table 5.1). Flexibility exercises should be performed daily, both before and after strenuous activity. The body should be "warm" prior to performing flexibility exercises, but the heart rate should not be elevated above 100 beats per minute.

Although flexibility can be increased in a number of ways, static stretching exercises are usually preferred. They enable a person to slowly stretch a joint/limb to a point of voluntary contraction (the point of mild discomfort or tension). Also, the risk of injury is decreased and less energy is required to perform the exercises. Each stretched position should be held for five full breaths (or between 10 and 30 seconds). The comprehensive flexibility program described will require between five and ten minutes to complete.

Strength

Gone are the days when basketball coaches believed that strength training adversely affected shooting accuracy, or that strong, well-muscled athletes lacked flexibility, or that strength training made a person "muscle bound." Although these myths were believed for a number of years, they have been disregarded by most successful coaches.

Basketball players who have physical prowess are often held in awe by coaches, players, and spectators alike. These athletes can be seen "attacking the boards" and diving for loose balls. They certainly do not lack confidence and are generally aggressive on the court.

Physical prowess is developed in the weight room through a sensible strength training program and effort. However, this does not imply that athletes train using the PTA method (pain, torture, and agony!). In strength training, the emphasis should be placed on getting the most work done in the shortest possible time period. This is best accomplished by utilizing isotonic exercises (exercises which involve a muscular contraction being applied throughout a muscle's full range of motion). An example of an isotonic exercise would be the standard bench press exercise.

When performing an isotonic exercise, the focus should be on the negative or lengthening phase of the exercise. In other words, the weight should be lowered more slowly than it is lifted. Other major focuses include the development of balanced musculature, physical size, overall strength, and power. To accomplish this, a program should develop all of the major muscle groups of the body with no special attention given to one or two "favorite" areas. The athlete who focuses the training program on only specific body parts and neglects others increases the injury potential substantially. Sites often affected by such poor training habits are the knee and shoulder joints. Through a solid foundation of strength, many injuries can be avoided (see Tables 5.5 and 5.6).

Endurance

Basketball uses all three major energy systems of the body: aerobic, anaerobic (ATP/PC and anaerobic), and lactic acid. However, most authorities classify basketball as being 90 percent anaerobic; the trick then is to train athletes for basketball by training primarily the anaerobic energy systems. This is done through high intensity activities such as interval training, sprint training, and actually playing basketball. Anaerobic activities result in heavy, laborious breathing (oxygen debt, oxygen bankruptcy).

With these all-out, intense workloads, the body must pay the price of extra long recovery periods before it can return to normal function. When an athlete gets a quick steal, sprints up the court, and slam dunks the ball, the anaerobic energy system is in use.

In-Season Strength Training for Basketball		
Order of Exercise	Reps	Sets
Bench Press	6-12	1-4
Seated Rowing	6-12	1-4
or		
Lat. Pulldown	6-12	1-4
Multi-Hip (each way)	6-12	1-4
Situps	12-24	2-3
Hyperextensions	12-24	2-3
Wrist Curl	6-12	1-4
(Effort should be 60% to 85%)		

Table 5.5

Off-Season Strength Training for Basketball		
Order of Exercise	Reps	Sets
Power Cleans	2-3	3-5
Situps	12-24	2-3
Bench Press	4-6	3-5
Squats	4-6	3-5
Seated Rowing	4-6	3-5
or		
Lat. Pulldowns	4-6	3-5
Leg Curl	4-6	3-5
Wrist Curl (and Reverse)	4-6	3-5
Calf Raise	8-12	3-10
(Effort should be 60% to 95%)		

Table 5.6

The aerobic or oxygen system, although not the primary energy system utilized in basketball, is still important and must not be neglected. By being "aerobically fit," the athlete improves recovery time, delays the onset of fatigue, is capable of playing for extended periods of time, develops cardiovascular fitness, and controls body weight. Long, slow, distance (LSD) training (30-plus minutes in duration) should be incorporated, especially in the off-season, to build a year-round aerobic base.

Summary

Today's basketball players are bigger, stronger, and faster than ever. One of the reasons is year-round conditioning programs, with development occurring during the off-season and maintenance occurring throughout the on-season. Basketball coaches today must not only perfect skills, devise strategies, and prepare for opponents, but also condition their teams in terms of flexibility, strength, and endurance.

COACH – CONDITIONING

Jerry Krause

Coaching basketball is one of the most challenging and rewarding of all professions. As a helping, service profession, coaching is an emotionally draining experience that can take a great toll on a person. I therefore strongly recommend that coaches develop a personal wellness program. This is a total approach to better living; focusing on prevention of problems before they occur, self-responsibility and taking charge of our own destiny when we can. This approach means addressing all wellness dimensions:

Spiritual - develop a well-defined philosophy and a clear set of values to transmit to your players.

Physical - commit yourself to a balanced, baseline development of health-related components of fitness.

Energy fitness (heart/lungs) - the minimum aerobic requirement is 3-4 times per week of movement for 15-20 minutes. Recent research reveals that we can get ourselves out of the high risk area much easier than previously thought with moderate movement for 15-20 minutes, and it need not be done continuously. This means that we can use functional physical fitness to gain those levels, such as by walking, climbing stairs, hiking, bicycling, and so on. Simple things such as parking farther away and enjoying a walk to your destination and avoiding elevators and escalators can make a great difference.

Muscular fitness (strength/endurance) - this area begins to decline when a person reaches the late twenties and early thirties. It is a key for weight control because muscle loss is commonly accompanied by fat gain, which fools you into thinking that weight stability means all is OK. Keeping muscle fitness up prevents injuries for coaches as well as players, but also is the key for body composition control. All that is needed for baseline muscular fitness levels is overload of one set of 8 to 12 repetitions with 40 to 60 percent of one RM for all major muscle groups (arms/legs/trunk) two to three times per week. A program of this nature will take 15 to 20 minutes to complete.

Body composition - nutrition and exercise (especially muscular fitness) are the keys. Cut out the fat and increase complex carbohydrates (fruits, vegetables, grains, cereals and pasta).

Flexibility - stretch after any energy or muscular fitness workout for best results. Focus on a prevention program for the lower back. Stretch all major muscle groups for 15 to 30 seconds (take five deep breaths). It is relaxing and also is a good antidote for muscle/tendon strains and pulls as the "ol' coach" proceeds along the career path.

Intellectual - balance your interests and challenge yourself by becoming informed in your profession as well as some other interest area.

Career - have a professional development plan to develop your knowledge, experience and contacts. Be active in a basketball coaching professional organization and enjoy each day you coach.

Emotional - develop a stress management program that includes exercise and control. Remember to focus on those things that you can affect and forget the rest.

Social - improvement and nurturing of social skills are a key to a satisfying family and professional life. Many key elements of social wellness are skills that can be improved.

Coaching wellness can result in increasing your life expectancy - not how long you live, but how well you live. Make your basketball coaching career one you can enjoy to its fullest. Remember also that one of the greatest gifts you can give your players is your best example. You should want them to not only do as you say, but do as you do.

Chapter 6   SCOUTING AND RECRUITING

SCOUTING

John McClendon, Jr.

The topic of scouting is very difficult to cover in a short period of time. I don't know how much scouting you do at your level, but I believe that it is an important part of the game. It has helped me a great deal through the years in my coaching.

At present, I am the basketball scout for the United States Olympic Team. I was appointed to this position by the Olympic Committee. No matter who the Olympic coach is, I am still the scout for the Olympic team. The Committee investigated and found that there were no records of foreign country competition. On file, we now have a record of all foreign teams and what they do. We know their personnel, what offense and defense they like to run, what their strengths and weaknesses might be, and any other pertinent information concerning the foreign teams. It was at my suggestion that these extensive files be kept.

In foreign competition, the thing that we must fight is our own arrogance. We have to realize that the other countries are working hard to build teams that can take away our basketball supremacy. We can't take anything for granted. This is the reason we must keep a comprehensive file on our foreign opponents.

What You Must Know About the Opponents

1. You need to be knowledgeable about your opponents and their strengths and weaknesses. You should know these things from an individual and team standpoint.

Some people use a tape recorder to scout, others use the standard method. How you take your information is not that important. Most foreign teams don't change personnel much from year to year. The United States changes personnel often, and I would consider it difficult to keep a good file on the United States teams. This helps us, because we can watch a player for a long time and pick up personal characteristics of an individual. At Tennessee State we scouted to keep from getting beaten too badly. If it did nothing other than accomplish this goal, it was worthwhile.

2. You need to scout to know their general ideas of offense and defense. Most teams have a primary and a secondary offense and defense. You must know them both and know their philosophy.

3. You need to scout to prepare your team psychologically. I coached college teams for 25 years, and used a scouting report for each game. My players felt better about their opponent because they felt they were prepared for their opponent. I also had a four-year file on the coaches. You might feel that is going a little too far, but I believe in scouting and I believe that it helped me to know about the coaches as well as the players.

4. You need to scout to prepare your team mechanically. This factor in scouting is obvious, because you must execute certain mechanical phases of the game to stop the other team.

5. You need to scout to minimize the danger of exceptional action by an opposing team or individual. Players should not be surprised by anything an opponent does, if that player or team has done it before. You and your players need to know the exceptional abilities of individuals (great jumper, quick hands, great shooter, great shot blocker, and so on).

6. You need to scout to minimize the opponent's ability to surprise with tactics and strategy. This refers to situation strategies such as late game tactics, presses, and delay games. You need to know when these tactics are used so that you can expect them.

7. You need to scout to know what special plays the opponent uses. With a few seconds left in the game, you need to know what type of play your opponent might use, such as an out-of-bounds play.

8. You need to scout to influence your approach to the game. Your strategy should not be so set that you cannot change or adjust. The scouting report broadens your approach to the game because you must be prepared for any event that occurs in a game.

What Must Be Done When You Scout

1. You need to take a good position in the stadium or arena. Your vantage point is important. The comment that the coach has the worst seat in the house is correct. When you scout, elevation helps evaluation.

2. You need a good process of taking notes. You need to have something handy that can be used easily. If you can film games it is good, but you don't get the panoramic view and depth that you can by being in the stadium.

3. You need the availability of statistics. Statistics are helpful, but using statistics from one game to make a judgement is a mistake. Players and teams should be judged on total statistics. One category that can be deceiving on a one-game basis is field goal percentage. Never decide what a player can do on a one-game performance.

Warnings About Scouting

1. Scout and prepare your team for what you can do. Don't do so much to prepare that you change what you are used to doing. You can confuse your players by giving them so many new things that they cannot execute.

I had an opponent when I was at Tennessee State that we defeated 16 consecutive times. During that series, that team was capable of beating us many times. Each time, however, the coach overcoached and his team was so conscious of what we were doing that it didn't do what it did best. Each time we won.

2. Always keep your credibility. Don't use scare tactics in your reports. Be realistic about your chances of winning. Don't, however, create overconfidence. I didn't want my team seeing the opponent play. I have had teams that thought they could beat anybody. Players often watch a team play and decide they will have no trouble with them. Even youth league basketball players react the same. I don't mind a couple of players scouting with me, however.

3. Don't report guesses as fact. If you don't see it, don't report it. If you are not sure, you may say what you think they might do in a certain situation according to their philosophy. But never report a guess as fact.

There is a value in scouting your opponent while you are playing it. Some coaches like to have a scout watch the first half from a high vantage point and then file a report to the team at halftime. If this is done, the report must be presented in quick and concise fashion. Halftime statistics are valuable, but they usually arrive late in the break period and you don't have much time to go over them.

Other Important Scouting Information

Other scouting information that can be important to a coach includes the following:

1. Condition of the court – what kind of surface

2. Type of lighting

3. Type of baskets

4. How close the seating is to the floor

5. The scoreboard – can it be seen from every vantage point on the floor?

6. Background at each end

7. Locker room facilities

8. Crowd reaction – attitude and actions

With scouting you are trying to eliminate surprises on and off the court. It provides you with information you need to know about the team and the coach. What distinguishes one coach from another? Some coaches do the same thing every year; others change every weekend. Through scouting you can find out these things.

SAMPLE SCOUTING REPORT

OPPONENT'S FIRST LINE PLAYERS

NO	NAME	POS	SHOOTING%	REBOUNDING	OFFENSIVE ABILITY	DEFENSIVE ABILITY	AGE	HT	WT	OTHER OUTSTANDING QUALITIES

OPPONENT'S BEST SUBSTITUTES

NO	NAME	POS	SHOOTING%	REBOUNDING	OFFENSIVE ABILITY	DEFENSIVE ABILITY	AGE	HT	WT	OTHER OUTSTANDING QUALITIES

TEAM OFFENSE			TEAM DEFENSE		
("Yes", "No" or Short Answer)			("Yes", "No" or Short Answer)		
Pattern Offense?			Aggressive?		
Type?			Type? (Press-Zone-MTM)		
Fast Break?			Defensive Traps? By Whom?		
Pivot Play Used?			Area of Greatest Pressure?		
Pivot-Post Position?			Multiple Defenses? Which?		
Offense Initiated By?			Zone-Press Alignment?		
Screens? Type?			Play Area or Zone?		
Players Usually in Screens?			Play the Ball?		
Out-of-Bounds Offense to Score?			Defense in Front Court?		
To Begin Offense?			Players Help Out?		
Strong Pivot Man?			Defense Inside Foul Line or 3 Second		
Guards Handle Ball Well?			Area?		
Guards Good Dribblers?			MTM Defense Involves Sliding?		
Strength of Offensive			MTM Switching?		
Rebounding Game?			Switching or Sliding on Pivot-Post Play?		
Forwards, FG Accuracy?			Good Defensive Floor Balance?		
Guards, FG Accuracy?			Good Against Screens?		
Speed?			Defense vs. Fast Break Good? Plan?		
Give and Go?			Zone in Front Court?		
Scissors on Post Play?			Zone Alignment?		
General Passing Game?			Fast Break From Defensive Rebound?		
Time of Offensive FGA in			Outlet Pass to?		
Relation to 30 Second Limit?			Defensive Rebounding Strong?		
Strongest Phase of Offense?			Strongest Phase of Defense?		
Weakest Phase of Offense?			Weakest Phase of Defense?		

Table 6.1

Your team needs confidence when going into a game against a certain opponent, and scouting can give this confidence. Through scouting, you may look at the individual player's attitudes. It is important that you know which player is most likely to hide in a pressure situation and which player wants the ball.

Some coaches even scout officials. I used to do this too. In international basketball this is very important. The players need to be prepared for the officials' attitudes. Each official has a temperament. It is important to know what that temperament is. Some officials like to make certain calls, which can influence the game. If an official is a poor official, tell the players so that they don't overreact during games.

Physical conditioning is a valuable part of basketball. What a team does after going up and down the floor must be included in your report. Going up and down the floor makes players "shorter." There are certain tips that indicate fatigue in a team or player. Look for these signs and try to take advantage of the team that is not well conditioned. I believe that a team can win one-third of its games on conditioning alone.

Scouting is a valuable and pertinant part of preparing your team for their opponents. It is a must to winning basketball games.

TIPS ON SCOUTING

Rick Majerus

We choose to scout a team at their fieldhouse when we are going to play them on their home court and scout them on the road when they have to come to our arena . Many collegiate teams, and this certainly is not as prevalent on the prep level, play differently at home than they do on the road.

We always arrive early to memorize the numbers of each player before warm-ups even begin. Once they take the court we want to be there. Also, it is often possible to judge the shooting abilities and favorite spots of certain individuals in practice. Watch for those who need to establish a rhythm to shoot (by movement or a dribble) as opposed to those players who are able to take the shot from a standing position.

Every good coach has a philosophy of the tactics he will employ. Before the game begins, try to be acquainted with his philosophy. During the first five minutes of the game, try to observe and determine just what that team's objectives are on offense and deense. We may chart a particular play, but at this juncture in the game we try to do as little writing as possible.

After the initial five minutes, begin to write down their patterns and plays. How do they initiate their attack and what do they do to designate which play

or pattern they will run? More often than not, the keys to watch for are the location of the center, a verbal signal (number, color), and a certain offensive set (stack, high, post). Do they key their attack off of a hand-off, dribble out, pass and screen away? Of course, be careful to distinguish a continuity pattern as opposed to a set play.

Once they are into their offense, the top priority is to ascertain exactly how they reverse the ball. We try to stop the reversal of the basketball because every good pattern and play is predicted on this concept, regardless of whether you play a zone or man-to-man defense. You are best able to distort an offensive concept (for example, the passing game) by denying the usual or easy route by which they swing the ball. For instance, against a zone will they relay on a permanent point, step a post out to the perimeter to reverse it, look to throw cross court by skipping a man, etc.? The next step is to prioritize the various techniques employed so we can force them to use the one to which they are least accustomed.

As the game progresses it is difficult to divorce the offense from the defense. For the sake of this article, let's stay with the offense. After charting how they swing the ball, the next objective is to determine who posts where and in what situations. Key point: It is just as important to know who can and will feed the post as it is to know who will be the post.

Always be aware of ball reversal situations from a wing to a point, because that is a difficult adjustment to make for a post defender. Do they look to punch it in from that point position on the reversal? Teams that run a passing game, or variation thereof, are especially adept at posting and historically have tried to create a mismatch by executing post exchange tactics.

Finally, after determining the set, ball reversal concepts, posting techniques, patterns, and plays, now try to note what type of break and early offense they're using. Who receives the outlet pass and who will fill the middle lane? Is it a "number break?" Are only predetermined players or a single player to handle the ball in the middle Is it a sideline break?

Next, how can the flow and timing of their break be disrupted? Perhaps the break is triggered to a designated outlet, as Michigan did with Rickey Green. We tried to counter this ploy by occasionally posting Green inside. This meant he wasn't able to go to the outlet area as quickly.

We are not overly concerned with the break. Occasionally we will jam an outlet, but generally the best way to contain a break is to hustle back quickly to play defense. If nothing else, this simple strategy entirely negates the concept of early offense. Marquette does not prepare for early offense. We have always tried to dictate the tempo of the game; there is no better way to counter a fast-breaking team than to frustrate them in this manner.

A point upon which we place what may be an inordinate amount of emphasis is the opposition's press offense. Most teams are stereotyped in their press attack so we mark down how they set up and inbound the ball. Usually a team will determine beforehand how they will line up on the lane for a foul shot and then they break to an exact spot to inbound the ball. This is usually a constant and that information has enabled us to really apply pressure to the inbounder and his first press.

Note whether or not the attack varies against a zone or man-to-man. The original set used to inbound the ball usually doesn't change. However, after that the philosophy normally does, based on whether they are facing a zone or man-to-man press. We are always searching the player against whom, or area in which, our trap will be most effective. An often neglected aspect of scouting a press offense is to decide what philosophy that team has once it has broken the press. Many teams prefer to merely break the press and then initiate an offensive thrust, as opposed to others who try to score off the press. Against the latter, watch for the long pass, shot selection once the ball has crossed midcourt, and trailer. Trailers on a press offense can pose a much more formidable threat than on a break.

Switching to what we look for defensively, we do not believe in the axiom "Never press a pressing team." Therefore, I am looking first of all for what type of presses our opponents will attempt. Do they pressure the inbounder? Try to give a direction of the inbound pass? At what point on the court or time in the game do they apply the press? Where will they trap, and how many traps are attempted? What keys a trap – the dribble, location of the ball, initial press set?

After seeing the press and getting a feel for its workings, pay close attention to the location of the back man. Can he be attacked? Will he commit early, thereby enabling your team to go for the two-on-one situation?

It is also important to watch for changing defenses and what brings about the change. Is it the score, the time, etc.? In assessing any defense, we first look at their pickup point. Remember though that this pickup point is predicted on quickness. If they are quick, the point may be extended when they play your team.

On their man-to-man defense, look for the type of pressure exerted on the entry pass. After that, observe how they play a cutter. Also notice how they react to a screen on the ball as well as away from the ball. Be very conscious as to where they want to influence you – to the middle or to the sideline.

In the backcourt, watch for free switching on a pressure cross. Also , do not neglect to look for a trap on a loss of vision and a false trap. Be wary of the run and jump. Do they use it on a loss of vision? Where is it most likely to occur?

On a screen or a split (scissors) will they switch or stay, go ball or man-side, and do they hold up cutters to disrupt your timing? These are the facts of defense that your players must be aware of to best capitalize on the possible alternatives the defense presents.

Every bit as important as their offensive post play will be their post defense. What is their decision line in relation to the location of the ball? How can we best void in the weak-side help if they front? Perhaps an even greater opportunity may be present because they overcompensate on their help. Will they two-time the post and try to rake the ball? Is everybody on their team prepared to play post defense? Who are we most likely to be able to flash post against? Another point to note is, what role does their center play in helping out? Will he leave the post or do they rely on the weak-side forward and cover down with an off guard to stop penetration by the forward with the ball.

Space limitations require that we mention only the following team characteristics to be charted: the opposition's rebounding techniques and tendencies, the delay game and freeze, out-of-bounds plays at side court, under the basket, and the play they most frequently revert back to when only enough time remains to take one shot.

YOUR NEXT OPPONENT

Dick Tarrant

Recommended Procedures

Before a game begins, a scout should follow these guidelines:

1. Obtain general information before entering the gym (from local newspapers, other coaching friends, and so on).

2. Get to the game site early.

3. Obtain a program – if none is available, get the players' numbers from the scorer's table well in advance of tip-off. If stats are available, get them.

4. Sit halfway up the bleachers, not at courtside.

5. Avoid all distractions.

6. Sit alone or with a person you brought along.

7. Observe the warm-up routine carefully.

8. Assess the players' sizes if a program is unavailable.

9. Try to perceive their "readiness" to play.

During the game, follow these procedures:

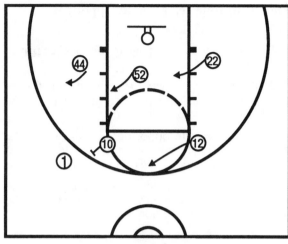

Figure 6.1

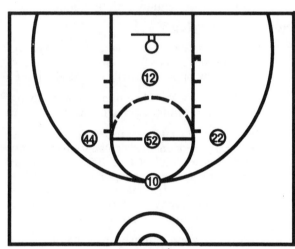

Figure 6.2

1. **Don't:**

   a. Become a fan – tonight you analyze!

   b. Get irritated and distracted with inept officiating.

   c. Take a lot of notes – especially early in the game.

   d. Get distracted by those around you. Try to isolate, if possible.

   e. Leave the game early.

2. **Do:**

   a. Totally concentrate. The only note-taking should be jotting down the starters by number and position.

   b. Observe carefully the general flow of the game for a few minutes. Take no notes. Zero in on

no individual or particular phase of the game. Be patient.

   c. Try to determine your opponent's game plan tonight. Might that also be the game plan for us?

   d. Jot down an early substitute or two. Why was this change made? Are they far less effective?

Team Defense (Basic Defense)

1. Where are the lines of resistance?

2. Do defenses change? How do they defend out-of-bounds plays?

3. Are they an active or passive team on "D"? Where? When?

4. When can we expect a press? Traps?

5. Transition to defense?

6. Where and when can we expect firmness?

Sample Notes on Team Defense

The following are notes a coach might make after scouting a game:

   1. M/M at 20 feet. (Man-to-man defense that picks up 20 feet out.) Poor support. Good pressure on ball.

   2. 1-3-1Z, OOB, under and sides, very tight, tough inside.

   3. Good box-out team. Strong on glass.

   4. 1-2-1-1 after made free throw, regroups to 1-3-1Z. Traps once.

Individual Defense (Their Match-ups)

1. Starting five. See Figures 6.1 and 6.2.

2. Establish in your own mind (without notes):
   a. Can we go inside against them?
   b. Can we attack at center?
   c. What kind of post defense do they play?
   d. Do they influence? Real pressure?
   e. Do they overplay the leads (passing lanes)?
   f. Do they "sustain" in their defense? This is important.
   g. Have they a defensive star? A stopper?

Team Offense

1. Do they fast break? When?
   a. Controlled?
   b. Wild and crazy?
   c. Cherry pick?
   d. Only off steals?
   e. Only on missed field goals?

2. How can we prevent their fast break?
   a. Discipline our shooting?
   b. Take high percentage shots?
   c. Get second and third efforts?

d. Tie up rebounder?

e. Jam outlets?

f. Special avenues of retreat on defense?

3. Their halfcourt game

a. In our M/M defense: What must we do to stop them? What must we take away?

b. In our zone: Do they have a good zone attack? Can we key off anyone? Who must we close out on more than others? Who are their perimeter shooters?

c. Their OOB's plays, if any. Must I alert my team to anything special?

Individual Offense

1. Can they handle pressure?

2. Are their guards one-size dominant?

3. Can we chase their best ballhandler off the ball?

4. Do their forwards work to free up?

5. Do their lane players work for position? Do they pin? Do they get after the ball on the glass?

6. Who are strong and weak free throw shooters? Know this for close end-of-game situations.

7. Where is their individual offensive strength?

Miscellaneous Notes to Take

1. Unusual jump ball alignment. Possession? To score.

2. Unusual OOB's situations.

3. Delay game sets (four corners, and so on) When?

4. Unusual substitution pattern.

5. When and what to write:

a. Time-outs and halftime.

b. Write in your first thoughts on your M/M matchups (F on F; C on C, and so on).

c. Their style of play.

d. Their team defense.

e. Their team offense.

f. Their individual offense.

After the Game

1. Review game and notes. Prepare a brief, concise, to-the-point report for your head coach and/or the team. Perhaps a different report for each. Include the following:

a. Starting line-up, with position, size, year in school, and so on.

b. Individual analysis (don't elaborate).

c. General comments on team's style of play.

d. Team defense.

e. Team offense.

f. Miscellaneous information _ out of bounds's plays and so on.

g. Recommendations.

Preparing Your Team for an Opponent

Before taking the floor:

1. Type a one- or two-page report for each player, if possible.

2. Read the report with the team either before or halfway through practice, if you prefer, to "key" at the end of practice.

3. Don't overrate opposing individual(s) or the team. Don't make your players fearful of a name opponent, regardless of his skill(s).

4. It's very important that you emphasize keys to winning. Be certain you know what has to be done to win. Be honest.

5. Ignore trivia (such as a player's favorite move).

6. Pump confidence into your team during the scouting report. Assign match-ups.

7. Ask players if they have any "pointed" questions before keying on the floor. Don't take more than 12 to 15 minutes with the report.

On-the-Floor Keying

1. Have an assistant coach take the reserves to the opposite end of the floor to go half-speed through the opponents' halfcourt M/M offense.

2. Spend no more than five minutes on readying your reserves in the above manner.

3. Key your top six to seven people against the reserves (opponents). Play man-to-man against their offense. Walk it first. Take away what they want to do! Make points of emphasis immediately, such as taking away certain cuts and certain passing lanes, putting pressure on their guards, stressing boxing out, and so on).

4. Key their zone offense against your zone defense, if you play it. Know your individual opponents (reserves) now!! Who do you shade off of? Who do you close out on very closely?

5. Key their out-of-bounds plays.

6. Key stopping their transition game, if necessary.

Offense Versus Opponent

Use your regular practice to prepare. Run your regular practice with emphasis on points of attack (toward their center, transition to offense, and so on). Work against your next opponent's basic defense as part of your regular practice. Let your reserves emulate the opponent's game. If the opponent presses a great deal, have your reserves press all day in practice without necessarily telling the team this is what to expect from opponent "X."

If the opponent is a good 1-3-1 zone team, have your reserves play 1-3-1 all day in practice without mentioning opposing players or positions in 1-3-1 unless it is important to your game plan. At the conclusion of practice, simulate the beginning of tomorrow's game. Go over the man-to-man match-ups.

1. Jump ball strategy, such as stealing the tip.

2. Out of bounds plays – home run pass against the reserves' press. Send your team off the floor bubbly, bouncy, and fully confident that your scouting report will greatly assist them in victory. Let them feel like they can't wait for tomorrow to shut down the opponent.

Game Night

Place a blackboard in the locker room to illustrate your game plan, including the following:

1. Match-ups.

2. Your defensive game plan.

3. Your offensive game plan.

4. Miscellaneous information.

5. "Keys" to winning tonight – review your basketball philosophy.

AGILE - MOBILE - HOSTILE

George Ireland

Give me players with that great love of basketball that drives them to constantly seek to improve their skills. They are the "horses" who make championship basketball teams.

My criteria in seeking promising high school players are, what I call, the "Three Iles" of basketball. The must be agile, they must be mobile and they must be hostile. By the latter I mean that they must be willing to scrap for ball possession at all times when the ball isn't in our team's control.

Players who fit that description are, in a nutshell, the ones I seek out for the Rambler squads.

It was five such players who carried Loyola to the national crown last year. Four of them are back this year along with another senior whose strong desire forced him to come back last season when many another ball player would have been content to sit back and watch the action from the sidelines.

Self-Discipline

It is players who have great desire who make a team click because they have one of the greatest assets that I look for in prospective players - rigid self-discipline.

This self-discipline showed up for us several times last season, but never so dramatically as in the championship game in Louisville. Although we were down by 15 points with only minutes remaining,

we would not and did not give up.

My starters were called "Iron Men" by the sportswriters because they played the entire game without substitution, using that hard running offense and pressing defense, and when the chips were down in the overtime period, five men - still without a breather - came on stronger and faster than during the regulation 40 minutes to win the national crown.

That is why I seek out and demand players with self-discipline. It's something each player must learn for himself. He must not have to question the need for rigid training and long and often grueling practice sessions. His self-discipline will enable him to put forth that 110 percent effort just when everyone expects him to have run out of steam. His satisfaction comes in playing the game right.

Many times last year, the Ramblers left their opponent exhausted because their self-discipline had taught them the need for peak physical conditioning - something the other team did not have.

Ours is a running style and it requires great love of the game and great discipline. Without these, there would be no enjoyment for the players - and the Loyola boys have a great time on that court.

Four of the starting five from last year's team are back - co-captains Ron Miller and Jack Egan at guards, Leslie Hunter at center and Vic Rouse at forward.

Joining them to fill the vacancy left by the graduation of Jerry Harkness is Chuck Wood from St. Catherine's High School in nearby Racine, Wisconsin.

Chuck was hospitalized with mononucleosis for nine games last year, but when scholastic problems sidelined our "number 6 and 7" reserves, Chuck rejoined the team and with a great amount of determination fought back to full strength and conditioning to become our number one substitute in the stretch drive.

Keys to Success

For players with this great self-discipline, other forms of discipline pose no great problems. Anything else just becomes second nature. And a team with great discipline as a unit is a team that cannot help, in the long run, to be a success.

But aside from discipline, other factors play a part in my choice of ballplayers, skill quite obviously being an important one.

But I also look carefully as a prospect's attitude toward the game and toward his fellow players. We have no individuals on the Ramblers. We have no place for them. Each ballplayer is a member of the team. Our national championship was a team effort. Had we tried to make it as individuals, we would never have won. We didn't have the five best collegiate ballplayers in the country, but we did have the best collegiate team - and they proved it in the national tournament.

I get the best rebounders, the best ballhandlers and the best shooters with the above qualities that I can find and make sure each has great speed. Speed is the key to both our offense and defense.

We teach our players our uncomplicated offensive system, but don't over-coach them. We demand that they produce their utmost, even in practice, and soon they develop that deep pride in their individual performances and in the performances of the team.

Practice Habits

We work hard to develop outstanding rebounders and, in Rouse and Hunter, we have about the best combination in collegiate circles. We teach the boys to fast break at every possible occasion. "Don't walk if you can run" is a good motto.

Our practice sessions last one hour and 45 minutes, with the greatest emphasis placed on shooting. About 40 minutes of each session is devoted exclusively to shooting at a rim about one inch in diameter narrower than regulation to promote greater accuracy.

This also requires self-discipline, because many a player will get discouraged in having to work with the small hoop which requires a "thread-the-needle" shot to score.

The good player keeps himself in shape at all times without having to be told.

THE ROLE OF THE HIGH SCHOOL COACH IN THE RECRUITING PROCESS

Dennis Wills, Bob Hallberg, and C. Eric Gronbech

A number of articles have recently appeared in consumer journals dealing with the exploitation of college athletes. For the most part these were written only to report accusations of impropriety leveled against college athletic personnel. A few incidences were documented with the purpose of casting suspicion on all. Coaches defended their means by pointing to the pressure placed on them to win, rationalized that "everyone does it," and defended their programs by reflecting the blame on the athlete who would let himself be exploited.

Realistically the blame must be shared, and although the stories of scandal made for interesting reading, the only positive results were a general increase in consciousness and some evaluation of entrance requirements. Scientists in the area of sport sociology most all agree that although college programs have brought the problems to light, they have been caused much earlier in an athlete's career.

It is not the purpose of this document to delve into the intricacies of exploitation. This paper is written to present some of the specific circumstances that contribute to a feeling of exploitation or of having

been exploited and what high school coaches can do to prevent it.

Matching the Athlete with the School

Coaches have long recognized the impact that they have on their athletes' lives, and many have almost total control of their athletes college destiny. Athletics are inseparable from the student and a major part of his personality; anxiety here can be the start of many other problems. A coach must use his powers of influence constructively to prevent this.

Most important is the fact that your athlete as a person comes first. Athletics serve the person, the person does not serve athletics. An athletic career is shorter than an individual's life span. The child existed and functioned before he was an athlete and shall have to effectively interact with society long after his playing days are over.

For a human being to perform consistently and realize his potential, he must be happy. Superior athletes are happy competing for starting positions on their teams as well as against the opposition. They are not happy sitting on the bench. A fighting chance to get off it is constructive; no chance is destructive. It is no longer practical to wait your turn because in a sport like basketball a reversal has taken place. No longer does a freshman or sophomore sit for a year or two before he plays; today he often plays immediately and even then is not assured he will again play next year.

Therefore, your athlete should go to a school where he has a realistic chance to play now, unless he is willing to sit. This means you must objectively look at the athletic potential of the school, who they presently have playing, and who they've recruited. Relative to this, you must realistically evaluate your athlete's ability and the competition which your schedule has previously afforded him.

Psychologists have recognized that playing is an addiction, and withdrawal from it is no less difficult psychologically than the withdrawal from dependency on drugs.

Along with athletics is the matter of obtaining an education. High school and college coaches say this is the important thing, but it does not have to be and in many instances it is not, neither to the coach nor to the athlete.

An honest approach is important. We can hope for the best, but some kids don't want a degree and won't get one. Some don't need one. It is not illegal to exploit athletics to gain an education, nor to exploit academics as the only possible way to showcase one's talent. An education is not a gift; you can be given the chance, but you must earn the degree. Many experts recognize the important educational changes that occur even when a degree is not attained.

The second point is to find a school that can cater to the athlete's interests, can provide the proper programs, and complements his academic potential.

It is important to remember that no coach can guarantee academic success. Only a fool believes he can. If the kid does not want it, the coach is helpless. If the kid does want it, he should inquire what type of help is available if needed and have his academic plans thoroughly thought out.

High school seniors should be mature enough not to pursue unrealistic academic goals. A "C" average and a combined 800 score on the college boards do not indicate potential in pre-med, especially with the added burden of big-time athletics. Interest and aptitude bring about academic success; the right choice of a major can make this possible. A kid who might be academically successful at a small liberal arts' college may be doomed to failure at a large university.

A third point to consider is whether going away or staying home is in the player's best interest. If your kid runs with a bad crowd, if his responsibilities at home are overburdening or even if he just needs some independence and humility, going away is probably best. But if your kid needs constant motivation and support from his family and friends, or a strong hand to keep him in line, he may be best off staying home. More than one athlete has lost a promising career to home sickness, and many careers have been cut short by well-intentioned families and friends. Many need a year or two of seasoning at a junior college to bring up their grades or just to mature as a person. The investment is certainly worth some time, research and discussion.

The first three points require integrity on the part of the high school coach. Although it is nice to say, "I have a kid at Notre Dame, one at Alabama and another at De Paul," in the long run people are more impressed by what the athlete becomes than where he went to school. To fight one's own ego as well as a star athlete's, his parents and fans and to remain objective is a difficult job – but a necessary one.

The fourth consideration regards the student's social life, a point often overlooked. The college experience includes more than just academics and athletics. In the 1950s it was difficult for blacks from northern cities to play in the South because they were not accepted socially. The only blacks on campus were athletes, and athletics for women, as we know them today, did not exist.

Things have changed, but similar problems still exist. Can a kid from Detroit's inner-city be happy at the University of Wyoming? Some kids assimilate and interact well, others do not, and a coach should know the difference. It is certainly beneficial to sample other lifestyles, but again the kid must be happy. An athlete is socialized through his athletic experiences, but his family, school, peers and church have had the major effect, and some continuity must be retained.

Intricately bound in the social life is the economic requirements of the prospective college. Without full financial aid, the cost of college is still high. The financial cost remaining after a partial grant-in-aid at one school might be more than a full financial burden at another, and within four years this may make attendance very difficult. The effect an economic reward for athletic prowess, no matter how insignificant, has on the ego may prove a very worthy adversary to making an intelligent decision. Even with tuition, room and board, and books many other costs exist. Can a kid from Washington D.C. afford the plane fare back and forth from U.C.L.A. to be with his family for Christmas, or in case of an emergency? Can his family and friends afford to go to see him play? Can he utilize the same wardrobe at Michigan State that he did in Mobile, Ala.? Can he afford to go to a show or get a late night snack a couple of times a week? Will the kid need a supplemental job (if allowed by rules) and is he capable of working, studying and playing?

The fifth consideration regards the athlete's self respect and the integrity of the recruiters. Anyone who is willing to cheat others, supposedly in your kid's behalf, will also be willing to deal dishonestly with him. Don't let your kid be misled. He has a choice. Consult players who have already participated in a prospective program, both the starters and the bench warmers. Coaches have idiosyncrasies, they have specific ways in which they consistently deal with their players, and they will not likely change. Will your kid be nurtured as a player and as a person under the coach's tutelage?

Programs also have tradition. Oklahoma will not become a passing football team just because your kid is a passing quarterback, and Indiana won't play freelance basketball no matter what the recruiter says. What are your kids strengths, as an athlete and as a person, and will the coach and program augment them? What are his weaknesses? Will they be corrected, or will they be antagonized? Is his position secure if he is injured? If he becomes ineligible? If he does not produce and wants to continue his education? Or will the stress be unbearable?

If you have a superior athlete, it's a safe bet that at some time he has thought about playing professionally. Relatively few college coaches can tell whether a high school player will be able to play professionally, and even fewer high school coaches can. Out of all the genuine pro prospects, only about 18 per year make it and stick. A professional career is not a realistic consideration for the vast majority of high school athletes. Any recruiter who plays to this pipe dream by quoting the number of pros who have come out of his program is an exploiter.

The high school coach's obligation is to stop these ideas as soon as possible. Discourage his ego and counsel the best choice. For each kid who has found a better life through professional athletics, thousands have been left behind chasing an impossible dream.

The kid's present and future must come first. Forty-odd years is a long time to carry a chip on one's shoulder, a chip that in the beginning was just a speck of stardust.

The last advice is to let the kid make the ultimate decision, because he has to live with the choice every day. A factor you might think is silly, such as your kid's girlfriend, might be extremely important to him. Stand behind your athlete, not in front of him; don't overplay or underplay your role. A wrong decision costs him two years of his life at the very least – the one he endures and the one he is ineligible to play for if he chooses to transfer. Many things can happen in a year or two. If he does not correct a wrong decision, much more may be lost. Expect for the careers of a very few in five years, all that will remain are the memories. Help him make them happy ones.

College Suitability Rating Scale

1. A chance to play: (a) freshman starter, (b) starter within four years, (c) sixth or seventh man, (d) ride the bench.

2. Athletic potential: (a) national Top 10 team, (b) competitive Division I team, (c) small college power, (d) traditionally weak team.

3. Current players: (a) five underclassmen starters, (b) majority of the team underclassmen, (c) majority of team upperclassmen, (d) not competitive.

4. Incoming recruits: (a) depth at all positions, (b) complement present players, (c) majority transfer and redshirts, (d) all new freshmen.

5. Previous experience of recruits: (a) excelled in top state-wide competition, (b) excelled in good sectional competition, (c) were competitive in league, (d) played against weak competition.

6. Educational objective: (a) degree is required for a specific field, (b) degree is important, (c) degree is a possibility, (d) degree is relatively unimportant.

7. Academic assistance: (a) academic advisement, tutors and files are available, (b) faculty shows respect and concern for athletes, (c) faculty shows neither favoritism nor prejudice toward athletes, (d) athletics and academics are separate entities.

8. Academic major: (a) in line with potential, (b) of interest but difficulty, (c) not important, (d) impossible.

9. Location: (a) fits students needs, (b) will require some transition, (c) negative influence, (d) unimportant.

10. Social consideration: (a) cultural similarities, (b) culturally dissimilar but positive, (c) social life is limited, (d) antagonistic.

11. School finances: (a) all needs are met, (b) school meets most needs, (c) the challenge is difficult but not impossible to meet, (d) athlete will not be able to meet financial requirements.

12. Personal finances (wardrobe, commuting, visitation, entertainment): (a) extraneous finances are available, (b) a job will meet extra financial needs, (c) limited extras, (d) no extras.

13. Recruited integrity: (a) all above-board, (b) anxious and pressing, (c) questionable, (d) illegal.

14. Coaching idiosyncrasies: (a) complement athlete, (b) don't infringe on athlete, (c) require adjustment for athlete, (d) antagonize the athlete.

15. Athletic tradition: (a) very positive, (b) varies, (c) average, (d) none.

16. Other variables: (a) all positive, (b) mostly positive, (c) half positive-half negative, (d) mostly negative.

17. Athletic termination: (a) experience will have life-long positive effects, (b) experience will be educational, (c) experience will be frustrating, (d) experience will probably abort career.

References

1. Axthelm, P. "The Shame of College Sports," *Newsweek*, September 2, 1980.

2. Berger, P. "Forever On Tryout," *Inside Sports*, May 1980.

3. Gilbert, B. "The Gospel According to John," *Sports Illustrated*, January 1981.

4. McDermott, B. "A Legend Searching For His Past," *Sports Illustrated*, October 12, 1980.

5. Miller, F.A. "The Ongoing Athletic Crisis—A Solution," *Athletic Administration*, Fall 1980.

6. Under, J. "The Shame of American Education—The Student-Athlete Hoax," *Sports Illustrated*, May 19, 1980.

7. "Another Year, Another Scandal," Editorial, *Scholastic Coach*, October 1980.

SMALL COLLEGE RECRUITING: A GAME PLAN

Greg Marshall

The recruiting practices of UCLA and Westmont College are worlds apart. We both have the same goal: sign the best players available. However, it would be a serious mistake for Westmont to try to match UCLA's recruiting efforts. Instead of going head-to-head with major colleges, most small college programs wait to sign the best of those not picked by a Division I school.

At last count, there were approximately 290 Division I schools and 980 others (NCAA Div. II, NAIA, NCAA III, NCCAA, NLCCA). We have the majors outnumbered, but that is about all. The top players today are interested in attending programs that provide ideal playing conditions, which means national television coverage, large crowds, demanding schedules and the status of playing for a Division I school.

The title "Division I" does have a status symbol ring to it. It is the most visible of all the divisions, and players there are perceived to be the best. A friend once told me, "I'd rather be the Vice-President of General Motors than the President of Chrysler." (This, of course, was before Lee Iacocca was pulling down $15 million a year.) The point was that he would rather be second in command at a company considered to be the best than to be the top gun at No. 2. There is some logic to this, but while one organization might be stronger than another overall, No. 2 can have some redeeming qualities. After all, would you trade your LeBaron convertible for a Vega?

Some institutional restrictions limit small college recruiting success, such as the following:

1. Smaller staffs. Very few small college programs have staffs to match their Division I counterparts. While the desire to match the effort might be present, there just aren't enough bodies to produce similar results.

2. Multiple duties. Most small college coaches and assistants do not coach exclusively. We are usually required to perform other duties, such as athletic administration, teaching, fundraising, or admissions. As a result, we cannot devote as much time to coaching and recruiting as we might like.

3. Budget. It is difficult to accumulate frequent flyer points when your school Visa limit is $300.00. Smaller budgets restrict travel, limiting the geographic area you can cover. It is imperative, therefore, to do a good job of recruiting local talent.

Most small colleges are at a disadvantage in the same way most small businesses fail: they are undercapitalized and overly optimistic.

Work Smart

Because resources are limited, it is important to use what you have efficiently. We strive to achieve maximum results with all our recruiting efforts. Working hard is not the key; working smart is! Here are a few areas in which we try to maximize our time and money:

1. Computers. Word processing allows us to personalize all recruiting letters. We combine our PC with a Laserjet printer and can mail-merge a letter to all of our recruits in less than an hour. Work-study students are utilized in the correspondence tasks.

2. Tournaments. High school and JC tournaments enable you to see a larger number of teams in a smaller time frame.

3. Resources. We will contact friends of ours who are Division I recruiters and get input from them. They put in a great deal of leg work and they usually share information on players with schools they are not competing against.

4. Tryouts. Campus visits for our best recruits will continue to be time well spent for us. However, over the years, we noticed we took up a lot of time with players we either didn't know much about, or weren't that excited about. Now, we set one specific date for all these players to visit. We see them play with our players and against each other. The time saved has been impressive, and we feel we have eliminated a lot of guesswork in the evaluation of these young men.

Overcoming the Obstacles

We still go after players a little too good for us. Until someone comes up with a better system, we will continue to joust with windmills. Here are some tactics we try to employ when talking to players of the upper echelon:

1. Don't get impatient. Just as we coaches rank our top recruits, players also rank schools by preference. I think it is a mistake to make a "take-it-or-leave-it" scholarship offer. Bide your time and wait for your chance.

2. Keep in contact. Be the friendly alternative. Keep your name in front of them and follow up with an occasional call.

3. Don't take the first "no." Always try to leave the door open until they have signed a letter of intent. If we think a player is going to tell us no, one of the assistant coaches calls first. This gives us a chance to analyze why he turned us down, before the head coach calls and takes his shot.

4. Leave it on a positive note. The final decision for most players is a time of highs and lows. They are excited to have selected a school, but also are faced with telling several schools "no." When the big one gets away, don't burn your bridges. We let him know we are disappointed he's not coming to Westmont, but we also encourage him about his decision. It is best to be remembered positively. Players have been known to change their minds or transfer later.

What We Look For

When we zero in on a player, we are interested in determining the following information:

1. Has he played on a winning team? We love to get guys who know how to win and who have received good coaching.

2. Is he tough-minded? We rarely get the great athlete, so we try to recruit the fierce competitor.

3. Can he succeed academically? It is not fair to the player or to our school if he cannot make normal progress toward a degree.

4. Is he a starter or a project? If he's a starter, is he better than the people we have now? Over-recruiting is a problem we try to avoid, especially with the junior college and Division I transfer players. If a player is a project, how will he get better? Does he need to grow, develop strength, gain agility? If we take a chance on a project, it is usually a big man.

5. Will he fit in with our players? After each recruit visits, we get feedback from our players. If our players give us negative reports, we immediately re-evaluate to see if we have made a mistake in judgment. We believe that a great player who is a jerk will never help you. It's a long season, and we want to be around people we like.

Standard Operating Procedures

We try to recruit by the I.C.C.C.E. method. The following is an outline of this process:

Identify

The first step is to identify our needs for the coming season. We then identify a pool of players for contact. We get names of players through recruiting lists, summer leagues, all-star camps and alumni. Many players also will write or call us for information.

Contact

Our initial contact with a prospect includes a personalized letter, questionnaire, return envelope and a four-color brochure that highlights Santa Barbara activities (obtained from the local Chamber of Commerce). When a questionnaire is returned, we immediately write back. This is generally a handwritten note on a postcard thanking them for responding.

To help us determine whether a recruit will be accepted academically we have started sending a transcript release authorization form. The recruit signs this, returns it to us, and we forward it on to his school's records office.

Cultivate

If we do a good job building a relationship with the recruit, the battle has swung in our favor. We keep a file on each recruit that contains records of all letters, personal contact and highlights from phone conversation. The phone has and will continue to be a primary tool in recruiting. Our goal is to gradually disclose information about Westmont, as opposed to shooting all of our bullets on the first call. We expound on a specific, pre-determined topic each time we call.

This is also the time to identify our competitors. After we know what other schools are recruiting a player we want, we can formulate a game plan. We always try to highlight the strengths of our program, as opposed to tearing down the opposition.

Closing

Finalizing the commitment can be tricky. Home and campus visits are crucial events and should be carefully planned. During campus visits, we match the recruit with a player with whom he will be compatible. When signing day gets close, all schools in the hunt intensify their efforts. Be ready to do the same!

Encourage

You've wined 'em, dined 'em, and signed 'em. The last step: encourage them about their decision. Make the good feeling last. Drop them a letter and call frequently. Letters and calls of congratulations by players are also an effective way to firm up the commitment. We also get the local paper to do an article on their signing and send them a copy of this.

Part II FUNDAMENTAL SKILLS

* *

The game of basketball – no matter what the level, the rules, the strategy of the personnel – is simply a matter of executing fundamentals.

— Lewis Cole
in *A Loose Game*

Coaching and playing basketball revolve around fundamental skills. It would seem that both coaches and players would spend most of their efforts and concentration on these basic skills. However, it is my belief that this is far from the case. Most attention is given to the peripheral elements of the game– everything from the hoopla surrounding the game to the emphasis on style (instead of execution) when playing the game. Even though many people stray from the fundamental core of basketball, the game is and should always be rooted in the basic skills.

Players, coaches, and spectators have a variety of reasons for their interest in basketball. However, it seems that everyone who shares a love for the game has several things in common.

Most of us enjoy the struggle of true competition– the individual rivalry as well as the group contest.

Close games and competitive balance can exist only when teams with lesser talent function better as a team or possess better fundamental skills.

The ability to develop a sound philosophy of playing or coaching is also rooted in a solid foundation of fundamental skills. It has often been stated that "what one does isn't as important as *how well* one does it." Execution of basic skills is necessary to carry out any plan or strategy. The ability of any individual or team to utilize their strengths and avoid their weaknesses (to stick to their own game) is highly dependent on the use of basketball basics.

The beauty of basketball is rooted in the development of all of your players' fundamental skills. Teach them to execute the skills correctly first (do it right) then execute them at game speed (do it quickly).

COMPACTNESS IN BASKETBALL

Bruce Drake

Editor's note: This article by Hall of Famer Bruce Drake, inventor of the shuttle offense, was the first fully developed technical article that appeared in the Bulletin. It was published in 1949.

In basketball, as well as in any sport in which accuracy is involved, the more compact we keep our actions, the more consistently we can perform.

A person addicted to golf has often heard, "That person is certainly in the groove." Just what does "in the groove" mean to a golfer? To me it means that Mr. Golf does not have any lost motion during his swing, and that he has worked on the fundamentals of his swing so diligently that each swing is the same: the same, that is, if the elements are alike. At the top of his swing he is very compact, and his downswing and weight shift are the same each time with no lost motion. When he rips into the ball, his left side is always against a stone wall, and his chin is on a barrel of swords. He doesn't bob his head up and down during his swing and gamble that he will be at the correct position each time he swings at the ball. He keeps his head "fixed," knowing that in so doing the hub of his swing, the left shoulder, is always where it should be. His left arm is straight. Thus he has eliminated all the error in a golf swing that is humanly possible. He has accomplished this by hours of practice and has chucked overboard any movements that were not necessary in making a shot or putt.

It stands to reason that no matter what sport we are coaching, if we can rid our athletes of lost motion, the accuracy curve will mount rapidly and consistently.

In boxing we associate the word "haymaker" with a wild swing of the arm that starts with the box seats and ends up in the second bleachers. That type of flow seldom hits pay dirt. The stinging punches of Joe Louis are very compact with very little lost motion. He finds his target consistently. Very seldom do you see him take a very wild punch. When he executes his piston punch, take a look at him from the hips down and watch his feet and knees at work. There's no lost motion there, which all adds up to a champion in the boxing world.

In my quest to rid players of lost motion in basketball, whether they play offense or defense, I can think of no better example to substantiate my practice and belief than a baseball player by the name of Frank K. O'Doul, better known as "Lefty." Frank came up from the Pacific Coast League to join the New York Yankees when the Ruppert guns were mowing down the National Leaguers with deadly accuracy. Lefty was a pitcher, but in short order that arm went dead and he was shipped back to the Coast League. There he broke down the art of hitting. He wasn't a slugger like Ruth or Williams, but more of a punch hitter. He practiced his theories so much that these fundamentals were with him to stay. He knew his hitting and could apply it. In short he was in the groove and was compactness personified. He came back to the National League as an outfielder and was rewarded for his hard work by winning the National League batting championship twice with averages of .398 and .368 respectively. He compiled a batting record better than .300 in seven of the eight years he played in his new position.

Did you ever watch Sammy Baugh chuck a football? If you have had that delightful pleasure, you may have noted that Mr. Robin Hood cocks that arm up by his ear, then – boom – strike! There is no lost motion, consequently, he doesn't miss that running target very often.

I'm not going into footwork in basketball, which is equally important on defense as well as offense, but will confine myself to compactness as applied to shooting.

First, I want the hands and arms always in as nearly the natural position as possible. Just stand up and let your arms fall loosely down. Take a look at the position of the hands. Those are the tools we work with, and I want to eliminate all tension if possible by keeping them in as nearly this normal position as possible whether they are hanging down in front or are up in front of the eyes for a long two-hander. Now raise them up slowly in front of the eyes and just relax and take a look at the surface of the hands. If I can get my boys to operate in this normal way, I'm throwing out the window any tension which would be present if we get away from the normal, natural position.

I have brought my Oklahoma team east any number of times and have had plenty of opportunities to study their two-handed set shots, and I know that Clair Bee, Nat Holman, Howard Cann, and a host of other Eastern coaches have picked up a few pointers on the Western one-hander. But whether it be one- or two-handed, your great shots are, and always will be, men who don't "crank up" their shots. Think of the greatest long shot you have seen, and nearly all of them keep the ball well out in front of the eyes, with the hands fairly close together and slightly on top of the ball. They are also well balanced when they deliver. The palms are facing down when they complete the shot. Their wrist action is compact. The

knees straighten with the delivery. In short, they can repeat their performance more consistently if they can throw out all action that isn't necessary to make the shot.

On free throws we use the underhanded two-handed throw with a staggered stance in preference to both feet up to the line. The staggered stance is the natural position you would normally take. If a person would go to the edge of the Empire State Building and look down at the specks on the pavements, would he go up to the edge and place both feet up to the edge, or would he stagger his stance?

I believe he would place one foot up and the other back and then bend the waist. He would do this because he would be better balanced. That's the normal position. I have better balance with this stance, and when I bend slightly at the belt, my arms and hands are hanging slightly away from the body where they will be with the ball – without tension. I have my players plant their feet wide enough apart so that the weight isn't shifted to the outside of the balls of the feet as the knees are bent. I never have them bend the arms on these charity shots, nor do I have them break their wrists in executing the shot. The wrists are used, but the weight of the ball does the breaking, and since the weight of the ball is consistent, the break is always the same. I insist on a short swing with a little knee break. Foremost in their minds is compactness and natural, normal position.

Having led the Big Six in this department by three percentage points over a period of nine years, you can see that using this form and keeping these fundamentals in mind has paid off at Oklahoma. No matter what sport, you will always find that the fundamental you are teaching requires elimination of all the motion not necessary in doing that one thing. Then you will find a marked increase in efficiency and accuracy.

TEACHING INDIVIDUAL SKILLS
Pete Newell

Introduction

The past four summers I have spent time teaching individual skills to basketball players. Most of these players have been established NBA players and in some instances college players. It has been a labor of love in a sense for me as the players have asked me for help and their cooperativeness, receptiveness, and desire to improve have been extremely rewarding for me. I have always been stimulated by the aspect of teaching basketball to receptive people.

I believe the game should be more openly discussed between player and coach. I spend a great deal of time talking the game with my players, challenging their thinking, discussing many of the "whys" of basketball. They seem to really enjoy these cerebral sessions, and I hope they learn from them.

I have taken one phase of the game – a forward one-on-one situation – as the basis for teaching footwork and balance. I teach it in more forms, but the drills I include here are what I use to teach my players, and I have guards and centers as well as forwards executing these moves.

The Importance of Teaching Footwork

I believe there is less individual teaching of footwork, balance, variable use of individual skills, and individual movements offensively than ever before. What we have more of is coaching team offense and defense. We have come 180 degrees from a game too individually oriented to a game that is now too five-man oriented. In short, we have an overcoached and undertaught game.

The skills of clever movement and good balance have been sacrificed in many coaches' minds for high jumping and physically overpowering skills. There is a tendency to emphasize the height of a player's leap to the detriment of his balance and movement. The offensive movement many coaches employ stresses "off the ball" rather than "on the ball." While I will concede that the one-on-one concept was not and is not the answer, I don't believe five-man motion is the total answer either. Somewhere between the two would be my thinking.

Because of the off-the-ball coaching emphasis, there is a growing lack of player skills on the ball. This referred-to emphasis has caused an erosion of the fundamentals of balance – individual footwork skills, indirection of movement drills, pivots and various turns, and creation of the shot on the ball. Motion offense does not lend itself well to breakdown or part method teaching. The result is a minimum of coaching attention to the individual's needs of improved balance, footwork, and movement.

How much time is given to individual needs in the practice plan that the coach devises for his team? What importance is given to proper movement; correct body stance while in motion; maneuvering speed; ability to stop, change direction and accelerate? Can pivots and turns be properly executed and with some knowledge of why they are being executed? Naturally the practice plan is particularly conceived for the offensive movement the coach believes in or, better, knows the most about. If the coaches know only motion offense with little or no breakdown, it stands to reason that fewer coaches understand teaching individual skills and refinement of those skills because they have been taught by these coaches who have been exposed only to the same five-man game. As a result we have fewer and fewer teachers of the game. This is not meant as a knock at present coaches, but merely fact.

If I were asked what one phase of the individual's game has eroded more and needs attention the most, I would reply footwork. To properly refine one's footwork, balance should be strongly stressed. To emphasize my point, I will relate something that occurred this past year. The occasion was a Golden State Warriors practice. I had a group of eight players around me and I was about to describe a drill. I asked for a basketball and a player handed me a ball. I held the ball up and asked the senior member of the group how many minutes of a 48-minute NBA game did he suppose he would actually have the ball in his hands. He thought for a while and said he guessed about 16 to 18 minutes if he played the whole game. When I said at the most 10 percent, or about 4 1/2 minutes of that 48-minute game, he was incredulous. After I explained that his team could only expect it 24 or less minutes, he then understood. I then asked him how many minutes of that 48-minute game he would play with his feet. Not wanting to be so far off again, he thought for a while and then said 48 minutes. I then asked the group to think about the amount of time they spend refining their footwork as opposed to working on their shot. None admitted to even thinking about the need to improve foot movement. What happened here would happen similarly in the great, great percentage of high school, college, junior college, and NBA programs. Little attention is given to this important part of the individual's offensive and defensive play.

Let me dwell on footwork and balance. Is there another word in basketball that has the many connotations of the word "balance?" We talk about floor balance, team shooting balance, body balance, rebound balance, balance in defensive retreat, individual shooting balance, balance between offense and defense, and balance of personnel. No one balance I have described is more important than the balance attributed to and necessary for proper footwork.

How do players improve their footwork and balance? Is it done with a piece of chalk or a vocal exhortation by the coach? Through threats and pleas? Films? How, exactly, can it be accomplished? I have never been privileged as a coach to be able to improve skills by any of the above methods. I have tried, but failed. Early in my coaching I came to the conclusion that a physical response can only be conditioned by a repetitive act. After I realized this, I devised drills to bring about proper stance, weight carriage, and footwork. I employed a fundamental as old as the game, "proper habit is the result of proper repetitive act." In practice, I constantly stressed this movement in the various part method teaching drills and supplemented it with a "hands-up" type drill that demanded a flexed knee stance and a constant directional change. I will later detail the drill and its "why." In summary, I believe in doing it, not talking about it.

Why are footwork and balance so important, and how do they improve the individual's game? Here are a few examples.

Shooting

When shooting is discussed at clinics, hand action is strongly stressed, and squaring to the basket is a popular advancement. Follow-through and proper hand action are described as absolutely essential, yet without a good base and proper balance, these important fundamentals that clinicians describe would be of much less importance. Good balance must be employed by the shooter. To oversimplify shooting, the shooter is normally faced with two problems on most shots – declinations and deviation (two gunnery terms from the Navy). Declination, or depth, is of immediate concern to most shooters, while deviation, or lateral adjustment or float, is given little thought. If both declination and deviation are adjustment problems, the shooter's accuracy is bound to lessen. If the shooter could almost totally eliminate deviation, he would then increase his accuracy abundantly. Good balance will accomplish this to a great degree as lateral sway or float by shooters is the result of poor balance in most instances. Obviously, if we only have to be concerned with depth, we have increased our shooting percentage potential. To repeat, a good, balanced base is necessary for effective shooting.

Creating a Lead

Creating a proper lead in an offensive area is extremely important to an offensive man, whether it is the motion offense or a post-type offense. To create this proper lead, we must deploy the defensive man into a screen or position him so that he trails the receiver. It is important for most offensive men to receive the ball in specified areas of normal operational zones. The defense is instructed to prevent this reception, so footwork and balance are absolutely necessary if the offensive man is to be the shooting, passing, or driving threat he is meant to be. If this same offensive man cannot deploy his defensive man properly, he will be operating from unnatural zones, which reduces his shooting accuracy, passing efficiency, and driving ability.

Body Control

Body control is particularly necessary in a fast movement game. "Out of control" is a widely used term to describe a player prone to mistakes in movement, such as offensive charge, progress calls, fumbled balls, and an inability to properly execute a stop. Without proper weight carriage and footwork balance, good body control cannot be achieved. The body control can only be achieved by a constant practice application and attention. I don't mean to minimize the need of body control in a slower movement game, as it is a must of either tempo, but it is a more apparent need in a faster game.

Without proper balance, the ability to stop quickly when running at a fast rate of speed is difficult. Not being able to execute this necessary stop can cause you to lose a chance to receive a pass in a close scoring area. Acceleration will often beat a defensive man, but it is difficult to accelerate if not under control. Changes of direction often fool a defensive man, but balance and footwork can only effectively accomplish this offensive maneuver. Pivots and turns are the result of a good base and low balance and are ineffective if executed in a high position. Rocker steps, step-off fakes, and other individual skill movements are effective only with the proper balance necessary to refine these movements.

In teaching footwork, a coach should realize that ambidexterity applies to feet as well as hands. Players are either right-footed or left-footed. They usually prefer a jump shot in one direction over the other. Their drives to the hoop often indicate this subconscious preference. What often happens is that a player will reduce his effectiveness because these preferences are detected in scouting reports. If a player only dribbles right, the defensive problem is greatly reduced because the overplay will cause him great problems. If a player is accurate going only one way and because of a float or sway loses accuracy in the other direction, he will have the same problems with the defense. As ambidexterity of hands is stressed by constant encouragement to use the weak hand, drills emphasizing proper footwork should be used on each side of the court to encourage use of either foot in movement, step, and shot.

Forward One-on-One Drill

Before going into detail, I would like to explain what we are trying to accomplish:

1. How to properly create a lead.

2. The importance of receiving the ball in a normal operational zone.

3. Various individual moves against pressure defense and insistence on proper footwork.

4. Distinguishing the type of defense – i.e., soft or aggressive.

5. Various individual skill moves.

6. Reading the type and position of defense and reacting accordingly.

Players are urged to recognize what the defensive man is giving and taking away. He is strongly taught to react to this defensive position rather than presupposing what it will be. Too often a player decides before he receives the ball and this is often a mistake. Reading and reaction are stressed. The why is emphasized so that each player knows what is open and why.

Initially in teaching this drill I will use signals for the defense to denote to them what type (pressure or soft) and what position (overplay right or left) I want employed. I will initially concern myself more with a proper offensive response than with the actual execution of the movement. Again, I am more concerned with reaction and reading in the early stages.

Forwards' Basic Position

Figure 7.1 shows the initial position of the forward in creation of lead from the guard.

      F — Offensive forward
      O — Defensive man
      X — Guard with ball (passer)

In Figure 7.2, F gets his inside leg across the defensive man and moves to receive the ball in the operation zone.

In Figure 7.3, F can come to the foul line for blind-pig action on the guard-to-guard pass.

In Figure 7.4, F can undercut the defensive man should the ball be reversed to the weak-side forward.

In Figure 7.5, F can empty the area should the guard beat his man coming downcourt.

Note: It is *extremely important* that the forward does not move for the lead, as in Figure 7.2, until he sees his guard's second hand go to the ball. This signifies that he is picking up the dribble. Timing between the passer and the receiver can be greatly improved if the receiver is moving toward the ball when the guard is ready to pass or has picked up the dribble. This timing will allow for the move shown in Figure 7.5 should the guard keep the dribble and beat his man.

Means for Forward Creation of the Lead in His Normal Operational Zone

1. The forward should attempt to get his inside leg across the defensive man, hold him for a short count with his leg, and dart toward the operational zone.

2. Should the defensive man play him high and without ball vision, the forward can circle man from inside and receive the lead in the operational zone (see Figure 7.6).

3. Should the defensive man overcommit in contesting the lead, the forward can develop a back-door threat.

It is important that forwards learn to develop leads against active, aggressive, defensive play. Overplays can disrupt offensive play if forwards are operating in extended areas as passing angles become too sharp and passing lanes too long, and defense can loosen up and invite the longer-range shot. The loosened defense reduces the passing threat inside and the threat of a dribble is minimized.

Normal operational zones for forwards and guards ensure good passing angles, normal distance lanes, and threat of an outside shot or fake shot and drive. Also cutters have better angles and timing on cuts. The importance of normal operational zones should

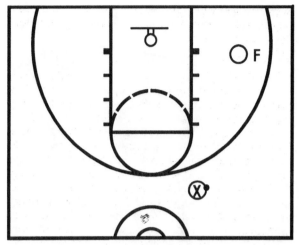

Figure 7.1

Figure 7.2

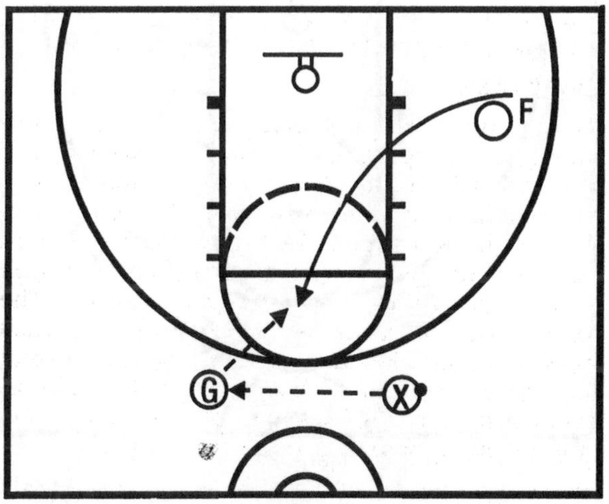

Figure 7.3

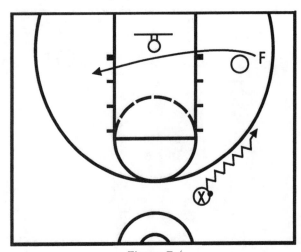

Figure 7.4

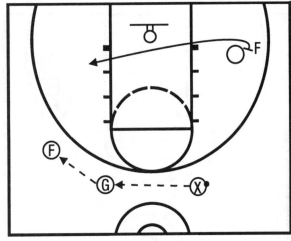

Figure 7.5

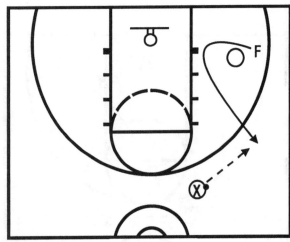

Figure 7.6

never be minimized in offensive planning or in defensive strategy and planning.

Practice habits are game habits, so create a game condition in this drill and make offense work against game-type pressure to create the lead.

Individual Moves Against Pressure Defense

1. The inside foot should always be the pivot foot established by the forward, for the following reasons:

   a. A reverse turn to the basket is a real offensive threat only if the inside foot is the pivot foot.
   b. A reverse turn with handoff to a circling guard creates a difficult defensive problem.
   c. The forward is several feet closer to the basket when he makes the fake to the hoop after receiving the ball as shown above.
   d. The ball is better protected by the body against aggressive defense.

If the outside foot is established as the pivot foot, an effective reverse turn to the basket is reduced, the forward can't create good guard motion, several feet are lost in the turn toward the basket, and a front turn can cause the defense to steal or tie up the ball.

As stated earlier, there is a need for ambidexterity of feet as well as hands, so these drills must be developed on both sides of the court. Footwork is reversed as the inside foot on the right side (above) is the right foot; on the left side it would be the left foot. This drill will ensure development of the weaker foot.

Individual Moves Against Softer Defense

1. When the defense allows the lead without a contest, a quarter turn or front turn should be employed (see Figure 7.7).

   X — Pivot foot
   • — Outside foot
   O — Defense

2. When the defense is aggressive, a reverse move can loosen the defense (see Figure 7.8).

   • — Non-pivot foot is reversed toward the basket, and the threat of a reverse drive to the basket will loosen the defense.

Drills against both defenses are used so the forward can learn to react against the type of defense he is confronted with. This is part of the offensive reading that is being taught.

A quarter turn against the soft defense caused the defensive man to react to the quick threat of a shot. He is then vulnerable against the drive to the basket as he moves toward the ball.

A reverse turn will cause the aggressive tight defensive man to react to the reverse threat of a drive. The forward comes to immediate shooting position from this fake reverse drive. The defensive man is vulnerable as he recovers from the reverse fake and moves toward the ball.

Individual Skill Moves for One-on-One

1. The forward should immediately look toward the basket when he receives the ball under normal conditions (see Figure 7.9).

2. Development of the baseline drive and drive over the top (to the middle) to the basket (see Figure 7.10).

3. Drive to the baseline for a jump shot — drive to the middle for jump shot (see Figure 7.11).

4. Drive to the baseline for a jump shot with a pump fake; drive to the middle for pump fake jump shot. On this drive the right foot is toward

the baseline (see Figure 7.12). Note: The difference between this and number 3 is the footwork.

5. Drive to the baseline for a step-back jump shot and drive to the middle for a step-back jump shot. On this drive the right foot is stepped back toward the sideline, not the baseline as in number 4 (see Figure 7.13). Note: The step-back is with the right foot.

6. A delay off the dribble as step-back is faked, dribble continues toward the baseline and basket (see Figure 7.14).

7. Drive to the basket after taking a rocker step toward the basket. The rocker step is an upper torso and head fake with the lower torso kept

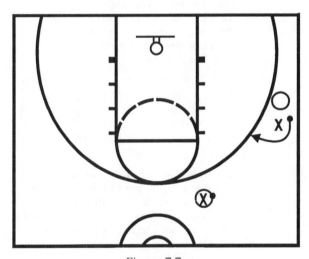

Figure 7.7

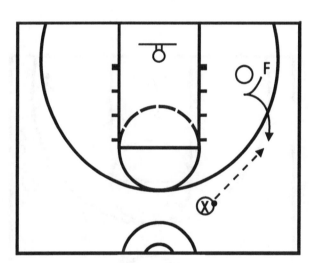

Figure 7.9

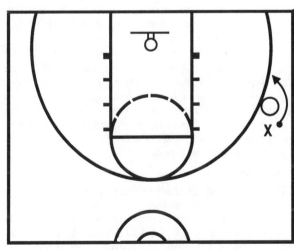

Figure 7.8

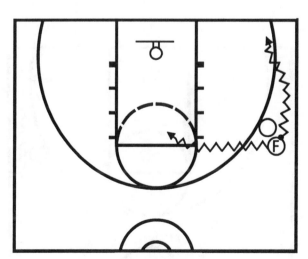

Figure 7.10

Figure 7.11

Figure 7.12

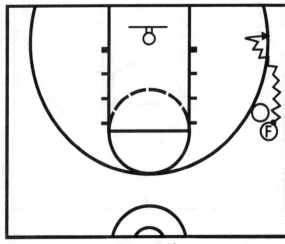

Figure 7.13

in a flexed knee position. The drive is to the baseline toward the basket and to the middle toward the basket (see Figure 7.15).

8. Drive to the basket after a step to the basket and quick explosion on the drive to the basket. The drive is a baseline or over-the-middle drive. This move is a quick move as opposed to the move in number 7, which is a slower, more deliberate move (see Figure 7.16). Note: This is a step with the left foot and a kickoff with the right foot as soon as the left foot touches the floor.

Reading the Defense and Employment of the Proper Move to Combat the Defense

1. Overplays to the middle by the defense.

   a. Baseline drive to the basket, rocker step, and step-off fakes.
   b. Baseline jump shot and pump fake.
   c. Baseline drive and step-back move.
   d. Baseline drive and dribble delay off step-back move.

2. Overplays to the baseline.

   a. Drive to the middle to the basket.
   b. Drive to the middle for jump shot and pump fake.
   c. Drive to the middle for step-back move.

3. Loose play.

   a. Quick turn to the hoop for shot.
   b. Shorten up side lead to force defense play or allow shorter range shot.
   c. A quick turn opens up drive potential if defense reacts to the turn and potential shot.

4. Aggressive, tight play.

   a. A reverse turn and drive to the basket.
   b. A reverse turn and quick look or shot off the reverse fake.
   c. A reverse turn and quick look and fake shot, and drive either way for drive or jump shot.
   d. Use of rocker step and step-off moves.

It is imperative that offensive reactions are the result of defensive positions rather than preconceived moves. Too often charge fouls are the result of predetermined movement. Other offensive mistakes are the result of this same predetermined movement, so proper reaction to the defense is strongly stressed and demanded in this drill.

Summary

The basic laws of teaching are readiness, exercise, and repetition. Mental awareness must be added to the mix. Mental awareness implies an intellectual appeal. Too often the physical demand by the teacher or coach completely submerges the intellectual appeal. Too often the "how" of doing something is so strongly advanced that the "why" is forgotten. Of the two, it is my belief that the why is much more

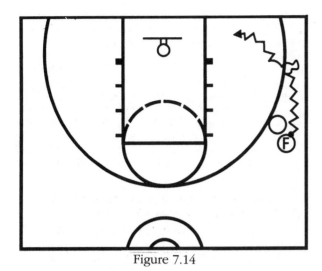

Figure 7.14

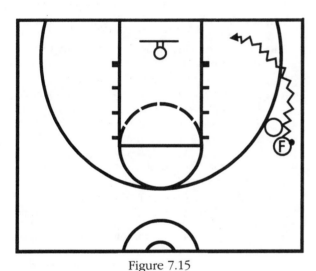

Figure 7.15

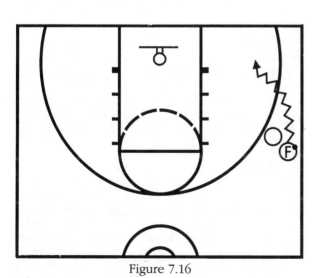

Figure 7.16

important. It is only simple logic to deduce that a player who understands why and how to do something will perform more capably that the player who only understands how. Often a player gets the job done because he understands the why and his how may not be fundamentally correct. In summary, a teacher should never neglect the intellectual capacity of a player, regardless of what he may think this capacity is. An animal can be taught to react, but only a human to think and react.

As I have explained earlier, footwork and the various arts of footwork are mainly neglected at all levels of teaching and coaching basketball. Basketball is a movement game, and what could be more important than the feet in movement? Exercise and repetition instill the proper habits of movement. In the drills that I have described, the demand for movement, step-offs, stops, and turns of either foot diminishes the tendency for the player to overuse or rely upon only one foot. He will learn to execute these footwork moves equally well with either foot. A player's confidence is often reflected by his effectiveness as a player, and the player that can execute his footwork in a superior manner is the confident performer. The great players of the game – such as Hank Luisetti, Nate Holman, Oscar Robertson, Jerry West, and Elgin Baylor – were tremendously adept with their foot movement.

Balance, as footwork, must be taught by exercise and repetition. It is more difficult for the taller player to create good habits of balance because his center of balance changes as he grows. The center of balance is a hypothetical line extending laterally through a person's hips. Too often the growing, clumsy youngster is neglected because he can't immediately perform to the coach's standard. A coach or teacher should recognize that one of his most important responsibilities is the recognition of the total needs of the player. This taller player's need for better balance can be remedied by an observant and patient coach.

I am strongly convinced that physical needs are met with physical exercise and repetition. A coach can berate a player with constant admonitions – "stay low, flex those knees" – but they are at best a finger in the dike. Only through programmed drills can a dependable game habit reflex be conditioned to perform properly.

Few knowledgeable coaches, if any, would dispute that all motion emanates from a flexed knee position. I have never seen an effective player running stiff-legged on a basketball court, but I have seen many standing in a stiff-knee position. If, then, a player must be in a flexed knee position for quick offensive or defensive movement, what do we, as coaches, do about creating this accepted fundamental position of flexed knees? Do we have each player write it 50 times a day on the board, do we expect our voice to instill the reflex, or do we expect a natural physical maturation will take care of this deficiency of the upright player? The coach must recognize the need for constant repetition for instilling the physical habit and increased exercise to condition and strengthen the muscle to allow the player to maintain this position.

An adage in boxing is when your knees stiffen, your head gets hit. Boxing fundamentals and conditioning are very similar to those of basketball. A boxer shadow boxes for interminable periods to build leg strength so that the body can be supported in a flexed-knee position. He keeps his hands up to build muscle support so that he doesn't drop his hands. Correct position of a basketball demands arms and hands up and away from the body. Offensively having the hands up ensures better ball reception, fending off an aggressive defensive man with the forearm, readiness for rebounds, as well as defensively fending off a screen, slowing a cutter, directing a dribbler, and creating a wide extended positioning for a defensive rebound. These defensive maneuvers can only be accomplished with the forearms and the arms up and away from the body. To ensure strength of arm support, we use drills. I will describe a drill that serves the needs of the basketball player with reference to the flexed knees and the raised arms that is as effective as shadow boxing is to the fighter and his needs.

Hands-Up Drill

The main purpose of this drill is to create the proper habit of movement on a basketball court. The drill demands a flexed-knee, defensive-type crouch. The weight should be equally distributed, with the right foot forward and the right hand and arm extended and up. The hand and foot should vary as the drill progresses – equal time for the left foot extended and left hand up. The movement is a shuffle with the feet never crossing. The direction of movement is determined by the coach as he gives these directional changes – right, forward, left, and rear. The coach should change the tempo of the movement constantly and vary the direction of the movement often. The alignment of players should be six to eight feet apart, spread over an area of the midcourt. The drill commences from this position.

This drill forms proper habits of court movement, builds calf and upper leg strength, and serves as a stamina and endurance builder. It helps build better body balance, as the constant directional changes cause weight shifts. It conditions the feet and toughens them to the rigors of a season ahead. It builds muscle support in the shoulder area, which enables a player to keep his hands up without impairing his shooting accuracy. Arms must be up in the shooter's face if good defensive habits are to be taught, but if the arm is tired the hand is often dropped. Shooting accuracy is likewise affected because of this tired arm. Muscle strength and muscle reflex is built through this drill.

This drill should be a part of a team's early conditioning regimen. It is best served in the first part of a practice session. At the college level it should be programmed for the first three weeks of a six-week pre-season program. As in all conditioning drills, the buildup is gradual; that is, in the first practice go four minutes; two with the right foot forward and two with the left. Add a minute to a minute-and-a-half each day. The team goal is 20 minutes. The drill should never be stopped until the time limit is reached, including the midpoint when the foot placement is changed. A limit of 12 to 14 minutes is the highest amount of time I would suggest for the high school lad.

Because this drill is extremely demanding physically, I have preferred vocal direction. Some coaches use hand direction, others a player as the directional guide in front of the group. I have found by voice inflection I can exhort them to better movement, forcing a tired, weak arm upward and keeping legs flexed that want to go upright and stiffen. A player learns to "gut it out," and that is a good practice habit to acquire. The team that develops mental toughness in practice will win the close, tough games. Most players and teams are reduced in efficiency as tiredness sets in and will give in to tiredness if a mental toughness isn't practiced.

I have found this drill rewarding in many ways. As odd as it sounds, one of the dividends is poor practice shooting. The arm muscles get extremely tired in the initial stages of the drill as muscle support is being built. This tired arm produces inaccurate shooting. Too often the individual player believes he is ready for the season's opener if he is hitting his shots in the early practices. Sometimes he gets lax about the other phases because of this. If the player is not shooting well, he will generally work harder in other aspects of his game – rebounding, cutting, transition, defense, and so on.

I would never employ this drill during the regular playing season or just prior to it. It is a fine early pre-season drill for the specific functions it accomplishes, but it would be counterproductive during the playing season.

Good morale should be a team objective. Teams with good morale have mutual respect for one another, as well as pride. The Marine Corps is a good example of squad pride, morale, and mutual respect. It grows out of the rigors of its training program and its physical demands. Each man knows the others endured demanding drills, and respects them for that. I believe arduous drills intelligently taught can bring about this same team feeling in basketball.

BACK TO THE BASICS

Fred "Tex" Winter

We coaches must be sold on ourselves. I honestly believe that I know as much about basketball as anyone in the profession. I am a student of the game and have spent many years developing my coaching philosophy and coaching techniques and methods.

Young coaches must believe that they too possess a vast understanding of basketball – so much that it is impossible to teach all that they know. Acquiring the knowledge requires each of us to be alert, and to concentrate on the many opportunities to learn and observe the game from television, videotape machines, attending clinics and seminars, visiting with fellow coaches, and being creative with the situation and material at hand. Grasp those good ideas and disregard those ideas that are of no value to you.

It is very important to realize that you do not have to teach all the basketball that you know to be a good coach; you won't have enough time. Therefore, you must be selective and convey to your players the most important information. The coach must set the priorities. Furthermore, you cannot take what other coaches teach and coach and make it yours. You must develop your own philosophy, methods, and coaching style, using ideas of others when you can, but you must teach your personality because you are the only one that truly understands your own situation and circumstances. You must coach according to your particular situation. Be flexible and able to adjust to changing situations. Each job demands a unique understanding of the setting and the situation.

Essentials of Coaching

1. The answer to success in coaching does not lie in some form of super strategy or some ultra super plan.

2. Success, overall, does rely on basic sound teaching abilities. The ability to teach the fundamental skills (basic basketball) to the individual athlete is critical. Your players must understand that their natural ability can take them only to a certain level.

3. Athletes must strive to break those physical barriers of endurance, speed, coordination, reflex action, jumping ability, and so on to truly become a better athlete.

4. Coaches must develop and organize out-of-season programs that promote greater total development of their athletes, so that they can break those physical barriers.

5. Total preparation of the mental, emotional, and physical aspects of athletes permits greater technical preparation.

6. A player has not learned a fundamental until it becomes second nature (a habit). Automatic reaction is the goal of skill execution. No thought process is necessary – just react.

7. Basketball is a game of total quickness, a game of reaction.

8. Athletes have not learned a skill until they can perform it correctly, quickly, and automatically while involved in game situations.

9. The coaching objective is accomplished through continuous repetition of drills and exercises.

10. Practice makes perfect, but only if the proper techniques and mechanics are being used. Proper techniques become movement habits.

11. Repetition must be done with high levels of interest and enthusiasm and in an exciting manner until it becomes an instinctive reaction.

12. One thing that highly disturbs me is the fact that I see so many bad habits being practiced today at all levels, from junior high to the professionals.

13. We must demand correct execution of basic skills.

14. Design practice time and situations so that it provides the technical know-how for the individual and the team of all the phases of the game that we plan to use in the total game plan.

15. Practice sessions must be so designed to lead to superb physical conditioning. Basketball is a game that cannot be played properly, unless you are in the very best possible physical condition.

16. Evaluate your practices to determine if they are designed to prepare the individual player physically, technically, mentally and emotionally. If these factors are included, then we should be able to visualize victory (see victory in the mind's eye).

Discipline and Coaching Behavior

I have always been very much concerned about the many ideas and practices of controlling or disciplining a team. I have researched this area in great detail and offer these findings to you.

1. I have no set rules of discipline or method of punishment.

2. Each situation is unique and depends on the coach, the team, and the individual(s) involved.

3. We are dealing with different types of individuals (different mentalities, different backgrounds, different experiences, and different expectations). A good coach must relate and adjust to these individual differences.

4. Each disciplinary case is settled on its own merits, rather than according to a bunch of preset rules. The player and I sit down and attempt to arrive at a solution based on what I think is best for the basketball program –

not necessarily what is in the best interest of the player. I try to save the individual if I can, and they know this.

5. We have some basic practice rules, as follows:
   a. Always be on time.
   b. Keep everybody busy learning the basic basketball skills we utilize.
   c. Correct all errors to assure each individual attention and success.
   d. Praise all proper conduct and execution of skills.
   e. Offer constructive criticism to the players and team to help bring about improvement.

6. I criticize the act, not the individual. Coaching should build rather than destroy, and all criticism is offered in a personal, one-to-one, private session, not as a squad function. Sarcasm is seldom desirable.

7. Rules are for prevention rather than cure.

8. Each player is labeled either as an asset or a liability. Each decides his position by his conduct and effort.

9. By keeping practices interesting and alive, we eliminate boredom, which might be a major cause for lack of attention.

10. As coaches, we must keep our temper under control. If we expect a poised ball club, we must be poised coaches. The controlled temper is a very strong motivational force.

11. Avoid carping and nagging. Take corrective action, then, drop the matter. Don't carry a grudge; it can become a deadly diversion between and among you and your players.

12. I believe that the very best coaching and teaching is being done at the junior and senior high school level, and that is where it is needed.

13. As teachers/coaches we must always consider the individual differences of age, playing level, experience, personality, emotional stability, and makeup. Know the total person and remember that the younger the athlete, the more sensitive he will be. At the pro level you are dealing with the overinflated ego; he must have that type of ego if he ever expects to make it in the pro ranks. But be aware of the level you are coaching. Junior high athletes are not miniature pros.

14. Team members must understand that your primary concern is what is best for the team – with an attempt, of course, to do what you can for the individual, so that each fits into the overall scheme. Try to avoid personality clashes. Do not deal in personality – personal vanity should not enter into the picture at all. Disciplinary problems are not taken as personal affronts. Revenge is not in your heart.

At the age of 36, I was a National Coach of the Year. My Kansas State team had won 25 and lost 2, and I thought I was the greatest thing since sliced bread. Today I am twice the coach I was then.

Practice Sessions

1. Be prepared, study past practice schedules, films, drills. Evaluate everything you plan to use this season.

2. Outline a complete yearly practice schedule.
   a. Pre-season.
   b. Seasonal (first day of practice to NCAA Finals).
   c. Post-season.
   d. Off-season.

3. The secret of success is organization. Add what you want to add, and delete what you want to do away with.

4. When you step on the floor, know:
   a. *What* you are going to teach.
   b. *How* you are going to teach.
   c. *Why* you are going to teach.

"The Six Honest Serving Men of Experience taught me all that I know, they are: who, what, where, why, when, and how." (R. Kipling). Know and use these six elements in developing a plan of action.

5. Daily practice should be held two hours a day from the first official day of practice until November 1, if the gym is available (2:30–4:30). All players are on the floor at 2:00 for individual practice with the assistant coaches. This time is the opportunity for the assistant coaches to teach their expertise, their special skills. Notice that when the head coach comes onto the scene the players stop paying attention to the assistant coaches; the players want that head coach's attention.

I have always had too large a team. I can't cut people, but regardless of how many we keep, everybody gets the same, equal opportunity to work. After I pick the starting five, or the top ten, I have the necessary information on which to base my decisions. But I truly believe I have a duty to give everyone that I invited out to the team an equal chance to make that team. All of you know that the greatest problems we have are from those players who are sitting on the sidelines who want to play and in their own minds know that they can play equally well as those out there playing.

6. We jump rope every day (365 days a year) for speed and hand-eye coordination. I recommend that players jump twice a day for

five minutes. This helps to develop quick feet. If you cannot move your feet, you cannot play basketball.

7. It is important that players do some slow stretching prior to practice. It is a good idea to bring in someone who is an expert in teaching stretching exercises – the trainer, a physical education teacher, maybe a dance instructor. Stretching helps to prevent injuries.

8. We use ballhandling drills to develop quick hands (behind head, behind back, around the torso, through the legs, and so on).

9. We want the players to thoroughly know the ball: feel, touch, smell, listen, and taste it. Be detailed in your introduction of the ball. How much does it weigh? How big is it? How large is the goal? They must be totally familiar with the tools of the game. Teach relationships: Little ball–big basket.

10. Take advantage of the many teaching tools and aids, the toss-back rebound machines, and so on.

11. The use of drills that are part of the actual game situations you plan to use are important. Don't drill just for the sake of drilling – make drills realistic.

12. Drill example: We teach drills that include all phases of our game, such as conditioning, floor spacing, ballhandling, offensive and defensive fundamentals, and the like. In one of our drills we stress running at three-quarter speed and maintaining 15 to 18 feet spacing. This spacing is a critical distance in many phases of our game. The players must instinctively know that distance.

13. Basketball is a full-court game – end line to end line. Use drills that use the whole floor – change of speed and direction drills, pivot and sprint drills, jump and run drills, or anything that you plan to teach in the total game concept.

14. Don't let your players practice bad habits – demand that each practice bring the team closer to the team's goals.

FUNDAMENTALS IS THE NAME

Mike Kunstadt

We feel that the foundation for any sound basketball team is based on both offensive and defensive fundamentals. Any team has to have good players to win consistently, but a team can partially overcome a lack of talent with solid fundamentals.

The first thing a coach must stress is to quickly and properly execute the fundamentals, and to do them on balance. Players aren't likely to execute fundamentals correctly when first taught, but they should do them properly. As they become more skilled, they will be able to do them quickly as well. Our responsibility as coaches is to devise drills that are going to be consistent with our coaching philosophy. In teaching fundamentals, keep in mind the following:

1. You should follow difficult drills with easier ones, and vice-versa.

2. New drills should be taught early in practice while the players are still fresh and alert, and all drills should be repeated often (some each day).

3. Do not spend too much time on any one drill, and have a variety of drills to cover the various aspects of the game.

4. Fundamentals should also be designed to aid the conditioning of your players so that running for conditioning purposes only is not necessary.

Obviously, certain fundamentals must be mastered by all players, regardless of position. Other fundamentals are specific to a position. Your fundamentals must be carefully planned and carefully organized to be most beneficial to fit into the concept of your daily practice. It can't be an "I'll decide what to do once I reach the practice floor" approach.

Some basic fundamentals that we believe all players should be taught are:

1. **How to get open.** You must move to get open. Timing between the passer and receiver to get the ball to the open man when he is open is very important.

2. **Defense.** The fingers should be spread, hands out and the feet shoulder-width with the head on the midpoint between both feet. Other points to be stressed on defense are: a) body positioning when guarding the man with a live ball, dead ball, dribbling, one pass and two passes from the ball; b) not reaching; being on balance.

3. **Shooting.** Be on balance. Your feet should be shoulder-width apart, the knees flexed and bent, the ball at chest-level and close to the body, the forearm perpendicular to the floor and the elbow in. Jump straight up and down (balance) and drive the arm up and through, with wrist follow-through. The forefinger is the touch finger and the last part of the finger to touch the ball on the shot. These fundamental techniques apply to all perimeter shots.

4. **Rebounding.** The first thing to do is *assume the shot will be missed*. Second, get your hands at least shoulder high, block out, and go after the rebound. If on offense, three go for the rebound, the shooter goes to the hash mark in the free-throw line area for the deep rebound, and there is a protector. If on defense, form a triangle and have two outside players become side rebounders. The hands should be open, fingers spread, and elbows extended. Timing and getting your hands on the ball at the maximum point of your jump and bringing the ball to the chest position with the head turning to the outside and elbows wide should be stressed.

5. **Passing.** A must for team play. Most of our success as a team has been when we were able to score most of our baskets off the pass. Pass by the defense, not over or around it. Work on passing to a spot and get the timing coordinated between the passer and receiver.

6. **Dribbling.** Don't overuse the dribble. The dribble should be used only to: a) advance the ball into a scoring area, or b) if no pass is available. Don't dribble too much – this lends itself too much to one-on-one basketball.

In teaching these fundamentals we believe in applying the four basic laws of learning:

1. Explanation – explain why and how the fundamentals should be executed.

2. Demonstration – demonstrate how the fundamental is to be done.

3. Imitation – players imitate the way fundamentals are to be done with coaches making corrections.

4. Repetition – the players repeatedly do the fundamentals daily to develop them into a habit.

Coaches must know their players and their fundamental strengths and weaknesses. They must be able to analyze and tell their players the following:

1. Who can/can't shoot from certain areas of the floor.

2. Which type of pass can/can't be made from certain areas of the floor.

3. Who can/can't dribble within the framework of your offense.

4. Who can/can't play defense against certain personnel on the opposite team.

Remember, a sound knowledge of and the ability to properly execute the fundamentals are absolutely essential for successful play.

PROGRESSIVE FOOTWORK DRILLS
Steve Brennan

Basketball is a game that features explosive and lightening-quick movements. It follows, then, that footwork is essential to compete effectively and successfully.

Slam-dunking, driving layups, cutting to the ball, screens, picks, and rebounding are just a few examples in which correct footwork is needed to successfully complete the desired movement. Coaches who stress correct footwork in their programs know that the effort will pay off for them during games. Players will also be able to see the results of correct footwork through increased success in all phases of the game during competition with an opponent.

Drills used to develop correct footwork are as varied as the offenses and defenses that coaches use in their programs. There are no "perfect" drills for footwork, just as there are no sets of drills that are "better" than others. What you consider is right or proper for your team, players, and program is the perfect or better program. The following drills are only ideas that can be expanded or changed as coaches see fit to do so. These simple drills are a good starting point, but not an end-all for footwork.

Drills

This footwork program is a set of nine drills which are broken into two sequences. The drills are progressive, meaning that each drill is an extension of the previous drill.

The two sequences start at different areas on the court. Sequence One begins at the free-throw line extended and ends at the baseline. Sequence Two begins out of bounds at the sideline and can start from one of two spots: the free throw line extended, or the lane box extended. To facilitate maximum player involvement, drills can be started from each side of the lane.

Sequence One — Drill 1 (Figure 7.17)

Movement: Jump stop on the baseline. Explanation: This is a simple, yet extremely important drill. Have the players run from the starting spot and execute a fundamentally correct jump stop. Stress balance and feet placement at all times.

Sequence One — Drill 2 (Figure 7.18)

Movement:

1. Jump stop

2. Reverse pivot (left and right)

Explanation: Begin each player at the starting spot and have each execute a jump stop at the baseline. After executing the jump, designate a reverse pivot (left or right). Again, stress balance on the jump stops and, most importantly, minimum vertical movement of the body on the pivots. The head and eyes should stay level throughout the pivot. As a coach, always correct the "jack-in-the-box" movement. This is an up–down body movement a player often uses when executing a pivot. Stress the need to stay level in the movement at all times.

Sequence One — Drill 3 (Figure 7.19)

Movement:

1. Jump stop

2. Reverse pivot

3. Power step outside

Explanation: Drill 3 is similar to both Drills 1 and 2. The new movement is now a power step (push–push step slide technique) to the outside. Keep a critical eye focused on the jump stops and pivots as usual, then stress staying low and not crossing the feet on the power step.

Sequence One — Drill 4 (Figure 7.20)

Movement:

1. Jump stop

2. Reverse pivot

3. Front pivot

4. Power step outside

Explanation: The new wrinkle to Drill 4 is the addition of the correct execution of a front pivot. Stress the correct balance, foot placement, and lack of vertical

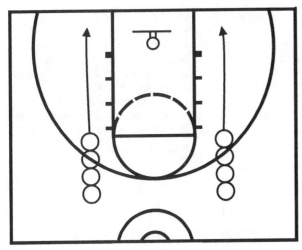

Figure 7.17

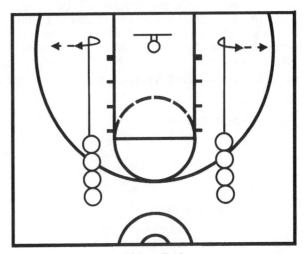

Figure 7.19

Figure 7.18

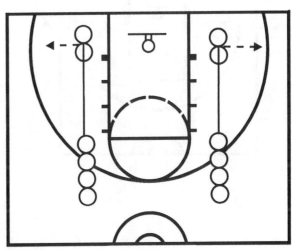

Figure 7.20

movement with the front pivot, just as you would with the reverse pivot. With the end of Drill 4, Sequence One has been completed. Let's now continue the footwork program with the explanation of the drills in Sequence Two.

Sequence Two — Drill 5 (Figure 7.21)

Movement:

1. Side to the box

2. V-cut

Explanation: The V-cut, or diagonal cutting, is used in many types of offenses. The player drives hard to the box, plants the outside foot, and executes a V-cut to the wing area. Stress planting the foot and the balance needed to execute the plant; then on the V-cut itself, stress the importance of staying low as they drive hard off the plant in a 45-degree direction. Always mention that the lower someone is to the floor, the quicker the movements will be during competition. As you can see from Figure 7.21, the drill begins at the sideline extended from the box. Both sides of the court can be utilized for maximum player involvement.

Sequence Two — Drill 6 (Figure 7.22)

Movement:

1. Sideline to the box

2. V-cut

3. Pivot on the inside foot

4. Square up

5. Dummy jump shot

Explanation: Drill 6 can easily be broken down into other drills before progressing to this drill. For our purposes, it's easier to put this final drill here and have each coach adjust it to his needs.

Again, stress low, quick movements on the plant and V-cut. On the inside-pivot movement stress balance, foot placement, and rotation of the body during the pivot. During the square-up, stress balance and foot placement, shoulder positioning, and the triple-threat position. During the dummy jump shot, stress the correct shooting form and follow-through, always being aware of the balance of the player, foot placement, angle of the shot, and shooting range for that player. Again, don't hesitate to break this drill down into additional drills if you see a need for it.

Sequence Two — Drill 7 (Figure 7.23)

Movement:

1. Run to the elbow

2. Push hard off the outside foot

3. Power step down the lane

Explanation: The final three drills all begin at the sideline extended at the free-throw line. Drill 7 stresses straight-ahead movement. Stress striding out and keeping low when running to the elbows. On the plant, stress cementing the outside foot and staying low while pushing off at a 90-degree angle. The players should stay low and move their feet quickly without crossing them on the power step. Again, utilize both sides of the court.

Sequence Two — Drill 8 (Figure 7.24)

Movement:

1. Run to the elbow

2. Reverse pivot

3. Power step down the lane to power layup

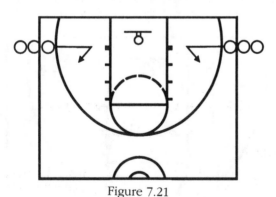

Figure 7.21

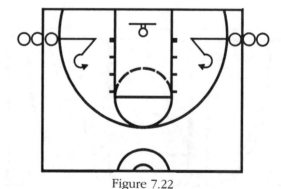

Figure 7.22

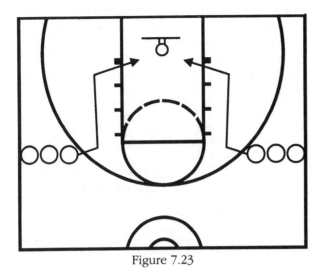

Figure 7.23

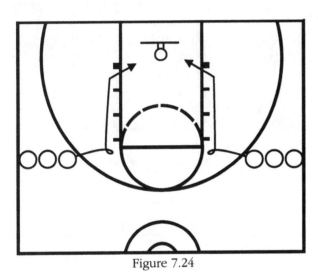

Figure 7.24

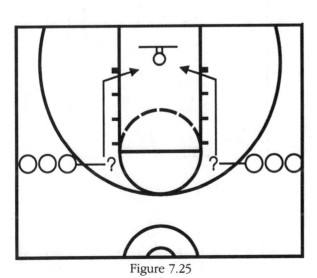

Figure 7.25

Explanation: Drill 8 is a combination of previous drills put in a different sequence of movements. Stress all the fundamental skills needed to perform the movements correctly.

Sequence Two — Drill 9 (Figure 7.25)

Movement:

1. Run to elbow

2. Listen for the coach's instruction: "Reverse pivot, V-cut," and so on.

3. Power step down the lane to power layup.

Explanation: The final drill of Sequence Two is again a combination of previous drills. The added skill is listening and reacting to the coach's instruction. Stress all the fundamental skills needed to complete the drill successfully.

Conclusion

Remember, there are many variations to these drills. The simple nature of each drill points in that direction. Don't consider these drills as the ultimate answer to footwork problems.

A basketball can be incorporated into the drills at the discretion of the coach. The use of a basketball was purposely omitted in the explanations of the drills, but a coach should feel free to use one at any time during the drills.

The last point concerns the placement of the coach or managers during drills. These were again purposely omitted to give each coach the opportunity to place himself or a manager in whatever position he so desires. Coaching positions can vary greatly, so position yourselves where you think the most benefit can be gained.

Even though the drills are extremely simple in nature, each is very important. These drills are only a stepping stone to the creative talents of each coach. The amount of time spent on footwork in practice might be that stepping stone to a championship season!

OFF-SEASON FUNDAMENTALS

Jim Valvano

Dribbling

It is most important that you work on the four basic dribbling moves with both your right and left hands. The following two drills are designed to work on the basic four, individually and in combination:

A. The basic four

1. Speed
2. Change of pace
3. Front change
4. Spin

Simply begin at half court A and using the right hand execute the speed dribble, then the layup. Then dribble to half court and execute the speed dribble with the left hand. Then go back to position A and execute the change-of-pace dribble, and so on, until you have completed the basic four dribbles (see Figure 7.26).

B. Time dribble

In a five-minute period, execute all the basic four moves, but in combination – that is, speed dribble followed by front change, then spin, and so on (see Figure 7.27). Also include behind-the-back and through-the-legs dribbles.

It is important that you dribble for the entire five-minute period nonstop going to your right and left for the drill to be effective. The full court is not needed. Use any available court space.

Shooting

To improve shooting percentage, you must work on two vital areas – first the shot itself (through drills) and secondly, shot selection (every time you play).

A. Standstill shooting

Stand in the perimeter 10 to 15 feet from the hoop and take five shots at a time from five different spots on the perimeter (see Figure 7.28). Change the five spots each time you do the drill. Do not move to another spot until you have made three out of five.

B. Twenty-five jump shot drill

This is a shooting drill we do every day (see Figure 7.29). We feel it is a great drill to develop your shooting if done properly. Player A is the shooter. Player B is the passer. His job is to keep A moving by passing the ball quickly and at times away from him. Player A must concentrate on the mechanics of his shot. He must try to receive the pass, square to the basket, jump straight up, execute the shot and follow through, land on-balance, and move again. He must never stand still and should make at least 13 of 25 shots. The breakdown of the 25 shots is as follows:

◆ Five no-dribble jump shots
◆ Five one-dribble jump shots
◆ Five one-dribble head fake and then dribble then jump shot
◆ Ten combination of all dribble moves, then shoot

C. Fake and shots

If you are alone, execute individual offensive moves. Fake right and go right, then fake left and go left, and so on. Take 15 to 20 jumpers.

D. Bet a pro

This is really a fun drill, yet it is challenging. The object of the game is to score 12 points before the pro you're competing against scores 12. The game begins with a foul shot. If you make it you get one point; if you miss, the pro receives three points. You

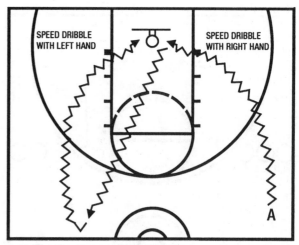

Figure 7.26

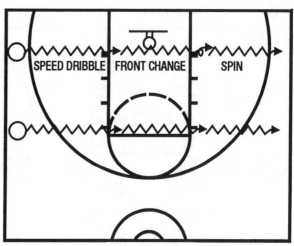

Figure 7.27

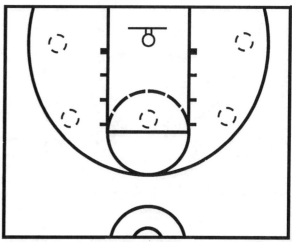

Figure 7.28

then take various jumpers from different spots on the floor, and for each basket you make you get one point. Each time you miss, the pro gets two points. Whoever gets to 12 first wins. Note: If you make the first shot, you must make a shooting percentage of 70 percent.

Inside Game

A. Tapping

The player stands to the right of the backboard and tosses the ball off the board and then taps the ball using his fingertips on his right hand nine times. On the tenth tap he taps the ball in the basket. The procedure is repeated on the left side using the left hand. The player must use proper jumping technique to get maximum use of the drill.

B. Two balls on the box

This must be done with a partner. The first player faces the basket directly in front. The other players line up under the basket, out-of-bounds (see Figure 7.30). Two balls are placed on the boxes on the foul lane. The player facing the basket reaches down for the ball and powers it up to the basket with a dribble. He then moves to the other ball as quickly as possible and powers it to the basket again. The other player must rebound the ball out of the basket and place it back on the same box. The goal is to make 20 power moves, 10 from each side as quickly as possible.

C. Inside shooting

The following three drills are designed to improve players' shot-making ability around the basket with both their right and left hands and to increase scoring chances in traffic with strong power moves and agility.

1. Standard right- and left-handed layup. The player stands to the right of the basket inside the foul lane area. The

drill begins with the player taking a right-handed layup, catching the ball before it hits the floor, and then executing the left-handed layup from the left side of the basket. This procedure continues for 20 made layups.

2. Reverse right- and left-handed layups. The player stands to the right of the basket inside the foul lane. He steps across the lane with his left foot and executes a right-handed reverse layup, catching the ball before it hits the floor, and executes a left-handed reverse layup from the right side. This procedure continues for 10 made reverse layups.

3. Power move. Players square off to the baseline inside the right foul lane area. Jumping to the basket, the player must execute a strong powerful move so that if closely guarded he will create the three-point opportunity (The key is to have the left elbow extended guarding the ball.) The player then catches the ball before it hits the floor and executes the same power move from the left side of the basket using the right hand. This procedure continues for 10 made power layups. Then using the same movement he executes 10 made power moves using the head and shoulder fake. (Left-handed shooters use the left hand in this drill.)

D. Offensive power moves from the box and medium post

1. Show ball middle – drop-step baseline

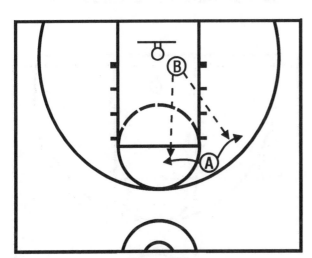

Figure 7.29

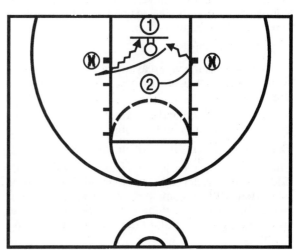

Figure 7.30

2. Show ball baseline – drop-step to middle
3. Show ball middle – turnaround jumper to baseline and follow hard
4. Show ball baseline – turnaround jumper to middle and follow hard
5. Step middle – turnaround jumper to baseline and follow hard
6. Step baseline – turnaround jumper to middle and follow hard
7. Show ball middle – fake turnaround jumper to baseline – one-dribble power move to the basket
8. Show ball baseline – fake turnaround jumper to middle – one-dribble power move to the basket
9. Sidney Wicks move – catch, turn, and pivot away from defender, then cross-over move in front.
10. Sidney Wicks move – catch, turn and pivot away from defender, then cross-over move in front of the defender and power to the middle.
11. Catch with back to the basket into quick baseline pivot – then one-dribble reverse layup
12. Catch with back to basket into quick middle pivot – then one-dribble reverse layup

All the above moves can be done either on the boxes or the medium post area, right and left sides. The main area of concentration is the low post on the boxes.

Defense

A. Shuffle drill

Assume a defensive stance in position A and shuffle the length of the court, concentrating on movement of feet and hands. When you arrive at the end of the court, execute a shuffle again. Do a minimum of three trips (see Figure 7.31).

B. Game defense

Every pickup game you play, try to defend the other team and the other team's best offensive player as best you can.

You cannot turn on and off. You must play defense every time you step on the court

Offensive Movement Without the Ball

This is one of the most important aspects of the game, and the least practiced. The following five moves are essential in becoming a complete player. The player begins on the right side of the court – foul line extended – and executes the following maneuvers:

A. Back-door

Cut behind the defensive man to the basket (see Figure 7.32).

B. Button hook

Take the man to the basket, pivot on the inside foot (foot closest to the basket), pin defensive man on back, and prepare to receive the pass (see Figure 7.33).

C. Square it

Take the man away from the ball to the foul line area, pivot on the inside, pin the defensive man on back, and prepare to receive the pass (see Figure 7.34).

D. Dip

This is the move to make when being overplayed. Start at the foul line extended and proceed to execute a back-door cut (see Figure 7.35). When the defensive man prevents by overplaying, simply take a quick change of direction and "dip" in front of the defense toward the hoop.

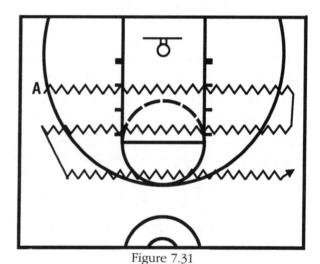

Figure 7.31

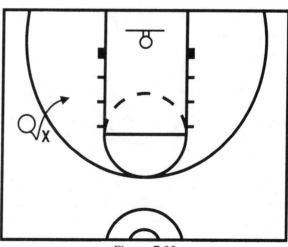

Figure 7.32

E. Hawk drill

This is a back-door move in traffic started with a square-it-up-the-lane move (see Figures 7.36 and 7.37). Two players start from the low box, one with the ball. The player with the ball rolls it diagonally up to the corner of the foul line (a little extended) and runs and picks it up. The other player cuts across the lane from his starting spot, then squares and cuts up to the foul line extended. Now the two players are exactly opposite each other at the foul line area. The player with the ball passes across the foul line. He then steps to the ball and cuts back-door. The other player hits him with a bounce pass for a layup, then follows to rebound. Now they do the same thing going to the opposite side. Make 20 quick but well-executed moves in a row, 10 on each side.

F. Optional change-direction drill (Figure 7.38)

    1. Number 1 passes to Number 2
    2. Number 2 drives to the basket and changes direction to make a layup on the other side

Running

A. Sprints

Players do 10 length-of-the-court sprints.

B. Suicides

I'm sure you have run this drill before, but possibly by another name. Player A must run from the baseline to the foul line and then return to the baseline, then to half court and return to the baseline, and so on.

Foul Shooting

You should take five foul shots between each of the four sessions and then take 25 at the end of the workout.

The basic ingredients of the foul shot are:

A. Repetition — establish a routine

B. Concentration — pick out the part of the rim you want to use as your target

C. Confidence — the result of the above

Optional Agility Drills

A. Tape drill

Two pieces of tape are placed on the floor with a maximum of seven feet between tapes. The player must start in position A and, using his feet together, jump to position B, then to position C, as indicated, going up and down as quickly as possible.

B. Quick feet drill

Simply place the ball on the floor and by alternating feet, touch the ball as many times as possible in one minute.

If time permits and you feel you need work on quickness of feet, then you should execute these two drills. These two drills should be done three

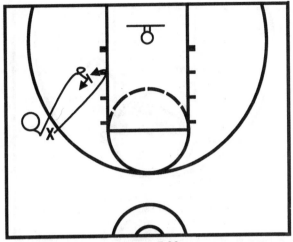

Figure 7.33

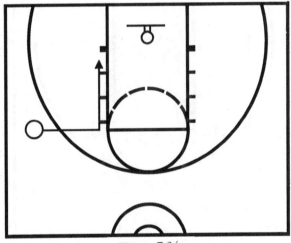

Figure 7.34

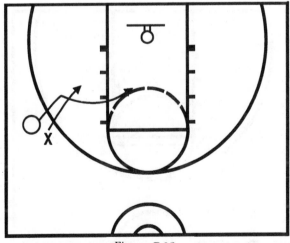

Figure 7.35

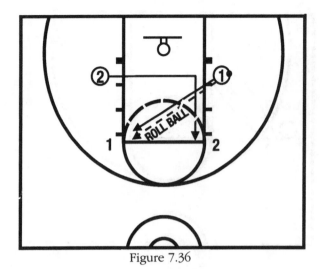

Figure 7.36

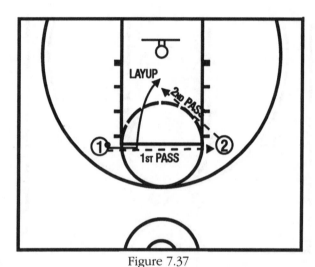

Figure 7.37

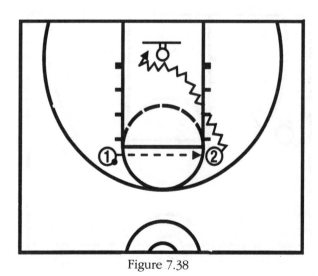

Figure 7.38

times during the program: for example, after dribbling, after moving without the ball, and at the end of the program.

THE 26 MAGIC NUMBERS
Alvin "Doggie" Julian

I realize that some of these rules overlap, but they are simple to remember and will help to impress the principles upon your players. Your players will get to know them and often inject a little fun into the practices by repeating one of these rules to a teammate who has made a mistake. We get a great kick out of them and find them very helpful. Fundamentally, we think they are sound, simple to teach, easy to remember, and will apply to any style of play or any group of players regardless of age.

Chuck Kaufman, a Dartmouth captain, once asked why I didn't say the ball was 24-karat gold. He said: "You know, Coach, the higher the karat, the more valuable the gold." I said: "Sure, Chuck, I know, But the higher the karat in gold, the softer it is. We don't want our basketball to be too soft."

1. The ball. It's 20-karat gold!

Too many players and teams are careless with the ball! Hang onto the leather! It's 20-karat gold! All too often a team will get the ball through an interception or a loose ball and lose it right back again because of a poor or thoughtless pass. Make haste slowly and be determined to hold onto the ball until you or one of your teammates gets a good shot. Bad passes and poor shots are the stock-in-trade of a poor team.

2. Be careful on a layup! It's money in the bank.

More games are won on layup shots than on any other. And more games are lost because of bad layup shots than by any other shot. The layup is the most important shot in basketball, but it is often missed because the shooter wants to be fancy or because he doesn't slow down before releasing the ball. It is better for the shooter to slow down after the drive and make the layup soft and easy than to look good on the drive and miss the shot. All players should learn to shoot with the left hand on the left side of the basket and with the right hand on the right side of the basket. Then they won't have to cross the backboard to shoot and their opponents can't concentrate on their favorite hands. Shooters should cut on an angle toward the basket, never in a semicircle.

3. Basketball is a game of motion! It's your move.

Motion on the court is vital! Many players stand still and "ball bet." This kind of player seems to think the ball should be passed to him in any situation. When he doesn't get the ball, he usually just stands there looking and watching the game. He should have a chair! In the balcony! When a teammate passes to a good player, he gets out of there and takes his opponent with him. This move opens up the court for someone else. All teams hate to play against opponents who keep the ball hopping and *move*.

4. Always fake direction! Remember "Wrong Way" Corrigan.

Faking is important because it tricks opponents into making mistakes! However, the good faker gives his opponent a chance to be faked and does not attempt to fake a "dumb" ball player. The dumb ball player won't react. The smart one will. The faker should also frequently go the way he has just faked. Then again, the good faker doesn't fake too much. He will often go without faking.

5. Move to beat the pass! Be where you ain't.

Beating and meeting the pass is the stamp of a good ballplayer! The player who moves and cuts and meets the ball makes it duck soup for a teammate to pass to him. Such action also keeps his opponent so busy that he can't find time to attempt to steal the ball. Hand in hand with beating and meeting the pass goes the fake to receive or meet the ball and the reverse cut (particularly when the defensive player is overshifting). When a player moves to meet or beat the pass, he should make sure he is in position to catch the ball, to return the pass and cut, to feed another cutter or the pivot, and to shoot.

6. When in trouble make a V for Victory.

A player in the wrong position can get right by making a V. A player never goes wrong when he feels he is in the wrong position if he makes a V, because he clears out and he takes his opponent with him. This is an important fundamental and is particularly good when more than one player cuts at the same time.

7. Don't think for the opponents! Be yourself.

Some players are more concerned with what they think the opponents are thinking than with what they are thinking for themselves. Frequently, when you ask a player why he did not go through with a cut or a play he will say, "Well, Coach, the defense was going to do this or that." How does he or anyone else know what a defensive player or team is going to do? The player should go through with his move and if the opponent or opponents play him right, he hasn't lost anything. If the opponent or opponents play him wrong, he has accomplished something. By thinking for the defense, the player has helped the opponents play their defense well, and he has also hurt his own team by a bad move and one which his teammates did not expect.

8. One player cuts at a time! Stay out of the act.

If a teammate is cutting and you are in his way, V out of the play. When a player starts a cut and sees that a teammate is also cutting, he should make a V. All players should remember: Only one cutter at a time! The good player realizes that two cutters will bring their defensive men where they will be in good position to double team the ball or stop the play. Further, two cutters often jam things up and frequently run into one another. The good player keeps cutting even if he does not get the ball and he realizes the vital importance of timing to his team's offense.

9. Grab it! Don't tap it.

Too often a player makes the mistake of tapping the ball under the defensive basket. This is bad because the ball often goes out of bounds and becomes the opponent's ball. Too, the tapper often taps the ball into the hands of an opponent and, not infrequently, into the opponent's basket. The good rebounder doesn't stab at the ball, he grabs it! Under the offensive basket it is all right to tap the ball back up, but, even here, a player is better off if he can grab the ball and then go back up with it for the shot. If he is in a poor position or is closely pressed, a deep back tap to his teammates in the backcourt is permissible.

10. Never force a shot! Look before you leap.

The opponents will never block a good shot. A shot should never be blocked if it is attempted at the right time. A team should be sure it has rebound strength under the basket before a shot is attempted. Good offensive and defensive balance is important and all offensive players should be sure their opponents are not forcing them to shoot unnaturally (bad arch on ball, shooting from a spot too far away, attempting shots they seldom practice). If the defensive man has been successful in making it tough for a player to get a shot away, he should pass off to a teammate and move. He will get his shot sooner or later. If a player's shot is blocked, he shouldn't have shot. A player should never shoot when well guarded by a defensive opponent (forcing the shot). He should fake a shot occasionally and drive or follow a fake with the shot. When under the basket, a fake layup followed by the actual shot is usually successful (particularly when an opponent is breathing down the shooter's neck). All players should take their best shots when the chips are down. All too frequently, a player will take his poorest shot at a crucial moment and, unaccountably, often take a shot he doesn't even practice. Don't ask me why! It's one of the mysteries.

11. Dribbling is an emergency measure! Bring your own ball.

Nine out of ten players dribble or bounce the ball before they do anything else! This is a bad habit and bad basketball because it limits a player's play opportunities.

12. Talk to your teammates! I've got a secret.

Talking on offense and defense builds team play! Talking encourages teammates, and a little verbal pat on the back goes a long way. Talking on defense is vital when picking up loose opponents and calling "stay" or "switch." Words of praise for a good play or effective offensive or defensive rebounding makes for a close-knit team. However, a player should not be a traffic cop – he should not stand in the backcourt and tell his teammates what to do.

13. Never turn your head on defense! The girl in the balcony....

A player should never turn his head to watch the ball when playing man-to-man defense. And, conversely, he shouldn't turn his back on the ball when playing on offense. Naturally, there are times when screens and picks force a defensive player into a situation in which the rule must be violated. Then, a teammate must help out. When a player changes from offense to defense, he should backpedal so that he can locate his personal opponent, point out a loose man, or help out in stopping the opponents' fast break. And, when changing from defense to offense, players should keep their eyes on the ball. Every fan and coach can recall a game incident in which a player who was changing from defense to offense turned his back on the ball only to miss a pass and lose the ball for his team.

14. Don't cross your feet on the defense! Why move so many feet?

Players should move only one foot at a time in defensive play. Many players move their feet in short steps when playing defense. Moving both feet almost at the same time is bad because it gives the offensive opponent a chance to beat the defensive player. The defensive player should move only one foot at a time so he will be in position to come back to a good defensive position or "go" with his opponent. A defensive player should not cross his feet on defense, especially on the first step. He should shuffle his feet because he can go just as fast shuffling as running sideways and crossing his feet.

15. Hands up on the defense! Shake hands with yourself.

Keeping the hands up is important to body balance and good defense. All offensive players dislike being harassed. Movement of the hands and feet discourages passing and shooting and often discourages the opponent. Besides, it shows that the defensive player is on the ball! Wants to play ball! And wants the ball! Further, use of the hands when guarding an opponent who does not have the ball discourages a pass to him and makes it difficult for him to move where he wants to go. There was never a good defensive player who didn't use his hands. A tight-rope walker uses his hands to balance his body and the good defensive player does likewise. Hands up!

16. Watch your opponent's belly button! The handle of the bread basket.

Where the belly button goes, he goes! We like our defensive players to keep their eyes glued to a part of the offensive ball player that can't fool them – the belly button! It is possible to watch an opponent's number, but there is always the danger of looking up and watching the eyes. We could say: "Watch the belt buckle!" But we prefer to use the belly button because we think it is expressive and easy to remember. An opponent can fake a defensive player with his eyes, head, shoulders, and feet, but wherever the belly button goes, the opponent must go. When playing against a corner man, the defensive player should be turned a little so he can watch the ball, but above all he should keep low and concentrate chiefly on his opponent.

17. Pick up the first man! First come, first served.

Pick up the first man down the floor whether he is your man or not! When you are back or coming down the floor ahead of the rest of your teammates, pick up the first opponent and call out to the teammate who is closest to your man and thus trade opponents. Some players point to the first man down the floor and yell for the assigned teammate to take him. However, the assigned teammate may be caught in a tangle, may have tried to follow in, or may find it impossible to catch up. So, the first player down the floor must take the opponent to save points and show he is part of the team. Any defensive player looks silly letting an opponent go down the floor unguarded just because he is not the man's assigned guard.

18. Don't leave your feet on defense!

After a defensive player leaves his feet, he is helpless. Why be a jumping-jack just because the opponent with the ball fakes? The defensive player should keep his feet on the floor unless he is rebounding, jump shooting, jumping for a held ball, or trying to block a shot after the opponent has released the ball. The good defensive player keeps his head up and his feet on the floor. If he goes for a fake, his opponent will drive.

19. Get position for rebounds! Position is everything in life.

Most players could get position for rebounds if they tried! Many players stand around like dopes when the ball is going up toward the basket. Instinct, and sensing the direction of the shot and the angle of the rebound off the backboard, will enable a player to move into the correct rebounding position at once. Many times the opponent's eyes will tip the defensive player off to the angle at which the ball is coming off the board. Offensive players should hustle for position instead of watching the ball until it is too late. If the offensive player gets position, he should try to tap the ball into the basket or back up on the backboard. Sometimes a fake can be used to get position. If a tap-in or possession is impossible, the long back tap should be attempted.

20. If you can't rebound you can't win! Join the union.

You could almost, though not quite, say that basketball today is: rebound and shoot! A team must rebound, however, or it will not get the chance to shoot. Players do not necessarily have to be tall, but it is vital that they block their opponents out and want to rebound. Too many players let the other fellow do it! If a player finds he is the loose man, if he is not being blocked out, or if his man stays out instead of following in, he should always rebound. We have a mythical organization on our team. We call it the "Union." The big men must make double figures (number of rebounds) to warrant membership. The little men must average six rebounds per game to qualify. Block out and *rebound*! Good rebounding affects the other team's shooting. They know they will not get another shot and the pressure is on the shooter. Good rebounding helps a team's own shooting and enables it to get two or three shots to the opponents' one. Good rebounding also limits the opponents' shots. This is the key to winning games.

21. The first fast-break pass must be perfect! A good beginning, a perfect ending.

You either have the fast break or you don't! The fast break must get started with the outlet pass – at once! If the first fast-break pass is a good one, the fast break is underway. After the fast break is started, it is hard to stop. That's why the first pass is so important. A bad first pass will bring on another and another and a team usually ends up losing the ball (certainly losing the fast break opportunity). Get off right with a good outlet pass! Wheel it!

22. You must make 70 percent of your free throws! Look a gift horse in the mouth.

Free throws are more important today than at any other time in the history of basketball! The value of free throws has been increased chiefly because of the bonus free throw. It is possible to be outscored from the field but still win the game through greater accuracy from the line. There is no excuse for being a poor free throw shooter. Practice, confidence, and the proper technique are the keys. On the basis of team play, good free-throw shooting upsets the other team and gives your teammates confidence. Players should use the free throw method natural to them and the one which gets the best results. (I give a trophy each year to the best free throw shooter on my team.) Get that one-and-one!

23. Keep the defense busy! It's hard to "move" on the bench.

Keep moving to keep the defense busy! If all five men keep moving, their opponents cannot afford to sag or float. Moving with or without the ball forces the defense into making mistakes because the offensive players know what they are trying to do and the defensive players do not know what to expect. The offensive team that moves keeps the opponents worried about their defense, and this stress upon defense affects their offense.

24. Don't cross the backboard to shoot! You take the high road.

Many players cross the backboard to take a shot with their favorite hand. This is a definite weakness, because the big objective is to get to the basket quickly and to get the shot away. A defensive player can catch up with the cross-over shooter because of the extra distance and the time required to cross over. Also, after an opponent discovers a player likes a certain hand for shooting, he will overplay his opponent and make it difficult for him to get any shot. A player should learn to shoot from both sides of the basket and with both hands. Shoot with the left hand from the left side of the basket and with the right hand from the right side of the basket.

25. Never underrate an opponent! Tall trees fall hard.

Every game is *the* game! This is more true today than at any other time. Years ago a five-point lead, with 10 minutes to go, was big. Today, a 20-point lead with 10 minutes to go does not mean the game is over. All teams start off playing better against an opponent if they think they are considered pushovers. But, if they turn out to be better than anticipated, even the great team can be upset. So, it is wise never to underrate or underestimate an opponent. If they are not as good as expected, you have lost nothing. Overconfidence can affect a team's play and it is wise to remember that it is only the underdog who can do the upsetting. Be ready!

26. Practice does not always make perfect! Do it right.

Practice does not make perfect if you practice the wrong techniques! Players often work long and hard and make little or no progress because they are practicing incorrectly. Stop them! Start all over! They will make better progress. In this connection, it is wise to supervise all practices (including three-man games). Start them right and keep them right! In shooting, start all practices with layups. Too many players start with long shots which they will never use in a game.

COMMON COACHING MISTAKES
Nat Holman

Without a doubt, some games are lost by poor strategy on the part of the coach, or even by specific errors made by the coach. Far more frequently, however, the results in a ball game will be determined by the common fundamental mistakes of individual players on offense or on defense.

We have listed below the most common errors on the offense and defense that are committed by players. By analyzing their individual techniques, the intelligent player will eliminate these faults and will help his team in its total efforts.

Even the finest players can make fundamental mistakes under the stress of a championship game. However, to the young player it is essential that he recognize basic mistakes as they occur during the course of a game. To the young coach it is vital that he correct such mistakes in the techniques of his players and keep them to a minimum.

Common Errors on the Offense

1. Dribbling every time you get the ball.

2. Failing to use a trailer on the way in and forcing a poor layup shot as a result.

3. Following up your own shot from out deep and setting up a fastbreak situation for the opponent.

4. Failing to clear out of the middle as two or three teammates move downcourt on a fast break.

5. Forcing a pass into the pivot when he is being closely guarded.

6. Running up the field on the change-over from defense to offense and taking your eyes off the ball.

7. Taking a long shot while your team is freezing the ball to protect a lead in the closing minutes of a game.

8. Failing to come out and help a teammate in distress during an opponent's pressing tactics.

9. Finding oneself trapped in the center of the court while teammates are moving the ball and not knowing where to go.

10. Remaining in the backcourt, and failing to uncover and to free oneself from his guard.

11. Not knowing where the defensive man is, which allows a closely guarding opponent to steal the ball and go in for a basket.

12. Making an unnecessary bounce pass, especially in the backcourt area; keep the ball off the floor.

13. Having poor offensive spacing.

14. Throwing careless crosscourt passes. On an interception, opponents move downcourt on a fast break.

Common Errors on the Defense

1. Playing behind a pivot man in and around the elbow of the foul line and offering no trouble to the passers feeding the pivot.

2. Turning the head to follow the ball as it moves behind a defensive player into the forward area.

3. Failing to box out and permitting an offensive player to follow up after a shot.

4. Slapping at a dribbler and letting him go by.

5. Dropping back too deep before picking up an opponent — and/or dropping back to help out and allowing an opponent to move into position for a shot.

6. Running out swiftly on opponents in the corner without boxing them or considering the proper spacing in defending which allows opponent to drive past (proper closeouts).

7. Leaving your feet to block shots and failing to box out as a result.

8. Failing to slide or to switch properly, which may cause defenders to block each other.

9. Failing to help out and to double-team an opponent's big man.

10. Watching the ball in a held-ball situation and permitting opponent to break downcourt unguarded.

11. Going all out on the ball in a two-on-one situation and permitting opponent nearest to basket to remain unguarded.

12. Going out for own man and permitting an opponent nearer to the basket to remain unguarded.

13. Failing to wave hands properly when the defender's back is to the ball.

14. Failing to point out and pick up on the defense (talk).

15. Failing to put your hands up on the defense to block any passes coming overhead.

16. Poor defensive spacing which prevents the defensive man from switching in time. Also, it prevents a teammate from sliding through to play his own defensive opponent.

17. Never let your man get behind you on the defense!

18. Two defensive men wind up playing one offensive man, leaving one offensive man free.

19. Trying to "ball-hawk," missing the pass interception and allowing opponent to drive in for score.

20. Failing to box out an opponent on a held-ball play.

21. Watching the shooter and following the flight of the ball, thereby permitting the offensive opponent to get between the guard and the basket for a good rebound position.

22. Failing to talk it up on the defense. Unnecessary defensive switch leaves offensive man with ball free for shot within scoring area.

23. Playing the pivot man too far in front, and failure of defensive men on the weak side to sag and to help out against the "big" man.

24. Playing the pivot man wrong, and allowing him to receive pass and score from a vulnerable defensive position.

MOVING WITHOUT THE BALL

John R. Wooden

There are so many styles or systems of offense and defense in basketball that it is almost impossible for a coach to have his team prepared for every possibility.

However, I continue to feel that the most difficult task that I have in regard to the technical development of my players is getting each individual to work properly on offense when he does not have the ball and to play heads up, alert, thinking defense in our man-to-man defensive system when his man does not have the ball.

If each player on the floor had the ball an equal amount of time, no one would have the ball over 10% of the playing time; so what each player is doing during the approximately 90 percent of the time he does not have the ball plays a tremendously vital part in the efficiency with which both the team and the individual will function.

It is true that the guards will have the ball a little more than 10 percent of the time when you are on offense, as they will usually advance the ball when possession is obtained, which makes it equally true that the forwards and center will have the ball less than 10% of the time. Therefore, they have even more time to operate without the ball.

I like to point out to my college players that most of them will have the ball considerably less than four minutes in a 40-minute game, because four minutes would be the maximum if each of the ten players would have it an equal amount of playing time, providing some player was in possession of it at all times.

At no time do I imply that what you are able to do with the ball when it is in your possession is not important. But you should continually emphasize that you will not have the ball the vast percentage of time, and none of that time should be wasted. Too many players, who are excellent players with the ball, do very little when they do not have the ball. Therefore, they are not complete players.

The offensive player without the ball has several things to do to keep him busy, and proper timing is essential for all of them.

Among the things that he must do when he is on the strong side are as follows:

1. He must be ready to screen at the proper time if the play or the situation call for it.

2. He must set his man up to run him into a screen if the play or situation call for it.

3. He must keep his defensive man so busy that he will not be in position to help a teammate.

4. He must make his defensive man turn his eyes away from the ball at the proper time.

5. He must constantly be working to set up his man so that he will be able to get open to provide an outlet pass for the man with the ball at the proper time.

6. He must constantly be working to get open and to receive a pass where he will be a triple threat man with the ball. In other words, he should try to get the ball in position where he is a threat as a shooter, as a driver, or on a pass and cut.

7. He must be ready and in position to cover the proper territory as a rebounder or as a protector in case a shot is taken.

8. He must be thinking constantly, as his moves will probably be predicated on the moves of the man who has the ball or the man who just passed the ball.

The offensive men on the weak side do not have quite as many things to do, but the things that they must do are of vital importance. If they do not keep their men busy and prevent them from floating, it minimizes the chances of the score from the strong side offense. Furthermore, because a weak side attack is of tremendous importance to the total offense, they must set their man up in order to be open to receive a pass in the proper position to immediately attack the opposite side if the ball is passed back out or over in case it did not penetrate the opposite side.

Because it is perfectly natural and normal for players to want to score, it is perfectly natural and normal for them to subconsciously work harder when they have the ball in their possession. In order to get them to put forth the same effort when they do not have the ball, we have to overcome, or at least compensate for, a normal subconscious reaction. This is not easy, but it is necessary to field the complete ball player and the complete team.

To help teach and promote this constant effort without the ball, it is necessary for a coach to use all of the psychology and ingenuity at his command. Because every boy is different and every team is made up of different individuals, it does not follow that what works with one will necessarily work with another. Therefore, season after season, the coach must keep searching for the right approach to a particular boy or a particular team.

Some ideas that I have found helpful are as follows:

1. Constantly emphasize the previously mentioned facts to your players by word of mouth, by

mimeographed material and by sight when viewing game movies.

2. Point out and give a lot of public credit to those who really keep working mentally and physically when they do not have the ball. Do this in your practice scrimmage situations and follow up in your game competition.

3. Get the cooperation of your sportswriters and sportscasters, especially your own school reports, in calling attention to these factors.

4. Be certain to indicate the preliminary movements of all those without the ball when diagramming plays of the offense. Explain the purpose of the moves of each individual.

5. Have the players diagram the offense occasionally and make certain that they show all the preliminary moves and fakes of those without the ball.

6. We do not want the players to criticize each other, but encourage them to critically analyze the play at all times and particularly watch those without the ball.

7. Run considerable offense without taking the shot so that the ball will always be brought back to the weak side and all options set up.

8. Stress constant movement without ever standing still or standing straight up. This encourages thinking and moving with a purpose.

9. Encourage your passing game by complimenting your passers at every opportunity. A fine passer will encourage men to work to get open to receive a pass, while a poor passer encourages a "what is the use?" attitude.

10. The development of a proper team spirit encourages everyone to work. I like to define team spirit as an eagerness to sacrifice personal glory for the welfare of the team.

Yes, offense without the ball is essential for the success of the individual player and for the team. I consider success to be peace of mind which can only be attained by self-satisfaction in knowing that you have done your best to become the best that you are capable of becoming. This cannot be achieved in the game of basketball without total effort by each individual with and without the ball.

I do not want my team to experience extreme heights because I feel that for every peak there is a valley, but I do want them to repeatedly experience the inner peace that is sure to come from an all-out effort.

As George Moriarity said in his poem "The Road Ahead or the Road Behind":

> *"Who can ask more of a man*
> *Than giving all within his span;*
> *Giving all, it seems to me,*
> *Is not so far from victory."*

Inside Shot

Chin-it
Jerry Krause and Jim Conn

Anatomy of a Rebound
George Raveling

Offensive Rebounding
Bailey Howell

Defensive Rebounding
Jim Brandenburg

The Rebound Game
Bill Leatherman

CHIN-IT
Jerry Krause and Jim Conn

After observing basketball players of both sexes and all age groups at basketball camps, games, and practice situations, we concluded there must be a technique developed that both sexes at all age levels could use to protect the basketball. By protecting the basketball the writers are referring to the offensive player gaining possession of the ball and being able to quickly adjust the ball to a position so the defensive player will be unable to remove the ball from the offensive player's possession, or force the offensive player into a jump ball situation by simultaneously grabbing the ball. This position or technique should be flexible so that once the offensive player has gained possession he can readily use other offensive skills such as shooting, passing, and dribbling quickly and efficiently. It is felt that the "chin-it" technique is appropriate and provides the player with a skill that produces confidence in protecting the ball. The writers will attempt to describe the chin-it position, how the ball is protected, and the offensive skills that can be used from this position.

Description of Basic Chinning Position

Stance: The feet are parallel, slightly wider than the shoulders. The weight is evenly distributed on the heels and balls of the feet. The head and eyes are up, looking for an outlet opening (pass, dribble, or shot). The hands are placed on the side of the ball flexed at right angles to the forearms. The forearms are parallel to the floor in an abducted position (elbows out). The ball is held firmly on the chest just slightly under the chin.

The ankles are flexed. The knees are flexed between a 90- and 120-degree posterior angle depending on the strength of the player's legs (the stronger the player's legs, the smaller the angle). The hips are flexed such that the back is at a 45-degree angle with the floor. This varies with the individual and is adjusted to enable the player to maintain an erect head position. The fingers are spread comfortably on the sides of the ball with the thumbs slightly behind the ball.

Protecting the Ball

If the defensive player attempts to slap the ball away from the side, he risks fouling by either striking the offensive player's hand, wrist, or forearm. To protect the ball from the reaching defensive player, the individual chinning the ball will keep pivoting away from pressure to prevent the jump ball situation.

If the defensive player attempts to reach from behind to remove the ball, the offensive player's head or face is in a position to receive the blow which constitutes a foul on the aggressor, and once again the offensive player can pivot away from pressure.

If the defensive player attempts to make contact with the ball from underneath the ball, the ball will be driven into the offensive player's chest or possibly the chin depending on the angle the defensive player delivers the blow. Possession can still be maintained even after a forceful blow.

Movement from the Chin-It Position

Once in the chinning position, it is possible to maneuver the body and ball into a triple-threat position (an offensive position in which the offensive player can shoot, pass, or dribble) quickly and efficiently.

Shoot (right-handed shooter): Using the left hand, push the ball to a position slightly below the right eye. Slightly rotate and pronate the right hand a quarter turn behind the basketball in a flexed position. Drop the right elbow from a parallel position to the floor to one of a right angle to the floor directly below the basketball, and the offensive player is now in a shooting position.

Pass: From the chinning position, the offensive player will step in the direction of the target and push the thumbs through the ball.

Dribble (right-handed dribble): Push the ball to the right side of the body with the left hand. With the ball on the right side, the right hand will rotate and pronate a quarter of a turn to the top of the ball and slightly behind it (opposite with the left-hand dribble).

Developing the Chin-It Technique

Since the technique has been used at the high school and college levels as well as with boys and girls in summer basketball schools, players using it have developed self-confidence in protecting the ball. An observer in practices and games will quite often hear players communicating with each other reminding teammates to chin it when they acquire a rebound or when they are being pressured heavily by a defensive player. The coaching staff can communicate this technique readily with a positive verbal reminder to chin it on rebound and other congested possession situations. When concluding basketball drills or changing to another segment during practice, the players with a ball chin-it when the whistle is sounded as a matter of quick reaction. The remaining players assume the chin-it position without a ball. All players focus their attention on the coach for instructions.

ANATOMY OF A REBOUND
George Raveling

"There is no glory in rebounding – just victory."

Rebounding can be learned. Since it is not an inherited trait, it requires courage, aggressiveness, pride and hard work. Like defense, rebounding is a fundamental area of basketball in which the unproductive scorer can become a valuable asset to his team. Size and jumping ability are definite assets in rebounding but they can be neutralized by the use of proper rebounding techniques.

Most practice sessions are scheduled with defense getting 35 percent of the practice time, offense 60 percent of the time, and rebounding five percent. The greatest degree of emphasis is placed on an area of concern in which players spend 90 percent of their leisure practice time. Coaches are putting less emphasis on ball control or rebounding, when more is required. There is no shortcut to improvement in the mechanics of rebounding. Sound coaching must specify aggressive rebounding in relation to any given offensive or defensive situation.

The coach with the most complete rebounding teaching techniques is generally a consistent winner. His plans are not confined to the offensive rebounding factors of the game. They must also encompass the techniques, tools, and tactics for defensive rebounding as well. Further, these plans must be broader than the team concept of offensive and defensive rebounding. They must include the essential activities for individual rebounding skills as well.

In this article we will concern ourselves with a description of certain tactics, tools, movements, and knowledge which can be applied individually or collectively in various rebounding situations.

The mechanics of individual or group rebounding may be classified into four areas: 1) position, 2) stance, 3) approach, and 4) recovery. These are not different entities. They function in a very close relationship.

Position

Rebounding position should be considered as the precise position on the court from which players can most effectively compete for the missed shot. This position remains static only as long as the offensive player makes no move toward the basket or until the ball has hit the rim. Seldom will the offensive player remain in one position and not compete for the rebound. Defensive position will be determined by the location of the offensive players. Offensive position will be dictated by offensive movement and the position on the floor from which the shot was taken.

Establishing a sound rebounding position is extremely important in individual rebounding. It is the primary position from which the player initiates all his rebounding. The offensive rebounder has an advantage over the defensive rebounder because he knows approximately when the shot will be taken or when the next offensive move will be made. The defensive rebounder can only anticipate the action of the offense. Improper defensive position will give the offensive player further advantage.

A good rule of thumb for the defensive rebounder to remember with regard to positioning is: Always keep yourself between the offensive player and the basket when the shot is taken. From the offensive player's standpoint: Always position yourself in the general area in which you think the shot will rebound.

Rebounding position is the focal point from which the approach toward the missed shot is started. If this position is faulty, difficulty with retrieving the rebound will magnify.

Stance

The rebounding stance represents the posture of the body parts in a manner that allows the player to contest for missed shots. Principally, the parts of the body that are most important are the feet, elbows, fingers, eyes, arms, legs, and head. Other important considerations are body balance, spread of the feet, bend in the knees, and location of the proper center of gravity.

The correct stance is a must for individual rebounding. A player must have the ability to move in any direction quickly and easily. Position is the core of rebounding, but stance is the actual medium for rebounding. The stance should be assumed as soon as the player is in position to rebound the missed shot. Stance has only one important function, and that is to place the player's body in the most advantageous position for the performance of his rebounding duties.

The basic features of the rebounding stance are as follows:

1. **Feet.** The feet must be spaced apart. The ideal placement of the feet would be directly under the shoulders. Normally this affords a comfortable and natural spread. A vital factor in the positioning of the feet should be personal comfort. The feet should be placed parallel.

2. **Knees.** The game of basketball cannot be successfully played from a "straight up" position. A player must have flexibility in his knees. Never lock the knees. They should be slightly bent, with the hips dropped in a like manner. The body weight is on the balls of the feet. The legs must be flexed at all times to insure freedom of movement.

3. **Trunk.** The trunk of the body has a slight lean forward in the direction of the basket. This position affords the player the freedom to move forward, backward and sideways.

4. **Hips.** The hips will be lowered, bringing the body into a semi-crouched position. This position will allow for an explosive movement toward the missed shot.

5. **Elbows.** The elbows must be out and away from the body. This frees the arms to move liberally and quickly in any direction. When the elbows remain at the side of the body, an opponent can apply body pressure causing the arms to be "locked" to the side of the body.

6. **Hands.** The proper positioning of the hands and fingers is vitally important in rebounding. Keep the fingers spread apart. They should be pointed upward in the direction of the basket or rim. The hands must be fully open. They form a cup shape so that the ball can fall into the cradle of the hands. Keep the hands relaxed, flexible, and dry whenever possible.

7. **Eyes and head.** The eyes center their primary vision on the flight of the shot to determine in which direction the ball will rebound. While the primary vision is focused on the flight of the ball, the eyes attempt to cover a broader visual span. This gives the player awareness of position and player movements. The head is stationed up and straight. The exception to this would be when a defensive player is blocking out his opponent. In this case his number one responsibility is to block out his opponent first, then contest for the rebound.

8. **Body balance.** The weight of the body must be placed in such a manner that it allows for quick and easy movement in any direction. Place the weight of the body equally on both feet. Do not get caught leaning forward or backward so much that it results in overbalance.

9. **Toes.** As the player begins to make his last thrust motion from the floor toward the ball, he lifts the heels off the floor and lets the weight of the body shift down to the legs and toes. Then he pushes up off the toes as his body leaves the floor. Do not jump flat-footed. A greater degree of spring will be realized if the player leaves the flat surface from the toe position. The high jump principle is applicable here and not the broad jump method. The initial stance is valuable because it establishes the basic posture from which the approach toward the ball begins.

Approach

The approach toward the ball is aimed to provide the proper movement from the stance to the actual competition for the missed shot. This involves the performance of a variety of specific fundamental actions. Proper utilization of these skills will result in many successful recoveries of missed shots.

The player's initial motion from the floor must be a quick and aggressive move toward the ball. The jump must be perfectly timed so that he can rebound the ball at the highest point that he can reach. The player does not wait for the ball to come to him. He must go after the ball.

As he moves toward the ball his arms must be fully extended. The elbows should not be bent. Extend the arms above the head in the direction of the ball. Full arm extension allows the player extra inches in reach. Rebounding is a game of inches.

Upon making contact with the ball, grasp it tightly with two hands. It is more "crowd-pleasing" to rebound the ball with one hand, smacking it loudly into the other hand as it is brought down. But for maximum protection of the ball, it must be rebounded with two hands. If the player is banged or his arms are pulled, two hands on the ball reduces the chance of it being jarred loose. The basic rule to follow is "never rebound a ball with one hand if it can be retrieved with two."

The ball should be caught, not slapped. The only occasions when the ball may be slapped are to start a quick break, to tip the ball to an open teammate, or as a last resort to prevent the opponent in good rebounding position from securing the ball. Once the ball has been rebounded, bring it down in a quick jerking motion (like pulling an apple from a tree). As the ball is being brought down keep the elbows out, away from the body. Let the upper body bend slightly over the ball as an added protection.

As the player descends toward the floor, he should spread eagle. This position requires the body to be spread wide on a firm body base. The spread must be performed on the way down, not on the way up. Attempt to make your body as large as possible without losing balance. In the descent the knees should be bent, the hips relaxed, and the ball should never be lower than the chest.

For the time being we will deal only with the defensive rebounder's responsibility. Obviously, the offensive rebounder would attempt to score.

While descending with the ball, the player should turn his head to the side (normally toward the outside of the court) in an effort to look over the shoulder to spot the open teammate or outlet man to whom he will release the ball.

The rebounder must execute a half turn in the air as he makes his descent. The body should be turned to the outside of the court (the sideline nearest the rebounder). Constant practice will be required to master the technique of the half-body turn in the air. This will afford the rebounder the privilege of clearing the ball away fom the basket quickly and effectively.

To land without making this half turn would result in the rebounder's having his back stationed to his offensive end of the court. Vision of the entire playing area is extremely poor. He must make at least two additional movements in order to free the ball from the rebounding area. The rule to follow here is: "Never rebound the ball and land with your back to the offensive end of the floor."

Upon reaching the floor, maintain good body balance. Keep the feet spaced properly under the body. The body weight should be equally distributed on both feet. Position the body so that it can be moved quickly in any direction. The knees should be slightly bent and the hips relaxed. Be certain to keep the body between the ball and the opponent. This will give the ball meaningful protection.

Once the rebounder has spotted an outlet or open teammate, a sharp and direct pass is made to him. The two-hand, over-the-head and the baseball pass are the most commonly used passes in this situation. More detailed information can be found on the outlet pass in a later chapter.

The use of the dribble should be viewed as a last resort tactic. Most big men are not good dribblers. The rebounding area is a highly congested place. This makes dribbling even more difficult. When the rebound has been recovered and the rebounder cannot find an open man to clear the ball to, then he can resort to the dribble. It is important to save the dribble as a safety valve or last resort. As the rebounder brings the ball out from under the basket with a dribble, he should be alert to look for an open teammate. Apply this rule for dribbling after a rebound, "Never dribble the ball if you can pass it to an open teammate."

When under extreme pressure by the opponent in the area near the basket, the rebounder must remember to keep the ball well protected. In some situations it is often better to be forced into a "held ball" than to make a bad pass.

The use of each technique as a complement of the other will increase the value and hasten the performance of both the offensive and defensive rebounder.

OFFENSIVE REBOUNDING

Bailey Howell

I will discuss offensive rebounding, and I chose this as my topic because: 1) it is an important part of the game; and 2) it is the part of the game that is often overlooked.

You have so much to do as a coach to get ready to attack a zone, a man-to-man, a full-court press, to execute a full-court press, etc. Sometimes offensive rebounding is overlooked.

If you emphasize offensive rebounding with your team, it will give your team another aspect of the game which the other clubs will have to respect. It will be more difficult for other teams to get ready for you. You will be a better team. Your players will be better players. I know that as a player, I worked really hard on the boards. It was the part of the game that allowed me to excel. I was never a great jumper, I just made an effort to get to the offensive boards. First, how do you teach offensive rebounding? You teach it by emphasizing it like anything else. Some of you may be an excellent defensive coach or offensive coach. Emphasize whatever it is you are good at teaching.

I know a lot of coaches have an emphasis of the day. For example, an emphasis may be taking the charge. Each time a player draws a charging foul, the coach stops practice and praises that individual. Your emphasis of the day could be offensive rebounding. It wouldn't have to be handled that way. It could be that when you're working on your offense and carry it through to the rebound, you could stop the play and praise the offensive rebounder.

If one of your players picks up a foul going to the offensive board, he should be praised for making the effort. I played pro ball for a number of years, and Bill Russell was coach when I was with the Celtics. One night there was a big snowstorm in Boston and some of our team had trouble getting to the game. The opponents were already in town and had no problem getting to the game. We finally arrived, except for Bill Russell who couldn't make it because of traffic. Red Auerbach took the team that night and I had never played under him, but because of his reputation as a coach, I wanted to play really well for Red. It was just a natural thing. We started the game and I had missed my first five or six shots and at a time-out I was moaning about not being able to hit my shots. Red told me, "Let me worry about missed shots, you just keep shooting."

It is unreal how that helped me not to worry about a bad night but to just go out and shoot the ball. Sure enough, the shots started going and before the night was over I had contributed quite a bit to the club. You will have your own way of doing things and you can handle that the way you like. Spend some time on offensive rebounding and emphasize it.

I depended on Coach Babe McCarthy in college to get me ready for games. You must spend some time on emphasizing self-motivation because the coach can't get a player ready to play. There are some people that just can't be motivated.

When I got to pro ball we played 82 games. There was no way for the coach to prepare a player to play 82 games. That had to come from within the individual. Because it was my responsibility, as a rookie, I was inconsistent and that was because I was doing a poor job of motivating myself.

Think of a catchy phrase that will help emphasize your point. If your big man is standing around and watching, you could say, "Don't be a spectator." This will emphasize to him that you want him to go to the board.

Let me tell you why I think offensive rebounding is important.

1. It is demoralizing to the other team.

2. It helps to stop the opponents' fast break. This is probably the most effective way you have to stop the fast break. Of course you can play the outlet pass, but the most effective way to stop the break is to keep pounding the boards. Even if the opponents rebound, they have had to work so hard that they have a tough time making a quick outlet pass. If they can't rebound it, they should tip the ball and keep it alive on the board. If they have to, tell them to knock the ball out of bounds, because that at least will stop the opponents' fast break.

3. It helps get opponents in foul trouble. If you go to the board in the wrong manner, you can get yourself into foul trouble. If you get the ball on the offensive board, many times they foul you on the return.

4. It promotes the three-point play. A power move on the rebound can get the three-point play.

5. It is the best way that your team has for getting more shots than the other team. This, to me, is the most important reason for emphasizing offensive rebounds. You can get the same on turnovers, but usually there isn't that much difference in turnovers. If you out-rebound the other team, you can be shooting lousy and still even the game. Wouldn't you like to know that you were going to get 25 or 30 more shots than your opponent?

In offensive or defensive rebounding, I strongly feel that position is the most important thing by far. Some of you may disagree. You see some of these guys who can jump and almost touch the top of the board, but still position is the most important factor. It is more important than jumping ability, and I think it is more important than height. Therefore, to be a good offensive rebounding individual or team, you must give the effort to get the position on the rebound.

Your forwards and post men need to be told that they will go to the board on every shot. In the first part of the game you want them to go to the board. If you are in the last three minutes, you want them to go to the boards. On every occasion you want them to go to the boards. On certain set plays you might have your big man prevent the fast break, but unless he is assigned to that specific job, he should go to the board on every shot. That is all it takes.

When I played professionally, I was an adequate jumper. I worked a great deal on my timing and my ability to be a quick jumper.

Tips for better offensive rebounding:

1. Rebounders should and can read where the ball is coming off of the board. Play percentages on the shots.

2. Coach your big men to stay close enough to the board that they have time to get there to rebound.

3. The best way to get to the board is through picks.

4. The rebounder should go to the board with his hands up.

5. Try to get your inside shoulder past the opponent.

6. When rebounding, keep the ball high.

7. Go to the board on every shot.

8. Try to get in on all of the fast breaks. Basketball is a sport that you can work on by yourself and make yourself a better player.

I worked really hard to jump quick, with power, to be able to stay on the boards several times in a row. There were a number of drills I used. They include:

1. Jumping as high as possible, reaching 95 to 98 percent of your jumping ability each time you jump. This helped me to jump over and over.

2. Working on tipping with alternating hands and then with both hands for 10 to 20 times (rapid jumping).

3. A friend can join you on the board and you can tip the ball across the goal to your buddy.

4. Do the same drill, but don't use the board.

5. Get three guys in a drill with each player tipping the ball and moving in a circular motion. (Keep the ball on the same side.)

6. The same drill can be done without using the board.

7. A drill I really like is the aggressive rebound drill. The coach shoots the ball on the board with three rebounders. The player who rebounds is now the offensive player and tries to score. The other two become defensive players and try to keep him from scoring.

Offensive rebounding is important. If you are to have a team that can be effective, you must emphasize the importance of it to the players.

DEFENSIVE REBOUNDING
Jim Brandenburg

Very little is mentioned about the skill of rebounding, and many coaches are convinced there's not a lot you can do with your players to make them better rebounders. However, I believe there are things you can teach which will help your players become better rebounders and, thus, help win a few more ball games for you.

The first thing to remember is that the rebound does not go to the tallest player nor does it go to the highest jumper. The rebound goes to the quickest jumper, the one who can get to the ball most quickly as it comes off the rim.

The second point to remember is that all good rebounders are two-footed jumpers. I have never seen a good rebounder who does not jump with both legs. Once I had a high jump track star on my team. He could jump 7'4" but he wasn't an effective rebounder because he wasn't going up in a strong manner.

The third thing to talk about in a great rebounder is the amount of area he can cover. If a player can rebound two players removed, then you've got a winner.

Rebounding requires strength, footwork and balance. These things are usually inherent in a player, but you can help. Fear is an important ingredient here. Everyone has a fear of something, and after years of observing basketball players, it is my opinion that a great many of them subconsciously, if not consciously, fear contact. So often I see a player who looks like he's trying to get the ball but he's conning himself and you because much as it looks like he's trying, he never gets the ball. And getting the ball is the desired end result.

The hands are key. Think about how many times you see the player go up with one hand to get the ball. What is the other hand doing? Protecting him. Watch for the player who goes up with two hands, exposing his body. That's a guy with courage, and probably a great rebounder.

I try to teach players to go up with both legs and come down on both feet. I want them to extend both arms and be quick to the basket. Having said that, I've told you all I know about rebounding.

What all this means to you as a coach is it isn't what you teach but what you emphasize. We emphasize rebounding. More than that, we demand that our players be good rebounders. And there are a lot of psychological things you can do to emphasize this to your players. The best one I've found is to sit them down.

I'd like to start here by giving you some of the terminology we use. A lot of people call it a block-out; we call it a cut-out because of our philosophy. We'll step to an offensive player, have brief contact, and go for the ball. If you have a player who blocks out the offensive man and holds him there for a period of time and then reacts to the ball, you have a negative teaching concept. Make sure your players locate the ball, and after you've made contact and have the area walled out, go after that ball. Emphasize getting the ball and not making contact with the offensive player.

Teaching a youngster when to release and when to go after the basketball is one of the most critical teaching problems we have. In addition, we must teach our players to read the rebound. In other words, the length of the rebound from the basket is related to the length of the shot. If we are at 21 feet and we've got some guy shooting the ball at 23 feet, we can expect the rebound to be a long one. Make certain your players think about the fact that a longer shot means a longer rebound and adjust their position accordingly.

We need to make players think about angles as well. If the ball is shot from a certain angle, then it is probably going to come off at the same angle on the other side. If the ball is shot in the deep corner, there will be much less angle and it can usually only come off long or short. The entire premium is reading the shot, and the more effectively a player does that, the better rebounder he is likely to be.

When we have a shooting drill, and wherever we have a shooter, we make sure our rebounder gets into the optimum area for the missed shot. We want him with his feet on the ground, arms up, and fingers spread apart in anticipation of the ball coming to him. In our drill wherever the shot is taken, we like to have the rebounder continually work on getting into the right position for a rebound. We also insist that the retriever not let the ball hit the floor, so we have players working on their shooting. At the same time, we've got our rebounder working at reading the ball off the rim.

Another area we need to talk about involves the type of defense you are playing and the effectiveness of your fast break. These two things will have a great effect on your rebounding.

In my early years at Wyoming we weren't a very good team, so we used a lot of zone defenses. Even now we're probably about 65 percent zone and 35 percent man-to-man, and the one important thing that philosophy has allowed us to do is to keep our big rebounders around the basket. It also helps to organize our two guards so we can get out on the fast break a little more quickly than some teams who use man-to-man defenses. We have a very good fast break and that makes the other team respect you in terms of offensive rebounding. We don't get a lot of people trying to crash the offensive boards on us.

I want to digress for a moment and talk about the two keys – strength and balance. You must have these two ingredients to rebound well. Our weight training program has helped us a great deal. We've been involved in an aggressive weight program for the past four years and it has really helped. We don't attract some of the great athletes that some of the other schools have, but our guys are big, strong, and aggressive.

We actually continue our weight program right through our regular season. Some coaches will say they don't want their players lifting weights during the season because it affects their shooting. I disagree. Our team has shot around 53 percent the last two years, and in my four years at Wyoming we've never been under 50 percent. If you are doing your stretching and flexibility exercises, the weight training will not affect shooting.

What happens is the weight training makes you play stronger at the very height of your jump. It will make you quicker and give you more body strength which allows you to rest and maintain balance. Basketball is a game of balance, whether it is rebounding or pressure defense. If you can make your opponent play on one leg and off-balance, you'll beat him.

Most of our weight training is free weights; the reason is to develop balance. An apparatus does not help poor balance.

We also use a number of other drills to achieve improvement in our players' footwork. We believe in jumping rope. We also bring in a football dummy and have our players jump back and forth over it, being careful to jump with two feet, land on two feet, and maintain balance. We'll also jump to squares. We also use the three-man weave (see Figure 8.1).

Number 1 throws the ball on the board and interchanges with Number 3. Number 2 catches Number 1's throw, then throws it back to Number 3 and interchanges with Number 1. Number 3 catches Number 2's throws, returns it to Number 1, and interchanges with Number 2.

We also have a drill called a Superman drill (see Figure 8.2).

Number 5 throws the ball high onto the board, steps across the lane, and rebounds the ball. He pitches it high on the board again, jumps back across the lane, and rebounds it again. He goes back and forth.

Another drill we use is rim touches. For some teams it may be known as net touches or backboard touches. We stress using two hands and landing on two feet. In our Ring-Around-the-Rosey drill (Figure 8.3) the following things happen:

1. The defensive man blocks out.

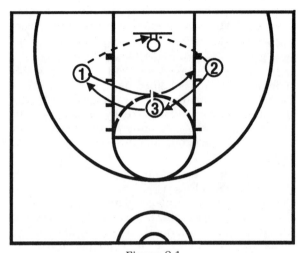

Figure 8.1

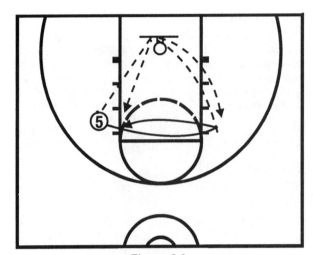

Figure 8.2

2. The offensive man works his way around the defensive man and then becomes the block-out man.

3. We repeat this over and over.

Finally, our on-the-board drill (see Figure 8.4).

1. Each player throws the ball high on the board and jumps for the rebound.

2. After catching the ball the player makes a quarter turn and throws it out.

Two arms, two legs, quickness. That's what each drill is designed to do because that's what rebounding is all about.

THE REBOUND GAME

Bill Leatherman

The rebound game is, without a doubt, the finest drill I have ever seen for teaching offensive and defensive rebounding. It is a drill that is so tough and competitive that you will find it necessary to tone down your team's aggressiveness.

At one time or another every coach has asked himself, "What can I do to improve our rebounding?" There just doesn't seem to be as many rebounding drills to choose from compared to defensive, offensive, fast break drills and others. I have used this drill in every one of my 19 seasons as a coach. For 13 years as a high school coach and six at James Madison University, I can almost guarantee that it is the only rebounding drill you need to make your team "better off the glass."

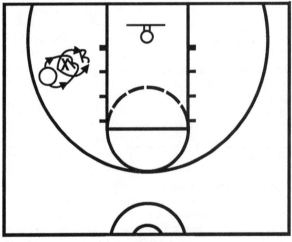

Figure 8.3

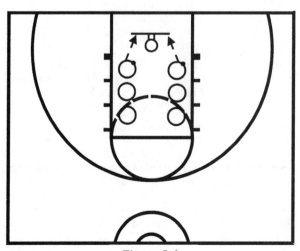

Figure 8.4

Rules for the Three-on-Three Rebound Game

Divide your squad into four teams of three players, consisting of a big man, a forward, and a guard. Number your teams 1, 2, 3, and 4. (If you have more than 12 members on your team, just add them equally to the four teams and they can rotate in after each shot attempt.)

Using your managers as perimeter shooters, pass the ball back and forth several times before shooting to ensure correct weak-side and ball-side defensive positioning (see Figure 8.5). Offensive rebounders should be active and in constant motion.

Team 1 should wear one color jersey, and Team 2 wears an opposite color. Team 3 will wear the same color as Team 1, and Team 4 will wear the same color as Team 2. Rotation always remains the same; therefore, there will be no jersey conflict.

Team 1 (defensive rebounders) is "under" first. They stay in that position for as long as they can maintain control of the rebound, or are fouled by Team 2.

Team 1 is credited with one point for each rebound that is cleared inbounds. The points are kept by a coach (see Figure 8.6). The emphasis is on control of the ball in game situations. Team 1 stays until they do not control the rebound.

There are two ways Team 2 (the offensive team) can score; if it gets an offensive rebound it receives one point; if it scores off the offensive rebound or gets fouled on a controlled shot, it receives two points. We try to discourage Team 2 (the offensive team) from just slapping the ball out of bounds, but that can be used as a last resort to illustrate how Team 1 failed to box out properly. When Team 1 fails to control the rebound, it moves to the back of the line and Team 2 becomes the defensive rebounding team, with Team 3 moving to offense. (Team 1 is always boxing out Team 2, Team 2 is always boxing out Team 3, Team 3 is always boxing out Team 4, and Team 4 is always boxing out Team 1.)

We go through three complete rounds each day, usually requiring about 10 minutes of practice time. The winning team gets a three-minute break, while the three remaining teams run sprints.

Points of Emphasis:

1. Box your man outside the lane.

2. Coaches cannot allow the offensive team to push the defensive team. This will result in a foul and the defensive team is credited with a point just as if it had cleared the rebound. The defensive team continues to be "under."

3. Managers should pass fake before shooting. This will eliminate standing around.

4. Encourage players to dive for loose balls, etc., and give credit for retrieves.

5. Remember, the defensive team should always have position advantage. The offensive team should try to take that advantage from the defensive team with constant offensive movement.

I know this drill will greatly improve all facets of your team's rebounding, offensively as well as defensively. The competition is fierce and the improved skills are obvious.

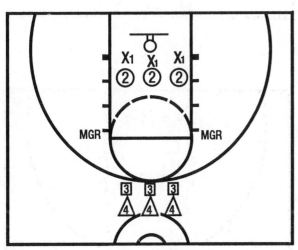

Figure 8.5

REBOUND GAME CHART

Date ☞									
Team 1									
Team 2									
Team 3									
Team 4									

Rules: 1. Circle all offensive rebounds, whether scored as one point or two.
2. Stay in defensive position as long as you maintain ball control.
3. Team with most total points after three rounds is the winner.

Figure 8.6

Chapter 9 **B**ALLHANDLING

PASSING – CATCHING

Branch McCracken

Players on a good passing team will be successful in getting open for their good shots. They will have the ability to get the ball to the open man at the right time and in a position from which he can get his shot off as quickly as possible. I have two sayings:

"Look where you are passing."
"Pass where you are looking."

Be clever, but never fancy. Fancy passing will backfire more often than it connects. You will fool your own teammate more often than you will the opposition. The straightaway pass with a little cleverness will get the job done.

I had a player a few years ago who could pass behind his back very accurately. I thought I would let him use it for show. During the first game of the season he threw several passes of this type. The crowd gave him a big hand. The next game the other four boys tried to get into the act, and the ball was up in the crowd more than it was on the court. The ball is too hard to get, and it is too far from one end of the floor to the other to throw the ball away without getting a good shot.

General Advice on Passing

1. Take pride in your ballhandling.

2. Be clever, but never fancy.

3. Be relaxed; don't fight the ball.

4. Have good body balance.

5. Learn to pass with either hand.

6. Learn to receive and pass in the same motion.

7. Fake one type of pass and use another.

8. Maneuver as close to the defensive man as possible when throwing a pass by him.

9. Pass only to a receiver moving to meet the ball unless he is cutting away for a lead pass to the basket, then give him a suitable lead. Don't make him reach back or down.

10. Keep the ball moving with sharp, accurate passes.

Catching Technique

The type of catching employed will depend upon the location of the ball, the position of the defensive man, and the offensive maneuver which is to follow. In teaching the techniques of catching, the coach should explain and demonstrate the method of performance. Then after letting the players try it themselves, he should correct and advise them as they progress. It will be necessary to observe closely each player's technique throughout the season.

Position of the Hands, Fingers and Eyes

1. The hands are carried waist high when moving into position to receive a pass. The arms are relaxed and the elbows are free from the body. The hands are extended to meet the ball. As the ball is about to be received, there should be a slight natural receding of the arms and hands to relieve any impact that causes fumbling.

2. The fingers should be well spread, not enough to cause strain, but in a comfortable position. The ball is caught with the first two joints of the fingers and the thumb. Never palm the ball. Handle it with the fingers and thumb.

3. A high pass is caught with thumbs pointing toward each other.

4. A low pass is caught with the little fingers pointing together.

5. In all catches, if not passing quickly from the receiving position, bring the ball in position for protection and also in position to execute any number of passes.

6. On all catches, the hands should be on the sides and to the rear of the ball.

7. The pass receiver's eyes must be on the ball until it is in his hands. He must never try to do anything with the ball until he gets hold of it securely.

Getting into Position to Receive the Pass

1. Semi-crouch, bending at the knees, employing a stance from which the pass receiver can move quickly in any direction.

2. Take a step toward the ball.

3. Catch the ball with one foot forward. From this stance the pass receiver is in position to start quicker. Also, he is in good shooting position.

4. Always be moving toward the passer, except when cutting away to get a lead pass for a shot.

5. Be relaxed. Never fight the ball.

THE LITTLE THINGS

Robert J. Nichols

This article will emphasize the little things in our offense. We think the little things are very important. As a matter of fact, a good offense consists of doing the following three things well: 1) the little things, 2) the fundamentals, 3) effort, especially the second and third effort.

Passing a basketball is, of course, one fundamental. Passing may be a lost art, for many players do not pass properly. We have four two-minute passing drills. One of these two-minute passing drills is used each day during practice. We alternate drills from day-to-day.

I won't describe our passing drills, as you probably have your own which could be as good, if not better, than ours.

Little Things We Emphasize in Our Passing Drills, in Practice and in Games

1. Use two hands on the ball for each pass – you can pull a string on the pass with two hands on the ball.

2. Do not throw the pass unless you can see the man you are passing to.

3. Make the next pass the safest pass. This is *important*! We are not interested in sensational passes. We discourage them in practice and games. Avoid them!

4. Pass away from the defensive man.

5. Aim for the target hand or aim the pass for the outside shoulder, shoulder height.

6. The passer knows when you are open; get the ball to him when open.

7. Any doubt about throwing the pass – *forget it*.

8. See the man you are passing to; the picture is always changing.

The passer is to blame for 90 percent of all bad passes. The other 10 percent belongs with the receiver. Usually the receiver should continue to come to the ball.

Concerns For The Receiver

1. Keep coming to meet the ball. Drill on this!

2. Square up and face the basket immediately upon receiving the ball. We drill on this!

3. When you square up with the ball, think three things, pass-shot-drive.

4. Look inside with a two-second hold on the ball. This helps to see things develop inside.

Almost all of these points have been broken down into drills.

Other Important Points

1. Never pass and then stand still. Move in some manner or direction.

2. Don't come to the ball unless you get a screen. Exceptions:
   a. Fill to keep 12- to 15-foot spacing on court.
   b. Help break pressure.
   c. Come if you are open.

3. Know where the ball is at all times. This is vitally important in our offense. Read the defense. Very often you are open, but because you do not know where the ball is, you are unaware you are free. You can be setting a screen and really you are the open man. Know where the ball is at all times.

4. If you are open, ask for ball and come to it. If the receiver of the pass has squared up (faced the basket) and put a two-second hold on the ball, he will see that you are free. Pass him the ball.

Screening

Screening is the most important, but it's usually not done. Be sure to screen the defensive man. Never run by one single defensive player. Points to teach the screener:

1. Run at a normal gait.

2. Anticipate the angle at which you will meet the defensive player.

3. Make yourself firm and wide in normal stance – shoulder width.

4. On contact, do not move. Fall down if they try to go through you.

5. If they switch, roll back to the ball in the open area. Remember: Screen the defensive player, never run by him.

I began by referring to the little things. We emphasize these little things and we invent drills for them. When we find things are going badly during the season, it is usually time to review some small area of the game of basketball. Every play is important. You will never know what one little play will lead to.

THE PASSING GAME

Ralph Miller

Passing is our chief weapon on offensive attacks. A player's first responsibility is to create a situation so he can pass to a teammate for a shot. This exudes a team feeling. Seventy-five percent of our baskets last year came from assists.

Passing and catching head the list of offensive skill requirements. You can teach both with the same drills. I have found that more errors are caused by catching than passing.

Two learning laws that we apply to our practices and drills are:

1. Any physical act has to be learned the hard way – by doing.

2. Repetition, over and over again.

Skills are only part of the whole. You have to apply them to competition. A coach is responsible to condition skill reaction in competition. The reaction is actually more important than the skill. You as a coach are a teacher and should know the subject material and know how to best teach the material.

While I was coaching in high school, I began to ask myself several questions. Why use pressure defenses only part of the time? (At that time, teams dropped back after missed baskets.) Why not pressure all the time on defense? We came up with the idea of instant conversion, either way, as the ball changes hands. We wanted all of our offensive patterns to start with the break. I didn't create anything new. I just looked into the past and used ideas. I took these ideas with me to college in 1951 and haven't changed.

Our system is based on the pass and cut. In my opinion, the pass and cut are the two most difficult things to defense in basketball. There are three ways to create offensive openings: 1) one-on-one dribbling, 2) screens, and 3) pass and cut. Even though we feel pass and cut is the most important, we want to put all three together.

In our system the player must be able to shoot, pass, or drive the moment the ball touches his hand. We have our players use the jump stop. The key result is the time it takes to get the shot off. A player should be able to shoot in one second as soon as it hits his hands. The secret of successful shooting is to get ready as the ball is being passed to you. Once the man has the ball, we authorize only two fakes – the shot and the pass. We want to teach three areas: 1) skills, 2) competitive reactions, and 3) related knowledge (When? Where? How?). We feel the following six drills do these three things.

Drill 1: Two-Lane Shooting (Figure 9.1)

Use two balls.
A 45-degree angle running at full speed.
Work from the left side also.
Must make approximately 30 layups in a row before the team moves on to another drill.

Drill 2: Split the Post (Figure 9.2)

Number 1 passes the ball to Number 2 and follows the ball. Number 2 dribbles the ball to the Number 1 position and then passes the ball back to the man who originally passed the ball to Number 2 in the Number 2 position. Number 1 passes to Number 3 in the free-throw circle and Numbers 1 and 2 then split off the post.

When the two men out front exchange lines (positions), they use jump stops and reverse pivots to face each other again. In this drill we practice three types of shots – layups, short hooks and short 17-foot jump shots. Post men slide to the basketball side, receive the pass, and work on their shots.

Drill 3: Breaking (Figure 9.3)

The ball never touches the floor and players go at full speed. Down and back is one trip. Go until the group has 30 or so error-free trips.

Drill 4: Wide Three-Man Weave (Figure 9.4)

Down and back, run it wide, again, require players to make a certain number in a row before you move on to another drill. Two things are accomplished by requiring players to make a certain number in a row – team concept and it lets the team know who's the boss.

Drill 5: Three-on-Three Full-Court (Figure 9.5)

Drills 5 and 6 are the bread and butter drills. Players cannot pass the ball over the midcourt, they must dribble the ball.

Players must switch on all good screens. If the offense gets the rebound, the same players remain on defense. If the offense misses the shot, the defense tries to fast break while the "new" defensive players pick up the man who was guarding them.

Drill 6: Full-Court Four-on-Four (Figure 9.6)

Always starts at half court. Go up and down the court three or four times, then change all eight players.

These six drills teach the skills that are necessary to play the game.

I would like to make a few comments about defense. The palms should be up to be in a ready defensive position. Why? 1) it assists with body equilibrium, 2) it's more natural for your body, 3) fewer fouls are called by the officials.

The defensive man must learn to cover the ball, be a helper, and learn to screen the boards.

Our two general rules regarding pressure defense are:

1. Do not deny wing passes. Be ready to steal if the passer makes a mistake, but don't overcommit or try to steal. We don't want to let the other team pass when and where they want to pass.

2. Perimeter rule. Guard-to-wing passes are no problem. As soon as a pass breaks the perimeter (goes inside), everyone runs in a straight line to the basket and gets in front of the ball. We always want pressure on the ball. We want to pressure the other team both offensively and defensively.

TEACHING PRESSURE PASSING

Vinnie Mili

How many times at the end of a close game have we said to ourselves, "If only we hadn't thrown the ball away, the outcome might have been different?"

Teaching the proper fundamentals of passing with players executing those skills is a key factor to becoming a fundamentally sound basketball team. But an aspect that must be dealt with in terms of our teaching breakdown is that passes made in an actual basketball game are made against pressure by the defense. How many times in a game can you throw a pass without a defensive man on you? Very seldom or never.

The ability to pass the ball determines the flow of the game and the execution, regardless of the offensive system employed. Since passing is the foundation for scoring, we as coaches must not underestimate its importance.

Because of the overwhelming pressure defenses now employed, players must learn and be conditioned how to react and pass versus aggressive pressure. Once players become confident in these types of situations, they will respond positively. The passer must maintain his poise and realize it is actually very difficult for the defensive man to take the ball away from him as long as he is under control.

Teaching players not to pick up their dribble until they know they have a pass keeps the ball alive versus pressure and gives the dribbler an opportunity to create better passing angles. The importance of ball fakes and pivoting must not be underestimated, especially if the passer has used his dribble. Showing the defense the ball by faking freezes them and often opens passing lanes to possible receivers. We constantly stress for our players to "be active with the ball," under control, always looking for a near outlet.

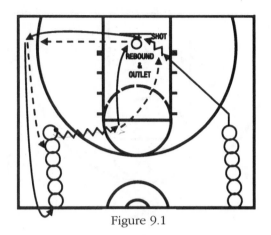

Figure 9.1

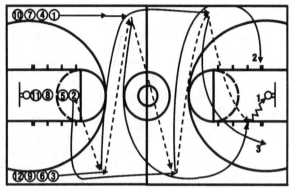

Figure 9.4

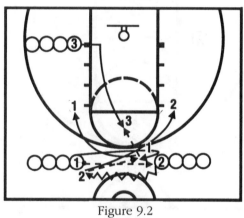

Figure 9.2

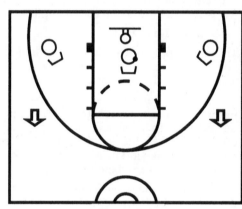

Figure 9.5

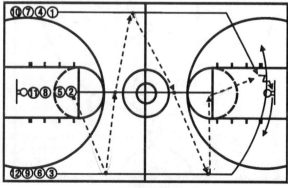

Figure 9.3

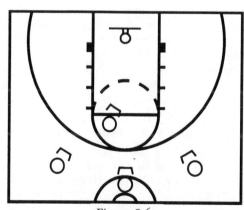

Figure 9.6

Although it isn't a good habit to hold onto the ball too long, we must realize that this situation can occur in a game. The passer must be ready to make the quick, accurate pass right off the dribble or after receiving a pass from a teammate. The ball must be moved quickly with a purpose. As Coach John Wooden says, "Be quick, but don't hurry!"

In the case in which the defensive man is applying pressure after the offensive player has used his dribble, the use of pivoting is vital. The passer is to drop slightly lower, pivot, and step at, around, over, or through, attacking the defense, protecting the ball, keeping his head and eyes up at all times. By pivoting and being active with the ball, he should be able to relieve the pressure and make the pass.

Many times a bad or errant pass is the simple case in which the passer tries to make the difficult or crowd-pleasing pass. Emphasize to the passer to "make the easy pass."

Teaching and repeating these realistic game situations in practice sessions and drills can only have the carry-over effect into the game, and that is obviously what we as coaches are trying to accomplish.

Pass to the Box Drill

This is a multipurpose drill incorporating passing versus pressure, defending the discontinued dribble, and a strong offensive power move (see Figure 9.7).

The dribbler, Number 1, speed dribbles to the free-throw area where his penetration is stopped by the defender X. The defender must "belly up" to the offensive player and employ the "windmill" with his arms to make it difficult for his opponent to see or pass, without reaching in.

Number 1, on the other hand, is to "be active with the ball" and pivot, attempting to pass. When the coach feels both have done an adequate job, he yells "pass," and Number 1 passes to any one of the two post players, Number 2 or 3, who are shaping up on the blocks. The post player who doesn't receive the ball is automatically on defense and must stop his opponent from scoring. No more than one dribble is allowed by a post player. The rotation of the players will be clockwise.

Adding the two defenders at the free-throw line now makes the passer react to a double team (Figure 9.8). The two defenders are to double team the dribbler as he attempts to make the pass.

Points of Emphasis. Offensively: pivoting, being active with the ball, inside power move. Defensively: playing the discontinued dribble, bellying up, windmill the ball.

Three-on-Three Pressure Passing Drill

Number 1 will again penetrate to the free throw area where he is met with an aggressive double team by X1 and X2 (see Figure 9.9). Number 1 is to attack the double team and pass to either post player Number 2 or Number 3, who are defended only by X3.

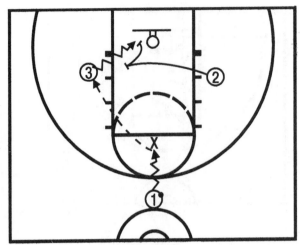

Figure 9.7

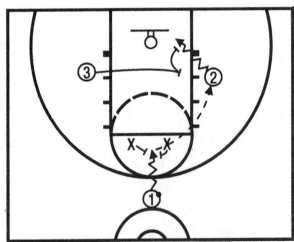

Figure 9.8

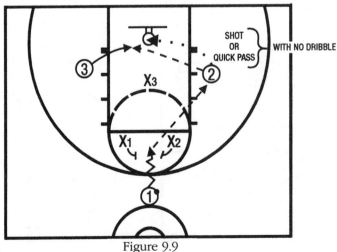

Figure 9.9

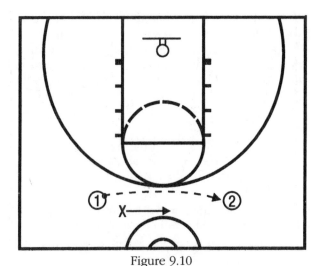

Figure 9.10

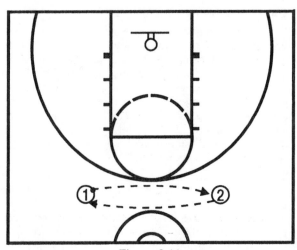

Figure 9.11

Once a post player receives the pass, he is to attack the basket and the defender, looking to score immediately or pass for a quick score versus the lone defender (X3). No dribbling is allowed by the post players.

Two-on-One Drill

The old passing drill where one defender is in the middle while the two offensive players must pivot, fake, and pass versus the aggressive defender (Figure 9.10).

The passer cannot throw the ball above the defender's head. The man in the middle must play closer to the passer than the receiver. He cannot defend the middle.

On a deflection, bad pass, interception, and so on, the violator is now in the middle on defense. The passer is to attack the defender by pivoting and ball fakes.

Bad Pass Drill

Since not every pass made will be perfect, the receiver must be ready to catch any pass that might be off the mark (see Figure 9.11). The players pair up about eight feet apart and for two minutes and throw bad passes to each other; low at their feet, high and away, at their head, away from the hands. (A manager or coach can throw the bad passes so as not to let the players form bad habits.)

Receivers are to catch the ball with their eyes and feet first, then their hands. See the ball into your hands and make your feet take you where your hands have to go.

Teaching and emphasizing these concepts in practice can pay tremendous dividends when game time arrives. It is not what we coach, it is what we emphasize.

BALLHANDLING

C.M. Newton

Ballhandling and Motivation

My topic is ballhandling drills. I had the unique opportunity to be able to take a program at Alabama and build it to suit me. As you know, in a large state university you are expected to make your team into a state representative. We had a successful season this past year and of the 16 players on the squad, 12 were from Alabama. We were very proud of that fact. The reason that I mention this is because I believe we have a responsibility to motivate the young players throughout our state, so that someday we might have those players interested in us. We have a responsibility as coaches to motivate young players. I am talking about elementary and junior high age kids. We as basketball coaches must help future basketball players. There must be some way for college coaches to encourage young kids to learn good ballhandling skills.

When my son was about 7, he was getting "turned on" to basketball. We decided to see what could be done. We started with 22 youngsters and used a drill team approach to basketball. It takes a great deal of desire and patience to develop proper skills.

I am totally opposed to the Little League approach to basketball. There are a lot of kids who get "turned off" to basketball at an early age because of failure in a Little League program. Their size and skill and coordination are different, and it is harmful to some kids to play in competition that early. They must be able to feel success, so we decided to begin to work with kids and try to give them confidence through success in basketball. You can give up on kids too soon. I think ballhandling is the easiest skill of all to learn and shooting is the most difficult.

It's important to motivate your players because the only way they will learn is through motivation. Players of all ages, even at the college level, must be motivated to work on their own. A number of things can be done to motivate youngsters:

1. Players must have a situation in which the opportunities to succeed are increased and the opportunities to fail are minimized.

2. The characteristics of size, quickness, and agility should be minimized.

3. The size of the equipment should fit the players' level of maturity. Volleyballs could be used for smaller players.

4. Create the homework basketball concept in the youngsters. Allow them to do things at home that allow them to succeed.

We told the youngsters they must have three things to master these skills.

1. Fingertip control. They must have a feel for the ball and develop a touch to allow them to handle the ball properly. I don't care whether they are dribbling, passing, or shooting; they must control the ball on their fingertips.

2. Quickness of the hands. They must be able to handle the ball quickly.

3. Ability to use both hands with confidence. They must believe they can do exactly what they want to do with the ball.

I held 30-minute sessions and showed the kids the skill I wanted them to learn. We first asked the kids to assume a basketball position and then began with the basic right- and left-handed dribble. We had them go to an alternate hand dribble. We told them those were the only three ways they were allowed to dribble the ball.

There were other drills that went along with teaching the use of the right and left hands more skillfully. The other dribble drills are:

1. Punching bag: An alternate dribble of the ball between the legs, dribbling with the alternate method except the hands are used in back and in front of the legs.

2. Lying down: Players dribble lying down on their back and side and then they continue the dribble as they get up and down.

3. Figure 8: This drill is just like the standing Figure 8 except the ball is dribbled. The ball goes in and out of the legs. (Do this on one knee.)

Once the kids learned the dribble, we told them to do it with quickness and with their heads up.

There was a series of dribbling and ballhandling drills that we worked on standing still first and then on the move. Our players at Alabama do a similar series of drills to learn good ballhandling technique.

The ballhandling drills which do not include dribbling are:

1. Pretzel: This is when the ball is put between the legs. The hands are alternated in back and front, and the ball is dropped and caught between the legs.

2. Seesaw: Pounding the ball from one hand to another in an arch in front of the body.

3. Ricochet: Bouncing the ball between the legs and catching it in back.

4. Catch ball behind the back: The ball is passed into the air and caught waist high, behind the back.

Our Offensive System

In order to talk about our offensive system, we must first talk about our philosophy. In order to decide what kind of offensive system to use, I have to evaluate my personnel and see if they fit the system I want to use. It is every bit as important to evaluate players' weaknesses as well as their strengths. In the off-season, we sit down and evaluate our players' strengths and weaknesses and try to motivate them to improve on their weaknesses and make their strengths even bigger assets.

The second part of this exchange of philosophy is the breakdown of the fundamentals that have to be mastered. The first is ballhandling, which I have already discussed. To me, ballhandling involves passing and catching the basketball. Ballhandling is the most important thing in an offensive system. Shooting, of course, is important but a shot comes as a direct result of ballhandling. If you can master handling the ball well, then you can become a pretty good offensive player.

One ballhandling skill that is very important and yet overlooked is catching the basketball. We spend a great deal of time learning to catch the ball. As we evaluated our turnovers in our game films, we found that most of our turnovers came about because of a poor catch rather than a poor pass. We try to tell our players that concentration is important. On the fast break many times a player will take his eyes off the ball for a split second and that causes a turnover and points. We tell our players that at the same time we work on passing, we must work on catching the ball as well. There are two things that are important in catching the ball:

1. Look the ball into the hands.

2. Catch the ball by feel.

This is one of the reasons we do the catch-behind-the-back drill. The players must catch the ball by feel in these drills, and it makes them stronger ballhandlers. It is important particularly in post play. I mention this skill because I think it is overlooked.

Naturally, to be effective on offense you must be able to shoot. We insist our players use the bank shot. On layups we want them to shoot the layup shot properly. Our post men must develop the power layup or power play.

Rebounding is extremely important in offensive basketball. We teach rebounding to all our players – centers, forwards, and guards. In our estimation, good offensive play demands good ballhandlers first.

Second, basketball is a team game and our team is only as good as its players. Therefore, we must insist on a team concept. How do we approach this idea of team play?

1. We stress that the assist is more important than the basket. We give great praise to the assist. I don't care how simple the pass, we always praise the assist to reinforce that part of the game.

2. We always criticize failure to get the ball to the open man. We don't stop practice a lot, but we do in this case and emphasize to that young man that he needed to get the ball to the open man.

3. The single most difficult thing to get a player to do is put the team above himself.

The third basic belief is the progression in building an offense. It goes as follows:

1. Individual play: One-on-one basketball. We believe any offense ultimately breaks down into a one-on-one game. No matter what kind of offense you run, your players must be able to play one-on-one. We like every player on our team to be able to play in the five post areas of the court. These five areas are low post (both sides) of the lane, mid-post (both sides) and the high post (foul line). This is something you have to teach. It is a high percentage area. The foul situation and the control of the foul situation is a critical part of the game. The team that can force the opponent into the bonus situation early in the game really has the upper hand.

Our thinking is that you don't get people to foul you playing on the perimeter. You get people to foul you playing inside. We have an automatic rule that any time any of our players gets his player with their third foul, he takes his man to the post area. We feel we have to build something into the offense to get him there. This, we think, is critical. We want to challenge him right then. If they substitute for him, that is fine too, because not many players have more than five, six, or seven players who are of equal

ability. If they change defenses, we have a great psychological advantage.

2. Two-man game: In our system our two-man game always involves a guard-to-forward exchange.

3. Three-man system: We add the post at the mid-post area

4. Five-man system: We call this two alignment single post.

This is the building process we use to create our offense. The fourth basic belief is, regardless of what offense you must focus on execution and balance.

OFF-SEASON BALLHANDLING
John Beecroft

It is a real shame that far too many times a young aspiring basketball player spends many hours during the off-season trying to improve his basketball skills; but all this effort is too little or to no avail. How many times have you met a young player who will spend time each and every day on his individual game, yet has shown only minimal improvement? It is the author's conviction that the only real difference between these young men and those who significantly improve is their knowledge of "How To Practice."

Enclosed in this article you will find many drills and exercises the author firmly believes will improve many facets of your players' games. As coaches, we must convince our players that hard work and dedicated practice during the off-season is imperative for their own development and the success of the team. Although this program should prove beneficial for all players, there is very little emphasis on the big man's inside game. Consequently, the author suggests that each coach supplement the program with a specific set of drills for your big men.

I. Ballhandling

As an initial exercise to improve your game, the author recommends ballhandling drills. These drills should not only help get you in the right frame of mind to practice, but also improve your hand quickness and fingertip control. The following drills should be helpful in improving your ballhandling skills in only 5-10 minutes. Each should be performed for approximately 30 seconds.

Note: Do not look at the ball. Keep your head up. Only use your fingertips.

1. "Fingertip Control." Keep your arm straight and your elbows stiff, begin by tapping the ball from one hand to the other at arms' length

in front of your body. Move the ball from the head area to the waist in an up and down manner.

2. "Around the World." Using only your fingertips, begin passing the ball around your head as quickly as possible for about 20 seconds. Then repeat the procedure around the waist, and then the ankles. Finish by passing the ball around the right leg, and then the left leg.

3. "Figure 8." Begin with feet shoulder width apart and the ball in the middle with your right hand in front and your left hand behind. In this drill, pass the ball from hand-to-hand in a "figure 8" motion without allowing the ball to touch the ground. Remember to keep your head up and eyes looking forward. This drill should be done as quickly as possible. Also try this drill while using short, snappy dribbles.

4. "Running Figure 8." This drill is the same as the "Figure 8" except you must pass the ball from hand-to-hand while running from endline-to-endline.

5. "Drop and Catch." Begin this drill with your feet apart and the ball between your legs, with the right hand in front of your body holding the ball and the left hand behind. Release your grip on the ball and switch the position of your hands (now the left hand is in front and the right hand behind). You are to make this switch and catch the ball before it hits the floor. Be quick. Once mastered, drop the ball, clap, switch hands and catch the ball before it hits.

6. "Imagination Dribble." You are to dribble while moving from endline-to-endline, keeping your head up and eyes forward. Use your imagination while dribbling. Don't be afraid to dribble behind your back or between your legs.

Note: This is critical. This drill is only profitable if there is no clowning around. You can use any type of dribble as long as you don't look at the ball while the dribble is in progress.

II. Mikan Drill

This valuable drill should be completed after the ballhandling drills and before beginning either the shooting or offensive moves part of the program. The purpose of the "Mikan Drill" is to improve one's "feel" for the backboard. During the course of a game players are faced with situations where they must adjust layup shots to accommodate the arms and hands of opposing players. Unfortunately, many players are not familiar enough with the backboard to successfully utilize it from various angles. Begin this drill standing directly beneath the basket with a ball in your hands. Stepping off the left foot, shoot a baby hook shot with your right hand. Rebound and chin the ball and, without a dribble, shoot a baby hook with your left hand. Repeat this procedure, shooting baby hooks with alternating hands for one minute.

Note: No dribbling is permitted and be aware of going off the proper foot; the right foot on the left hand hook shot, and the left for a right hand shot.

III. Shooting

The object of the game of basketball is to score more points than your opponent. Consequently, the ability to put the ball in the basket is of prime importance, and thus much practice time should be spent improving your shot.

An excellent drill to improve shooting is "Spot Shooting." In this drill use 12 spots of varying distances from and at varying angles to the basket. You are to shoot jumpers from the first spot until 10 baskets have been made. Then proceed to the second spot and make 10 more shots. Proceed to the remaining spots until 10 baskets have been made from each spot. Any misses should be followed up and laid in. It is a good idea to keep a record of how many shots you must shoot to make 10 baskets from each spot. Records are a good way to measure your progress and improvement. Figure 9.12 shows 12 spots that shots are commonly taken from during the course of a game. It is recommended that you choose those spots from which you shoot most of your shots.

IV. Offensive Moves

The purpose of this series of drills is to help you become more of an offensive threat. Keep in mind that to be profitable, these drills must be performed as though a game were in progress.

1. "Jab Step." One of the most effective ways to beat a defender is to become proficient at the jab step. In this series of moves you will get the defender to react to a jab step (a quick short step directly at the outside foot of your defender), and then beat him. To be effective you must assume a triple-threat position (one where you could either pass, dribble or shoot the ball) and make good jabs at the defender. There are three basic moves in this series. First, when you jab at the defender and he doesn't react, take a second step with the same foot and you will be by him for the drive to the basket. Second, when you jab at him and he reacts by taking a half step back, cross over with the foot you jabbed with and drive by him. When you cross over, place your foot beside the defender's lead foot, thus keeping him from recovering. Be careful not to travel by changing your pivot foot. The third and final move in the series comes when the defender reacts by jumping back a full step. When this occurs, shoot the jumper.

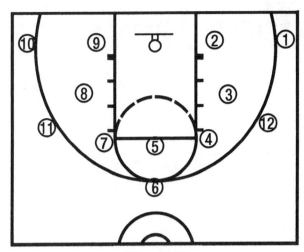

Figure 9.12

Below you will find an outline of the drills for working on the jab step. Keep in mind that everything is done in series of five. The author recommends the use of a shirt or towel or some other object as a mock defender. Place this object foul line extended a few steps from the lane.

a. Right side of court — The left foot is the pivot foot, and jab with the right foot. All layups from this side must be shot with the right hand. Do each move five times.

1) Jab-drive – layup.

2) Jab-crossover – layup.

3) Jab-jump shot.

4) Jab-drive – jump shot.

5) Jab-crossover – jump shot.

6) Foul shot.

b. Left side of court – The right foot is the pivot foot, and jab with the left foot. All layups from this side must be shot with the left hand. Do each move five times.

1) Jab-drive – layup.

2) Jab-crossover – layup.

3) Jab-jump shot.

4) Jab-drive – jump shot.

5) Jab – crossover – jump shot.

6) Foul shot.

2. Moves with the dribble. This is the second and final series of drills for the improvement of individual offensive moves that the author includes in his practice program. Whereas the jab-step series utilizes offensive moves where a dribble has not yet been established, this series comprises moves that will make a player more of an offensive threat after he has already established his dribble.

Below you will find an outline of the drill for improving your offensive moves with the dribble. Again, just as the jab-step series, everything is done in series of fives.

a. Right side of the court. Begin about 20-25 feet from the basket at the foul line extended area. All layups from this side must be shot with the right hand. Do each move five times.

1) Begin with right hand dribble – cross over to left – layup.

2) Being with left hand dribble – cross over to right layup.

3) Begin with right hand dribble – spin dribble – layup.

4) Begin with left hand dribble – spin dribble – layup.

5) Begin with right hand dribble – change of pace – layup 5X

6) Begin with left hand dribble – change of pace – layup.

7) Begin with right hand dribble-head and shoulder fake dribble – layup.

8) Begin with left hand dribble – head and shoulder fake dribble – layup.

9) Foul shots.

Repeat the moves but end each one except the foul shots with a jump shot.

b. Left side of the court. You are to repeat the eight moves listed above from this side of the court, ending the moves first with a left hand layup and then with a jump shot. Be sure to finish with five foulshots.

V. Tipping Drill

An excellent way to end any workout is by using the tipping drill. Standing under the basket on the right side; throw the ball up on the board; jump up as high as you can and tip the ball with fingertips of your right hand 10 times. Try to tip the last one into the basket. Repeat from the left side using your left hand.

FIELD GOAL

SHOOTING

Sonny Smith

Shooting is the most important fundamental in basketball and the least taught. Why is it the least taught? 1) When you try to teach a person to shoot right, it may change his shot and it doesn't feel good and it won't go in so he won't do it. 2) The ball won't go in the basket, so consequently he has no confidence in what you are telling him, so you just don't get anything done.

I am going to give you a way to help young players learn how to shoot the basketball. If you do this, you must sell them on the facts that, number one, it's not going to feel good; and, number two, it's not going to go in the basket for a while. They are going to have to shoot the way you tell them to for at least two weeks. If they will do this, it will start to feel good and it will start to go in the basket. What happens over the years is that players shoot the basketball with muscles in a strain, but they get in kind of a groove and even though they are not shooting it correctly, the ball is going in the basket so they don't feel any need to change.

What I am going to do is have you teach your players how to shoot in two ways: 1) alignment – line yourself up with the basket, and 2) judgment – you do not teach alignment and judgment at the same time. And that is where we make a really big mistake in teaching shooting. Judgment is this: a) how far to push it, b) how high to push it, and c) when to push it. Judgment has nothing to do with alignment. Alignment is getting everything in a straight line going toward the basket and using the least amount of muscles that you can. The more muscles you use, the more mistakes you make. I am going to give you a method of shooting in which you use the least amount of muscles.

1. **Feet.** You have to establish a shooting foot. If you are a right-hander, your right foot is your shooting foot. You line your shooting foot up directly with the center of the goal. You don't toe in; you don't toe out. This is on every shot you take. (Make sure you only work on one phase of shooting at a time.) Your other foot is

for balance. Get your feet shoulder width apart and establish a heel-toe relationship with both your feet. You may turn your balance foot out. Seventy percent of field goal attempts are shot off the dribble. The shooting toe must be pointed straight, but you may get better balance if your balance foot is turned a little, just as long as both feet are shoulder-width apart. That is the key.

2. **Knees:** If you bend too much, you lose your balance. You bend just enough to slip a coin in under the heels. You never bend down to where it throws you on the balls of your feet because you are off-balance when you do that. Use this statement with the players you are teaching. "The farther you are from the goal, the less you jump. The closer you are to the goal, the more you jump."

3. **Elbow.** The biggest mistake made in shooting is the elbow. The elbow must be lined up with the center of the toe, because the toe is lined up with the center of the basket. There are three positions in which you can carry the elbow as long as it is directly above the toe:

   a. Low elbow lift: The elbow is even with the armpit. Who would shoot that? Sixth, seventh, eighth, and ninth graders. Don't let anyone else shoot that.
   b. Medium elbow lift even with the chin.
   c. High elbow lift: Move the elbow up even with the eyes. You progress up with age.

4. **Wrist.** Sometime during the shot, the wrist has got to be parallel with the floor. That is called wrist cock. The reason for that is this you have got to tell a player to push up and through the ball. If the wrist is not cocked properly, i.e., half-cocked, you will push the ball at the basket. You don't push the ball at the basket. You must push up and through the ball so that the ball is coming straight down as it gets to the basket. If you shoot the ball at the basket, the ball will only go through half the time. It will only go through the back half. With proper wrist cock, and by pushing up and through the ball, the ball can go through the front half, back half, or either side. To prove this to the players, you get two balls and push them through the rim at the same time.

5. **Grip.** Most shots are taken off the dribble. When players dribble, they put their hand in the center of the ball. If you pick the ball up with your hand in the center of the ball, your elbow goes out. Show your players that first. Now here is what you do. You take your shooting finger (the index finger of your shooting hand) and line it up with the valve core. You don't have to touch the core, just line up with it. Your

other shooting finger, your middle finger, when combined with the index finger is called the shooting fork. You line up your shoot finger with the valve core and spread your fingers until they start to feel tight. That is the way you grip the basketball. You must teach them to grip the ball this way off the dribble. When the index finger is lined up with the valve core and the ball is picked up, the elbow is automatically lined up. The fingers should be spread tightly, but not so much that the flat part of the thumb touches the ball. The thumb should be turned sideways so that the outside quarter of the thumb touches the ball. If the flat part of the thumb is touching the ball on the snap through, the thumb will come in and that puts an unnatural sideways spin on the ball. If you have your outside quarter of your thumb on the ball on the snap through, the thumb will go straight down and will not put a sideways spin on the ball. This is a very important point in teaching shooting the basketball. Also, do not tell a shooter not to palm the ball, because this takes the ball off the shooting pads. The off hand is used purely for balance.

Now, to judgment. In judgment, the first thing to teach the players is where to aim. Do you aim at the back part of the rim, do you aim at the front part of the rim, what do you do? Here is what you do. Have a player go out on the court with a partner. Line him up in his range and pick one spot. Tell him to shoot 100 shots from that spot. The partner will have a chart with 100 circles on it signifying the rim. Each time the shooter misses a shot, the partner is to make an X on the circle where the ball hit when it missed: front, back, either side. After he has shot 100 shots, there will be a pattern. More shots than not will have hit in one certain spot. If more shots have hit the back of the rim, tell the shooter to aim at the front of the rim. If more shots hit at the front of the rim, tell him to aim at the back of the rim. The partner is to put an X inside the circle if the shot goes in. If most of the X's are in the circle, tell the shooter to keep aiming where he has been aiming.

If most of the X's are on one side or the other, the shooter has an alignment problem. Then you take the alignment problem and work on it one phase at a time: feet, knee position, elbow position, wrist cock, push up and through the ball. This chart will tell you what needs to be taught.

Now, how high do you push it? You push it high enough so that it comes straight down when it gets to the center of the basket. Ask the player if he is shooting a high arc – coming down in the center – a plus, low arc — shooting at the basket.

Why would you shoot the medium arc as opposed to the high arc? The reason is this. It takes muscles to shoot a basketball. The more muscles you use, the more chances you have of making a mistake. So, if you have the ball coming straight down with a medium arc, why use extra muscles? It will make an effect on a player late in a ball game. The more he works at the high arc using more muscles, the more fatigued his body is. Teach the player to use the least amount of muscles to get the shot off.

Next point: When do you shoot? You shoot the ball when you are in your range. Here is how to find a player's range. You start the player out shooting bank shots from right under the basket with his toe lined up. Every time he makes it, have him back up a step. When he is feeling a strain, he has reached his maximum range. You tell him to stay within that range. The next point on when to shoot: You shoot when you are wide open in your range and there is no one else wide open closer to the basket than you are. That is called teamwork and team play. Ask the players, "Was that a good shot or a bad shot you just took?"

Now let's go to the balance hand and the follow-through. The balance hand is very important. Most shots are taken off the dribble. When most dribblers pick up the ball, they put their balance hand on the bottom of the ball. If you pick up the ball with your balance hand on the bottom, you do not have a clear vision toward the goal, because your two forearms are in the way. The balance hand must be moved to the side of the ball. Here is the way you sell this to your players. You tell him to take his shooting finger and hold it up in front of his shooting eye. You look straight out into the distance with both eyes open and you will find that you cannot judge distance with your right eye. With one eye blocked you cannot judge distance. You need both eyes on the target to judge distance. If you have a one-eyed shooter, shooting into half a basket, he's got your contract in his mouth. You have to sell the player on the fact that when he changes his shot, it is not going to go in and it is not going to feel good. You must spend time working on it over and over until it does start to go in and it does start to feel good.

Follow-through: Shooters usually follow through too much or not enough. The only thing the shooter needs to do is make sure that, at the end of the shot, the shooting fork needs to be pointing down in the basket (toward the floor). It can be the shooting finger, or the shooting fork. If it is any more than that you are getting a curve on the ball. The other two fingers need to stick up slightly. Don't tell them to put their shooting hand in the basket because then they are going to lead with their little finger and get a curve ball.

What is going to happen when you first start teaching a player to follow through? The first thing that is going to happen is that they are going to start shooting long. They must also push the ball up before they follow through.

Here is how you get kids teaching kids. Have one player stand in front of the other player who is shooting. The player standing in front and watching the shooter should watch for these things:

1. Is his foot straight?
2. Is his elbow lined up with his toe?
3. Is anything in front of his vision?

Have the player shoot three shots and look for each thing, one at a time during the three shots. Next, have the player move to the shooter's shooting side and have the player shoot three more shots looking for these things:

1. Are the knees slightly bent?
2. Is the wrist cocked properly?
3. Is the elbow at one of these three positions: armpit level, chin level, eye level?

Next, the watcher stands behind the shooter watching for:

1. Is the shooting fork lined up over the shoulder joint?
2. Does the ball have a backward rotation on it after it is released?
3. Are the feet shoulder-width apart?

If you check these things in that manner, you are letting kids teach kids. One more thing, when the watcher is standing in front, he should look at the shooter's eyes to see if his eyes are following the ball toward the basket. If his eyes are following the ball, you make him stop. Make him fix those eyes on the rim and leave them there.

MENTAL IMAGERY IN SHOOTING

Paul Westhead

There are many components of making someone a good shooter. Certainly good coaching and many long practice hours are important ingredients. But there are some areas of the shooting game we have overlooked. In order to be an excellent shooter, you must have the proper mental image. This begins with feeling good about yourself.

Cybernetics

If you have a positive attitude, you will respond favorably in all situations. Don't leave it up to luck to have a good shooting day.

This self-esteem or self-image can be whatever you decide it to be. This concept was discovered by a plastic surgeon, Dr. Maltz, who discovered the dramatic changes in the lives of people undergoing surgery.

A man has facial scars removed and he then becomes successful in business, gets along with his family, and is liked by his neighbors and is cheerful. All because of a few scars? Not exactly – once the scars were removed, he changed his self-image from negative and doubtful to positive and assertive. Because of the new self-image, he began to experience success.

The scar removal is not the basis for success or failure. In Prussia, where dueling is the highest from of masculine acceptance, to have facial scars is an attractive addition, not a blemish.

Therefore, your physical situation does not determine your status – your self-image does. You act and feel and perform according to what you imagine to be true about yourself. If you have the label of "non-shooter," you will fulfill that image. You have the option to imagine negative, doubtful, and destructive things or positive, assertive, and constructive things.

Your nervous system cannot tell the difference between an imagined experience and a real experience. Thus, the merit in role-playing. Select the role of a successful person and rehearse that role. In business, this would mean imagining yourself in various sales situations, then solving them in your mind until you know what to say and what to do whenever that situation comes up in real life.

This is why the practice of mental picturing has great merit, because it is the natural process for the brain to learn. Get into this habit of dwelling on desirable ends.

This concept of cybernetics deals with the power of the brain to perform exactly what it learns to do. It means the great capacity of our muscle memory – namely, once we learn how to do something, we never forget.

Examples:

1. My 12-year-old daughter, Patrice, one day was rummaging through her room and found her recorder, which she hadn't used in a year. She picked it up and played a flawless rendition of "Can-Can." Her finger timing was perfect because her muscle memory had it down forever and all she did was call on it. She simply let it happen with no conscious interference, i.e. pressure to remember, pressure to perform well. She simply played and let her fingers do the talking.

2. A situation with two basketball managers carrying hot coffee and one not looking at it. Jim would go out for coffee, and it would be spilled all over. He would come in and apologize and promise it wouldn't happen the next time. But sure enough it would, and even worse. Mike would go out for coffee and never a spill. I asked him his secret, and he said he never looked at it – he just walked through campus talking and laughing with friends. The

secret was that he allowed his automatic muscle memory of balancing to operate and he never spilled. This is exactly what we need to do in shooting – allow our muscle memory to operate. It is like an airplane put on automatic pilot.

Scientific Facts About the Brain

The muscle memory becomes even greater the more you groove the activity in your mind.

If you clearly picture the action, it registers in your brain as actually doing it, that is, making clear, vivid mental pictures of the ball going through the hoop is just the same as making the actual basket with your arms on the court.

Therefore the saying, "practice makes perfect" is only half true, for so does "mental practice make perfect." With this in mind we came up with a foul shooting drill which combines both.

1. Shoot five – physical practice.

2. Picture five – mental practice.

3. Close eyes picture five – mental practice.

4. Close eyes and shoot five – physical/mental practice.

5. Open eyes five – physical practice. We had players making three to four out of five with their eyes closed. This drill surfaced itself during a crucial moment in our Villanova game.

6. Gladden – two seconds, one and one foul, down one point. Close your eyes and fire away. This is no time for screwing around. He didn't close his eyes, but he did go out and rely completely on his muscle memory and pictured the ball going in. Because he pictured it going in, he was expecting good things to happen. You must be positive and expect your shot to go in.

There are some highly technical things in shooting, for example, keeping your elbow in close to your body; your forearm perpendicular to the floor, and your wrist cocked forming the letter "U", not a "V". But more important is the attitude of the shooter. He must have a clear picture of the ball going in and the expectation of scoring.

This is true in other sports.

1. Tennis – get the first serve in.

2. Golf – putting – expect the ball to drop.

3. Football – passing – expect it to be caught

4. Baseball – expect to hit it every time. Some kids expect to miss it every time.

What mental practice is doing is conditioning ourselves to win. We have every reason to believe things will go well because of our great capacity. There is so much energy and excellence within our body if we only learn to call upon it.

In basketball keep your eye on the RIM and expect the ball to go in. (Make a mental picture of the ball swishing through the hoop as you are in the act of shooting.) The key to mental imagery in picturing the ball going in is you do not allow any interference to alter your shot process, like the antics of the defense, or the game circumstances (for example, the last shot). You simply "look through" the defensive man because, in fact, he is not on your mind. A mental picture of the ball going through the basket is the only object on your mind. The mental picture is not of this actual shot but of any or all of your shots.

It is placing all your concentration on the successful making of a shot and thus allowing your natural memory of how to do it run its course in this actual shot.

The key to success is the ability to still your mind and thus allow yourself to concentrate on one thing – making the basket – at the exclusion of all else. An excited fluttering mind is not able to settle in on any one thing. The player must learn the act of shooting the ball with total concentration yet not care about the outcome. You expect it to go in; you have a clear, vivid picture in your mind of it going in, but you do not react to the results.

The quality of the process is your goal. The end result is not the be all and end all. It will take care of itself. Once you stop worrying about the outcome, you find you shoot much better. The best performance takes place when a player concentrates on his action (shooting the ball) without attachment to the fruits of the action.

The paradox to be understood is that the more you care about making the shot, the harder it is to make it. So too, the more you care about playing well and sticking out as a great player on your team, the harder it is to excel.

Conversely, the less you care about the shot going in, the greater the results, and the less you care about being the star on your team, the better you play. That is why when basketball performers play with abandon (that is, not caring about the outcome and feeling they have nothing to lose), they produce much more than when they feel they must win at all cost.

At LaSalle, I have a great athlete, Michael Brooks, 6'7", 220 pounds, strong, quick, agile, mobile, and hostile. Yet he shot 4 for 20 against Duke on a big TV game which featured him as Muhammed Ali versus Gene Banks as Joe Frazier. They were high school rivals (West Catholic versus West Public), and the whole city of Philadelphia was to see in living color who was the best. Brooks missed six layups and missed dribbles and passes. Poor results, all because he was overly concerned with the fruits of his actions. So, paradoxically, they were much worse than if he didn't try at all. The harder he tried to prove his greatness, the farther away it went from him.

Two weeks later against Notre Dame he decided to go out and let it happen, just go out, play hard, and follow our fast-break system and not worry about the consequences. He got 39 points and 16 rebounds.

The exact mental image in shooting the basketball should be that of a cat stalking a bird: Effortlessly alert, he crouches, gathering his relaxed muscles for the spring. No thinking about when to jump, or how he will push off with his hind legs to attain the proper distance, his mind is still and perfectly concentrated on his prey. No thought of missing his mark. He sees only the bird. Suddenly the bird takes off; at the same instant, the cat leaps. With perfect anticipation he intercepts his dinner two feet off the ground. Perfectly, thoughtlessly executed action, and afterward, no self-congratulations, just the reward inherent in his action: the bird in the mouth.

The lesson to be learned from the cat for a basketball player is clear. Shoot the ball and see only the basket. Know that once your muscle memory has learned how to shoot the ball in the basket, it will never forget. All you have to do is call on the brain – push the foul shot button just as you push the brush your teeth button, and it will go in. If you can recognize this reality and trust yourself, you could never miss a shot.

A key here is being able to picture only the ball going in and not all of the chances of it not going in. Then you are presenting distractions to your mind and planting the seeds of mistrust about your own proven ability. It is essential that you have complete trust in your body to perform.

Another key in proper mental imagery in shooting is the ability to ignore the defense. The shooter must blot out the attempts of the defensive player to distract him. All of the defensive man's ploys such as waving hands, the jab step, the karate thrust, yelling and screaming, and nose guarding must be blocked out by the shooter. Good defense is exactly this – distracting the shooter without drawing the foul.

Good shooting is sighting the basket without interference by the defense. (Fear of getting your shot blocked is the cause of many missed shots.) That anxiety of potential embarrassment plays havoc on the automatic process of the brain. Once you have made the decision to shoot, you must be totally committed to doing just that. Even if the defender jumps above you and is about to slam the ball down your throat, you must ignore him and shoot through him. Even if your vision of the hoop is blinded, you must allow your automatic pilot to take over. I had my players do five drive-in layups regularly, then imaging, then eyes closed with no ball imaging. They actually ran it with their eyes closed, shot the imaginary ball, and, with their eyes still closed, ran back to the end of the line exactly where they had started.

It gave me further evidence that the real challenge of being a good shooter was not the keenness of your physical eye but the confidence of your mental imaging, then eyes closed with no ball imaging. They actually ran it with their eyes closed, shot the imaginary ball, and, with their eyes still closed, ran back to the end of the line exactly where they had started.

It gave me further evidence that the real challenge of being a good shooter was not the keenness of your physical eye but the confidence of your mental eye. Physically, you can score with your eyes closed. Mental confidence is the factor that must be controlled and practiced.

LaSalle's fast-break system instructs first good open shot, fire away. Our players released the outside shot with greater consistency because they were encouraged to shoot. in fact, they were only scolded when they didn't shoot the open shot. This sense of freedom to shoot without fear of reprisal led to far greater accuracy. Our team had a 50 percent field goal accuracy (led by Michael Brooks with 58.8 percent), which established a new LaSalle mark.

Also shooting on the run created a more relaxed atmosphere because the decision had to be made quickly, not rushed or hurriedly, but quickly (John Wooden: "Be quick but never hurry").

It seems that the longer a player has to calculate his shot, the more difficult it becomes. Once you are set, that is, the whole body in a squared-up, balanced position, any further time is of no advantage. Therefore, to slow down ball control and wait for the clear, totally uncontested six-footer probably lends to less accuracy.

Our players were judged on shooting the ball from their proper fast-break position, not whether they made or missed the shot.

This year was the highest scoring team in LaSalle's history – 2,503 points; most field goals by an individua – Michael Brooks – 288; most field goals by a team – 1,047. We averaged 87 points per game and the highest field goal percentage in the history of the school – 50 percent.

We made scoring seem easy to our players, so they reacted accordingly and made it so. Their mental image of scoring a 20-foot jumper was as simple as brushing their teeth. Unfortunately for us, they carried this image with them on defense and stood around picturing the ball going in next time down. As a result, we gave up 84 points per game.

Who knows, perhaps we created an atmosphere that encouraged good shooting at both ends of the court because we acted like it was so easy. Free and easy scoring is contagious.

In conclusion, we need to expect good things to happen. When shooting the basketball there are some valuable techniques to follow. But more important is the attitude of the shooter. He must have a clear picture of the ball going in and expect it to score before he shoots.

Your positive energy will pour out in your delivery. You must form the habit of expecting to win a la Lombardi. Much of what you are is the result of habit. As Vince Lombardi stated, "Winning is a habit. Unfortunately, so is losing." We will show you how to form the winning habit.

As you ramble through life, keep your eye upon the doughnut and not upon the hole. We always have the choice to expect the positive or the negative. Awaken the sleeping giant within you – think with a positive mental attitude. Expect the ball to go in and it will.

SHOOTING DRILLS

Don Frank

Two years ago we came up with a positive way to work on shooting in practice that keeps players intense, competitive, and motivated and also allows us to take advantage of the three-point line. By using these drills we have seen range increase and accuracy improve. During the last two seasons we have shot 53.5 percent from the floor and have led our conference in scoring. Last year we finished second in three-point baskets and this year we led our conference in both three-point percentage as well as in total three-point baskets. As players see their improvement, they have become more motivated to continue the hard work necessary to stay sharp.

To put it very simply, all we have done is taken some concepts given to players at summer camps and incorporated them into team drills. By doing these drills with intensity, you will fatigue your players so that they will be shooting under game-like conditions. Try these drills. At first scores will be low, but as players increase their speed, quickness, and endurance, scores will improve. We believe that your team's shooting percentage will improve as well.

We do not do all of the drills every day, but we do try to have two shooting sessions per practice that can last from five to ten minutes each, depending on our schedule. We shoot competitively every day. We work hard the day before a game as well as later in the year, although our time on the drills might be reduced to a minimum of 30 seconds. We never shoot less than 30 seconds or more than a minute per shooter per drill. These short, explosive bouts of work help to keep intensity and concentration.

All drills are done in pairs. All drills are timed. Players must call out their score as each basket is made. After each particular drill or "event," each player's score is recorded (we record after both players have shot). If the drill lasts for one minute, then it will take a little over two minutes to do the entire drill and then we record.

The player with the most baskets or points for the entire team wins that particular event and will get his score circled. For each circle a player gets, he receives five bonus points to his total score at the end of the day. Each individual drill is competitive, and each player's score for every drill counts toward his final daily total. We run a couple of sprints for shooting after practice. The top three shooters for each day do not have to run these sprints. It's amazing what this little incentive will do to motivate.

Shooters are encouraged to shoot their outside shots just behind the 19'9" line. Our strictly inside players do not go beyond the line. We believe that this quick, repetitive, and competitive shooting grooves the shooter for the three-pointer. Players are really interested in their scores and will work hard on these drills.

The Drills

1. Hustle shots. Players start under the basket, shoot a lay-up or a dunk, let the ball go and sprint to the free throw line. They must touch the free throw line with their hand and then go pick the ball up, shoot it from where they pick it up, leave the ball and sprint back to touch the free throw line (see Figure 10.1).

2. Layups. The shooter starts with the ball at the short 17 right side. At the signal he drives in with his right hand, shoots a layup, and rebounds his shot as it goes through the net. He then speed dribbles out to the opposite short 17 with the right hand and then turns and drives back to the basket with his left hand, lays it up and rebounds the ball as it goes through the net and speed dribbles with his left hand to the original starting point where he again switches hands and continues on (see Figure 10.2). These first two drills really get the players working and get them ready to start their outside shooting sequence. We work very hard on these early in the year.

3. Toss and shoot. The shooter starts at short 17, shoots a jump shot and gets his own rebound and tosses the ball back to the opposite short 17. He then sprints around and catches the ball on the bounce, squares up, and shoots. (He is passing the ball to himself.) He then rebounds and goes to the opposite short 17 (see Figure 10.3).

4. Wing to wing. The player starts at the wing beyond the three-point line. His partner is under the basket as a rebounder. The shooter shoots the ball and sprints across the court to the opposite wing beyond the three-point line. The rebounder gets the ball and passes it hard back to the shooter. The shooter shoots again and sprints back to the original side. This continues for the duration of the drill (see Figure 10.4).

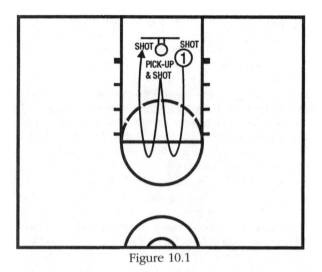

Figure 10.1

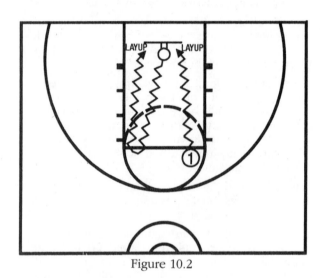

Figure 10.2

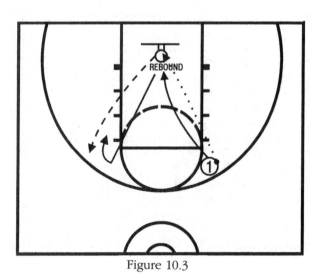

Figure 10.3

6. Baseline sprints. The shooter starts in the corner beyond the three-point line. He shoots the ball, sprints, and recovers the made or missed shot. His partner is at the free-throw line. When the shooter retrieves the ball, he passes it back out to his partner at the free throw line and continues to sprint to the opposite corner. The shooter must touch the sideline with his foot and come back to the ball, which will be delivered sharply by his partner. He catches, shoots, follows the ball and passes it back to his partner and then sprints to the opposite sideline where he touches the sideline and comes back to the ball (see Figure 10.6).

7. Closeout and shoot. The partner passes the ball to the shooter and then sprints and closes out on the shooter. The shooter catches the ball and goes straight up for a jump shot over the pressure. The shooter follows his shot, retrieves the ball, passes back out to his partner, and closes out on him. (Players continue to change spots in this fashion until the time period is up remembering to verbally call out each basket they make.) A good variation of this drill is to up-fake before the shot and take two power dribbles either way and then shoot (see Figure 10.7).

8. Spot shooting. The shooter starts at the top of the key. He has spots on the floor that are worth points to him when he makes a basket from there. They are: five points from the top of the key, four points for a baseline jump shot, three points for a jump shot from short 17, two points for a dunk, and one point for a layup. (You

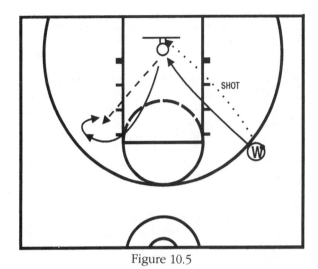

Figure 10.5

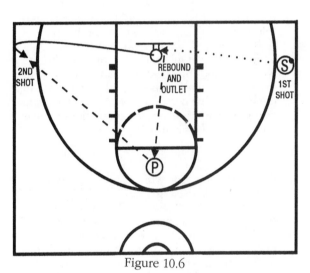

Figure 10.6

Figure 10.4

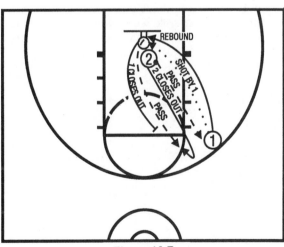

Figure 10.7

can only shoot two layups in a row.) Sometimes we do not allow more than two attempts in a row from any spot. A good score on this is over 60 points in a minute (see Figure 10.8).

9. Double white line. This drill is so named because we have two white lines on each side of our court. In this drill we put two groups together on the main baskets so that we have eight players working on the main court. Everyone else uses the side baskets. The shooter stays on one side of the floor and after each shot must pass to the feeder who is beyond the double white line on our court. The passer is about 10 feet from the top of the key. We have two shooters and two passers on each of the main baskets. The shooters are required to shoot two shots: the jumper from the short 17. Each time he shoots the ball, he must rebound it, pass it out hard to the feeder and move quickly to the next spot. The other pair of players on this particular basket are doing the exact same thing on their half of the court. Both shooters start at the red square and come to the ball giving a target. One side starts by going to the wing first and the other side starts by going to the short 17 first. In this drill the ball starts in the hands of the passer. Shooters shoot the same two shots on the same side of the floor for the entire drill (see Figures 10.9 and 10.10).

10. Free throws. We shoot two free throws at a time and shoot a total of 10 during each drill. When the coach blows the whistle, players sprint in a counter clockwise direction to the next basket on a two man fast break. This will eliminate standing around, eliminate needless talking, and increase concentration. You can score this drill in one of two ways. You can count total free throws made out of 10 or you can score it this way: Shoot 10 free throws two at a time and switch positions. A swish is worth two points. A made free throw that hits the rim is one point, and a miss is a minus one point. In this way the highest possible score would be 20 points for 10 made free throws without hitting the rim.

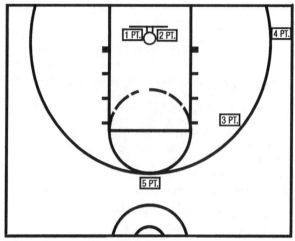

Figure 10.8

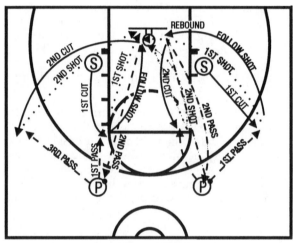

Figure 10.9

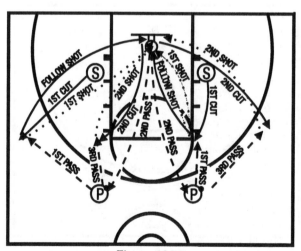

Figure 10.10

"55 SECOND" OFFENSIVE DRILL

John Kimble

Each coach has to maximize the small amounts of time he has to teach and practice his team. To establish and maintain interest and intensity levels of players at a peak, we try to incorporate into every drill maximum game realistic conditions. We try to incorporate into our drills the techniques and methods we have attempted to teach with repetition; but repetition that is not dull or boring or lacking of action. We try to eliminate individuals or groups of players from standing around. Our drills have game realistic conditions; they are fast-moving, and do not last longer than four to five minutes (before moving on to another facet).

We have changed the name of this particular drill from 55 Second Shooting Drill to the 55 Second Offensive Drill. The reason for the change is to emphasize to everyone that the drill is not just a shooting drill, but a drill that emphasizes several different facets of the offensive game besides shooting.

This drill is designed to work on the proper footwork and the proper "handwork" needed in getting open, catching the ball, and shooting the ball as quickly as possible (while remaining under control). Other techniques emphasized and practiced include offensive rebounding, making and catching outlet passes, making different types of passes to moving receivers from different floor locations, and finally receiving those different types of passes while moving to "get open." The drill is set up to provide maximum game realistic conditions.

Similar to other drills, this drill strives for intensity, teamwork, competitiveness, individual and team performance goals and objectives with game-realistic factors such as floor location, fatigue, individual and team pressures to perform well.

When the drill is performed properly, it will improve an individual's conditioning, his mental toughness and competitiveness, his self-confidence, and the other following skills: jumping, rebounding, proper pass selection, passing accuracy, cutting without the ball, catching the pass while on the move, proper footwork and handwork of his shot and his shooting accuracy.

The drill is set up in three-man groups at each basket. There are three assignments; a Rebounder, a Passer, and a Shooter. After 55 seconds, the Rebounder rotates to the passer's position, as the Passer becomes the Shooter, and the Shooter becomes the Rebounder. The process is repeated again and again. It requires just three minutes on each side of the court for the

three players to complete the cycle. The drill is then moved to the same spot on the floor on the opposite side.

It takes 55 seconds to perform the drill and 5 seconds for transition to rotate to the next phase, or a total time of three minutes.

The Rebounder (R) should rebound all shots as "misses." He should pull down the rebound off of the rim or out of the net. The Rebounder should pivot to the outside (away from the imaginary defense), and make a two-hand overhead pass to the Passer. All rebounds should be made with maximum effort and all outlet passes should be two-hand overhead passes thrown with maximum effort and accuracy.

The Passer (P) should time the shot, the rebound, and the outlet pass with his cut back to a predetermined spot on the floor to catch the outlet pass. The Passer should have made a cut before he caught the outlet pass. He should then make a passing fake in one direction (high or low) and then make an accurate pass "around or over the 'imaginary' defense" to the Shooter (S).

Almost all passes made by the passer (except "skip" passes) should be bounce passes around or over the imaginary defense preceded by some type of game-realistic fake.

The Shooter (S) should be moving quickly but under control as he cuts without the ball to the designated spot for his shot. He should have the proper footwork and handwork in preparation of catching the basketball. It is stressed constantly that the hands are in proper position with the proper footwork being a pivot off of the 'inside heel.' It is also stressed repeatedly that the shooter should not float, drift, or fall away after taking his jumpshot. The Shooter should go straight up and straight down. The proper follow-through is constantly stressed also.

In this drill, we are trying to simulate game conditions. We can add individual and/or team statistics to be kept to put more emphasis on performance. Proper practices lead to success. Success leads to confidence. Confidence leads to more success and the cycle rolls on and on. Another common phrase that is spoken by many is "practice makes perfect." We disagree with that; we have modified that statement to "perfect practice makes perfect."

For additional game realistic conditions, the man and zone offenses should be analyzed as to where the majority of the individuals' shots in that particular offense are being take in the actual games. The shot location of each player is determined and the movement of the shooter that preceded the shot are analyzed and studied. The types of passes and the direction from where the passes come from should also be studied and evaluated. After the evaluations are made, the "Offensive Drill" can be modified so your Shooter where they most generally start from during actual games when that particular offense is being run.

That way the players practice making 'game-like' passes. Two examples would be when using bounce passes to players for inside post shots, or making 'skip passes' when working on zone offense shots. Also the shooter will receive 'game-like' passes from the same general area that they will be receiving passes from during games, in addition to the same general area where that individual takes the majority of his shots during the games.

The following diagrams (Figures 10.11 through 10.22) are general examples of where you can position your Passer and Shooter in regards to particular types and styles of offenses you may generally run.

Evaluate the drill. Try the drill. Modify the drill to meet your specific needs for your particular program. Good luck!

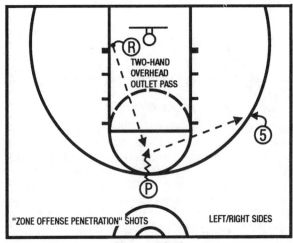

Figure 10.13

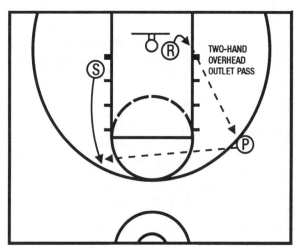

Figure 10.11

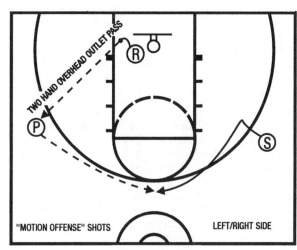

Figure 10.14

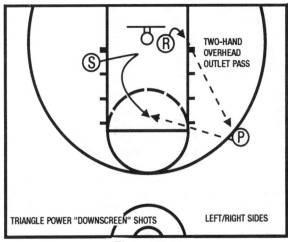

Figure 10.12

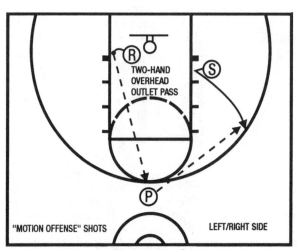

Figure 10.15

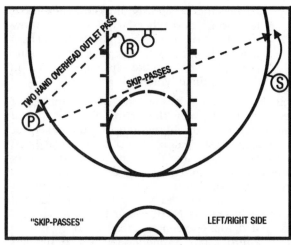

Figure 10.16

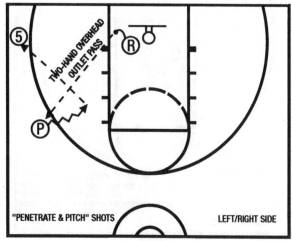

Figure 10.19

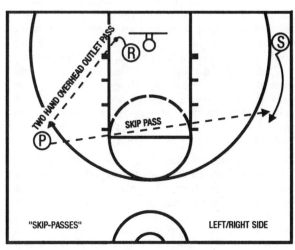

Figure 10.17

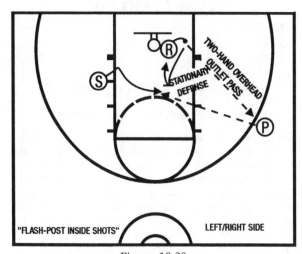

Figure 10.20

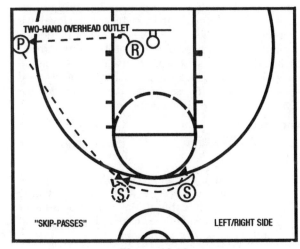

Figure 10.18

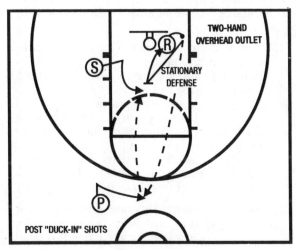

Figure 10.21

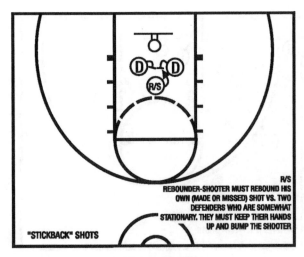

"STICKBACK" SHOTS

R/S
REBOUNDER-SHOOTER MUST REBOUND HIS
OWN (MADE OR MISSED) SHOT VS. TWO
DEFENDERS WHO ARE SOMEWHAT
STATIONARY. THEY MUST KEEP THEIR HANDS
UP AND BUMP THE SHOOTER

Figure 10.22

FREE THROW

SCORE ON THE THROW

Jerry Krause and Dan Hayes

Is 70 percent still an insurmountable barrier for free-throw shooters in the United States? NABC Research Committee statistics show that free-throw shooting percentages in men's college basketball have remained relatively constant, just below 70 percent, for the past 20 years (actually between 68 percent and 69.7 percent). This has occurred even though field goal shooting has improved steadily for over 40 years. There are many theories that might explain the reason for this lack of improvement in such an essential basic basketball skill. After studying free-throw shooting for over 15 years, we feel that free-throw shooters can break the 70 percent barrier, and free-throw shooting will improve if the following steps are taken:

1. Practice during the season in proportion to scoring importance in a game (over 20 percent). For a practice evenly divided between offense and defense, this would mean that 10 percent of total practice time should be spent on free throws. In a two-hour practice session, this would translate into at least 10 minutes spent solely on free-throw practice. A simple guideline for determining allotted free-throw practice time would be five minutes for every hour of total practice.

2. Practice free-throw shooting regularly in the off-season. How many players have a regular routine to shoot free throws during this time?

3. Coaches and players should know the proper techniques and other factors for free-throw shooting. Coaches should know what and how to teach free-throw scoring, including learning principles to meet the challenges of a skill that are primarily mental.

With these possible ideas in mind, a coach and player need to decide why they should place special emphasis on free-throw shooting. It is our belief that in a college basketball season of approximately 28 to 30 games, we have determined that four to six games per year are decided at the free-throw line. An example of this would be a recent Oklahoma Christian season in which 14 games were decided by five or less points. NABC research statistics confirm also that 20 to 25 percent of a team's scoring is from the free-throw line. As mentioned before, this has important implications in terms of the amount of team practice time that is devoted to the skill. We also regard a free-throw situation as an opponent's mistake in the form of a foul. One of our teaching points is that players should make opponents pay for their mistakes as a proper mental approach to shooting free throws. In our opinion, free-throw shooting should be thought of as a team skill. This implies that each and every player on the team can and will become a good free-throw shooter. Finally, if the national free-throw percentage has remained at that same level for the last 30 years, then it would seem important for us to try to improve in this area and progress as coaches and basketball players.

The critical question then becomes how to become a successful free-throw scorer instead of someone who merely goes to the free-throw line to shoot a charity shot. The first step is to set appropriate goals of free-throw shooting so that expectations of players can be raised. In our opinion, the appropriate goals from the junior high school level through the senior high school level to the college and professional levels are 60 percent, 70 percent, 75 percent, and 80 percent, respectively. If it is recognized that there is always some game slippage, then we should adjust our practice goals so they are 5 percent higher than our game goals. This means that, at the college level, we set a regular practice goal at 80 percent or higher for any individual. Next, we feel that it is important to put a KAP on your shot. KAP is an acronym to remind us of the three critical areas in becoming a good free-throw scorer. Those three areas are: knowledge (K), attitude (A), and practice (P).

Knowledge

The correct techniques for free-throw shooting are as follows:

1. Get a ritual; this means do what you do. The same thing is done the same way every time you shoot a free throw. Make the same number of bounces each time. Take a deep breath (to relax) as part of your ritual.

2. Get down on the same spot in the same position every time. On a wood floor, there is a drill hole on the floor that is marked as the exact center of the free-throw lane. This should be used for consistent alignment each time a shot is taken. The shooting foot should be aligned relative to that spot so that the foot is pointed to the basket. This means that a right-handed shooter should put the right foot slightly to the left of the drill hole and point it at the basket. The non-shooting foot should be aligned so that it is in a comfortable position about shoulder width and slightly behind the free-throw line. It will be pointed approximately 15 to 18 degrees away from a line that goes from the shooter to the basket.

3. Get forward with the weight and the follow-through.

There is a tendency for players to pull back away from the free throw, especially in pressure situations. Therefore, we strongly recommend that players keep their weight forward and also hold their follow-through (upper arm at 30 to 35 degrees from the vertical) as close to the basket as possible (make a parachute or put your hand over the rim and in the basket) until the ball goes through the net. The shooting motion is carried out with controlled tension and the eyes stay forward on the target, not the ball, until the ball goes through the net. Note that the trunk should be kept near vertical or slightly back even though the weight is forward.

4. Finally, it is important to get to the bottom of your shot.

Pause at some place during the shot motion, preferably in the shooting pocket, and use all positive motion from that point on. This means that there is less chance for error if you go from the pause position to the completion of the shot. This means eliminating dipping-type motions and allowing the legs to be used for power.

Some shooters also make the mistake of staying on the floor. Instead, you should rise up on your toes or leave the floor slightly and use your legs for power. Another guideline for younger players (elementary age) would be to use a low basket (nine feet), a smaller ball, and a shorter free-throw line (12 feet).

Attitude

A proper shooting attitude is developed in the form of the three "C's." *Concentrate* means to focus on the proper mental approach. We believe you should, as a player, focus on making the opponents pay for their mistakes. *Cotton* is for developing a proper mental image. It is important to see and say the word "net" before every shot. This is a trigger word to develop the mental image of the ball going through the net. *Confidence* stands for developing respect. On a made free throw, it is important that the player build confidence by remembering that free throw and providing a mental pat on the back. For missed free-throw situations, it is also important to develop respect by analyzing the shot and forgetting it as soon as possible (analyze and forget). It is important to know how to analyze and adjust your miss; for example, if the shot is short, you should use more legs. If the shot is long, less leg power is needed. If the shot is left or right, then adjustments need to be made on alignment (drill hole, foot, elbow, shoulder, wrist).

Practice

This is the most important final phase of putting a KAP on your shot. The two phases of practice are physical and mental. During physical practice, we believe it is important to groove your shot when developing your confidence both on a long-term and a short-term basis. The second part of physical practice is learning how to compete in a variety of pressure situations. These need to be structured by coaches during practices and by the players during the off-season. A good free-throw scorer will know what a good shot looks like, sounds like, and feels like. This can be gained by mental practice. By this, we mean that mental practice can be carried out by removing all distractions, closing your eyes, and vividly imagining a successful free throw (see it, hear, and feel it). The critical thing that must be carried out is to vividly imagine as much of the free-throw situation as you can including all sights, sounds, and feelings of the total situation. After a player is able to put a KAP on the shot, he is now ready to plan and carry out a specific free-throw shooting program.

A Free-Throw Shooting Program

The basic program that we recommend in the off-season is called The Foundation 5,000. At the college level we believe that a thousand free throws should be shot after the completion of the season while school is still in session. The basic format is to shoot 100 free throws per day on a five day per week schedule. A written record of those free throws is kept. Players need to imagine each shot as a game shot. Basketball shoes must be worn. It is advisable to use some type of toss-back as a retriever unless the players want to shoot in pairs.

The final purpose of this Foundation 5,000 series is to set an 80 percent practice goal (college level) and use that as a measure of status to establish a player's shooting level before a season begins. This I used with an "adapt or adopt" principle. If a player is able to meet the 80 percent goal in the off-season, then we ask that player to "adapt" one or two things that might improve his free-throw shooting. If a player does not meet the 80 percent goal, he must "adopt" the whole free-throw shooting package.

During the summer, the player will shoot another 2,000 recorded free throws. This can be done in a four-week period of 500 free throws per week. During the fall season before formal practice begins, we also ask players to complete 2,000 additional free throws in a four-week period of time.

Coaches could modify the 5,000 so that they get a basic foundation during the off-season in any fashion they desire. Good free-throw shooting technique based on this foundation is then developed during every practice session. Also, have a pre-practice period of time devoted to free-throw shooting. The pre-practice time is simply another daily session in grooving the free throw in which a player is asked to go to the line and make 20 free throws before every practice session and record those on a record card. If this is done on a regular basis, it gives us a regular spot check on the 80 percent goal as well as allowing that player to regularly groove that shot before practice every day.

Other outside practice incentives include a membership in a Free-Throw Club. A series of awards can be set up for making 25 free throws, 50 free throws, or 100 free throws in a row on a player's own time. The only rules to free-throw club membership is that the consecutive free-throw goal must be witnessed by another player. During practices and in preparation for the season, one of the first steps that is carried out is to give the team a free-throw shooting clinic in which all the basic principles are reviewed and they are given a small free-throw shooting reminders card with all the basic principles listed. A mini-clinic emphasizing one of the basic principles is given once a week prior to a free-throw shooting session during regular practice; for example, we may use a short mental practice session prior to a five minute free-throw physical practice session in order to teach what we call "de-icing" technique.

During the practice sessions devoted to free throws (five minutes per hour), we try to cover all situations that a player might face in a game so that no surprises are faced in game situations. Each player has faced all the possible free-throw situations under a variety of pressure during practice. Following are some of the specific techniques that we use:

1. All free-throw situations that occur in a game: one-shot, one-on-one, and two-shot situations.

2. Row free throws: individually, in groups of two or three, and as a team. Row free throws are consecutive free throws that the individual, group, or team must be able to shoot during the five-minute practice period. Example: row five for individuals shooting a one-on-one would mean that each player in a group at a basket must shoot a one-and-one and rotate around until they individually have made five in a row during a five-minute period. It is usually desirable to have no more than three or four players to a basket in doing this so that they can get plenty of attempts. At the college level, we would usually try row four up to row seven for either individual or groups as a competitive practice situation. Any group that doesn't meet the goal during the five-minute period would have a minor punishment.

3. Sprint free-throw: this is a competitive drill in which groups of three or four players are placed at each basket and asked to shoot one-and-one situations (the bonus). If the shooting player makes both free throws, then a rotation is made and another free-throw shooter steps to the line. If a shooter misses the first free throw, then a penalty is assessed against the non-shooters. Non-shooters must sprint to touch four opposite walls in the gym while the shooter who has missed the shot continues to practice until they are finished sprinting. If a second shot on the one-and-one is missed, then the non-shooting players must sprint and touch two opposite walls before they come back and rotate to the next shooter.

4. Net free throws: a drill in which players must set a goal of four to eight shots that are successful and only touch the net. This is sometimes called "swish free throws."

5. Free-throw progression: a review of form and technique is carried out with a goal of row three or row four in the following manner. The first progression is taken from the imaginary dotted line in the lane (nine feet from the backboard). At this point a one-hand shot is taken without the use of the balance hand emphasizing form and holding the follow-through until the ball touches the net.

    The second shooting position is halfway between the dotted line and the regular free-throw line. At this location, the shot is taken completely the same as a regular shot except that it is at a closer distance. Again, the emphasis is upon perfect form and technique. Finally, a regular free-throw situation is completed with the same goal that was set for the day. Free-throw progression is used when a free-throw shooter has been having difficulty with the shot and may be in a slump or wants to review the basics of free-throw shooting.

6. Eyes closed free throws: on a regular basis, usually once a week, we shoot free throws with eyes closed to remove vision as the dominant sense. This forces the player to learn the proper feel of a good free-throw shot. Teammates act as the shooter's eyes and give appropriate feedback. Our goal here is row two to row four depending upon skill level of the team and the period of the season.

7. De-icing: this is a technique used to mentally prepare for a free throw when a player has to face the situation of a wait or time-out before a free-throw shot is taken during a ball game. We ask the player to relax by deep breathing and contracting and relaxing the arm muscles. The eyes are closed and a mental picture of the ball and the rim is created so the player

visualizes the ball going through the rim and touching the net. At this time we ask them to paint a perfect picture (PPP) by mentally shooting three free throws in preparation for the end of the time-out. Coaches need to be innovative in order to provide a variety of situations and to place players in competitive pressure situations that simulate the game contest.

The purpose of our total free-throw shooting program is to simplify the skill and teach players so that they can develop confidence in their ability to become a free-throw scorer. They must develop a muscle memory pattern with every free-throw shot being the same. Like eating, you shouldn't have to think about the free throw. Babies have to think, and we train them with a spoon and not a fork because there is no muscle memory pattern. There are many basketball players who never develop the proper muscle memory pattern and the confidence to shoot the free throw the same way every time they shoot. It is our conclusion that these methods will work. The Gonzaga University basketball team, using this program, improved its free-throw shooting from 65.6 to 70.1 percent during the first year and from 70.1 percent to 75.3 percent (13th in the nation) during the 1986-87 season. This included a school record performance of 79.8 percent during the West Coast Athletic Conference season. John Stockton improved to over 80 percent the last two years with Utah. He exemplifies the free-throw shooter who has developed into a player who can "score on the throw."

Chapter 11 INDIVIDUAL OFFENSIVE MOVES

Inside Shot

INSIDE PLAYERS
Post Play
John Thompson

Big Man
Joe B. Hall

OUTSIDE PLAYERS
Moves with the Ball
Hal Wissel

Playing the Point Guard Position
Don Eddy

INSIDE PLAYERS

POST PLAY

John Thompson

A. The Big Man's Role

1. Post men must have a positive self-image. They are conspicuous. Make them proud that they are tall.

2. It's important that the big guy touches the ball. Get him involved even if his primary role is defense or rebounding.

3. Show the big man how to receive the ball.

4. The pivot man is always closely guarded. It is where the defensive man is which determines where you pass him the ball.

5. Teach the big guy to seal his man.

   a. Your rear end is a pressure point used to hold off your defensive player.
   b. Spread out, "create a space," hold your arms out – bend over.
   c. The key is to learn how to hold and not to push. Don't get called for fouling.
   d. Create a passing lane or protect a passing lane with your upper and lower arms. The legs are overemphasized.
   e. Keep your shoulders free so you have flexibility. Your lower body (rear end) should be making the contact.

6. One way of receiving the ball is to start by going away from the ball and then holding your man behind you until the ball comes back to your side. Or you can flash the strong side at the proper time.

7. Another way to get free for a shot is to screen for the ball and then roll to the basket when the defense switches.

8. If I am close to the basket, I will set a screen with my back side. If I am on the outer perimeter, I set a screen with my front side. In close it takes too long to roll to the hoop with a front screen.

9. When going away from the ball, keep your eye on the ball—skip across the lane. Take your man away from the spot where you want to get the ball.

10. Don't assume that your big man can pivot. Teach him the pivoting moves.

11. Big men must know how to dribble the ball so they can help clear it.

12. Big man shooting
   a. The key on offense is to get the post man to keep his arms up. The big man can get a lot of garbage if his hands are active.
   b. The hook shot is a great offensive weapon.
   c. He must be a good foul shooter.

13. Big man defense
   a. Try to front the low post position.
   b. Once the post man catches the ball, the forwards and guards must help.
   c. Make the big guy the defensive leader because he sees the whole floor. This will help his ego.
   d. Post men don't talk enough. They are defensive traffic cops. Direct the defense by talking.
   e. Keep your arms up in the ready position to cover passing and cutting lanes.

B. Big Man Rebounding

The head, legs, arms and hands are all important.

1. Head
   a. Be aware of where the shots are coming from.
   b. Be aware of who is shooting.
   c. Anticipate the shot being taken and get in position for the rebound. Don't always wait for the shot to be taken before you seek your rebounding position.
   d. Talk to your big guys about the opponent's gym. Tell them the floor is a good rebounding floor.

2. Legs
   a. The legs are more important, as relates to position rather than jumping.
   b. Rapid jumping is more important than high jumping.
   c. Horizontal jumping is more important than high jumping.
   d. Rebounding drills
   (1) No jumping drill: Play three-on-three underneath–cannot leave your feet to get the ball–it teaches your big men to use their arms, hands, quickness, and position.
   (2) Timing drills

   (3) Passing drills off the backboard are good for reaction.
   (4) Rim touches.
   (5) All rapid game situations off the backboard are good drills.

3. Arms — Keep the arms high in the ready position. Keeping the ball active on the offensive board is important.

4. Hands
   a. Developing strength in the hands should be done with the basketball. Forget the gimmicks, i.e., fingertip pushups, squeezing a tennis ball, hand squeezers, and so on.
   b. One-hand rebounding is only effective on the offensive board. You can keep it alive this way, but you must use two hands on the defensive board.
   c. Learn to pivot and hold the ball once you have caught it.

5. Boxing out in rebounding.
   a. Always turn in the direction the player is going–front pivot.
   b. Make contact before you turn.
   c. Rebounding off the foul shot is very important. You should not hold your hands up high because this can alert your opponent. Your arms should be in a position to lock your opponent's arm.
   d. In weak-side rebounding if you are in a sluff position you should go out to meet your opponent before boxing him out.

6. Your big men should have positive learning experiences. If you need to, have your manager or your lower-line players drill against your main guys so they can have success. If you always battle your best against best, there can be a negative experience which could be detrimental.

7. Rebounding off the floor (loose balls) is also important. If one of your offensive rebounders gets a piece of the ball and deflects it to the floor, your players' horizontal movement is significant in coming up with the loose balls.

8. Zone boxing out: Form a triangle and take up a space in the key rebounding area.

BIG MAN DRILLS

Joe B. Hall

In the past seven years, our system has been extremely effective with the use of two big men in the same lineup. We began by using Bob Guyette and Rick Robey together and then were fortunate enough to win the national championship with the use of Mike Phillips and Rick Robey.

Despite the ever-present criticism that this system would not work, we worked extremely hard with our big men on a daily basis through various fundamental drills and inside moves. Toward the end of each season you can actually see the big-man drills being put to work effectively in game situations. The secret is: 1) repetition through hard work in the drill sessions each and every day, 2) patience with slow developers, and 3) a dedicated commitment to the two-big-man system.

The following drills and moves are ones that the big men in our program work on every day.

1. Mikan drill: Continuous hooks with each hand. Right hand hook, left hand hook, continued.

2. Tip drill: Throw the ball on the board, tip with your right hand in the basket. Then use a left-handed tip. Work up to five or six tips with each hand.

3. Rebound-stuff drill: Throw the ball on the board, go up with one hand and stuff. Use both hands. Then go up and stuff with both hands. (Do three sets.)

4. Beat the rim: Throw the ball on the board, go up and get it, then beat the ball against the rim before coming down. Beat the rim twice, then three times.

5. Power up: Throw the ball on the board, go up and get it, then bring it down. Keep the ball at shoulder level. *Do not bring it to your waist.* Then go up very strong and shoot a power layup off the glass.

6. Pump fake–power layup: Same as the power layup, only this time use a pump fake with the head and ball. Do both these drills on each side of the basket.

7. Superman rebound drill: Start outside the free-throw lane. Put the ball on the board above the basket at an angle and go rebound it on the other side of the lane with both feet outside the lane. Then throw it back to the other side and go get it. Do this continuously for 30 seconds. Work up to a minute.

8. Two-ball Superman drill: Place a ball on each block. Begin by picking up a ball and power move it to the hole. Quickly go get the other ball and power it to the basket. Continue this sequence for 30 seconds. Work up to a minute. You will need two other people to help you with this drill.

Big-Man Moves

1. Low side/power move: Post up big and wide on the block. The defense is three-quarters fronting you on the high side. Ward him off

with your left arm, receive the pass, and power move straight to the basket without a dribble. Then, utilize one dribble in your power move. *Go up strong!* Do this on both sides.

2. High side lane hook: Defense is now three-quarters fronting on the low side. Ward him off with the right arm, spread wide, give a BIG target, receive the pass, and then one step in the lane for the baby hook. Do this on both sides.

3. Lob pass play: Defense is totally fronting. Get position on the block. When the lob pass is thrown, keep both hands high; then when the ball is directly overhead, release from the defensive man and go get the ball – a power layup. Keep your hands high to avoid a pushing-off call by the official.

4. Turn and face: The defense is playing completely behind. Establish position with good, big post-up, then if you feel pressure, receive the pass, pivot, and face your man. Drive him right or left, or shoot the jumper. If you feel no pressure, receive the pass then, and shoot the quick turnaround bank shot.

OUTSIDE PLAYERS

MOVES WITH THE BALL

Hal Wissel

Basketball is a team game. By playing together and complementing each other's talents, a team with less individual talent can beat a team with greater talent.

This does not mean there is no place for one-on-one opportunities. On the contrary, the game is a series of one-on-one confrontations involving different aspects of the game.

The aspect of one-on-one involving moves by the offensive player with the ball against his defender is extremely important. It occurs every time the offensive player receives the ball. The player with the ball can help or hurt his team depending on what he does with the situation.

A distinction can be made between a selfish one-on-one player and a team one-on-one player. The selfish player does not see the entire team situation and guns the ball at the basket or plows to the basket like a bull driving into trouble. No matter what the defense, man-to-man, zone, or match-up, the objective is for each defender to be conscious of the ball and help his teammate guarding the man with the ball. These team defenses, with players who are adept at leaving their men and blocking the shot or drawing the charge, prevent the selfish player from succeeding. The team one-on-one player is one who gains an advantage over his defender with a solid fake or penetrating drive which forces defensive help from another defender and creates an opening for a teammate to score.

Looking at the one-on-one situation in another way, average players are only able to score when they receive open shots. Great players work to receive the ball in a position to be a triple threat to shoot, pass, or drive.

Any player desiring to be better than average must be able to:

1. Make the outside shot.

2. Pass to the open man in better scoring position.

3. Drive to the basket and complete the play with a shot or pass.

Being a triple threat is no easy task. It takes the desire and determination to spend countless hours alone perfecting one's offensive skills of balance and footwork, shooting, passing, driving, and passing off the drive. More than this, it takes the experience gained from competition to react to a given one-on-one situation and decide what is to be done.

Oscar Robertson was possibly the game's greatest all-around player, and he led the NBA in scoring and assists in one season. When asked what was the most difficult part of the game for him to learn, he responded with a profound statement, "when to shoot and when to pass."

The game's most exciting players–Bob Cousy, Earl Monroe, and Julius Erving–were all great one-on-one players who not only created their own shot, but would draw other defenders to themselves and get the ball to their open teammates for the score. This concept of one-on-one basketball is an integral part of team play.

Classification of Moves

Moves with the ball may simply be classified as low post (back to the basket) moves and one-on-one (facing) moves.

The low post may be considered as the area inside the middle hash marks on the free-throw lane and below the dotted semicircle line in the lane.

Getting Open in the Low Post

Work to get open by using a mentally strong and balanced stance with your feet spread at least three feet apart, knees flexed, back straight, rear out, and at least one hand up for a target. Try to seal (keep in one position) your man on one side warding him off with your back and upper arm while giving a target with the opposite hand high. Do not allow the defender to get his lead foot over your foot, but keep his pressure on your back and rear.

If you are not open you can:

1. Move away a few steps and quickly come back.

2. If you are completely fronted by the defender, take him higher up the lane a few steps, above the middle hash mark and cut back-door.

Receiving the Ball in the Low Post

Meet the ball, catching it with two hands. Use a jump stop, both feet landing together above the box, with the weight back on the heels and the knees flexed so that you have excellent balance to react to the defender with the correct move. Protect the ball by keeping it in front of your forehead with the elbows out.

Reading the Defense

Reading the defense means determining how the defender is playing you and then reacting with the correct move. It involves seeing the defender or feeling his body pressure against you.

In the low post, you read the defender's position by feeling whether his body pressure is coming from the top side (toward the foul line) or from the baseline side. In both cases you would drop-step with the foot opposite the pressure, or when in doubt he is probably directly behind you. In this case, use a front turn and face him to see how he is playing you.

Before you receive the pass, you can anticipate the defender's position by being aware of where the pass will be coming from, meaning corner, wing, or high post area, and by being aware of the defender's position in preventing the pass.

Three Basic Low Post Moves (Without Dribble)

A. Drop-step to baseline and power move.

1. Reading the defender's position to the top side, make a ball fake by showing the ball above your shoulder to the middle.

2. Drop step with your inside (closest to basket) foot, maintaining your strong balanced stance, getting your shoulders parallel with the backboard, your defender on your back, and the ball protected in front of your forehead with your elbows out and away from the defender.

3. Make a head and shoulder fake keeping your knees flexed and getting the defender to jump or at least straighten his legs.

4. Explode to the basket off of both legs, emphasizing position and power rather than height.

5. Shoot the ball with two hands from the protected position in front of your forehead.

6. Be in balance with your knees flexed to rebound a possible miss with two hands, and go up again with as many power moves as it takes to score.

B. Drop-step to the middle and hook.

1. Reading the defender's position to the baseline side, make a ball fake by showing the ball above your shoulder to the baseline.

2. Drop-step with your outside (away from basket) foot, pointing it at the basket, maintaining your strong balanced stance.

3. On the drop-step, move the ball to the "lock-in" position with the shooting hand under the ball and the balance hand on top of the ball. Do not lead with the ball, rather "step and hold" keeping the ball back and protected by your head and shoulders.

4. Hook the ball by lifting the ball to the basket with the balance hand on the ball until the point of release. Follow through with your wrist and fingers pointing to your opposite ear.

5. Be in balance with your knees flexed to rebound a possible miss with two hands and go up again with as many power moves as it takes to score.

C. Front turn to the baseline, cross over to the middle and hook.

1. When in doubt as to your defender's position, front turn to the baseline pivoting on your inside foot and drive step (jab step) with the other foot and fake a jump shot by showing the ball high toward the baseline. (If the defender does not react, you can shoot the short bank jump shot).

2. As the defender reacts to your showing the ball high, bring the ball low below your knees as you cross over with your lead foot.

3. On the cross-over step, move the ball to the lock-in position with the shooting hand under the ball and the balance hand on top of the ball. Do not lead with the ball, rather "step and hold," keeping the ball back and protected by your head and shoulders.

4. Hook the ball by lifting the ball to the basket with the balance hand on the ball until the point of release. Follow through with your wrist and fingers pointing to your opposite ear.

5. Be in balance with your knees flexed to rebound a possible miss with two hands and go up again with as many power moves as it takes to score.

One-on-One Moves (Facing the Basket)

A player may be a fine shooter and one-on-one threat, but if he can't get open once the defense is on him, his ability with the ball is worthless. Always see the ball. Scoring opportunities may be lost because the receiver does not see the pass.

Move without the ball to free yourself. You cannot stand still. Constantly change your pace and direction. Use moves such as the V-cut, back door, pop, fade, or flash. Work to use screening techniques to get open. Cut off screens with the roll, pop, or fade.

Receiving the Ball in Your Shooting Range

Get open to receive the ball while in your shooting range. Your shooting range is the distance within which you can consistently make the outside shot. Try, through disciplined practice, to develop a consistently good shot from a range of at least 15 to 17 feet.

By catching the ball in the area where you are a threat to make your outside shot, you can be an effective triple threat. If you do not catch the ball within your range, the defender will be able to sag off you and play your pass or drive thereby negating these moves.

Two Techniques for Receiving the Pass

There are two techniques for receiving the pass, depending upon the size of the opening created between yourself and your defender.

A. Catch the ball in position to shoot (after creating a good opening).

If you have created a good enough opening between yourself and your defender, catch the ball in position to shoot.

1. As you come to meet the pass, turn your body to face the basket.

2. Give a target with your shooting hand in the position from which you start your shot.

3. As the pass is thrown, jump behind the ball letting the pass come to your shooting hand. Do not reach for the ball.

4. Catch the ball with the "block-and-tuck" method. Block the pass with one hand and then tuck your non-shooting hand under the ball and your shooting hand behind the ball.

5. As you jump behind the ball, land in balance in position to shoot.

B. Turn and face the basket (if you are forced to reach for the ball).

When tightly guarded, beat your defender to the ball and turn and face the basket. A common mistake is for tightly guarded players not to face the basket and be an offensive threat. Poor players have the habit of bounding the ball immediately after receiving it.

1. Go to meet the pass. Reach for the ball with two hands. Land with a one-two step.

2. It is good to learn to land the inside foot (establishing it as a pivot foot). You can then protect the ball with your body and also be in position to execute a drop step (with the opposite foot) should your defender overcommit himself when going for the pass.

3. After receiving the pass, use a front turn and face the basket.

C. Triple-threat stance.

Upon receiving the ball, face the basket and become a triple threat to shoot, pass, or drive.

1. See the basket and your defender. By focusing on the basket you can see the total picture, including an open man under the basket or the man who passed you the ball starting a play. When seeing your man, read whether he is playing your shot, pass, or drive.

2. Drive step. This is a short (10 to 12 inches), aggressive jab step with one foot straight at your defender that fakes a drive and forces him to make a retreat step.

3. Weight on your pivot foot. Your weight should be on your pivot foot with your knees flexed and your upper body fairly erect. A common mistake of players is to lean with their weight on their forward foot. This limits quick reaction to the defense being played.

4. Square to the basket. Be square to the basket with your body facing straight ahead. This provides good position for a shot, and a pass or drive in two directions, right or left. Another common mistake is to face too far to the right or left, which limits your move with the ball to that direction.

5. Move the ball close to your chest. Keep the ball moving close to your chest above your waist and below your shoulders.

6. Keep your hands in shooting position on the ball. It is easier to change your hand position from shooting to passing than the opposite.

D. Reading the defense.

Reading the defense means determining how the defender is playing you. It involves seeing how the defender reacts to your aggressive drive step.

From the triple threat stance there are three basic moves: 1) drive step, jump shot, 2) drive step, straight drive, and 3) drive step, cross-over drive. All three moves start with the drive step. The move to be made will depend upon the position of the defensive player after he has reacted to your drive step.

If the defender retreats, come back for your jump shot. If he plays you tight, drive straight or cross over and drive depending upon his position in regard to your drive step.

The weakness in a defender's stance is his lead foot (the foot that's up). It is more difficult for the defender to stop a drive toward his lead foot because it necessitates a long drop step with the lead foot while reverse pivoting on the back foot. A drive toward the back foot only necessitates a short retreat step. The defender should protect his lead foot by moving his stance half-a-man over, placing his back foot in line with the midpoint of the offensive player and his lead foot to the outside.

You should read the defender's stance and position of his lead foot. If the defender plays you tight and head on, drive by him to the side of his lead foot (weakness). Use a straight drive or cross-over drive depending upon which foot is your pivot foot.

It is extremely important that on your drive step you stop and hold your position for a count of one to read your defender's reaction and position.

Do not make the common mistake of hurrying your move, causing a poor shot, or charge. Keep your balance physically, mentally, and emotionally.

E. Three basic one-on-one (facing the basket) moves. From the triple-threat stance there are three basic moves all starting with an aggressive drive stop.

1. Drive step, jump shot.
   a. Make an aggressive drive step. Stop and read the defense.
   b. If your defender reacts by retreating, quickly bring your drive step foot back into your balanced toe-to-heel shooting stance and shoot your jump shot.

2. Drive step, straight drive.
   a. Make an aggressive drive step.
   b. If the defender does not react with a retreat step, take a longer step with the same foot used to drive step.
   c. Take a long dribble forward with your outside hand, then push off your pivot foot. Do not make a traveling violation on this move. The ball must leave your hand before you lift your pivot foot off the floor. Also, be sure not to drag your pivot foot. By keeping you weight on your pivot foot during the drive step, you can prevent traveling.
   d. Protect the ball with your inside hand as a guard hand and with your body.
   e. Drive in a straight line to the basket keeping your body close to the defender and trying to cut off his retreat by "closing the gap" between your body and his possible retreat step.

3. Drive step, cross-over drive.
   a. Make your aggressive drive step.
   b. If the defender reacts by playing you tight in the direction of this step, swing the ball down below your knees and cross-over step with your drive-step foot in the opposite direction. Do not bring this foot back to your starting position before crossing over.
   c. Take a long dribble forward with your outside hand, then push off your pivot foot.

d. Protect the ball with your inside hand as a guard hand and with your body.

e. Drive in a straight line to the basket, keeping your body close to the defender and trying to cut off his retreat by "closing the gap" between your body and his possible retreat step.

Remember, on your drive step, stop and read the defense, keeping your balance – physically by keeping your weight on your pivot foot, mentally by making the correct move, and emotionally by knowing the total team situation and keeping your poise.

One-On-One as a Part of the Team Concept

On your drive see the total team picture. There is no greater offensive play than driving by your defender causing another defensive man to react to stop you, and then passing to a teammate spotting up in an open area for an easy shot. This concept of unselfish one-on-one basketball that creates openings for teammates is team basketball at its best.

PLAYING THE POINT GUARD POSITION
Don Eddy

General

A. Every position on the team has an important role to play in the success of this team. But the Alpha (the beginning) and the Omega (the ending) or importance is in the position of the Number 1 guard. This player must be the most completely skilled and, even more importantly, must have the intangibles of leadership and the coach's perspective of the game. Much of this is gained by years on the court, being coached and liking to be coached, and also enjoying and studying the strategies and technicalities of the game. He is the coach on the floor and this applies to practice as well as games. Sometimes it comes down to taking a stand at the risk of being unpopular for the good of the team.

B. You keep your teammates in touch with the coaches and you keep your coaches in touch with your teammates. This is on the court and off the court. A difficult challenge is for you to see the coach's perspective as well as that of the player. This will better enable you to be the team leader which you and the coaches want you to be.

C. Strive to help your teammates maintain a positive line of conservation between each other. It is never acceptable to tear a teammate down. This is often done under the camouflage of humor. It is in poor taste and is very destructive to team attitude to "humorously" poke fun at a teammate's game or any part of his person–such as his number of shots, shot

selection, speed, body build, looks, hands, and basketball intelligence. You should not criticize any of these things, and you should stop any teammate who is inclined in that direction. Only the coaches can be critical of a player's performance. The exception is during the flow of a game or scrimmage when you are the coach on the floor and have to keep individuals in line with the team concept and team goals.

D. Basketball is a team game and unity is of utmost importance, although every team member is an individual. The same general standards are applied to all players, and in working with each player to reach those standards, some may need to be treated differently than others by the coaching staff. You understand this principle also from the standpoint of being the "coach on the floor."

E. You know the 10 attitudes that build winners and how they apply to your individual and team success.

F. The qualitites of a clutch player are your goals to be or become. Study them and make them a part of your being.

G. During the flow of the game, the position you play puts you in "front" of your teammates at all times. You initiate most everything. On offense, you start the offense with the ball. On defense, you set the defense by how you first meet the ball with intensity and pressure. Your teammates key off all this. If you are poised and smart as you start the offense, the team will be as you are. If you are intense and tough defensively, your front line will play the same way. So the bottom line is that it all starts with *you*! You can create much of the attitude and atmosphere for the players around you.

H. Keep a watchful eye on your teammates during the course of action. Watch for fatigue and loss of concentration. Communicate your findings to the coach.

Attitude

Attitude is everything. In a nice way (or whatever way necessary), keep pettiness and bickering out of the game. Your teammates will honor your leadership and stand against this sort of thing.

Practice

A. Daily practice is what you love and where you really excel. You set the example for intensity, concentration, and execution from the time you set foot on the floor until you leave the court.

1. Non-basketball talk is taboo.

2. Enthusiasm is a must *every day*!

B. As practice moves from drill to drill and situation to situation, you lead the way in getting organized and getting things going.

C. "Hurting" and being tired are an important part of every practice and every game. *You play above it –*

you react by stepping up the pace and increasing the enthusiasm.

Intelligence and Leadership

A. You have studied the game plan until it is a part of you, and where possible have studied films of opponents so that you can visualize all game possibilities before they happen.

B. On game day and night, you know all the mechanics and procedures to be followed that day. You understand that each part is important to the outcome of the game that night and to games ahead. Because of this, you make every effort to have yourself and your teammates get each part done in a proper way.

1. The time in the locker room before the game is of utmost importance. The attitude of seriousness and thoughtfulness must prevail in an atmosphere of peace and calm. Loud talk, non-basketball talk, horseplay, etc., is absolutely unacceptable.

2. The pre-game warmups are a key get-ready time. Enthusiasm, concentration, and execution are the theme.

C. Know that your team wins from the inside and keep them honest from the outside. The most productive play on offense is to draw the foul in an attempt to score and this can be most successfully done from the inside.

1. At the start of a game the tendency is to fire away from the outside: Hitting or missing it will beat you in the long run.

2. The start of a game must feature good passing, penetration inside by pass or dribble, and player movement. We gain a definite psychological advantage in a lot of ways: You have established to the opponent that you can hurt him in his most vulnerable area, and you have all of your teammates involved and "playing."

This will pay dividends defensively as well as offensively.

D. As you are playing the game at its present point, at opportune times such as between plays or when the clock is stopped, your mind is playing ahead preparing for possible upcoming situations. You want your teammates to be doing the same thing and you must be talking to them all the time about possibilities.

E. Know the strength of the team you have on the floor at any given time, and look to play to that strength. If you are bigger and stronger inside, you must be careful not to outrun your strength while still keeping the pressure on and challenging your big men to get up and down the floor. If your strength is quickness, then you up the tempo and go that way.

F. As a point guard you are not looking to score as a first priority. If the opportunity is there then capitalize on it, but your first priority is to look for opportunities for your teammates.

G. Be a calming influence. You have poise! Do not try to force passes, shots, drives, low-percentage steals, and so on. When you force the issue, the rest of the team has no guidance or direction. Play within your physical ability (each of us is different). Be patient and allow the game to come to you.

H. Know the offenses and defenses inside and out. You must know the movements and responsibilities of every man on the floor.

I. *You are in charge!* Everyone in the gym must know that by how you conduct yourself on the court. Confidence and leadership "ooze" out of your being!

J. You must maintain continuous communication with the head coach. As time goes on you will find yourself thinking more like him. Every direction coming from the bench you can apply in detail using every option and also being confident enough to deviate when the situation warrants it.

K. *Do not be afraid to make a mistake!* Fear has no place in your makeup. You know the percentage of success for everything you do, so fear has no part of you. When your teammate makes a mistake, "pick him up" and help him put it behind him.

L. You must be a good public relations man on the floor, creating lots of goodwill with the following.

1. Your teammates

2. The officials

3. Fans in the stand

M. You must act by planned thought, not by impulsiveness. In other words, you condition yourself to do what is called for in a given situation, not what all of a sudden you may "feel like doing."

N. It is OK to say, "I don't understand," or "Someone else could do it better," if these situations arise. Ego and pride must take a back seat to team success.

O. Know the time and score at all times!

P. When calling a time-out in the frontcourt, bring the ball inside the five-second hash mark before calling time out. This is so we can effectively execute the SLOB (sideline out of bounds) play.

Q. Constantly compliment your inside people for sprinting up and down the floor, hitting the boards, taking the charge, intimidating defensively, playing smart, passing it back out, and so on. In other words, there is always grounds for being positive in your communication. This lays the proper groundwork for them accepting constructive criticism positively from you when that is necessary.

Offense

A. Keep in mind that you have a dominant hand and that your mind subconsciously works to that side.

Even though you use each hand well, your tendency will still be to start the offense to the right if right-handed, to look to your right as soon as you catch a pass, and so on. So you must make a conscious attempt to work both sides of the court equally. The team suffers if the lead guard is "one-sided" as opponents capitalize quickly on these kinds of tendencies.

B. Know and understand spacing on offense, both in transition and in the set. While the basic responsibility for spacing is the players without the ball, you can also help. Try to maintain a general midpoint between two receivers. Too close to one (less than 12 feet) means you are too far from another (more than 18 feet). On the set you will usually have two immediate receivers and sometimes three. You keep the offensive pressure on by maintaining a position that allows you to play effectively with all immediate receivers.

C. Sense when you have a teammate that is in really good rhythm (hot hand), has a mismatch, has an opponent in foul trouble, etc. Know the offense in depth so that you know what options to run and to which side to increase the scoring opportunities for him. At the same time you do not disorient the offense to benefit one player.

D. Give the ball up freely and quickly. This way your teammates are always anxious to get the ball back to you. It is very dangerous to make judgments like ignoring an open teammate in an attempt to wait for an opening for a scoring pass underneath. This is what we call the "big play syndrome." The first open man gets the ball!

E. Your head and eyes are always centered on the basket. You should have all four receivers in your field of vision. Learn to use your peripheral vision to find teammates. Some eye movement is necessary, but you should not move your head.

F. Know that a set defense is toughest the first 15 to 20 seconds you face it. Move the defense with two to four basic passes before you attack it. This also gets your teammates into the act handling the ball while breaking the defense down. Now is the time to look for the penetration drive or pass.

G. Penetration does not mean that you beat your man and get a shot off. Penetration also does not mean that you drive as hard and as fast as you can and then be forced to do something with the ball that is not desirable.

1. Know and learn what to expect when you penetrate. Know ahead of time from where the defensive pressure will come and react to the pressure.

2. Do not have your mind made up before you penetrate.

3. To penetrate and charge means you are out of control, and that is the poorest of offensive plays. As you are learning to play against tough defense, you will charge some – just learn by it!!

4. When penetrating, always get at least into the lane before picking up your dribble.

H. Equal and skilled use of both hands goes without saying (almost). Allow no opposing scout to even entertain the thought that you are not fully ambidextrous!

I. You execute the pass that meets the need of the situation. The spectacular pass/play is not made to please the crowd. In the natural course of action this type of pass/play will sometimes be the only one that fits the need, but there is no place for manufacturing it.

J. Keep everybody happy by free distribution of the ball. You have got to know when a particular teammate has not touched the ball for a while and get it to him. That does not mean that he has to shoot it necessarily, but just handle it.

K. When playing against full-court pressure, double teams, and so on:

1. You have 10 seconds to advance the ball across midcourt, so no need to hurry.

2. Do not pick up your dribble in a double team.
   a. Use the backup dribble to get out of the double team.
   b. In backing out of the double team, look to split it by going to the low dribble and driving between the defenders.

3. All forms of presses, double teams, and so on load up on the ball side. Thus ball reversal is a must in beating the press.

4. Try to keep three angles of passing attack with the ball:
   a. Sideline.
   b. Middle.
   c. Release behind the line of the ball.

5. If you should receive the inbounds pass, after squaring up and "reading," you should try to advance the ball as far up the floor as possible to ensure a release passing angle behind you.

6. In getting open to receive the inbounds pass, stay out of the corners. They are double team territory.

7. After beating the press, your team should advance the ball all the way to the baseline.

L. Understand the value of the basketball and *take care of it*! Your opponents cannot put any points on the board without it.

M. Learn to move your teammates by eye contact, head movement, body language, and visual signals.

N. In crucial situations, know who ought to have the ball for the key scoring efforts.

O. If you get a half-step advantage when being pressured on the dribble in the backcourt, accelerate and angle in getting contact trying to draw the foul.

Defense

A. You set the tone defensively. You are the first line of defense and your front line will play with the same intensity and intelligence they see out of you. Executing every play soundly and enthusiastically will upgrade everyone's play.

B. Know what defense you are in and communicate that to your teammates at all times. When we substitute, you need to do the same relative to defense and offense.

C. The opponents' point guard is usually their key man just like you are. Thus, the better job you do on him defensively, the more difficulty the opponent will have playing in rhythm.

D. Defense is potentially the most consistent and successful part of our game. You must attach special significance to how well you play defensively. Playing hard-nosed, tenacious, intelligent, team-oriented defense will make you invaluable to your teammates. They will follow your example. Concentration is so important as you maintain proper position at all times. Then you have to go the second mile and do things to help your teammates that are not called for in the organized scheme of things. Taking the charge and diving for loose balls must be automatic for you.

E. The hustle, guts, and determination you display in transition defense are critical to the team. When an opponent is coming down on you on the break, you must be determined to stop him. Going through the motions and giving up a score is not acceptable. Your back is to the wall and you must work and fight a delaying action until help gets there. No lay-ups.

1. Talking continually on defense, especially in transition, is so important.

2. Demand that your teammates hustle back in transition. Good transition defense is even more important than transition offense.

F. Keeping the ballhandler as far off the center of the court and as close to the sideline is extremely important to the overall function of the defense. Understanding who is overplay – deny, support, and so on – is first determined by ball position.

Tempo and Transition

A. As the primary ballhandler, you determine the tempo to some degree by how quickly or slowly you advance the ball up the floor.

1. Try to catch some defensive player asleep in the final phase of transition.
2. Make your own teammates get into the offensive position as quickly as possible. When the ball is deep into the frontcourt and no opportunities are there, he keeps his dribble alive and brings it out to set up.

B. If you pace yourself you will find that you are leading a "lazy team." If you are nervous or anxious you will find the same thing in your teammates.

C. When you feel your big men are temporarily out of breath or the momentum is shifting the other way, you may slow it down and walk it up.

D. Feeling the movement of momentum is so important. If it shifts to the opponent, you slow it down. If it shifts your way, you increase the tempo as a rule. This is particularly true if you are playing on the road where the crowds are the big part of momentum. The more quickly the home scores come, the more the crowd enthusiasm builds and the situation becomes more disturbing. When this begins to happen, you put time between their scoring opportunities by controlling the ball.

E. Some reasons you might want to "up tempo":

1. You are on a roll–everything is breaking your way.

2. The opponent is sending four or five men to the boards.

3. Your team on the floor has a speed and quickness advantage over the opponents on the floor.

4. The opponent is not "deep" and offensive pressure makes fatigue a factor in your favor.

5. The opponent's half-court defense is unusually tough, so you try to beat it in transition.

F. Some reasons you might want to "down tempo" are:

1. "Big Mo" is going the other way.

2. You have a key player who is in foul trouble or tired and he must stay in the game.

3. You have not scored in three straight possessions, so you go for the sure basket.

4. Your opponent has scored three straight baskets, so you want to put some time between their possessions.

5. The team you have on the floor is at a speed and quickness disadvantage.

6. You have a real size advantage, so you play to the big men.

Conclusion

A. The most important contribution you can make is the height to which you can raise the determination, concentration, motivation, inspiration, and overall productive levels of the other players. A very important part of this is how well the team plays as a unit when you are in control.

B. You think of others first.

WHATEVER IT TAKES!

YOU ARE WILLING TO GIVE!

Part III TEAM OFFENSE

•••••••••••••••••••••••••••••

Unless you plan to out-rebound and out-shoot everyone you play, then you better learn to handle the ball.

—Henry Iba,
former Oklahoma State University
and Olympic coach

One of the basic purposes of the game of basketball is to score points. Team offense is highly dependent on team tactics and strategy as well as the sum of the individual skills each of your players brings to the team.

It has been said that your team's ability to compete successfully, if you have lesser individual talent, is especially dependent on your team offense. Balanced development of this phase of the game will allow your team to regularly meet the offensive objectives by obtaining good shots.

Inside Shot

Offensive Basketball at North Carolina
Dean Smith

DePaul's Offensive System
Ray Meyer

Missouri Offense
Norm Stewart

Offensive Philosophy
Bobby Cremins

OFFENSIVE BASKETBALL AT NORTH CAROLINA

Dean Smith

The object of basketball offensively is to score two points on every possession, and ideally three points. To me the best offense is one in which you get fouled. The biggest reason I'm against simply running the ball down and shooting the first shot available is that the defense doesn't have time to foul you. You have to give the defense the opportunity and time to foul.

Offensively you must be prepared for any type of defense. This is one of our jobs as a coach. If you have a player who can shoot the 15-foot shot with great regularity, it's your responsibility to find him the shot. As we approach offensive basketball, we should say that our goal is two points, with the board covered for offensive rebound possibility, and the opportunity for good shots. When talking about good shots, we're concerned with two factors: 1) distance from the goal, and 2) amount of defensive pressure. If your players have a good understanding of what a good shot is and are unselfish, then offensive basketball can be fun and easy to play. As a coach you need to convince players of their role on the team. Once each player understands his role, it will be easier for them to know what is a good shot for each individual.

At North Carolina, we firmly believe in the fast break. We always want to fast break after a missed shot or an interception. We act like we believe in it from a made shot, but I honestly don't think you'll get many of these breaks against a good team. However, by getting the ball in quickly, we discourage the opposition from setting up a full-court press defense. I have always thought that the toughest people for us to full-court press were the teams that quickly got the ball inbounds. We work every day on the closest man to the ball grabbing it, stepping out of bounds, and immediately hitting an open man.

Another area of the game that your team should be well prepared in is special situations. Make sure you practice your endline, sideline, and last-second plays. We even work on our offense from the free throw line by teaching the middle men to tip the ball back to a teammate. In addition, your teams should be prepared to attack any type of set defense. We number our offense in the following manner:

Number 1: 1-4
Number 2: T-game (continuity triple stack)
Number 3: Passing game
Number 4: Four-corner delay

T-Game

This offense can be used against both zone and man-to-man defense, but we've found it to be better for us against zones. We start every offense by giving the defense the same apparent look (see Figure 12.1).

We start our T-game by making the initial cuts shown in Figure 12.2).

1. Number 1 has the option of going to either side.

2. Number 3 goes to the same side as Number 1.

3. Number 2 breaks out opposite of Number 1.

We now are in the setup shown in Figure 12.3.

Once the ball goes to Number 3, Number 4 slides down the lane and Number 5 comes across (see Figure 12.4).

1. Against a zone, Number 1 will stay and look for a seam.

2. Against man-to-man, Numbers 1 and 2 will interchange.

3. Numbers 4 and 5 want to stay as wide as possible.

4. Number 2 stays away.

Against any zone, we want to start to one side and attack the other side. On all these plays, try to imagine we have started to one side and reversed the ball. In our T-game we have different options to score (see Figure 12.5 through 12.11, Options 1-7).

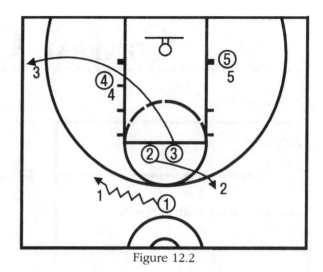

Figure 12.2

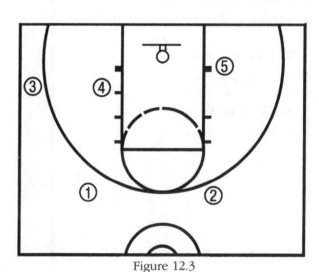

Figure 12.3

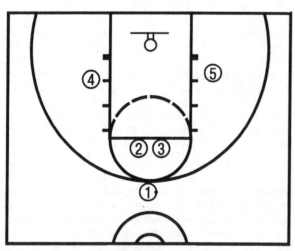

Figure 12.1

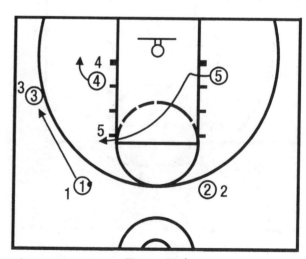

Figure 12.4

Figure 12.5 Option 1

1. Number 5 crashes the board.

2. Number 3 goes opposite the way Number 4 turns.

Figure 12.6 Option 2

1. High post Number 5 looks to Number 4 on low post and then to Number 2 finding seam.

Figure 12.7 Option 3

1. Perimeter people hold ball above their heads when there is pressure.

2. Throw cross-court quickly if Number 2 is open.

3. Dribble penetrate (split the defense).

Figure 12.7
Option 3

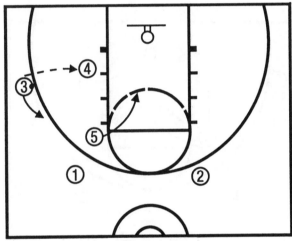

Figure 12.5
Option 1

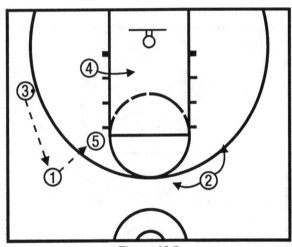

Figure 12.8
Option 4

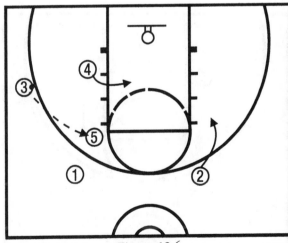

Figure 12.6
Option 2

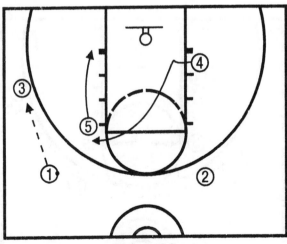

Figure 12.9
Option 5

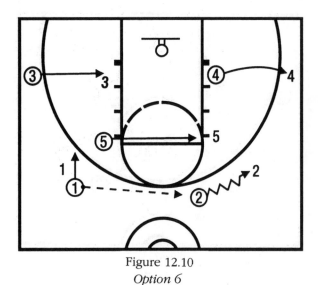

Figure 12.10
Option 6

Figure 12.8 Option 4

1. Number 1 looks for Number 5. If Number 5 gets the ball, he looks for Numbers 4 and 2.

2. Once Number 1 has the ball, Number 2 centers up. If 1 doesn't want to reverse the ball, he has the option to "kick back" the ball to 3.

Figure 12.9 Option 5

1. Number 5 drops down and Number 4 comes to high post.

When the ball goes from guard to guard, we're reversing the action.

Figure 12.10 and 12.11 illustrate Options 6 and 7.

As you can see, the opposite side then has the same options as the first side had. In this offense, if you have a big man Number 5 who can't shoot or handle the ball very well, we place him as the initial high post (see Figures 12.12, 12.13, and 12.14).

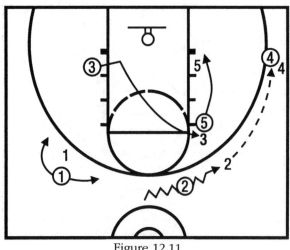

Figure 12.11
Option 7

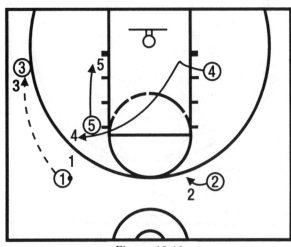

Figure 12.13
Left

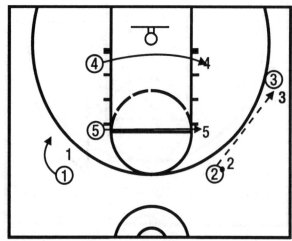

Figure 12.12

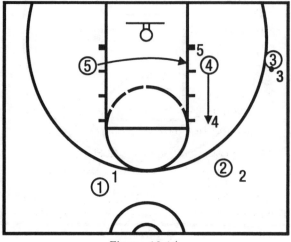

Figure 12.14
Right

Number 5 simply goes high and low, low and high.

Our whole philosophy on offense is to get the ball into the center of the court and then change sides. We feel the best places to have the ball are under your basket and in the middle of the court. Therefore, we teach defensively to try to deny the ball from those two areas.

Passing Game

We have two entries into our passing game: 1) When the Number 1 man brings the ball downcourt, and 2) at the end of our secondary break. As Number 1 comes down the floor, we set up in the following manner (see Figure 12.15).

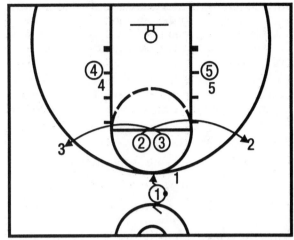

Figure 12.15

Numbers 2 and 3 help each other get open. To me, the key to the passing game is developing an unselfish attitude. In some way you have to congratulate the people who set screens and make the passes. I feel it is essential to encourage the man setting the screen. We tell our people that usually the man setting the screen will be the one who is open. This concept obviously generates some interest in setting picks! I constantly stop practice to ask players, "What did you do to help a teammate?" They need to be thinking about their teammate at all times. The most important thing in our passing game is movement. Don't pass and stand!

We believe in moving the defense before penetration. This is where our "three-pass rule" comes into effect. The exceptions to this rule are any layups and if your defensive man falls down. The three passes help us by: 1) making three players happy because they've touched the ball, 2) we've reversed the ball because the high post must get the ball every third pass, and 3) for some reason the shooting percentage gets better in relationship to the more passes we make. I also feel the passing game is a time saver, regardless of the level of competition. It also lets the players think for themselves and work to become true basketball players. I want to start with the "high-low post" passing game. We use this against man-to-man, zones, and for court balance (see Figure 12.16).

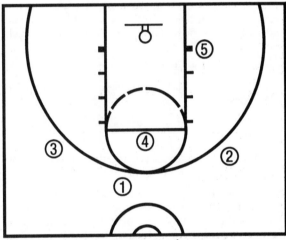

Figure 12.16

Our basic rules for the man with the ball are:

1. Pass and screen away.

2. Pass and go to the goal.

3. Pass and screen the man you pass to (after three passes have been made).

4. Pass and slide the perimeter (against zones).

The high post area includes (see Figure 12.17):

   1. Number 4 is one pass away from the ball at all times.
   2. Number 4 has to be able to get open.

The low post area includes (see Figure 12.18):

Number 5 needs to leave room for people to go to the corners. Whenever Number 4 gets the ball, Number 5 goes to the goal. When Number 5 gets

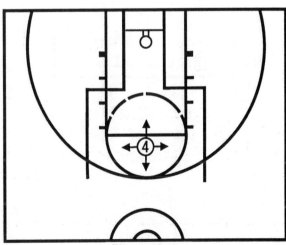

Figure 12.17

the ball, Number 4 goes to the goal. The man on the high post always looks low and then to the weak side. The hardest one point we had to teach was that the top of the key belongs to the high post man.

To work on our high-low post passing game, we divide the team into two groups, with the post men at one end and the perimeter people at the other basket.

Post Men (Figure 12.19)

1. Offense stays as long as they score.

2. If manager throws the ball away – switch.

3. Should build confidence because it's much easier to score two-on-two.

Perimeter (Figure 12.20)

1. Must pass to coach every third pass.

2. Offense stays if they score.

We begin work on our passing game early in the year by playing five-on-five without a basket. The game is to see how many successful passes each team can make.

Figure 12.21 illustrates another set.

1. Total score by adding number of passes in three possessions.

2. No dribble – this makes people move without the ball.

3. If the defense fouls, we add three passes to the other team's total.

Other drills that help in teaching the passing game include huddling with the offense and telling them that only the guards or forwards or center can shoot the ball. We try different drills to keep it interesting,

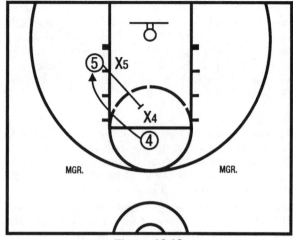

Figure 12.19

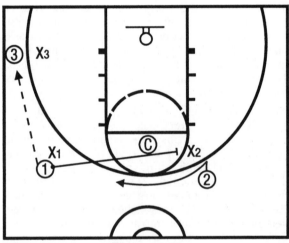

Figure 12.20

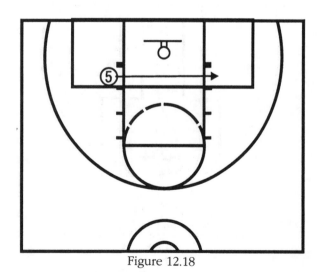

Figure 12.18

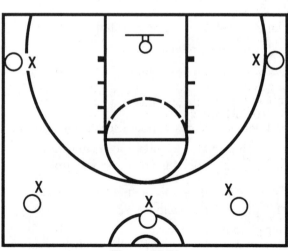

Figure 12.21

but we also stress movement and screening. When we use the passing game against a zone, we allow more dribbling by the guards and less screening by the post men. We stress that they find the open hole against the zone and be prepared to crash the boards. The biggest weakness in a zone is that it's difficult to block people out so we must take advantage of this situation.

Obviously, the object of the game is to win. However, we stress to our teams that they must do their very best. By doing their best, I mean working from the end of one season until the first game of the next one. You must work to improve. Once the game starts, I tell our players not to worry about anything and just play the game. I'm finally beginning to condition myself not to be upset if we play well and lose, and to be upset if we win and play poorly. Doing the very best you're capable of doing is the important thing.

DEPAUL'S OFFENSIVE SYSTEM

Ray Meyer

The offensive plan at DePaul University is based on a few simple philosophies. We try to beat the defense down the court and make an effort to outnumber them. Looking for the transition basket, our players are told to drive the defense all the way underneath so that we're able to get the 10- to 12-foot jump shot.

When the fast break doesn't materialize, we immediately go into our movement offense. The proper movement in the framework of our offense is to look for a good percentage shot. Basketball is a game of percentages. By probing the defense and working from inside-out, we have been very successful in taking advantage of the good-looking shot.

It's obvious that when the shots don't fall initially, the rebounding phase of our offense comes into play. The key to an effective performance is to limit your opponent to one shot and be able to get two or three when you're on the offensive end.

Every successful team must drill on their team-oriented principles at their practice sessions. All drills should be well planned in order to make sure the parts (individual drills) eventually fit the total offensive philosophy. The coach, as a teacher, is responsible for preparing the lesson plan – the practice session. By evaluating and organizing his talent properly, this chore becomes easier as the season progresses.

One of our early pre-season practice drills stresses squaring up to the basket prior to shooting the ball (see Figure 12.22). A shoots the ball, B rebounds and passes back to C who in turn passes the ball back to A for his shot. This drill normally runs for

about 30 seconds.

In the past, DePaul has been noted for developing the good big men – George Mikan and Dave Corzine, to name just two. A very simple drill, shown in Figure 12.23, helped develop our big men offensively. The player comes across the lane to receive a pass from the coach. After taking the shot he must rebound his own shot. The purpose of this drill is to teach the player to follow the ball on every shot taken.

At DePaul, we teach pressure defense. The players are taught not to stop and reach for the ball. If they don't get the job done the first time, they're asked to make a second and third effort. Most offenses start with a guard to forward pass. Our major concern is to put pressure on the man with the ball. After a few trips down the floor, the offensive player starts to think about that pressure. Basketball is a game of habit. If your defense can start to make an offense "think before they act," that offense has lost its advantage and eventually will deteriorate to some extent.

A big part of our offense is predicated on the fact that we must keep the weak side of the defense busy. In order to do this we run the diagonal drill (see Figure 12.24) each day in the pre-season and build on it daily. Basically it begins with the guard passing the ball to the weak-side forward after the forward has made a fake cut to the basket and then out to the foul line to receive the pass. Once the forward receives the pass, he has many options open to him, depending on how the defense plays him (reverse pivot or roll to the basket). Ideally we want him to always move toward the basket whenever possible.

Building on this drill might give us a situation as seen in Figure 12.25. Using one of our basic offensive principles (every time a pass is made somebody moves) as the forward receives the pass at the foul line, the opposite forward screens down for the

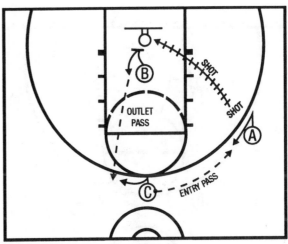

Figure 12.22

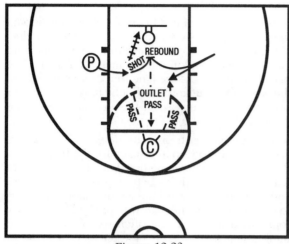

Figure 12.23

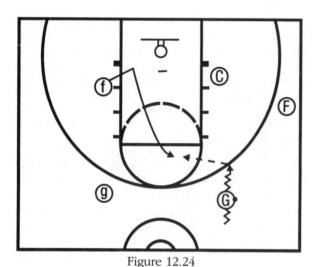

Figure 12.24

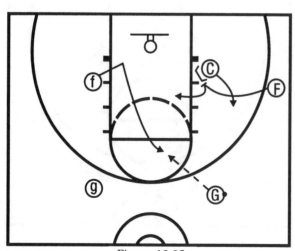

Figure 12.25

center. If the center is open, hit him with the pass. The opposite forward can also roll to the basket if the defensive man on the center switches. You can see that, with more players involved with this simple basic drill, more options become available offensively. Our players learn to utilize what the defense gives them off this formation so well it sometimes scares me. Once our offense finds a play that works continually down the floor, the defense will see it until they are able to stop it.

Speaking briefly about our offense against zones, a few simple statements can be made. We don't believe you can beat a zone consistently from the perimeter. We try to probe the defense inside first and the high post second. Alignment is another key to beating a good zone. Our players are taught to maintain good spacing (roughly 15 feet apart) with the positioning in the gaps of the zone.

Personally I don't believe you can beat the zone with only one offense. Defenses today are so sophisticated that they will adjust to an offense after seeing it a couple of times. Two things we try to do to disrupt a zone are: changing our offense occasionally and trying to get movement behind the zone. For us this has proven to be the best answer.

In all my years of coaching, I have learned it is much better to win than to lose. To make the job of winning easier, you must recruit talented players that fit your system, offensively and defensively.

MISSOURI OFFENSE

Norm Stewart

This is a game of percentages. You've got to know what works 70, 80, 90 percent of the time. You've got to have a knowledge of yourself, you've got to have a knowledge of the players, the game, the situation, so when that one time comes up, you can make a decision. It may not be tried and true, but you make that reaction, and if you know yourself and you know your players, it'll work.

If you catch yourself reaching for that five, ten percent, you're not going to get it. There are no tricky plays.

There are three areas on the court. The basket area, or the block, is the first; this is where we operate out of. This area is where the game is dominated. The boards, rebounds, close-in scoring, point-blank range — that is the game. What player plays there? I think you take a player who has to have some size, although sometimes your basket man can be somebody who just has the ability to play around the basket. He's got that ability to step around somebody, the ability to get his hands on the ball. If he can shoot the ball, we're going to keep him away from the basket.

The next area is what we call the midcourt. The middle-of-the-court player, I think, is the one the game was designed for. That's the player who can catch the ball, pass the ball, put it on the floor, has a fair shooting range, makes good decisions, can play in a crowd, is probably the best player on your team completely. Sometimes you've got to bring him out of that area to help you bring the ball down the floor but, primarily, he's in the middle-of-the-court area.

The rest of it becomes a perimeter area. You can talk about point guards, but I have trouble with the terms today. We just try to get players, put them together, and have one of them bring it up and throw it to the one who can shoot the best. We can isolate him and do some different things but, primarily, these three areas are what we are concerned about. Those are the three key areas. Who is in the basket area, who is in the middle of the floor, who are our perimeter people? They're going to move horizontally and vertically, but we know these are the three areas we are going to concentrate on.

Three Stages of Offense

1. The conversion for fast break – leads to the easy bucket.

2. The set – a basic form of organization.

3. "In between" a three-second period occurring perhaps 16 times a game, where the thrust to score remains between a fast break that doesn't result in a basket and the time when the teams set up their offenses and defenses.

The most important job the coach has to do is to select your personnel, people who are going to carry out your ideas of what you're going to do with your ball club. Staff selection, player selection, are the most important things you're going to do. To me, it's like being an artist. If I'm going to paint a picture, I don't want to hand the brush to somebody else. I want it to be my picture, so I've got to have people I can communicate with and I want them to carry that out. I want the picture that I see.

On offense, we play a weak-side forward-offset. It's extremely important for us to have the players understand their abilities when they're in that position. We play out of this offset alignment (see Figure 12.26).

Regardless of how we come in, we are going to this offset. It's an overload.

We like to break. We want the easy bucket, the first stage. We feel that's the one thing we can always do. I don't care how small our ball club is, or whatever the situation happens to be, we can get an easy basket. We've had some slow teams – not tremendously slow, but fairly slow in comparison to the people we're playing. Offside running can get you a lot of buckets. To me that is a key for conversion. How many people can you get to run

without the basketball? How quick you get the ball out doesn't have anything to do with it. That's one of the toughest assignments we have; everybody wants to break, but they all want to do it with the ball. Get that offside guy to run, that's the key. And you can run regardless of your quickness if you have mobility and ballhandling.

First Option at the End of the Break

Number 1 passes to Number 2. Number 2 passes to Number 5 and screens for Number 3. Numbers 4 and 1 clear.

Option for Number 4

Number 4 can come to the ball if the middle is open. Number 1 can pass to Number 2, and then look to Number 4.

Special Option

You look for certain ways to get your best player the basketball and get his shots. Ricky Frazier was a guy like that. The players knew when we had to have a shot at the end of a game, for example, the ball was going to him. This special option was run for Frazier. Number 1 (Frazier) passed to Number 2. Number 4 breaks high to open the basket area. Number 2 lobs to Frazier for the backdoor play on a direct pass over the top.

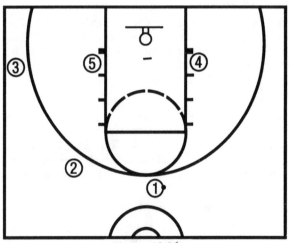

Figure 12.26

OFFENSIVE PHILOSOPHY

Bobby Cremins

Everyone should be skilled enough to fast break on missed shots. Fast breaks after made baskets must be flexible with the court spread and it is important to have open lanes.

Whoever takes the ball out for the inbound pass must have brains and courage. We have one of our big men, Number 4, assigned with Number 5 as his backup. Number 1, our point guard, always has the job of getting the ball. Numbers 2 and 3 are similar wing-type players that fill the outside lanes.

Fast Break After Made Baskets

Refer to Figure 12.27. Number 4 will take the ball for the inbound pass to Number 1, while the other big man Number 5 will go off center down the court first. After Number 1 advances the ball up-court, he passes off to the wing Number 2 and will stay around for the return pass. Number 5 will start looking for the ball at the top of the key, and it is vital that he attacks the defense on the ball-side block. Number 4 should go to the opposite block and face the ball.

Reverse Action

Refer to Figure 12.28. Number 2 will first look inside for posting Number 5. If not open, he should pass back out to Number 1. Number 5 will turn baseline and clear out behind the defense. Number 4 will flash to the ball in the middle looking for the pass.

Swing the Ball

Refer to Figure 12.29. Number 1 will put the ball on the floor hard so he can pass to Number 3 or penetrate. Number 5, our clear-out post, will attack the baseline from behind the defense. When not open inside after the swinging of the ball, we go right into our offense.

After the Swing Regular Offense

Refer to Figure 12.30. After Number 1 passes to Number 3, we like for him to rub off Number 4 outside but he might have to go inside. Number 4 will step to the ball if 3 can't pass to Number 1.

Passing Game

Refer to Figure 12.31. With the swing pass to Number 4, Number 2 will set the screen for Number 1 outside the lane. Our down screens should be set high enough so back-door is possible and low enough for the short jump shot. Number 3 can delay so that Number 5 can step in the lane for the lob or down screen for Number 5 to work for the short jump shot off the passing game pattern.

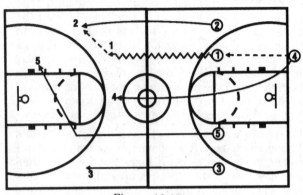

Figure 12.27

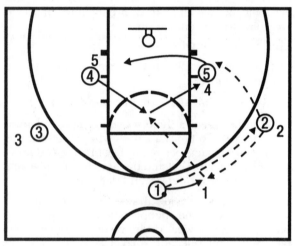

Figure 12.28

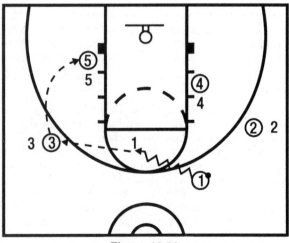

Figure 12.29

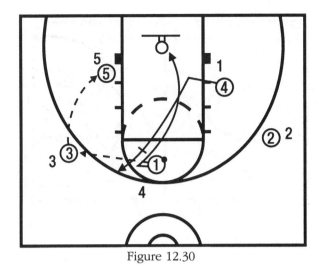

Figure 12.30

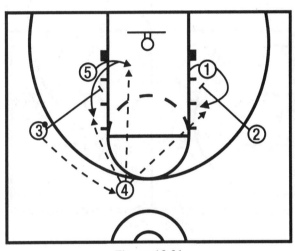

Figure 12.31

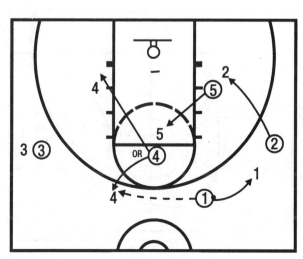

Figure 12.32

Fastbreak Elbow Position

Refer to Figure 12.32. Number 4 has the option to stop at the elbow. If he doesn't get the ball at the elbow, he goes to the opposite block for the regular pattern or pops out to the point for a swing pass to Number 4 from Number 1. Number 5 flashes in the lane looking for the ball, Number 2 replaces Number 5 and Number 1 slides over to Number 2's position.

Swing the Ball

Refer to Figure 12.33. Number 4 will look to pass in to Number 5, if covered. Number 4 will swing the ball to Number 3, with Number 5 looking for the ball down the lane. Number 2 will come up the lane to back screen for Number 4. Number 4 steps to the ball, then back-door cuts looking for the lob pass. Number 5 must attack the defense at the block and Number 2 pops to the point position.

Offense Versus Fullcourt Pressure

Refer to Figure 12.34. Number 2 and 3 wing players must check for press when flying down the outside lanes. If traps are set, they reverse hard for the ball with Number 5 remaining midcourt. Our first option should be to pass in to Number 1, the second option to the wing players, and third option would be Number 1, Number 2. and Number 3 screening for each other to get open. After the first pass, we want the other two onside players above the line of the ball. We want Number 1 attacking down the middle, Number 5 can go sideline or come back if needed, and Number 4 will stop in after his inbound pass, read the press, and then generally releases downcourt fast.

Dead Ball Situation

Refer to Figure 12.35. We need something for the end of the game and dead ball situations. Here we double screen with Number 2 and Number 3 for Number 1 around the lane. Our next option would be to get Number 2 or Number 3 open coming off their double screen. Number 5 will fly right away to clear out.

Free Throw Fastbreak Versus Fullcourt Pressure

Refer to Figure 12.36. Same rules as dead ball situations with Number 2 and Number 3 screening for Number 1 and Number 5 flying down the court.

Trick Play

Refer to Figure 12.37. Similar set with Number 5 coming hard to the outside wing, Numbers 2 and 3 screen first for Number 1 around the free throw lane. Number 3 will fly downcourt for a long pass if we do a good job of deceiving the defense into thinking we want the ball inbounded with a short pass.

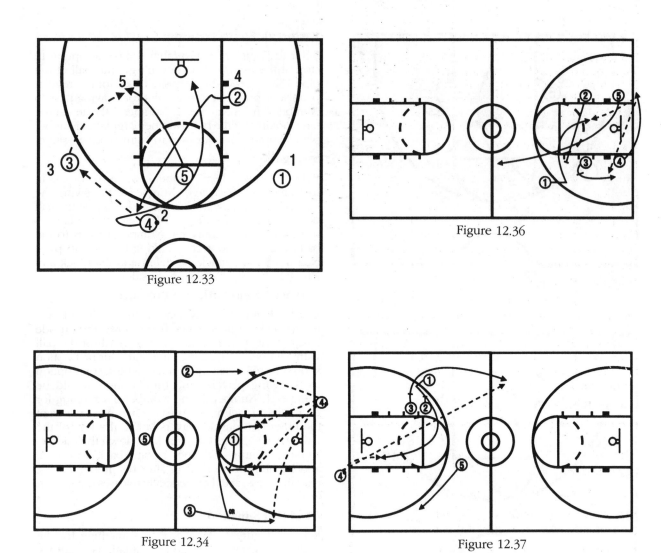

Figure 12.33

Figure 12.36

Figure 12.34

Figure 12.37

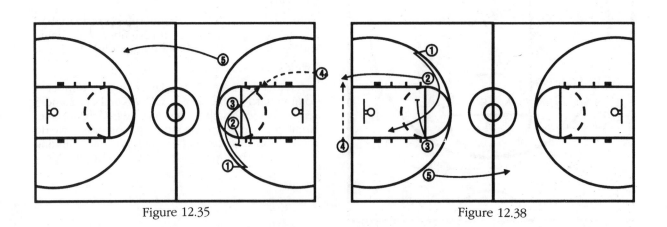

Figure 12.35

Figure 12.38

Against Fullcourt Denial After Time-Out

Refer to Figure 12.38. At times, we will have Number 2 jump out of bounds for the quick pass from Number 4, who will step inbounds for the first pass. Number 5 will fly, Number 3 will screen for Number 1, who will work hard to get open around the top of the circle and we are off with the fastbreak.

Half-Court Offense Versus Pressure

Refer to Figure 12.39. Our players Number 1-Outlet, Number 2-Weak-side, Number 4-Rover, and Number 5-Middle flasher must be drilled to react against the half-court trap. Our outlet and our weak side people are responsible for the outlet. Cross court pass to Number 2, our weak-side players, will hurt the half-court pressure but you must have courage to practice and use this outlet.

Halfcourt Rotation

Refer to Figure 12.40. If Number 1 reads halfcourt pressure on the first pass, he will go outlet, Number 4 will rove to the baseline, Number 5 will middle flash toward the ball, and Number 2 stays weakside. If the pass to the weakside Number 2, Number 4 will baseline cut, and Number 5 should step into the lane for the quick pass inside.

Corner Pressure

Refer to Figure 12.41. Similar options with Number 1 outlet to the sideline, Number 4 middle flash, Number 5 posting, and Number 2 weakside.

Georgia Tech Offensive Rules

1. Continuity – through patterns that are flexible.

2. Bust out for entry passes with dribble keys, screens, delay screens, and stack sets.

3. Breakdown splits – must teach cross screens.

4. Know passing options – look inside and weakside.

5. Deny options – use dribble option and weakside flash to the high post.

6. Shooting drills.

7. Use individual moves daily.

8. Rebounding.

9. Screens.

10. Ball movement.

11. Work against trapping defenses.

12. Special plays.

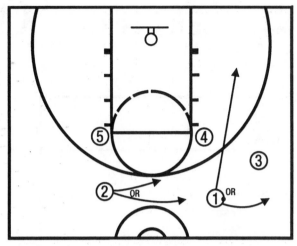

Figure 12.39

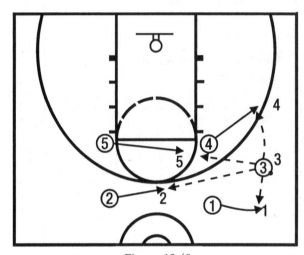

Figure 12.40

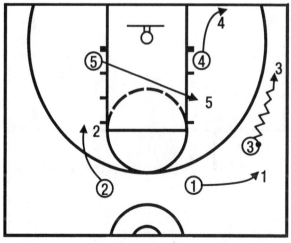

Figure 12.41

TRANSITION

FLOW TRANSITION

Harry Larrabee

I sincerely believe that most games at the college level are won in the transition phases. The same may be said of the high school game. Teams that reset well from defense to offense or from offense to defense have a built-in competitive edge. For instance, we would rather play three-on-three anytime rather than five-on-five because of the additional space our offensive men have to operate and crash the boards.

We have coined our conversion from defense to offense as the "Seawolf Flow" game. We refrain from using the term "fast break" because unconsciously it attempts to make our players rush, playing out of control. We have also found the concept of the "flow game" makes it easier for our players to execute our secondary break and to proceed smoothly into our offense.

Our flow game begins when we gain possession of the ball by either a defensive rebound or a steal. As soon as we gain possession of the ball, we attempt to push the ball up the court with our three primary ballhandlers (see Figure 13.1).

Rule 1 (and our only constant rule) is to make sure we maintain control of the basketball regardless if this means that we walk the ball up the court.

Responsibility of the principal ballhandlers is to advance the ball up the court as quickly and safely as possible with the middle and outside lanes occupied. We do not care who fills what lane. The important thing is to get to the lane that is easiest and quickest for each player.

Control of the ball is preferred in the middle lane but is not mandatory. We like to take the ball all the way to the baseline if we don't have the layup or the good 15-foot bank shot (see Figure 13.2).

We use the term "barge" for the fourth man who is the cutter toward the ball. We want him to make himself big and wide as he is cutting diagonally through the key toward the ball. We tell the perimeter people to "give the barge time to load up." As the ball is being reversed, the barge can either follow the ball if he has good position or he can step out and screen for a perimeter baseline player (see Figure 13.3).

Our last man down the court is called the "trailer." His primary responsibility is to be ready to defend our basket in case of a turnover or a quick rebound. Otherwise he fills the position opposite our point guard and becomes a perimeter player looking for the quick reversal (see Figure 13.4).

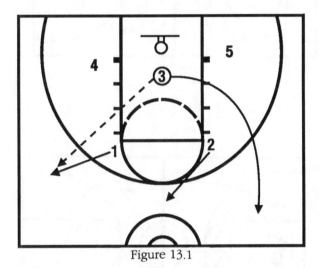

Figure 13.1

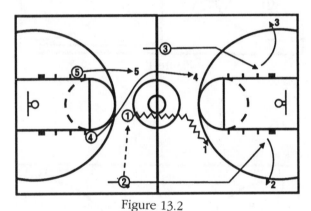

Figure 13.2

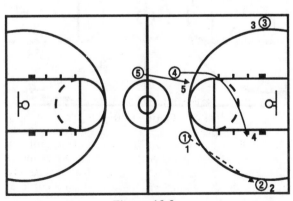

Figure 13.3

After the perimeter players have given the barge time to load up, we flow into our motion offense. This easy transition enables our offense to begin naturally so that we do not need to get everyone in a particular spot before we initiate the offense.

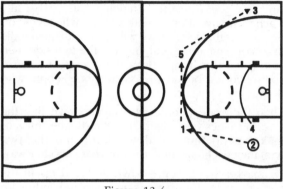

Figure 13.4

FAST BREAK

THE RUNNING GAME

Rollie Massimino

It's really a great opportunity for me to talk to you about what I consider the greatest game ever. What I'm going to try to discuss are offensive concepts in running the break and developing the offense.

Let's talk about the transitions. How are you going to run a fast break? Do you want to create the tempo of running up and down the court? Do you want to create the tempo where you're going to run, look for the break, look for open shots, make some movement off the transitions, then get into some basic offense? That's a decision you will have to make. There are about seven or eight different things you can come up with, but again this has to be what you want it to be.

How do you get the ball to go the other way? Missed or made fouls, field goals, steals, jump balls, and blocked shots. These are the ways to move into the transition and you must adjust accordingly. Do you want to pass, pass, pass, and get the ball stolen, or do you want to come down the court with some semblance of authority, try to outnumber the defense, and get a good shot?

Shot selection is very important. You must get good shot selection in your transition. If you don't make it clear what is a good shot to you, though, there will again be confusion.

Basically, what we're trying to do is exploit the defensive structure as you come down as a result of those changes.

First is the conventional way, shown in Figure 13.5, when the ball goes up on the board, is rebounded, goes out to the side, and everyone fills the three lanes and goes from there. In doing that, we basically teach the conventional break and say whenever you outnumber the defense, we will run it with the middle man stopping at the foul line and the two side men cutting to the hoop. Basically, we try to run a controlled fast break. We assign spots. People who do this are very successful.

Then there are people who come down like the Boston Celtics (see Figure 13.6) and either miss or make, whip the ball down-court and the two wingmen exchange underneath. That's another way.

Or maybe they'll come down and end up in the corners, with a fourth man coming in and ending up in the low post. Then play from there.

What we try to do is run an assigned break, with a controlled setup such that once the ball gets down the court we're set up and looking to take advantage of the defense.

In teaching this we can run several drills. We throw the ball up against the board and teach three very important spots (see Figure 13.7). The first spot is the 1 man and that's where the ball goes all of the time. When the ball comes off the board we try to get it to the 1 man. Not on the side, but to the foul line extended side where the ball comes off. If by chance they don't let the 1 man get the ball, we either power dribble it up or we give it to the 1 man on a flare cut to either side or on a button hook cut, but he has to get the ball. By doing this we're getting the ball up the court and we're putting the ball in the hands of our best ballhandler. This is the first spot that we teach. The second guy that we teach is our

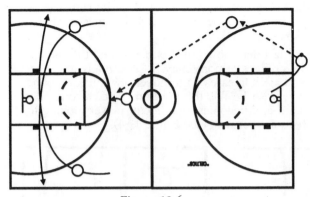

Figure 13.6

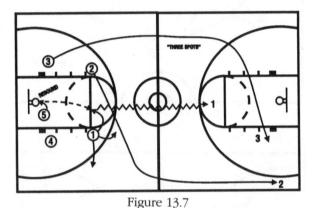

Figure 13.7

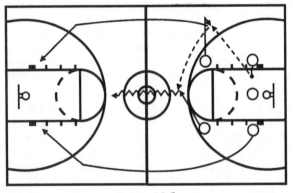

Figure 13.5

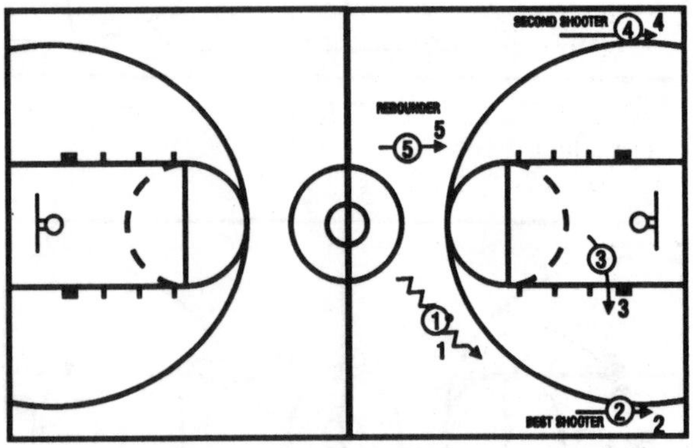

Figure 13.8

second quickest person and our best shooter. Say he comes down the right side of the court at the two spot. He is immediately prepared to shoot the ball. The third guy comes up the opposite side of the court and ends up on the low box. We assign these three people.

Then we bring the fourth man in and he goes to the opposite side of 2. Then we'll bring in the 5 man, who's the slowest guy in the group and probably the best rebounder in the group. Now these are the five spots that we assign. We just tell these guys that they have to get to these spots. The first possibility is a shot from 2. The second option is to drop it inside to 3 low. Outnumbering the defense is part of this philosophy (see Figure 13.8).

Next we say anyone can challenge for the 2, 3, 4, and 5 spot but the 1 man stays the same. Now what happens is everyone busts out of the gate and no one rebounds. So you assign 2, then let them go after the 3, 4, and 5 spot. Now after making a decision, you assign these spots and everyone knows where they should be on the break.

Occasionally we give a slight amount of freedom to 1 and 2. If the defense is set such that it's easier for 1 to go in the corner, he'll tell 2 to take his spot and we'll set up like that. That's really the only freedom we will allow between these two guys (see Figure 13.9).

The next drill is a five-on-three drill. Again to get them familiar with the spots. Then we'd go five-on-three boxing out, with two defenders back, but the three offensive men stay at that end after the shot goes up. We're still manipulating the situation so the offense will get a good idea of where they're supposed to be.

The next drill is what we call pop-up. We'll have five guys on offense, and six on defense. The rover in the mid-court area is only allowed to go within 15 feet of the center line to try to intercept the pass. What we're working on here is boxing out, outlet passing, and getting to the spots in a tough situation. Eventually the three offensive people are allowed to come back on defense.

Now to initiate or break down some of the aspects of this break, we use a variety of drills. We start with a regular three-on-two break, (Figure 13.10) with the side guys driving down the lane into a two-on-one situation (Figure 13.11). As the middle man comes down and passes, he is to go to the side he passes because that's how we teach our defense; the back man takes first pass ball side; the top man goes out back. Therefore, if the passers go to this side, it makes it more difficult for the top man to go back. As the ball goes up, the two defenders box out, the middle man drops back, and they come back playing two-on-one.

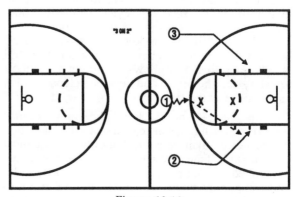

Figure 13.10

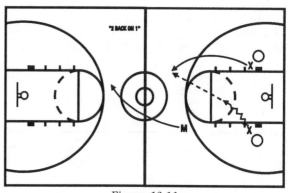

Figure 13.11

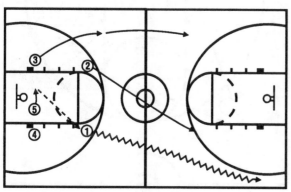

Figure 13.9

Now, to go along with that, we use another called three-on-two with help (Figure 13.12). The ball goes off the board, it goes to the 1 man, they come, and as soon as the ball crosses mid-court, a third defender chases, to help the two defenders already out on the court. The third guy tries to get in a position such that it is a three-on-three situation. Now as the ball goes up, they all box out, get the ball, and go back in the other direction (Figure 13.13).

The key to any kind of transition game is Number 1 getting the rebound and Number 2 getting the successful outlet pass to the right man. Too many times the kid will get the rebound, come down, turn, look, and pass. That is not a good start in my opinion. We set up a drill, with a simple line or two. The second guy throws up the ball, and the first guy in line must box the second guy out, get the rebound, and be facing the outlet position as he comes down with the ball. This is one key, to box out properly and get the ball to Number 1 quickly, and this drill should help that. This allows you to get the ball off quickly, start the break, and beat the defense, which is an object of the transition.

The first thing Number 1 does is he looks, because we don't want him getting called on the charge. Then he pushes the ball up-court, but only if he's almost unmolested. If he doesn't have it, fine, but we've controlled the tempo. I think tempo is one of the most important words in basketball. You've got to create the tempo that's best suited for your team. That's what must be established, based on the type of players you have.

Now we've brought the ball up the floor and we try to run to our spots. We like to hit in to 3, but it's not open we try to swing from strong to weak, from 2 to 1 to 5 to 4, while 3 comes across the lane, looking for the ball and sealing off his defensive man. Four also may get the shot, so after 5 passes he heads toward the low box. If 3 can't get it, he heads out.

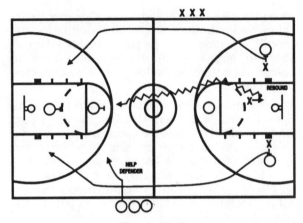

Figure 13.13

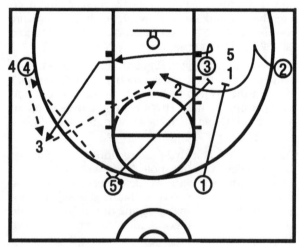

Figure 13.14

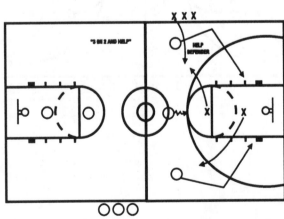

Figure 13.12

Figure 13.15

Now, the ball swings to 3 and 5 sets up a shuffle pick for 2 and we look. Next, the ball swings over to 5 and we set up the low exchange for 4. If it's not open, then we're in good rebounding shape as we screen 2 low, he pops out and deliver a skip pass to him for the jumper. If it's not open, you still end up with the little people outside and the big people low, which is the setup you usually start with. This is one way to run this transition. This can be a drill that you run in practice, five-on-zero just going through some of these options so that it moves smoothly and quickly. Another option for you on the same set is when the ball goes from 5 to 4, as 3 comes across, 5 goes through now, you've got a double set up for 2 as 3 pops out and gets the ball. This leaves you with a double away from the ball, which I think is very difficult to defend against (see Figure 13.14). Or if the defensive man gets caught behind the double, you skip pass over the top for the jumper (Figure 13.15).

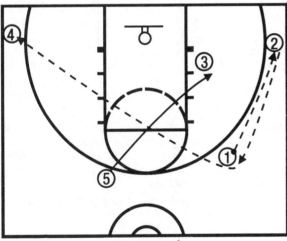

Figure 13.16

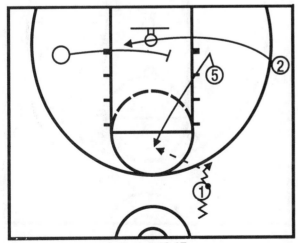

Figure 13.17

Now, you may have a problem with your perimeter people, when the passing lane gets cut off. If that happens, you send the guy through and skip-pass to the next man. The skip-pass philosophy must come into being, to set up certain things (Figure 13.16). We try to make our drills competitive and we keep stats on rebounds, bad passes, etc. We will make the players go through laps or something after practice as a result of these stats, if it goes beyond our normal limits. We have what are called three-minute drills, both for the break and for conditioning. We've got 12 guys, so we go six-on-six and keep score. First, we throw the ball on the glass and say first guy to shoot is Number 1 man. You say everyone must take a shot before anyone can shoot twice and you go back and forth for 1 1/2 minutes. After all five guys have taken a shot anyone can shoot. Then the next team comes out and tries to beat the total.

Another three-minute drill we use is going full court with three men we would pass, touch a sideline, one dribble only by the receiver, pass, touch a sideline, etc. and we try to score. Make sure they throw good passes, touch a sideline, and take one dribble. This continues with the same group for 1 1/2 minutes.

Another three-minute drill has to do with the break, even though we deviate a little from it. We play five-on-five now, the ball goes up, box out, and go down the court. For every offensive rebound the team gets a point. We try to work and see how many offensive rebounds they can get. Again, it's a competitive drill and I think it's helpful because offensive rebounding is very important. With this drill, we just keep running back and forth, trying for those offensive rebounds.

This next thing is probably the best thing that happened to us offensively all year. We call this a starter (see Figure 13.17). Regardless of what you want to do offensively, whether it be break or slowly set up plays, we've gone to a starter. We do this because, as you are scouted during the year, people come to know what you're going to do. If you continue to start your offense the normal way, you will be playing right into the defense's hands. This starter is something we do to go into our offense and you can really do it any way you want to.

For example, in a zone offense, your starter may be a dribble move which leads to a pass and whatever. You start something, see how they play you, then go ahead and do what you want to do. The same philosophy goes for a man-to-man. You want to see how they're going to handle you. You may run the ball up the court and have a guy flashing into the post. Off that, with the ball live in the middle, you might run a duck-in or a skip pass. If you can't get it in on this, you may run a low exchange and get the ball where you want it. This eliminates the "Coach, I can't get the ball" argument.

SONNY ALLEN FAST BREAK

Sonny Allen

We have a full-court offense – the fast break. The second we touch the basketball, we start our offense. Our philosophy is that anytime we get the ball, we want to advance the ball down-court as quickly as possible in an organized manner.

We get very few points off our defense. Most high-scoring teams get their points from their pressing defenses. I refer to our team as offensive specialists. We get our points from the fast break. We want the good percentage shot by outnumbering the opponents or getting the shot before the defense gets set. Our fast break is successful because it is easy to teach, easy to learn, and very adaptable. Two ways our fast break differs from the traditional fast break is that we give each player a definite assignment and our outlet pass goes to the middle man in the foul line area.

We believe this method is better because it is quicker and there is less chance of error since each player has definite responsibilities. The outlet pass always goes to the middle man at the foul area. This eliminates one pass and lessens the chance of making a mistake or getting an interception. Also, just as in football where the quarterback always handles the ball, our best ballhandler handles the ball 99 percent of the time.

In organizing our fast break we number each player by position. Number 1 is our middle man who is our best ballhandler and point guard. His size is unimportant but he must be strong and have good stamina in order to keep offensive pressure on the opponent for 40 minutes. Our middle man is a take-charge type of player with leadership ability. He must be a clever passer and dribbler, able to penetrate and at the same time possess the ability to hit the 15-foot jumper.

Number 2 is the other guard who fills the right side wing position. He is our shooting guard with good speed and good driving abilities.

Number 3 is our fast forward who fills the left side wing position. Speed is important as well as stamina. Number 3 is our third best rebounder who should be able to catch and lay the ball in on the move. The ideal player for this position is left-handed.

Number 4 is the trailer on the left side who is the slower but stronger rebounding forward. He must be a good outlet passer and able to crash the offensive boards. Speed is not that important here.

Number 5 is our pivot or safety. He is our best rebounder with a quick release on outlet passes. He must have good hands to get the shot out of the net

quickly to begin our break. A plus to have here is good 15-foot shooting range from the trailer position. In my fast break system, no player can change positions without my instruction. The outlet pass always goes directly to the Number 1 man who is at the foul line. The Number 1 man passes only when he is in trouble – that is, double or triple teamed, or when a teammate is open for a shot. The less passing, the better. We are looking for the layup, but we will take any good percentage shot within the normal course of the game.

As soon as we get the ball, all players have certain responsibilities to fulfill. The Number 1 man goes to the foul line and must get open. He must dribble the ball down to our end of the floor to the foul line. He must put pressure on the defense by making a feed or taking the shot himself.

The Number 2 and 3 wings must get the ball to Number 1 as quickly as possible and fill their respective lanes. They must cut to get open for a possible pass from Number 1. If they do not receive the ball, they must set up in good offensive rebounding position.

The Number 4 man, the trailer, also tries to get the ball as soon as possible to Number 1, He always trails behind and to the left side of Number 1. The trailer goes to the foul line extended, looking for the pass from 1. If 1, 2, or 3 shoots, 4 must crash the boards.

Number 5, the center, rebounds and outlets to 1 as quickly as possible. He walks down-court behind the play, acting as a safety in case of an interception or turnover. If we do not get a layup, he goes to any vacant spot and looks for a pass from 1.

Here is our alignment from our 2-3 defense (see Figure 13.18):

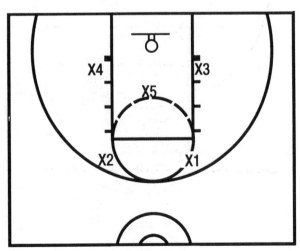

Figure 13.18

We fast break after an opponent's field goal in the same way as a missed shot except for only two small adjustments. As usual, when the shot is taken, 1 goes to the foul line. If the basket is made, he runs toward the right sideline to receive the inbounds pass from 5. Numbers 2 and 3 take off in their lanes. As the ball comes through the net, 5 grabs the ball and runs out of bounds toward the right sideline and inbounds to 1 at the foul line extended. From then on, the five players have the same duties as they did for a missed shot.

If our fast break is not successful, we execute a continuity offense at the end of our break (see Figure 13.19). Let's say the 1 man still has the ball. Number 2 comes back out about 8 to 10 feet for a shot while 5, our trailer, now takes 4's place. Meanwhile, 4 has cut to post low where 2 was positioned.

If 2 cannot shoot or pass 4 the ball low, he returns the ball to 1. Number 1 may now be open for a shot. Let's say that 1 was covered, 5 may now receive a pass for a shot or drive down the lane.

If 5 was covered, he can screen across for 1, who can then look for a shot in the foul line area. Numbers 3 and 4 are still positioned low for rebounding.

As you can see, our fast break is our logical approach to winning. There is a lot of action and both the crowd and players like it. Very few teams will press us because we inbound the ball so quickly. Our fast break allows us to utilize our personnel to the maximum. It has been very successful for me, and our teams will continue to use it as much as possible.

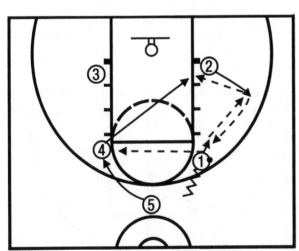

Figure 13.19

THE FAST BREAK
Jerry Welsh

The philosophy behind our fast break is this: Anytime that we gain possession of the ball we want to advance the ball downcourt as rapidly as possible in an organized manner.

We want to get the good percentage shot by outnumbering our opponents while they are adjusting into their basic team defense. The success of our fast break lies in its simplicity. This fast break is run differently than many fast breaks. It differs primarily in that each player is given a definite assignment and the outlet pass always goes into the middleman in the foul line area.

We believe this method is better because:

1. It is quicker.

2. There is less chance of mistakes because each player has definite responsibilities.

3. With the outlet pass going directly to the middleman at the foul lane area, there is only one short pass and less chance of interception.

4. Your best ballhandler has control of the ball most of the time.

In organizing the fast break, we number each player by the position we want him to maintain in our fast break alignment.

Number 1 – Middleman = best ballhandler, point guard

Number 2 – Left-side wingman = other guard, best outside shooter

Number 3 – Right-side wingman = fast forward

Number 4 – Trailer – down the middle and big forward

Number 5 – Safety man at the foul line = center

Numbering each player and giving him definite responsibilities helps to eliminate indecision by each player and reduces the chances of errors or turnovers. It also enables the players to react automatically to their responsibilities as soon as we gain possession of the basketball. Both factors lead to a better coordinated fast break.

Before listing the responsibilities of each position, a few important points about this fast break system should be understood.

1. The players should not change positions on their own; only the coach should make this decision.

2. The outlet pass goes directly to the #1 man.

3. The #1 man should be in the foul line area, and he should come to meet all passes.

4. The #1 man should be in the foul line area, and he should come to meet all passes.

5. We are looking for the layup shot but will take any good percentage shot if we have rebounders in position.

Responsibilities of Each Position

As soon as we gain control of the basketball, each player has the following responsibilities:

Number 1 – Middleman

1. Go to the foul line area and get open and call "Ball."

2. Spring-dribble the ball down the floor.

3. Put pressure on the defense and make the play in the foul line area.

4. Feed teammates or take the shot. He must make intelligent decisions.

5. Dribble to the right if your can not pass to either wing or the trailer and do not have an open shot. Look to pass to the #5 man at the foul line or the #2 man who has crossed under the basket toward your side. If you pass to #5, then screen away for #2 for a possible jump shot.

Number 2 and Number 3 – Wingmen

1. Get the ball to #1 as quickly as possible.

2. Fill your respective lanes very quickly.

3. Get open and look for pass from #1 man. Yell loudly, "I am on your left" or "I am on your right."

4. If unable to get a pass or a shot, cross under the basket and go out to the opposite side. The #2 or left wing goes closest to the baseline when they cross. They pass right shoulders. Number 3 should look to screen #2's defensive man as they cross.

Number 4 Forward — Trailer down the middle to the low left block

1. Get the ball to the #1 man as quickly as possible.

2. Sprint downcourt and go to the low left block while looking for a pass from #1 when he dribbles to the right of the free throw line. Be constantly yelling "trailer left" loudly.

3. Drive hard across the land if #5 gets the pass from #1 at the high post.

Number 5 Center – Safety man to the free throw line

1. Get the ball to the #1 man as quickly as possible.

2. Trail behind as the safety man. Go to the foul line and look for a pass from #1 to start the "secondary" break if there is not a shot on the "primary" break.

3. Constantly yell "secondary" or "foul line" to remind #1 that you are open to start the "secondary" break.

4. When you get a pass from #1, look for a shot or a pass to #4 diving low or to #2 or #3 for a jump shot.

5. When #5 passes to #3 or #2, he then cuts hard to the goal and #4 will then come up hard to the high post.

Mid-Break Positions

When the #1 man has the ball at the midcourt, Diagram 13.20 shows where all the players should be.

Fast Break Positions

When the #1 man has reached the foul line, Diagram 13.21 show the desired locations of all players.

Qualifications

Following are the ideal qualifications of each particular position that will make your fast break successful.

Number 1 man or middleman

1. Take charge type player with leadership abilities.

2. Must have good court awareness and be unselfish.

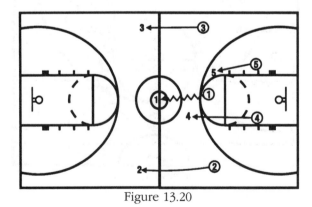

Figure 13.20

3. Must have stamina and strength to keep offensive pressure on opponents for full game.

4. Clever passer and dribbler.

5. Good penetrator with a good 15 foot jump shot.

Number 2 man or left-side wingman

1. Big guard or shooting guard.

2. Good speed and good driver.

3. Good 15 to 18 foot jumper.

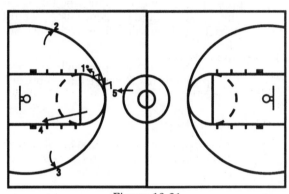

Figure 13.21

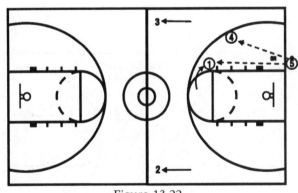

Figure 13.22

Number 3 man or right-side wingman

1. Fast forward with excellent speed and stamina.

2. Good rebounder.

3. Good hands with ability to catch ball on move and make driving layup.

4. Good speed and good driver with a good jump shot.

Number 4 man — Trailer to the left low post block

1. Strongest rebounding forward.

2. Fastest big man.

3. Good passer on the outlet pass.

Number 5 man — Center and trailer as safety man to free throw area

1. Excellent rebounder, strong and rugged.

2. Good, quick release on outlet pass.

3. Quick reaction on getting shot out of net; stepping out of bounds and making a firm, on-balance pass inbounds.

4. Good 15 foot jump shot from the free throw line.

Responsibilities after a Made Field Goal

Numbers 2 and 3 run the same pattern as on a missed field goal. Number 4 will go the right corner for a possible pass from #5. Number 5 will grab the ball from he net with both hands before it hits the floor. As he steps out of bounds away from the basket, he will look for #1 to the right of the free throw circle. If #1 is fronted and not open, #5 will pass to #4 in the corner. Number 5 will always use a two-handed pass.

Number 1 will work hard to get open and call for the ball to the right of the free throw circle. He must come to meet the pass from #5. If the pass has first gone to #4, then #1 will cut hard at an *angle* upcourt for a pass from #4.

Inbound Positions for all Players for the Fast Break after an Opponent's Field Goal (Diagram 13.22)

We dummy this numbered fast break every day in practice. The players must condition themselves to react immediately to all fast break opportunities. We emphasize talking on the break and carrying it through to the end. This is also an excellent physical conditioning drill.

We must flow from primary break to secondary break to half-court motion offense with good timing and without delay.

Reasons why we feel looking for the fast break opportunity is important on every transition from defense to offense.

1. Almost all players enjoy participating in a fast tempo game with both practices and games.

2. Nearly all spectators enjoy watching a fast tempo game with hard running, good passing and quick dribbling.

3. It gives an advantage to a team that is in excellent physical condition and/or one that has good depth on the bench.

4. It gives more players on the team an opportunity to play and contribute. A well-planned substitution pattern is important if a team is going to put pressure on for the entire game.

5. It is very difficult to apply a full court or half court press on a team that fast breaks in an organized manner on every transition from defense to offense.

6. The fast break is an excellent way to insure that your team is in excellent physical condition. This conditioning will help your team on other important aspects such as team offense, defense, and rebounding.

7. It helps teach good team and individual discipline as both are important if the break is going to be well-organized. Proper shot selection is necessary as the team flows fro the primary break to the secondary break and into the half-court offense with continuity.

8. Teams that you play will have to spend much time preparing to defend the break. This will take practice time away from other important part so their game plan such as half-court offense and defense as well as other practice drills. Teams may have a tendency to prepare against you negatively instead of positively. If your fast break is as good as it should be the opposing coach will constantly be telling his team in practices and pregame talk, "We must get back or they will kill us with their fast break."

9. I feel that this aggressive play will carry over and help your team defense, team offense and rebounding.

Chapter 14 PRESS OFFENSE

ATTACKING PRESSURE DEFENSES

Lou Carnesecca

I believe that you must decide your philosophy. The other team is trying to speed up your tempo with the pressure. In one game several years ago, we established our philosophy because we were picked to pieces. We have been beaten since, but not because we were not prepared.

The kids must be prepared for the defense, ready physically and mentally to combat the pressure. Let me warn you that you can be mentally and physically ready but still things may not turn out well. Don't ditch what you are doing. Stay with what you believe. Organize yourself and organize your team.

There are two kinds of attacks. There is the free-lance attack in which the players move to the open spots. The second type of attack is the control press attack. The kind of players you have will determine which attack you will use. I like the controlled attack better. This is the one we are going to discuss today.

What are some of the objectives of the attack against pressure? The first thing, of course, is to get the ball inbounds. The next thing you want to do is go into some sort of an attack. The most important thing you must do against any type of pressure defense is to score. So many times teams are satisfied to get the ball across the 10-second line. They don't try to score. I think that is a mistake.

What are some of the ideas about pressure attacks that we can build on? One thing that is very important is to place your men where they will perform at their best in the attack. The second thing is to determine either through your scout report or through playing them in the first half, what type of press they are using. Instill in your players and yourself that they must be calm. This is the third idea in handling pressure. Make sure your players know that they must stay calm and if they make one mistake, for goodness sake, don't make two. You can get so upset about throwing the ball away and giving up that hoop that you give away two and then three. When they feel pressure they must stay calm. The next thing they should know is what I call the three looks: 1) look up, 2) look before you pass, 3) look before you dribble. This will help if you instill this in your plays.

Little phrases that your players can understand and make them visualize what you are saying will help. There are many things that are important and many small things which will help.

In your practice schedule, make sure that you include time to work on what you want to do. The most important part of this presentation is that implementation of the principles of your attack is vital. Most of the patterns are very good, but the implementation of your ideas is the most important thing.

Execution of the fundamentals in your attack is the key. The back door is a good technique against the press. When you are taking the ball out of bounds, you don't want to rush or take the ball underneath the hoop. You should come to either side but step back so that you can see the whole picture. Try to eliminate the lob pass, the parachute pass. The passes should be firm and on target. Against Marquette we had a kid step to the ball rather than attack the ball. He waited on the pass, and a guy took it and scored. Little things like catching the ball are important.

I believe that you should center your attack, rather than bring it up the sideline, so that it will be difficult for your opponents to attack you. If you are bringing the ball up the center of the court, you have an option to go both ways.

The use of the dribble is very important when you are trying to get the defense to commit itself. Use your dribble, but use it wisely and limit the dribble in attacking zones.

In attacking pressure, it is important to use your post man. You need to decide who you will use as a post man. You will also need to decide if he can come to the ball, turn and feed the cutters, and start a pass and pull it back if the opening closes. Who you select is important and how you use him is important.

Offensive and defensive balance is very important. You need to use the entire court. You don't want your players to be disorganized and not alert to what is happening. Your attack should be simple, not complicated. These are some of the basics which you must think about in preparing your attack.

A lot of time should be spent in working with your players to teach them what should be done.

Placement of personnel is important, and in our attack we like to have certain guys in certain places (see Figure 14.1).

In our attack we call the man out of bounds the middle man. He is our best ballhandler. G is our second guard and F is our next small forward. P is our post man and S is the great scorer or a player you can hide.

There are certain things that each one of these players must be able to do. A key thing which we should tell our offensive players is that they should stay behind the defense to have the same effect as the blind-side cut.

Against pressure, when a pass is made, it is like the outlet pass for a fast break. The player who receives the ball must know where he has a pass to eliminate the pressure. There will be one area open in your outlet pass. If we are properly adjusted, against any type of a defense, we can execute. Against any defense you want to perform some kind of surgery.

There are many kinds of formations. The formation we use is shown in Figure 14.1. We always line up the same way, no matter whether against a man-to-man or a zone. This is where your scouting is used.

Usually the time to expect successful pressure will come after made foul shots. In order to attack any of them you must get the ball to your ballhandler, if you hit a full court press (Figure 14.2).

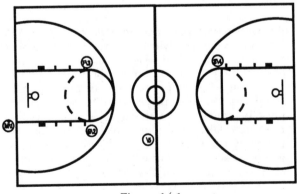

Figure 14.1

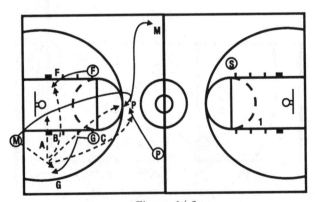

Figure 14.2

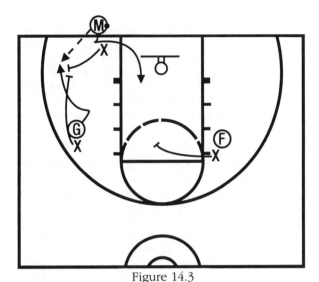

Figure 14.3

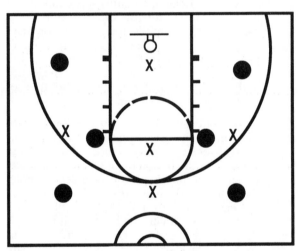

Figure 14.4

M looks over the floor and tries to hit G. When G catches the ball he must know that he has three passes. He can return the ball to M under the basket or when he moves to the center of the floor and button hooks. He can also hit F, who has moved to the ball and behind it. The third pass is, if M can't get the ball back, P comes to his spot, M moves away to the side. P can make three passes now, to F, back to G or to M, who has moved to the side. When P catches the ball, he must turn and look at the defense. All players must know what their outlet pass will be. The idea is to get the ball to the deep man. If he can score, he should. If he can't score you should get the ball back and attack their defense.

If you hurt their primary defense, their secondary defense will probably not be as good. Once you get through that facade, their defense will weaken. Teams that press a lot as their primary defense will have a secondary defense that will not be as good.

In our attack there must be a trailer. Condition your players to recognize that they have five seconds to throw the ball in and 10 seconds to cross the center line. That is a long time.

There are many teams that do a good job of blitzing the player with the ball on the throw-in (see Figure 14.3). Teach M to step inbounds and be ready for the ball. G should know that when he catches the ball, he should never have his back to the hoop. He must catch the ball and turn and look immediately. He must be able to see the floor. We must limit the dribble. Most of the time the pass goes back to M to bring the ball down the floor, but he must be ready to make the quick pass up the floor.

Sometimes the opponent starts playing the pass back to M. If they don't want to return the pass to M, posting in the middle, F can rotate over as the man who follows the ball and he will act as a safety valve (see Figure 14.1).

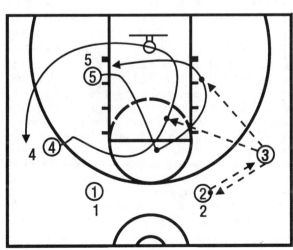

Figure 14.5

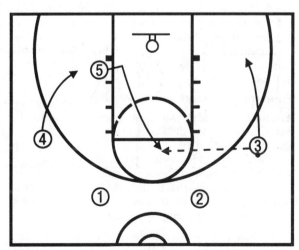

Figure 14.6

When the players are bringing the ball up the floor, tell them not to dribble to the trap area. They should stop before they get into a trapping area. Stop, but keep the dribble live.

Against a half-court zone there are several spots that you want to cover. These are attacking areas in the half-court trap (see Figure 14.4).

Figure 14.5 shows the rotation of the half-court attack without a defense. Number 2 passes to Number 3. Number 3 feeds either cutter. If he doesn't hit either cutter, he reverses the ball. After each pass, set up.

Figure 14.6 shows the movement of 3 and 4 when 5 catches the ball inside. We always use this. If we lost, it was lack of execution in a particular phase of the game.

If they are doubling, we try to clear out on them. This will make it difficult to double and also leaves a man open. I want to do what I want to do and can do well. We want to control the tempo of the game.

OFFENSES AGAINST FULL-COURT ZONE PRESS

Frank McGuire

One of the most successful renovations in modern-day basketball has been the use of various types of full-court zone presses. The object of these defenses, in whatever form, has been to pressure the offense into mistakes by means of such devices as double teamings, traps, anticipation of passes, and just pure harassment. Formerly, it had been thought that all that was needed to break any type of press was a good ballhandler. This may still be true against man-to-man presses and in the case of an exceptional player against zone presses.

However, we believe that to successfully break the zone press consistently, there must be extra emphasis put on certain fundamental areas of the game and on certain offensive principles. In this article, I would like to outline our philosophy against the zone press in these two areas:

Fundamentals and Offensive Alignment

A. Fundamentals. Our basic principle against the zone press is that dribbling leads to mistakes and that the ball must be passed up the court. We may use the dribble to force the opponent to double team and thus to commit themselves or to advance the ball in an area free of traffic, but we stress that to *beat* the press, you must pass the ball, not dribble it. For this reason, we emphasize the following:

  1. **Passing.** We teach the use of the two-hand chest pass and the long baseball pass, emphasizing both stepping in the direction of

the pass and following through. We use many drills employing these passes, stressing form both with the medicine ball and with the regulation basketball. We tell our players to look at the defensive man rather than their own teammate when passing the ball. It is also important in the fundamentals of passing to make sure your players fake before they pass so as not to "telegraph" the pass.

  2. **Meeting the Ball.** Perhaps the most abused area in basketball today and one of the reasons for the failure of a press is the failure of a player to meet the ball when it is thrown to him. We tell our players "to make a big hand" and to come toward the ball when it is thrown to them. We also instruct them to be prepared to be hit and to come at the ball in a strong fashion, catching the ball with legs spread and elbows out when it is received.

  3. **Look Up.** In dealing with the press, especially the zone press, probably the most important aspect is to look up the court so that you may spot an offensive man. If you are double teamed or trapped, then someone must be free, and by simply keeping your head up and looking around you should be able to spot an open offensive man.

  4. In our offenses, we usually employ two to three men who are 6'8" or better. In the past, press defenses were very successful against a team with such height. Realizing this, we insisted that our big players be able to handle the ball and advance it up the court. Perhaps the easiest way to train your big players to acquire these abilities is by making them go through all the drills you require of your backcourt men. There is no reason why a man 6'8" or better should not be able to dribble, pass, and catch a ball and to be able to advance it up the court. This perhaps is one of the most important fundamentals in our philosophy since we do believe in a pro type of offense in which two to three 6'8" or better players are employed.

B. Alignment. One good drill for employing all the fundamentals is the Four-Ball Give-and-Go Drill (see Figure 14.7). Once you have gotten your team to master the fundamentals of passing and catching the ball, you must have an offensive alignment which is suitable to breaking the zone press. It is our thought that you should treat the zone press much like you would do a zone – that is, by splitting the defensive men so that they cannot matchup, therefore forcing two defensive players to play one offensive player. For example: Against a 1-2-1-1 zone press, we would align ourselves 2-2-1 offensively (see Figure 14.8).

Against a 2-2-1 full court zone press, we would align ourselves in a 3-2 (see Figure 14.9).

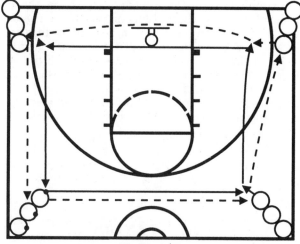

Figure 14.7

C. Advancing the ball up the court. For the purposes of this article, I will only discuss the 1-2-1-1 zone press. However, the same principles would apply if we are facing a 2-2-1 full-court zone press. The only difference would be the alignment of the players as previously explained in Figures14.8 and14.9.

1. Force the defensive team to double team and to commit themselves. In many zone presses there will always be a trap and then the players away from the ball will be anticipating the passing lanes (see Figure 14.10).

2. Fake forward and then throw back "across the grain." This is a very dangerous pass, but if practiced properly it can be done with a minimum of mistakes (see Figure 14.11).

3. Advance the ball down the sidelines of the court and not the middle. The power of most zone defenses lies in the middle and the safest area is on the sidelines (see Figure 14.11).

It is imperative that once the pass has been made and brought down the sidelines, the other players try to beat the defense down-court. We tell our players if they have a situation such as three-on-one, two-on-one or three-on-two they can go ahead and go to the basket. If the defense has gotten back, we tell them to go into one of the many offenses we have here at the university (see Figure 14.11).

Obviously there are no stereotype defenses. When we see a zone press making changes, then we have to change our offensive alignment to combat it. However, we feel that by stressing the fundamentals, we can switch easily into adjustments against any type of zone press.

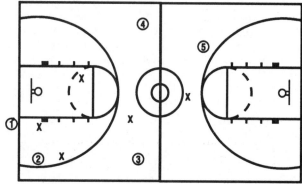

Figure 14.8

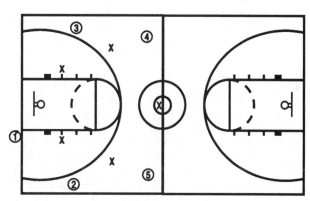

Figure 14.9

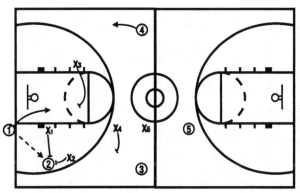

Figure 14.10

In this drill shown in Figure 14.7, four balls are used and the passing starts simultaneously in each corner on a whistle by the coach. A great variety of passes may be used. For example, the first pass from Number 1 to 2 is an over-the-shoulder, two-hand flip. Number 1 in each corner then breaks toward the next corner (counterclockwise in the figure) and receives a long baseball pass from Number 2. Number 1 takes the ball over his right shoulder while in a dead run. He then uses a two-hand chest pass to pass the ball to Number 2 in the next corner, who should be meeting the ball. Number 2 gives the ball to Number 3 with the same two-hand over-the-shoulder flip. This is repeated until a mistake results. The best way to teach this drill is to start out with one ball, then go to two and finally to four balls, one in each corner. In this drill, you have every fact of fundamentals that have been mentioned.

In our offense, 1 and 2 would be our backcourt men. Numbers 3 and 4 would be our swing men or corner men. Number 5, in most cases, would be our center.

In most cases the zone press will allow the initial pass inbounds. Number 1 passes to 2, then immediately 1 breaks to the other side of the court. Number 2 will dribble right at defensive players X1 and X2. In the stereotype 1-2-1-1 press, X3 will go toward the ball, X4 will go to the sideline anticipating the passing lane. X5 is usually back protecting against the long pass. For this reason we place 3 and 4 in the backcourt to serve as outlets and 5 is all the way back to drive X5 out of the play. Once 2 has been double-teamed by X1 and X2, he fakes forward toward 3 causing X4 to commit himself. He then pivots and passes to 1, who has the option of dribbling the ball himself or passing to 4, who can then advance the ball up the court.

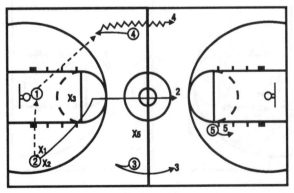

Figure 14.11

One deviation that we have made from these principles occurs when a situation pictured in Figure 14.11 occurs. Many times when 2 is double-teamed by X1 and X2, X3 is starting to play it smart and guards 1. In this instance, we still tell 2 to fake to 3 but to look for 4 breaking to the foul line. Number 4 is usually one of our big players. Number 4 then hands off to 1 and we try to bring the ball down so that we may have a situation of three-on-one, two-on-one, or three-on-two.

THE 2-3: AN ANTIDOTE FOR PRESSURE DEFENSES

Marv Harshman

There are some ideas I have that are not completely mine by any means, but are things I've observed that help us overcome pressure. I know that all coaches have had the problem of facing good pressure defenses, some average pressure defenses, and perhaps some that were not so good. When you're successful, you recognize that it's what you do on offense, I think, rather than the fact that it might be a lack of good pressure defense.

We have come up with some ideas that we've put into an offensive situation. First of all I'd like to read you a little statement that we have prepared, because it kind of gives our thinking about the philosophy of pressure defenses and what we hope to do. I've entitled it "The 2-3, an Antidote for Pressure Defenses." We've always played a pattern offense. The pattern means predictability, as you know, and perhaps makes it a little easier for people to pressure you. We feel that if that's the case, if you believe in pattern, and if you think there's some advantage in it, you're leaving yourself open for people to take away the things they know you like to do. In order to try to take away some of that advantage for us, that if they do try to overplay everything that we're going to get some easy baskets.

One of the things that we think is most important is player alignment. First of all, where we are playing, we find a lot of people that play pressure. Generally we used to play a situation where we'd have somebody in deep, and all that we found out in our conference was there were a number of big centers who zoned the area. The other four guys overplayed everybody so badly that you went to the basket and when you got there, you found somebody in your road. So the first thing we decided was that we were going to empty the baseline, because our philosophy was that we were going to take away support offside. So we went to the 2-3 set, which is far from new and which a lot of people do. The other reason is that our coaching is fairly simple, and we cannot have anything that is really too complicated.

There's one thing that I've observed over a number of years of coaching and that is when you put people on the floor you should try to give them the biggest advantage possible and you should try to make the defense cover as much area as possible. So we've always had rules of alignment which have to do with passing angles and cutting angles and distance that the defense has to cover.

Being a pattern offensive oriented operation, we became aware a few years ago of the need for an offense that by its player position and ability to take advantage of defensive cheating, we could negate a good share of the defensive pressure. Our answer has been the 2-3 offense.

Our belief is that we want to encourage overplay so we can get the easy basket. By emptying the baseline we take away the basket support necessary to complete overplay at wings and guards.

Player Alignment

Player alignment is as essential to successful execution as good talent. We believe that passing and cutting angles are analogous to execution, and player placement can ensure this to a great degree. (See Figure 14.12.)

1. High post above line and middle of lane.
2. Wings above foul line extended and dividing distance between lane and sideline.
3. Guard with ball at least at hash mark and splitting wing and post.
4. Off guard – splitting post and off wing and one step ahead of ball.

Execution Hints

1. Wings may start below and inside of receiving area.

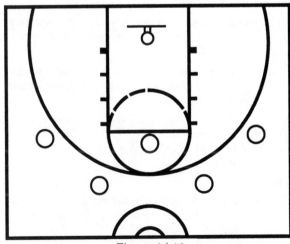

Figure 14.12
Basic Set

2. Wings may exchange as ball comes down.
3. Post comes high to be available not to ball side of lane (destroys cutting angle).
4. Guard penetrate to hash mark and pick ball up, not pass off dribble.
5. Off guard behind ball until it crosses midcourt one step in advance when ball is picked up.
6. All players come to meet pass.

Basic Entries

Basic entries are:

1. Wing on ball side – which can trigger two different basic operations.
2. Post – which can initiate back-door sequences.
3. Off guard – which many times is the simplest manner to relieve pressure (He goes in other side).

Player Responsibilities

Depending on personnel, we assign definite responsibilities of rebounding and defensive balance. It may be dictated by position on floor or by type of personnel in game. (See Figure 14.13.)

Hints

1. This offense works best against overplay.

2. Wings 3 and 5 should be foul line high and split the distance between free throw line and sideline.

3. Post 4 should be above foul line and head on the basket. How high he must come will vary with defensive pressure.

4. Guards 1 and 2 should split the distance between wings 3 and 5 and post 4.

5. When 1 has the ball 2 should be a step closer to basket and vice versa. (See Figure 14.14.)

Hints

1. Numbers 1 and 2 must be inside of hash mark before offense is initiated.

2. Numbers 3 and 5 should remain stationary or semi-stationary until 1 and 2 are ready to pass them the ball.

3. Number 4 must come high enough to get pass from guards. (See Figure 14.15.)

Key: Number 1 to Number 3, 3 goes diagonal for give-and-go or screens for 2 if defense won't let him go diagonal. Number 4 slides down to first hash mark, 5 closer to lane, 3 to 4, 3 screens for 2, 2 for jump, 1 out for defense.

Hints

1. After 1 passes to 3, he goes to the basket for return pass if defense allows. If defense chests

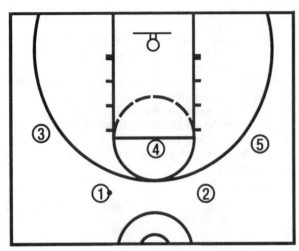

Figure 14.13

Basic Position

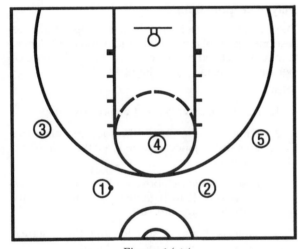

Figure 14.14

Starting Position

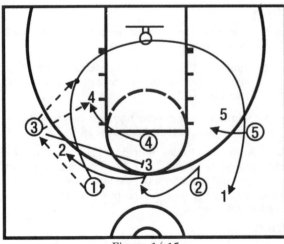

Figure 14.15

Basic to Wing

and makes him change his direction, 1 will screen for 2, who will run give-and-go with 3.

2. When cutter goes by and doesn't get return pass, 4 will slide to side post at first hash mark.

3. After 4 slides down, 2 will be head on the basket, 3 will hit 4 and run screen and cut-away with 2.

4. When 3 gets ball he thinks drive, give-and-go with guard, hit post, reverse ball to guard at top of key, or for opposite forward foul line extended, in that order. (See Figure 14.16.)

Key: Numbers 1 and 3, 3 diagonal, 4 slides to side post. Number 5 is close to lane, 2 head on basket, 3 to 2, 5 screens down for 1, 1 jumps out, 5 cuts away, 2 to 1 or 5.

Hints

1. Defense will not allow 3 to hit 4 or across to 5, so ball is reversed to 2.

2. Number 1 must hold his man for 5's screen by stepping to basket and then jumping out after screen is set.

3. We want a switch to occur so 5 will have a guard checking him inside.

4. When 1 jumps out he must turn in the air so his feet are facing the basket when he receives pass. (See Figure 14.17.)

Key: Number 1 to Number 4, 3 goes back door, 1 goes to foul line extended as a jump shooter, 3 continues through setting a moving screen for 5, 4 to 3, 5, 1 or goes on his own at any time.

Hints

1. As soon as 1 passes to 4, 3 will go back-door and look for the ball.

2. Number 4 will then turn and face. Number 1 will go to foul line extended looking for ball and jump shot.

3. Number 2 will stay and key his man away from high post. This may mean going deeper to the end line.

4. Number 5 now uses 3 as a screener. Usually going low after screen, but this is dictated by the defense. (See Figure 14.18.)

Key: Number 1 to 4, 3 back-door, 1 goes low and sets double screen with 3 for 5, 2 goes to jump shot area foul line extended, 4 to 3, 5 or 2 and 1 out for defensive balance.

Hints

1. This time 3 and 1 will set a double screen for 5. These six moving bodies caused defensive confusion.

2. Again, 5 must recognize opportunities to go on his own.

3. Number 2 must keep his man away from high post but if his man goes to 4, 2 must be in a jump shooting area. (See Figure 14.19.)

Key: On verbal signal 3 to opposite corner, 1 to 5, and 1 and 2 exchange, 4 to basket, 5 lobs to 4, *or* 5 to 2 on 1, 1 and 4 two-on-two action.

Hints

1. On signal, 3 must go all the way to the opposite corner.

2. Number 1 and Number 2 must exchange after 1 passes to 5 to keep defense honest.

3. Number 4 tries to slide to ball if defense won't allow this action. Four will wheel to basket for lob.

4. Four's path is not directly to basket but similar to angle drawn in Figure 14.19. This makes pass completion easier.

5. If lob is not open, ball is reversed by 5 for two-man action with 4. (See Figure 14.20.)

Key: Number 3 clears to corner, 1 to 5, 1 and 2 exchange, 4 slides to ball, 5 to 4, 3 back-doors, 5 screens for 2, 2 off pick, 5 to basket or stays high for jump shot.

Hints

1. On this occasion 4 is allowed to slide to ball.

2. When 5 hits 4, 3 goes back-door immediately for open pass and makes room for splitting action.

3. Number 5 picks for 2, 2 shoots jumper or passes to 4. Number 5 goes to the basket or steps out after the screen.

4. Number 4 goes one-on-one when he has the opportunity.

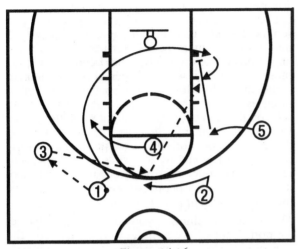

Figure 14.16
Basic to wing and reverse

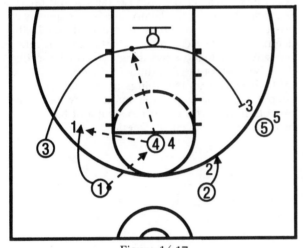

Figure 14.17
Basic to post-single screen

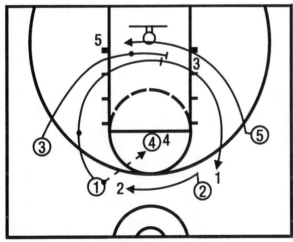

Figure 14.18
Basic to post-double screen

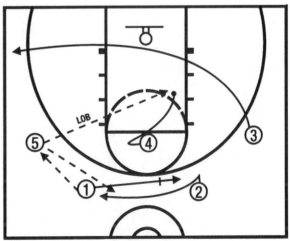

Figure 14.19
2-3 clear and lob

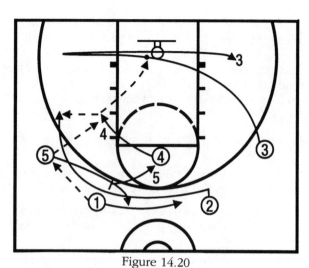

Figure 14.20

2-3 clear and splits

We used to run a lot of offenses, and we still believe in multiple offense, but in the last few years we have run the 2-3 more than anything else because we feel that it satisfied more needs. For people with some limitations in their mobility, it has been a very good offense for us and we have been able, we think, to come up with a lot of answers that some other offenses haven't provided easily. I'm not trying to sell you this. I'm trying to point out some things that I think can be helpful. If I were going to say one thing against pressure that I would demand of my players and I would try to sell coaches on, it is to explore what your offensive alignment is. Don't make it easy for the other people to pressure you and give them automatic support at the basket.

That's the first thing – you must remove basket support. If they have a big guy who can "tent" the area or if they've got a very active post man who can get back in there and help quickly, you better get him someplace a little farther away than he likes to be. I think that's the first premise that you must have. Secondly, try to get the layup situation as quickly as possible because you have to create doubt in the defense that they can afford to stay in that much pressure. You do those two things, you do the second thing because of the first thing in my opinion. Then try to have just as few things as possible to do – keep it as simple as possible and then work on the execution. And you can do this without having the best basketball players in America.

WHEEL OFFENSE

Garland Pinholster

I am not going to try to sell you our offense, I am not going to try to tell you that it will work all the time. We have been beaten when we were trying very hard to run this offense, so I am not going to tell you that it is the total answer to all you offensive problems.

It has been good to us, and without any apologies for it I will try to get into it and tell you what we do. We were forced into this offense. We didn't create it; our opponents created it for us. We ran the "first guard around and Sweet Georgia Brown" as Coach "Frosty" Holt says, and we were getting along pretty good and all of a sudden our opponents quit cooperating. It wouldn't work any more. So we kept making adjustments, and we kept making adjustments, and we finally flexed right into an entirely new offense over a period of time.

We were running one offense against the man-to-man and one offense against a zone, using one formation against a man-to-man and another formation against a zone, and a 2-1-2 single post setup against a zone. We were using a 1-3-1 rotating continuity against a zone, and a 2-1-2 single post setup against the man-to-man. Every time we went into our man-to-man offense, the defense would jump and lo and behold we were attacking a zone. So we had to bring it back out, set up, and start our 1-3-1 continuity and lo and behold they were playing a man-to-man. So we were forced into finding a formation that would be the same for attacking a zone and a man-to-man. These people were alternating their defenses, jumping defenses, and concealing their defenses, and they forced us into doing basically the same things against both defenses, of course eliminating the screens and adjusting the cuts when attacking a zone. If anybody comes along with an offense that will work precisely the same against both defenses, he will make a million dollars in a hurry.

We call this pattern the wheel because like a wheel it has a hub, pivot man, spokes, four other players, two guards, and two forwards, and the spokes rotate around the middle, revolve like a wheel, and like a wheel we can stop it or reverse it, we can run it slower or faster. Also like a wheel (unfortunately) sometimes it will bog down in the mud and in the sand when somebody knows it and can run it faster backwards than you can run it forwards.

There are certain advantages that we think we enjoy by running this particular continuity pattern. First of all, we have gotten away from the idea of having to use four or five different offenses, one against a man-to-man, one against a zone, one when they use combination defense, or man-to-man your guards and zone the base line, and another one when you don't know what they are doing, another one against a zone press, and another one against a man-to-man press. Pretty soon you've got so many offenses you've got more offenses than you've got players, and this is exactly what we had come to. So it gives us more versatility. We can use the same basic moves, with some adjustment, against all defenses except a zone press.

We can use it to get our first shot play and our last shot play; we can use it for a stall pattern; we can run it as an out-of-bounds play. We stick with basically the same thing at all times without having to teach quite so much, in the hope that what we do we can do well and more precisely.

We are able to maintain possession of the ball, generally, in most games longer than our opponents. In other words, we keep the ball more than they keep the ball. If possible, we would like to keep it about 25 minutes and let them have it 15. A lot of people have said that our offense is our defense, and I wouldn't argue with them too much after the way we finished the season. But we think that is an advantage, too, because if we are on defense only 15 minutes, we ought to be able to play real inspired defense and go real hard for 15 minutes. So if that is true, then we aren't ashamed of the fact. We hope to keep the ball longer than our opponents.

In doing this we have led the NAIA defensive statistics for three of the last four years. It might well be that our offense has done more for us than our defense has. I wouldn't debate that.

We get a little closer shot than we were getting. We hit 51.2 percent this year for the season, and layups and the number of close-in shots certainly brought our percentage up.

Offensive rebounding should be easier – because the players begin to know about when the shot will be taken and they can anticipate a move for the board, and this anticipation, I believe, is about 90 per cent of offensive rebounding.

Everyone gets to shoot. You might not consider this an advantage but I do. If you don't consider it an advantage, you can adjust it so you can wait until your good shooter comes around if you want to. You can turn the thing over as long as you want to and wait for your good shooter, but we like for everybody to get a shot with the pivot man getting slightly more, the guards and the forwards being almost completely interchangeable and getting about

the same number of shots. Everybody gets to handle the ball, and I think this keeps players happy rather than just being in there to defend or to rebound.

You don't develop many gunners because the shot is either there or it isn't. It is almost reflex action. A boy will take a shot or run the pattern almost reflexively, after a time. He is left free to think, free to watch the defense for a mistake, free to use his own initiative, to make a free-lance move off of it that will take advantage of the defensive mistake.

The big boys are forced to move. They can't stand around if they are going to run this offense. They have got to move, they have got to work real hard, and they get a little more mobility than our big boys were getting before we went to this pattern.

The opponents are forced to switch, creating the big man on the little man situation quite often, and generally it's a situation where the big man is on the little man right smack under the goal on what we call the first cut. You can just move everybody out a couple of steps and feed the big man in that spot if you choose to, or you can stay in the offense and bring him back around again.

The pattern blends well with the break if you want to fast break. We don't fast break a whole lot. We fast break sometimes with what we call an opportune break. That means if the other team falls dead – if all five of them fall dead – then we will run with the ball, but generally we don't break a whole lot. But we could and we might start doing it in certain situations.

All the team members are forced to develop more fully. They must be able to go right and go left. They come open on a cut to the left, a horizontal cut to the left or a vertical cut to the left. They have vertical and horizontal cuts right. They have drives right and left.

The team progress should be continuous throughout the year. Keep looking for little things, the timing, little adjustments. There should always be something new and there shouldn't be any real stale spot during the season. These are ideal situations which we know never occur but which we work for.

The pattern is fairly difficult to scout, although we have had some people who have defensed it real well. We have had others who had to come back the fifth or sixth time to get the pattern real good. We had one or two coaches move in with us, move in the dorm and just stay with us for a few days to learn the offense a little bit better.

The defense is checked out each time you come down the floor. With the movement that is involved, the defense gets checked out every time with the people moving around and cutting through. They can't change their defenses without you getting some hint of that if all five players are alert.

So much for what it should do. Now we will illustrate what we actually do. We chose the 1-3-1 formation as our basic pattern. We conceal the formation and we conceal the pattern in various ways. I think any pattern that is worth running is worth camouflaging a little bit, worth concealing a little bit, but basically we use a 1-3-1 formation, which is shown in Figures 15.1 and 15.2.

It is a sort of an overload 1-3-1 with three men in a line down the side of the key and one clearout man on one side of the floor. We have numbered them in the order of their moves and cuts. That is the only reason for the numbering.

The first cutter is the Number 1 man and we've got to give the ball to 5. We'll call him the feeder. We get the ball to 5 any way we can. It depends on what sort of concealment you use. We are going to take first the nucleus, just the basic cuts, the basic pattern, and then show you one or two ways that you can conceal it.

We will make a simple direct pass. We'll assume that 4 has it, and we will get it to the feeder, 5. And 2 sneaks up on the boy defending Number 1. Number 1 comes in the back door down the base line off that screen and we hope to hit him at the goal. Of course this doesn't always work. That is why we have continuity.

We can run that one either way. If the defense is switching, Number 2X will generally be lagging back on the base line waiting for Number 1 to come down. He might even be turning his head and turning his vision slightly. That is the ideal time for Number 1 to go over the top of 3 and bend in to the goal, putting his back to the defensive man in the corner and facing the receiver in a shuffling slide sideways step as he bends in over Number 3. This helps to put a little more pressure on the switch there between 1X and 2X. This is the first cut either on the base line, down the base line, or over the top (See Figure 15.3).

The second cutter is the screener. After setting this screen for Number 1 (who steps out, if he doesn't get it), he comes over the top, over 3, and 2 should cut tight. Number 2 cuts real tight off of 3, and 4 steps down the middle before 2 gets there and sets a double screen on the side of the post as 2 comes over the top (see Figure 15.4).

In the event they are switching, Number 2 should do everything he can to keep 1X on his back and not let 2X beat him to 3. If he beats him to 3, then he has got 1X running into the double screen or forced to go behind it. In either event 1X is in trouble. If he runs into this screen, of course, he is out of business. If he goes behind it he will be a step late. If he goes on the base line side and comes up, he will be a step late if the timing is good. The ball gets there as soon as Number 2 gets there.

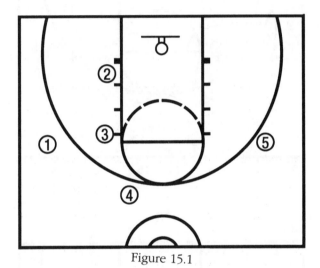

Figure 15.1

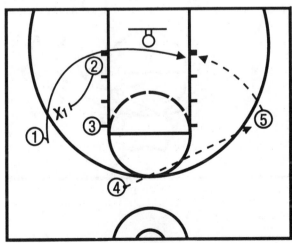

Figure 15.2

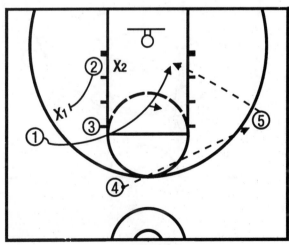

Figure 15.3

Now the third cut is by the Number 3 man (see Figure 15.5). He comes up just as soon as he feels 2 brush the outside of his hip. He can either face the play there or face the ball. He would face the ball in this case. If Number 1 had the ball he would be facing him. If Number 4 had the ball he would be facing him, and when the ball goes to 5 he will turn and face across the lane and spread out as wide as he can to be a screener. As soon as 2 comes off his right hip he comes up for the third cut to what we call the corner of the head of the circle, if there is such an item.

If his man is sloughing in there to pick up the cutters or to knock them down or to tackle them or for any of the things 3X can do in there, Number 3 must be able to shoot. Number 3X can do a lot of damage if he is allowed a good bit of freedom in there. Of course we know that most defensive players are allowed a good bit of freedom in this case because the referees are like everybody else, they're watching the ball, and Number 5 has the ball. So 3X can do a lot of damage if 3 can't shoot at that particular point. If he can shoot pretty well, he can keep that boy honest.

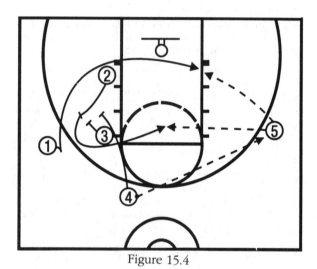

Figure 15.4

Figure 15.6

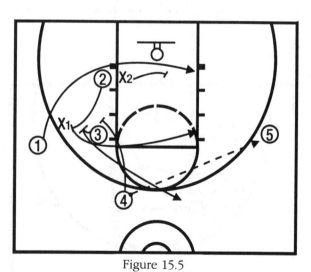

Figure 15.5

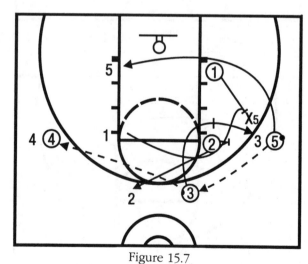

Figure 15.7

Now we get a turnover. We will run all the cuts and everybody will stay where they are, with the exception of Number 4 who will step out, and we are on the other side of the floor coming back around again, 5 with the ball, 2 becomes the dead screener, 1 becomes a screener, with 3 at the corner of the head of the circle, and 4 becomes the feeder on the other side (see Figures 15.6 and 15.7). Number 5 has the ball, of course. Just as soon as the ball leaves his hand, Number 1 will sneak up on his man, screen him, and Number 5 will cut to the base line or over the top, according to what the defense is doing, 3 will set his screen, 2 will become the new Number 3 cutter, and 3 will screen down and out and become the subsequent feeder on that side of the floor again.

Now from there on out you just run these same cuts from one side of the floor to the other. It is the same thing over and over.

I'll move on to what we call the counter moves. The defense can overplay you in any number of ways. Of course as you watch these diagrams the first thing you will do is figure the counter attack or the counter move, and of course there are a number of good counter moves that cause us a lot of pain, a lot of frustration, a lot of sleepless nights, but that is what makes the game interesting.

Let's assume we are at this side of the floor again and Number 1 has the ball and he is trying to throw it to 4 who has made his cut (see Figure 15.8). On the continuity, he would have been the screener on the side of the post, and then he breaks up to get the ball and he wants to take it from 1 and turn around and hit 5, but breaks up and he can't get the ball because his defensive player plays directly in line between him and Number 1. So he will turn and break the other lane hard and be a real threat going down the lane. This 4X is supposed to go with him, but some of these guys don't play the way they're supposed to, they won't be cooperative, and they'll stay right there. Number 5 will then come up, take the pass, we hope, and turn around and hit Number 4 who is breaking down the lane.

All it amounts to is an interchange between 4 and 5. If 1 can't hit 4, 4 and 5 will run an interchange with 4 trying to be as much of a threat as he possibly can as he goes down the middle.

You can do that two ways: He can break back and screen, set a pretty strong screen for Number 5, and bring 5 up as a potential shooter, or you can break Number 4 down the lane and let him be a potential cutter or receiver (see Figure 15.9).

One other possibility on this we call a shove-up (see Figure 15.10). When you can't make that pass from 1 to 4, turn and hit down the base line to Number 2, who would normally become a screener for this cutter. Number 1 will screen away and let 4 fake toward 5, fake the high-low interchange, come back for a possible shot over 3 and 1. If he doesn't get the

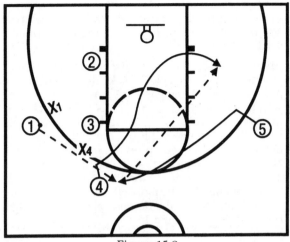

Figure 15.8

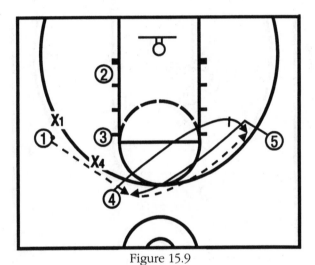

Figure 15.9

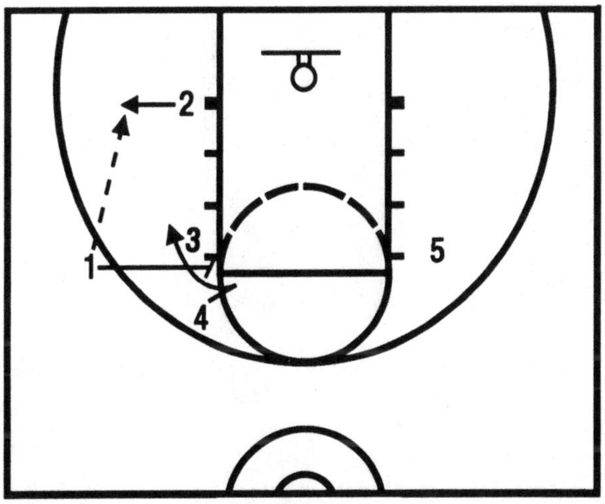

Figure 15.10

shot he takes the pass, and 4 and 1 simply interchange there, 4 turns and hits 1, and 1 gets the ball on down to 5. This is when the pass from the wing man to the point is overplayed.

Another pass we have to make is from 4 to 5. We'll assume we've been able to make the pass from 1 to 4, and as soon as he passes, 1 is going; he doesn't wait around to see if Number 4 is going to be able to make that pass, he is going but he gets under here, and of course 4 still has the ball because the defensive boy moved up on the side of Number 5. Number 5 can't receive, so he simply steps under and takes the place of Number 1, and everybody keeps cutting. It is the most effective counter move we've found when the defense plays up that high on that boy (see Figure 15.11).

Now if you just come down the floor and go straight in to this 1-3-1, you will have trouble first of all in initiating the offense. There are a number of ways you can conceal it. You can figure out more ways in 10 minutes to conceal it that you can use but I will just illustrate one very old maneuver, a very successful maneuver as an offense in itself and let it serve as concealment, camouflage.

In Figure 15.12, we set up in a 2-1-2. You see, we're just going to run this to get the ball in play and to get into the 1-3-1. We will start out with the 2-1-2 and run the guard outside. Four will drift across and as 4 comes across 1 runs first guard around and you can see how we got into this thing. This is what we were running at one time, so this is how we got into the pattern. I said we ran it "first guard around and Sweet Georgia Brown," but the defense wouldn't cooperate so we had to go one step further.

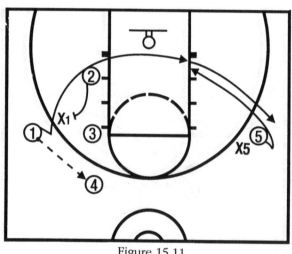

Figure 15.11

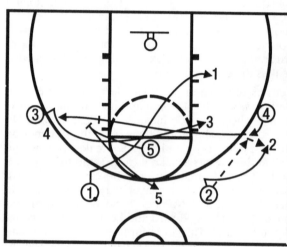

Figure 15.13

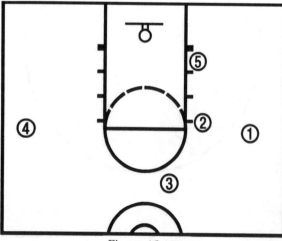

Figure 15.12

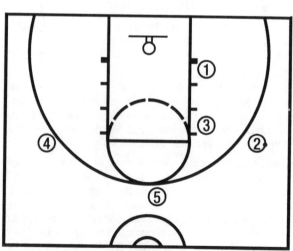

Figure 15.14

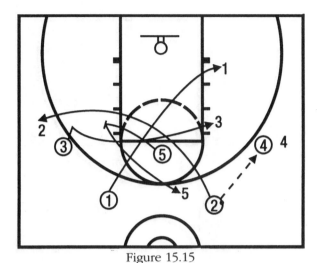

Figure 15.15

We ran this guard outside, and you see now you are in a 1-3-1 (see Figure 15.13). All you've got to do is let 4 step out and you are in a 1-3-1 ready to run the wheel. This guard outside is simply used as concealment. We have 2 with the ball, 3 has come in to the side post, 5 screens opposite and then wheels back up to the corner at the head of the circle, 1 runs the first cut off the tail of the forward drifting across, the forward drifting across steps out on the weak side and becomes a feeder on that side, and you are into the wheel, in your normal business.

Again, using the 2-1-2 for concealment, another good maneuver that brings you into direct alignment for the 1-3-1 without having to make it too hard is what we call the guard opposite (see Figure 15.14 and 15.15). Run the weak-side guard under, bring the weak-side forward into the middle, let the screening guard step out on the weak side, and again Number 5 comes to the corner at the head of the circle, and we are in our normal alignment for the wheel again.

This type of concealment we call "active" concealment. It is a little more complex. You can make your concealment as simple or as complex as you want to. We call this rather complex method "active" concealment. If you don't want to go to that much trouble and use what we call "passive" concealment, simply run a guard through and you see you are in your normal 1-3-1 alignment by letting 5 move over, you are in your overload 1-3-1 formation for running the wheel.

Of course that is not going to fool anybody very much. They are going to see right away that you are not camouflaging very much, but you are camouflaging some in that you move from one formation to another.

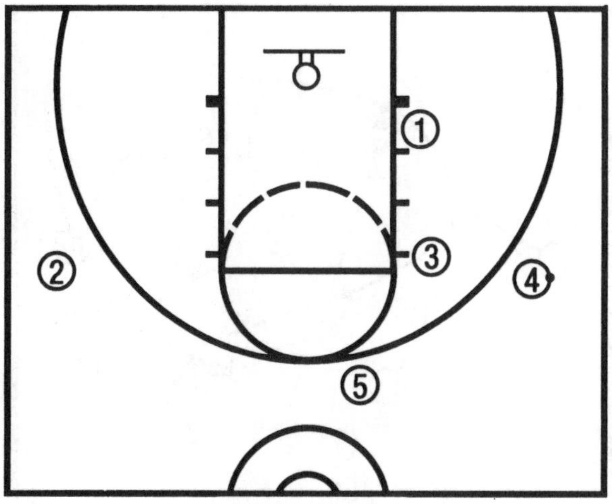

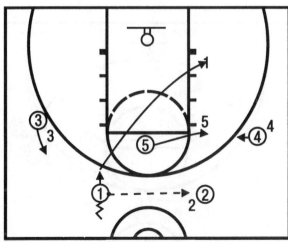

Figure 15.16

Figure 15.17

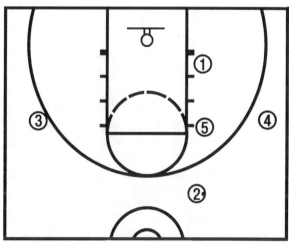

Figure 15.18

We run this same offense against a zone simply eliminating the screens, run the same pattern without the screens (see Figures 15.17 and 15.18). Take the most direct route, forget about running the wide route or the most difficult cut and just go directly to your new spot and a little more quickly and be ready to shoot when you get there. You get the double triangle on either side of the floor, the base line opposite, the middle option is always there, the point, the wings, the weak side.

HIGH POST OFFENSE

John Wooden

It isn't any one offense or defense that brings the most out of your player under your supervision. Your job is to get the most out of what you have and the more you worry what the other teams have, the less you are going to do with what you have. It isn't the style or system you use that will get the job done, it's the following three things:

1. Get them in best possible condition and keep them there.

2. Teach them not only the proper fundamentals, but quickly execute them.

3. Make them play as a team, and keep in mind that balance is the most important thing.

High Post Offense

I want the shots to come from the offense, not from some individual dribbling around to get open, except in certain situations when the defense makes a mistake. On the shot from the offense, we want triangle rebounding power underneath, a long rebounder, and a protector. Never pass to a player standing still and we must attack each side of the floor equally.

C – Our center will start the play on one side or the other of the foul lane (see Figure 15.19).

G – Our two guards will be just wider than the foul lane extended to the top of the key.

F – Both forwards should be one good step in from the sideline with the front foot even with the foul line extended.

F1 must be alert to cut to the high post whenever he sees the defense on the off-guard overplaying to deny a pass from G2 to G1 (see Figure 15.20). As G2 passes to F1, G1 cuts for the basket and F1 has the following options: Pass to G1 cutting, to G2 as a second cutter, G1 coming around double screen by C and F2.

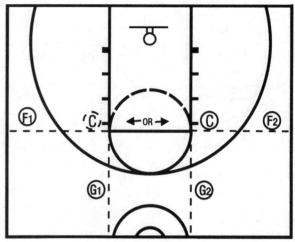

Figure 15.19

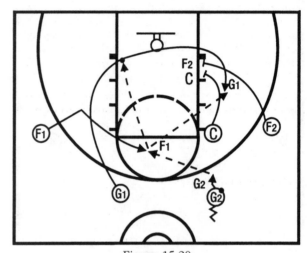

Figure 15.20
Initiation and first cutters

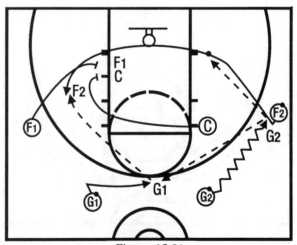

Figure 15.21
Continuity continued

F2 fakes up to meet the ball against the overplay, suddenly accelerates for the basket turning toward the inside, and looks for the pass if open (see Figure 15.21). If not open, F2 will buttonhook at the foul lane and look for the pass. If he doesn't get the ball on the buttonhook, he crosses the foul lane and comes around a double screen by the center and F1; now he looks for a pass from G1 to whom G2 has passed the ball. Never call the plays; let the defense call your plays by how they play against you.

If we see overplay by strong-side guard, F2 will come up to screen and roll with same three options as forward overplay in Figure 15.22.

G1 passes to F2 coming around the double screen and cuts for the basket, screening for G2 or getting an upscreen from G2 (see Figures 15.23A and 15.23B). G1 may pass to G2 coming up to the side post and cutting off of him for a two-man play, with F2 coming on back as the protector.

Remember that it's the little things that count, and each man must be set up in his position. Each player must know the type of passes to make as he receives the ball. He must have in mind an automatic progression in where he is to look first, second, and third.

The player without the ball on the weak side should be in position to make their defensive man turn his head away from the play so that he will not be able to bother one of your teammates. On the strong side, we need to work to get open to receive the ball in our advantageous position where we are a threat to shoot, dribble, or pass.

Both forwards reverse sharply looking for a pass from the center when a guard passes to the post (see Figure 15.24). G2 passes to G1, who passes to the high post C, who first looks for strong-side F2, then for F1 on short post underneath, then for G1 or G2 on the wings.

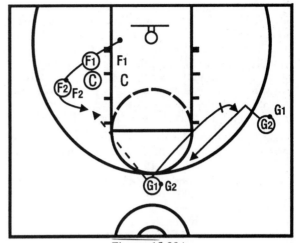

Figure 15.23A

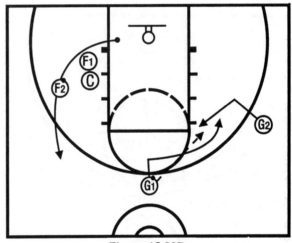

Figure 15.23B

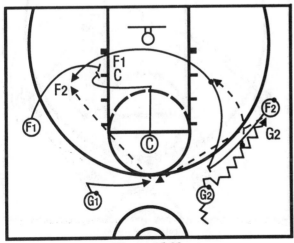

Figure 15.22

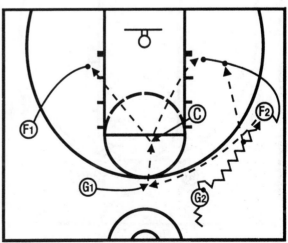

Figure 15.24

If C passes to either G1 or G2 on the wing, he should always take two steps toward the person he passes to and look for the ball going down the lane (Figure 15.25). The center can double-screen down low and can always come back to the two-man game on the weak side. Sometimes guard to center, guard to forward, and sometimes guard to guard. Each man when he gets the ball must know where to look first, second, and third so that we can run all options.

Guard passes to forward and cuts off either side of post (who should face the basket) looking for a pass if he gets open (Figure 15.26). Sometimes the post can cut down the lane if the defense makes a mistake. The forward should always look first for the post cutting, and then second, the guard cutting off the post. If they body-check our cutting guard, he can fake the cut and step back as the opposite guard cuts off of the post.

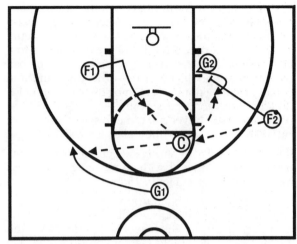

Figure 15.27

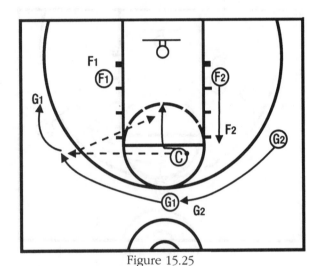

Figure 15.25

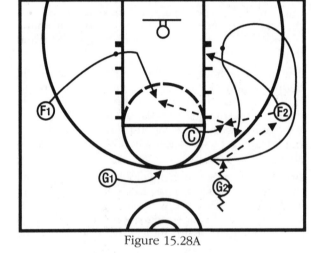

Figure 15.28A

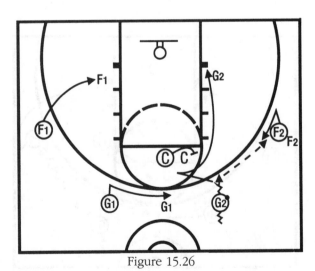

Figure 15.26

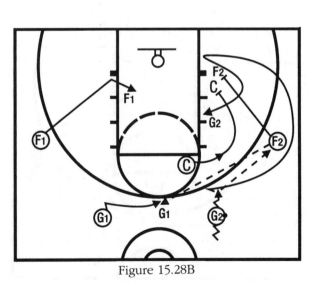

Figure 15.28B

Guard passes to forward and cuts off C (Figure 15.27). Forward hits post, takes two steps to the ball, and then cuts to the basket. If not open, post should look for G2 coming around the F2 screen and cut for the basket. High post should always look for the deep post and if neither G2 nor F1 can get open, we reverse the ball outside to G1 for the two-man game on the weak side with G1 and F1. We like to have two-man weak-side options and double screen strongside.

If guard can't get the cut, he steps back outside and goes to the ball (Figure 15.28A and 15.28B). G2 passes to F2 and cuts outside to the white box. F2 can pass to C for splits with the cutting guard or pass the ball back outside to safety G1 and then forms double screen with the center for the cutting guard. The out-guard, G1, can pass to G2 coming back off the double screen or pass to F1 for two-man side post option.

Cutting guard passes to F2 and gets the ball back on the outside cut. Now we have the same options with pass to low post, high post, lob, or reverse the ball back outside to the protecting guard for two-man weak-side and double screen options (Figure 15-29).

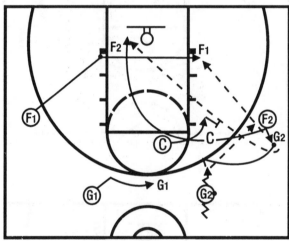

Figure 15.29

THE SCREENING GAME

Bob Knight

Offensively, Indiana is a team that relies on three things: passing the ball, cutting without the ball, and screening for each other so that we end up with a good shot. We define for our kids what a good shot is. What may be a good shot for Scott May is not always a good shot for another player, and we tell them this.

Offense at Indiana is not equal opportunity. Those players who can shoot best are going to shoot most. It is important that every player know his offensive limitations. It is also important that a player know who the best shooter on his team is. When a passer has the option of passing to two players, I expect him to get the ball to the best shooter. I continually stop practice and ask players who the best shooter is and I expect them to know. It is important that you get the ball to your best shooter.

We call our offense the "motion offense," but if a fundamental name were to be given to it, the offense would be called the "screening game." The screen is the most important thing in our game. Screens are the most difficult maneuvers to defend against in basketball. Motion and good passing will get you good shots, but if you can have motion, good passing, and screening you will increase the number of good shots you get.

There are a lot of reasons to run the motion offense. The motion offense is very unpredictable and this creates many good shot opportunities in itself. Unlike pattern play, there is no predetermined order of movement by either the players or the ball, which makes it very difficult for the defense to anticipate what the offensive team is doing. Another important point in favor of this offense is that the players enjoy it greatly, and because they enjoy it they work hard at it and frequently get good shots with it. I believe this is an important factor to consider.

It is my feeling that to prevent the offense from becoming stereotyped and predictable, the number of rules should be kept to a minimum. The rules serve as guidelines to the movement of the players and the balance of the offense. The more rules the offense has, the more closely it will be to patterned offense. We separate our offense into perimeter and post play and have a minimum set of guiding principles for each area. I have always felt that one of the most important things in offensive basketball is each player concentrating on what his teammates and the opponents are doing. As you will see, each of our principles is designed with this in mind. We use the following principles in our perimeter play.

1. **Don't make two consecutive cuts in the same direction.** This helps us avoid congestion in our movement by preventing three players from moving together in one small part of the floor. The offensive player can exercise four options in cutting without the ball (Figure 15.30).

    a. **Inside cut:** This cut takes one to the baseline and puts him in ideal position to come off a screen for the shot.

    b. **Basket cut:** One makes a sharp cut to the basket looking for a return, the chance to set a screen, or the possibility of posting.

    c. **Post cut:** The purpose is the same as in the basket cut except that a man on the high post is used as a rub-off screen.

    d. **Replace yourself:** This move is used when nothing else is available and will keep the defensive man occupied and allow a return pass.

2. **Face the basket for a count of two.** We found that our players were passing the ball too quickly on the perimeter without allowing enough time for things to be created by our movement and screening. Often we would get a man open, but the ball would not be in the right place for a pass to the open man. Facing the basket and holding for a slow two count, give things a chance to develop and the man with the ball can see where it should go. If a man is open for the shot, we would naturally forego the slow two count and make the pass. I have always felt it is better to be a little late than too soon on offense.

3. **Look below you to screen.** Since the vertical screen is such an integral part of our offense, we want to use it at every opportunity. Each time a player makes a pass on the perimeter, we want him to look to the baseline to see if he has an opportunity to set a screen.

4. **Maintain 15- to 18-foot spacing.** We think it is essential for offensive balance to keep 15 to 18 feet apart on the perimeter. We have found that this greatly facilitates our moving and screening. This principle also takes care of rotation and filling or replacing because of cutting. This principle applies to both a two-man and a three-man perimeter. It also makes it easy for a player coming out of the post to get into the proper position in the perimeter.

5. **Use of the dribble.** We want to do everything we can to reduce or eliminate the use of the dribble against man-to-man defense. We want to use it only to advance the ball against full-

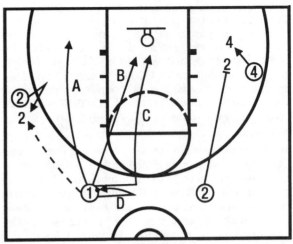

Figure 15.30

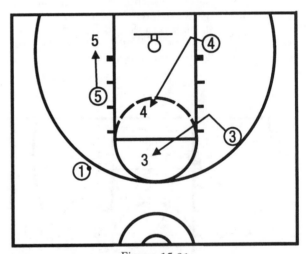

Figure 15.31

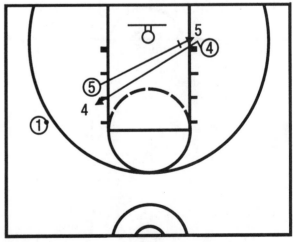

Figure 15.32

court pressure, to take it to the basket, to improve our passing angles. We try to put the ball on the floor no more than three times.

6. **Use of screening principles.** All of the principles of screening that we have previously discussed must be followed by all perimeter players.

7. **Cut to high post when it is vacant.** Anytime the high post is not occupied, we want somebody moving into it as quickly as possible. Quite often this will be a player sliding up from the low post. However, if no one is available in the low post we want a flash cut made from the perimeter to fill this spot.

Since each alignment of our offense is a combination of perimeter and post play, we have separate rules for each. Just as in perimeter play, however, we want to keep them as simple as possible. We use the following principles in our post play.

1. **The center is always in the post.** We do not allow a center who does not have all the skills to play the perimeter, or is far too valuable to take away from the basket, to play anywhere but the high or low post and we use him in both spots.

2. **Everyone on our squad is expected to be able to play the post.** We will naturally use some players in our post play much more than others. Many players are equally adept at either perimeter or post play and often the lineup may not have a particular player restricted to the post.

3. **The high post is ball side.** We want a player moving into the high post to go to the ball side of the foul line. He should hold his position for a slow count of two, and then he has three options.

   a. He slides low on the ball side to allow someone to replace him, who will come from the low post or from one of the perimeter spots (see Figure 15.31).

   b. He goes opposite the ball to screen for the low post as shown in Figure 15.32 and assumes the low post spot.

   c. If the player on the high post is not restricted to post play, he can step out to back pick for someone in the perimeter as in Figure 15.33. He will then become involved in perimeter play.

4. **The low post is opposite the ball.** Setting up in this spot places a player in ideal position for a screen from either the high post or a perimeter player away from the ball. This is the most likely place in our offense for a

double screen to occur, which would be set by the high post and a perimeter player following the principles of screening to the baseline. We spend a lot of time working with our players coming out of this spot and taking the shot. A perimeter player coming out of the low post has the following options if he does not get the shot.

   a. Fill the high post and remain for the slow two count as shown in Figure 15.33. This is done when the screen has come from the high post. Any time a player designated for post play only, comes out of the low post, he automatically moves into the high post.

   b. Move out to a spot on the perimeter as in Figure 15.34 and follow the principles of perimeter play.

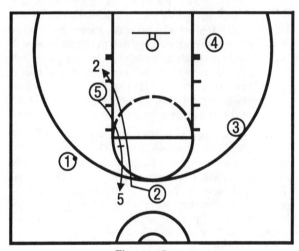

Figure 15.33

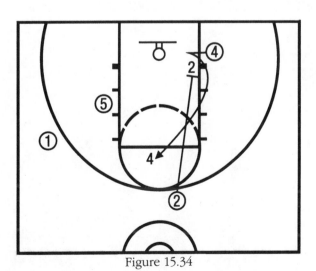

Figure 15.34

c. Back pick for a perimeter player who can move into the high post, screen the low post, or go through to the baselines as in Figure 15.35.

5. **Low post rolls on a feed to the high post**. When the ball goes into the high post, a player in the low post should roll to the basket for the high-low feed.

6. **When the high post is vacant – move into it.** If the flow of motion leaves the high post open, the first player to see this moves into it. A flash post cut from opposite the ball often results in a good shot or a back-door opportunity.

7. **Low post back pick**. At times the low post on the ball side may be occupied. We try to make the feed into him, if possible. However, if the feed can't be made and the ball is reversed, we like the player in the low post to step out and back pick for three as shown in Figure 15.36. This gives us an excellent cut to the basket against A, who may momentarily relax when three gives up the ball. Number 4 will have a good shot opportunity by stepping back if his man sags, or by stepping to the ball if there is a switch. This is the one situation where we let a designated player back pick on the perimeter.

It is by no means imperative that you use only the principles that we have outlined. The rules that you establish and use should be those that best serve your own needs. Everyone who works with motion offense will develop principles that he feels are best for his own situation. Keep in mind, however, that the more rules you have, the more you will be restricting movement and the closer you will be to a pattern offense.

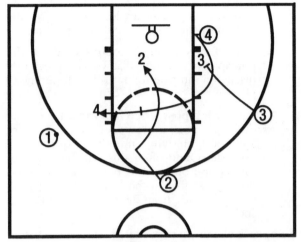

Figure 15.35

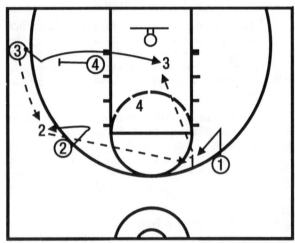

Figure 15.36

Chapter 16 ZONE OFFENSE

Inside Shot

Zone Attack
Jud Heathcote

Zone Offense
Lute Olson

Zone Attack
Jim Brandenburg

How to Attack Zones
Jack Hartman

ZONE ATTACK

Jud Heathcote

Don't try to get too much out of a clinic or book – try to incorporate some of the ideas into your own program.

Some Comments on Zones

1. Zones may be more effective in high school than college – offensive shooting is different by three to five feet – players shoot farther out in college.

2. If you're using zone offenses, you still must get it in close enough to get a good percentage shot.

3. Everyone zoned us because of Earvin Johnson. He's a great passer and penetrator but not a great shooter. Zones are more effective against this type of quarterback.

4. Zone match-ups are a trend today. We're going to see more and more of them.

5. There is more freedom to free-lance in zone attacks.

6. Make sure your shooters are getting the shots against a zone.

7. It's a myth that you should move the ball faster than the zone moves. Many times you pass up good shots in a zone pattern.

8. Zone attacks cannot be stereotyped because the same zone for one team is not necessarily played the same way by another.

9. There is less pattern in attacking zones today because of the jump shot.

Ways to Beat the Zone

1. Fast break – beat the zone down the floor–looking for the layup or the 10-foot jump.

2. Early offense – any shot you can make over 50 percent of the time.

3. Offensive rebounding is important because of the lack of screen outs.

   a. Offensive rebounding – not how high you jump but your position and going to the hoop.

4. Percentage shooting – must take the good shot.

5. Press a zone club because they may be slower– take away their opportunity to set up their defense.

6. Attack an area – get a man behind the zone at the baseline. Attack a man because he is a weak link in the zone.

7. Lob pass – must work on it.

8. Screen the zone – go after weakest man.

9. Drop off pass – go up for the jumper and drop the ball to the open man.

10. Drive the zone – must penetrate with the dribble and look to drop it off. If you do penetrate and find nothing, it's easy to kick the ball back out because the zone has collapsed.

11. Easy jump shot versius zone by going inside and pitching it back to the shooter.

12. Overload principle – flood the zone with more people than the zone can cover without flexing. Every overload goes back to the weak side or back to the original alignment and then back to zone again.

13. Must be a shooting "threat" – you don't have to shoot it.

14. Change your alignment – if you are in a 1-3-1 alignment go 2-1-2 or change men or positions within the alignment.

Different Zones Offenses We Use

Move 4 out to screen for ball (see Figure 16.1). Number 3 moves down to open area (gap). Number 5 flashes – back and forth in low. Number 2 finds a gap where he can get the ball.

Number 1 passes to 2 and cuts (see Figure 16.2). Number 3 steps out to receive the ball. Number 3 to Number 4. Number 4 passes to 1 coming off back pick.

Same start as special but 3 passes to 1 coming off double pick or to 4 on a roll across the pivot or to 5 on a lob underneath (see Figure 16.3). Can also run double keeping the point guard out and sending 3 through.

If nothing materializes, then we have the situation reversed and we double on the other side (see Figure 16.4). This is a four-man rotation with Number 5 the only man staying in the same spot.

Number 1 passes to Number 4 (see Figure 16.5). Number 3 cuts low. Number 4 passes back to 1 and we have the same options. Number 1 and Number 5 stay in the same spot.

Number 5 now rolls high and 2 rolls low to weak side. Now everyone exchanges positions.

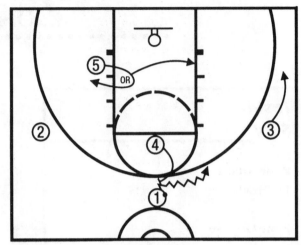

Figure 16.1
1-3-1 freelance offense

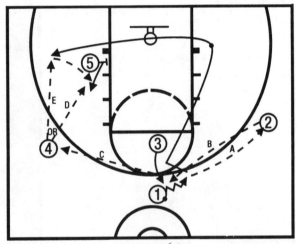

Figure 16.2
Special

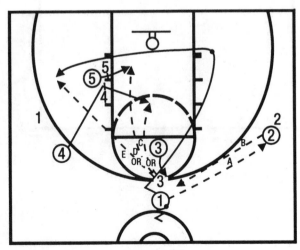

Figure 16.3
Double

A three-man rotation is shown in Figure 16-7. The point man and pivot man stay. Number 3 is slash man.

Now we have a four-man overload (see Figure 16.8).

If we get nothing and we go to weak side – 4 becomes the slasher.

If we get nothing from the Number 4 man slashing, we go back to the weak side and Number 1 becomes slasher.

What we are doing above is interchanging 1, 3, and 4 in an overload – reverse overload situation. It's hard for the zone to cover the slasher and the pivot man at the same time.

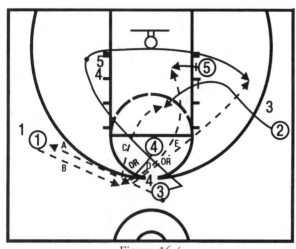

Figure 16.4
Four-man rotation

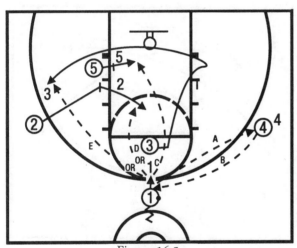

Figure 16.5
Double with three-man rotation

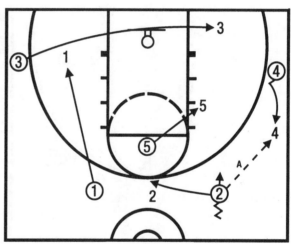

Figure 16.7
Slash

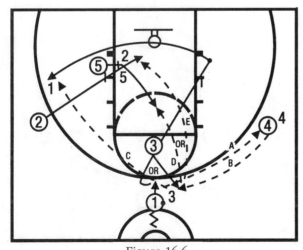

Figure 16.6
Double with five-man rotation

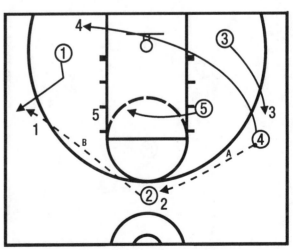

Figure 16.8

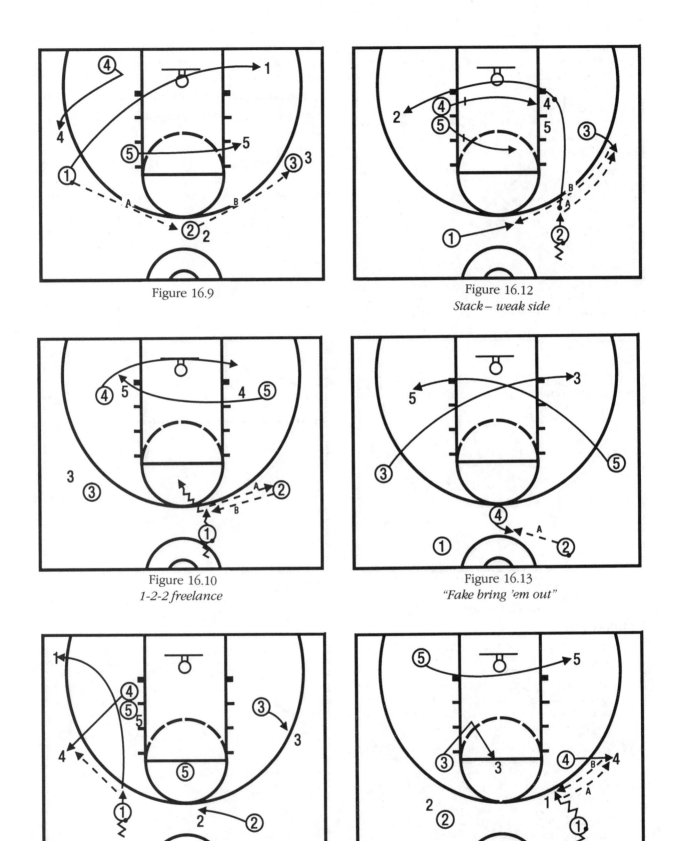

Figure 16.9

Figure 16.12
Stack – weak side

Figure 16.10
1-2-2 freelance

Figure 16.13
"Fake bring 'em out"

Figure 16.11
Stack – three man overload on strong side

Figure 16.14
Gap

We also use a 2-1-2 freelance by setting up in a 2-1-2 formation and trying to penetrate with the dribble and overload 4 men by breaking opposite corner man to the ball side.

In the 1-2-2 freelance, we pass Number 1 to 2 and hit low if possible. Number 2 passes back to 1 who penetrates and tries to shoot it. If nothing, 1 kicks it out (see Figure 16.10).

Number 1 is our Earvin Johnson. Every time the ball comes back to "E," he drives, tries to find the open man or shoot. If nothing, he kicks it back out and we try it again. Place your best shooters on the wings.

In a "stack" set, we will overload three players on the strong side as shown in Figure 16.11.

Figure 16.12 shows a weak-side stack set.

Number 2 passes to Number 3. Number 4 cuts low and 5 cuts high. Number 3 can go to 4 or 5, or 3 can be back to 1 who looks for 2 or the lob to 4.

"Bring 'em out" – play the clock – don't even try to score. This is best done from a 2-3 high set (see Figure 16-13).

We also keep guards out and play three-on-three from the past from the 2-3 set. When we hit the high post, Numbers 3 and 5 will cut to the basket.

In our "gap" set (Figure 16-14), we run a three out, two in alignment with the perimeter players dribbling into the zone gap. Number 1 looks for everyone but goes to 4. Number 4 gives it back to 1, and he tries to dribble again looking for gaps in the zone.

ZONE OFFENSE
Lute Olson

I. Philosophy

1. The offense must be adjusted to fit the personnel.

2. Movement, if it has a purpose, is valuable. Movement for movement's sake is of little value because a zone reacts for the most part to ball movement, not player movement.

3. Purposeful movement is necessary to eliminate match-up zone and combination defenses.

4. Our players are to play the "gaps" whenever possible to force the zone to move.

5. The ball must be moved rapidly, especially in attacking the weak side of the zone. Ball fakes, opposite the man we want to set up, should be used frequently.

6. If we get ahead we are not opposed to holding the ball. If we can force the zone to extend, they will be much less efficient.

II. The Offense

1. Our zone offense is a combination of a number of different zone offenses that have proved successful in the past.

2. We have attempted to incorporate variations of the 1-4, overload, give-and-go rotation, 1-3-1, and double post in our offense.

3. Our game plan will indicate the options we expect will be most successful against the next opponent. We attempt to "polish" these during the ensuing practice sessions.

4. We will throw a lot of cross-court passes from the wing to the opposite baseline, especially when our offside low post man is in position to screen the low zone man inside the lane. This forces the zone to cover baseline to baseline which will create inside gaps for our post men to flash to.

5. The following are a couple of our favorite options.

III. Stack and Gap Zone Offense

1. Stack set up below lowest defender.

2. Number 1 will drive away from stack (see Figure 16.15).

3. Number 4 will try to screen the defender while 1 looks for lob to 5.

4. If above cannot be done, then Number 4 will break to the middle of the zone (see Figure 16.16).

5. Number 5 follows Number 4's cut to middle gap as 4 continues to the baseline position (see Figure 16.17).

6. Number 3 now slides in behind Number 5's cut looking for lob.

7. If nothing materializes, 1 will drive the ball to the opposite side with 4 and 5 stacking and 3 popping out to the wing position (see Figure 16.18).

8. Any time pass is made to interior he will look to shoot or pass to other post or offside wing.

IV. Mid-Post Zone Offense

Options:

1. Get the ball inside of post.

2. If pass is made to Number 3, he will look to 5.

3. If Number 5 is not open, Number 3 will look for Number 2 behind Number 4's screen or for Number 4 slipping into the middle (see Figure 16.19).

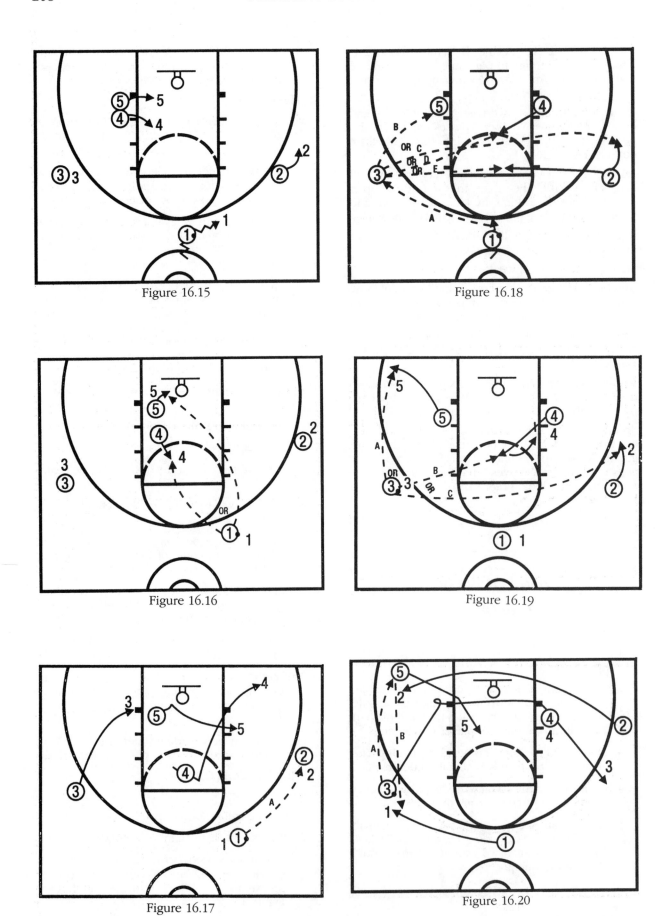

Figure 16.15

Figure 16.18

Figure 16.16

Figure 16.19

Figure 16.17

Figure 16.20

4. Number 5 will pop out to corner if Number 3 cannot make the pass to Number 2 or Number 4.

5. Number 3 hits Number 5 and then goes to the low post-up position looking for return pass (see Figure 16.20).

6. Number 1 fills the wing spot.

7. Number 5 passes to Number 1 and then moves into mid-post position calling for the ball (3 vacates to offside on pass from 5 to 1).

8. Number 2 comes from offside to ball-side baseline looking for pass from 1.

9. If Number 2 steps up to the top of the key (instead of going ball-side), then he will look for jumper or for Number 3 behind 4's screen.

V. 1-4 Dribble Chase

1. Number 1 dribble chases away from 2. Number 3 goes to the corner and Number 5 slides down and post up.

2. Number 4 pops out and receives pass from 1 (see Figure 16.21).

3. Number 4's first option is to hit Number 5 coming into the middle.

4. Number 4's second option is 2 who has slid into a gap in the zone (see Figure 16.22).

5. Number 4 goes to the offensive boards while Number 3 takes open part of the rebound triangle.

ZONE ATTACK

Jim Bradenburg

Things to Do Against Zones

1. You must establish a good inside game. (Not necessarily to shoot – but be able to get the ball inside.)

2. Go odd against an even front or even against an odd front – penetrate the seams.

3. Organize your rebounding – be sure to have offside coverage.

4. Use skip passes and dropoff passes when operating against zones.

5. Develop some set plays but allow for some free-lance as well.

6. Develop and practice good shots from within the high percentage range.

7. Insist that your players catch the ball squared around and ready to shoot or pass.

Slash Offense Versus Zone

We like to start the offense as indicated because it is hard to trap. Number 2 passes to Number 3 and screens away (see Figure 16.23).

After Number 2 passes the ball to Number 3 and cuts, the basic set will assume the positions shown in Figure 16.24.

Rules

1. Number 5 follows the ball.
2. When a forward (Numbers 2, 3, and 4) reverses the ball, he slash cuts through to the opposite block, then steps out (see Figure 16.25).

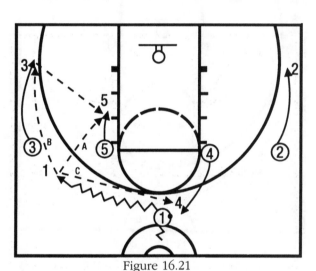

Figure 16.21

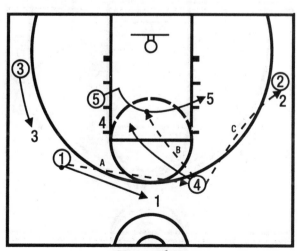

Figure 16.22

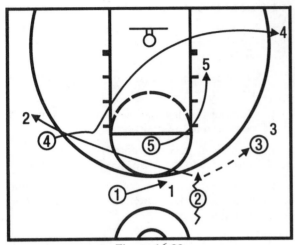

Figure 16.23

3. Cutter reads and times his move based on what the center (Number 5) does. When Number 2 receives the pass, he looks for Number 5 and Number 3 on the block. If nothing happens, Number 3 steps out and players are positioned as shown in Figure 16.26.

Keep turning the ball over constantly. This creates a high-low post situation with the Number 5 man and the slashers.

Special Plays From Same Offensive Set

Number 3 passes to Number 4 and Number 4 looks inside. If nothing is there, Number 4 passes to Number 1 who filled Number 3's spot (see Figure 16.27).

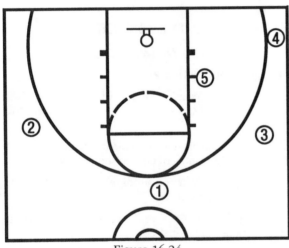

Figure 16.24

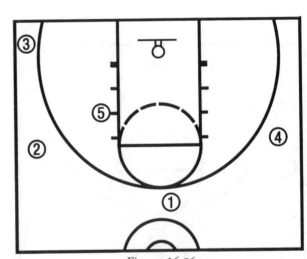

Figure 16.26

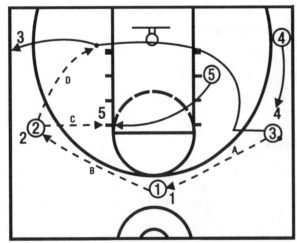

Figure 16.25

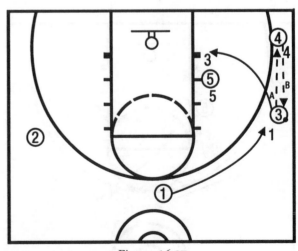

Figure 16.27

Number 5 rolls up toward Number 1. If the defender comes with him, Number 3 flashes back for a pass. If defense on Number 5 does not come with him, Number 1 looks for Number 2. If the defender takes him, the lob pass for Number 3 should be open (see Figure 16.28).

Special Plays for Slashers

Offense can convert into a 1-4 high set offense form the basic set.

When Number 3 cuts through, he comes straight up to the high post (see Figure 16.29).

After receiving the pass from Number 3, Number 1 dribbles left and hits Number 5 at the high post. Number 3 pins his man and cuts hard to the basket looking for the ball.

We Call This Play Number 10

Number 1 passes to Number 2. Number 5 rolls opposite the ball down to the black and sets a double screen with Number 4 on the baseline. Number 3 cuts to the middle of the free throw line for a shot if available or then hard to the block opposite side of the double screen (see Figure 16.30).

If Number 3 is not open at the block, Number 2 passes to Number 1 and reverses the ball.

Number 1 may take a dribble or two looking for Number 3 coming off the double screen (see Figure 16.31).

If Number 5's man takes Number 3, Number 1 looks for the lob pass to Number 5 at the basket.

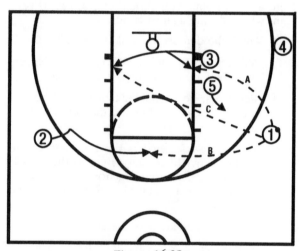

Figure 16.28

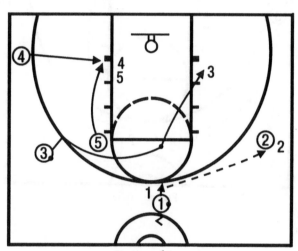

Figure 16.30

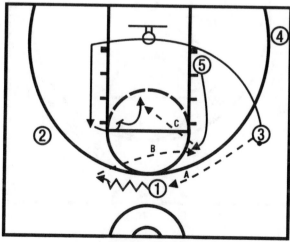

Figure 16.29

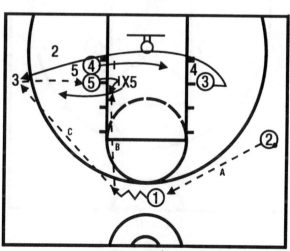

Figure 16.31

If nothing happens, Number 4 floats out opposite (for weak-side rebounding position) and we are back in the slasher offense set ready to go (see Figure 16.32).

Against Odd Front Zones

Numbers 2 and 3 play skip pass. Numbers 1 and 4 play skip pass (see Figure 16.33).

Everyone reads Number 5's defensive man, so he can pin on the skip pass and roll toward the ball. Look for the jump shots off the skip passes.

HOW TO ATTACK ZONES

Jack Hartman

Zone defenses give us all problems. All the different zones and what they can do dictate to the offense what it can execute. We are trying to get the ball to the right guy at the right place on the floor.

We as coaches should try to understand what zone defenses are doing or trying to accomplish. Two important things we should do are: 1) Assess our offensive and defensive strengths and weaknesses. 2) Have a good understanding of zone defenses and their strengths and weaknesses.

Here are ten points you should emphasize to your team when playing against zones.

1. Watch the defense as well as the ball.

2. Move the ball with a purpose. Tell players why they are doing the things they do.

3. Receivers, be available. Don't stand behind the defense or out beyond the defense. Take up slack.

4. The weak-side wing is pinched (see Figure 16.34). Why? It's easier to get to the boards from this position and action on the strong side may free a spot for him to cut to from the pinched area.

5. Step into open areas of the zone.

6. Take up slack space and look for the spot.

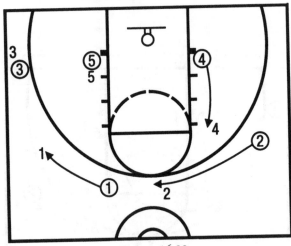

Figure 16.32

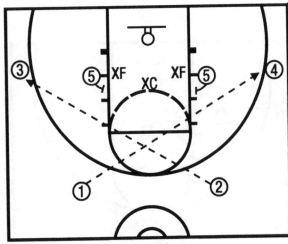

Figure 16.33

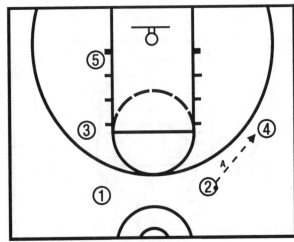

Figure 16.34

7. Emphasize the overhead pass.

8. The threat of a lob pass to the low post area has to always be there or you allow the defense to cheat.

9. Penetrate the zone with a pass or dribble. Take what the zone gives you.

10. Teams must get the ball inside. You have to attempt to score from three general areas on the floor to keep the zone honest (see Figure 16.35).

A player should do one of two things when he catches the ball inside – shoot or pass. Have your players familiar enough with your offense that they know their passing options when they catch the ball inside.

Here are two basic offensive sets against zones.

Against a two front zone (see Figure 16.36):
   –Start with a one guard offensive set.
Against a one front zone (see Figure 16.37).
   –Start with a two guard offensive set.

You must have some motion in your zone offense or your stationary set will be just that — stationary. Here are some patterns we run from our 1-3-1 set (see Figure 16.38).

1. Point guard should be offset to let wings know which is the strong side and which is the weak side.

2. Number 1 passes to Number 4.

3. Number 4 passes to Number 5 in the corner.

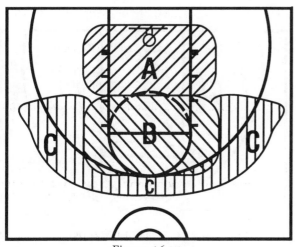

Figure 16.35

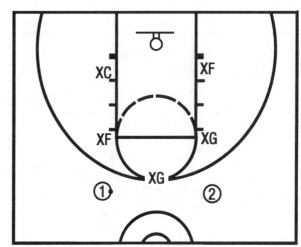

Figure 16.37

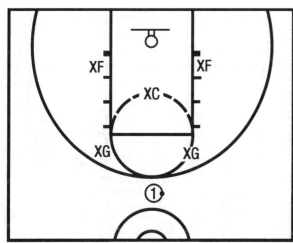

Figure 16.36

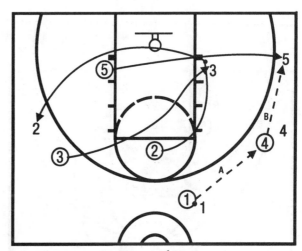

Figure 16.38

This keys the rotation of Numbers 2 and 3 with Number 2 cutting first and Number 3 coming right in behind him.

4. When the ball is swung back around, Number 3 rotates to the weak side (see Figure 16.39).

Here is another pattern or option starting with a two guard front.

1. As soon as Number 2 passes to Number 4 and cuts, Number 5 rotates over to the ball side and Number 3 pinches (see Figures 16.40).

2. If Number 4 can't hit Number 5 or do anything himself, he reverses the ball to Number 1. Number 1 in turn passes the ball to Number 3. If Number 4 can throw directly to Number 3, that is acceptable (see Figure 16.41).

3. For about a one count, there will be a two on one on the weak side. Number 3 should attack the defensive man and read him.

Against a 1-3-1 zone (see Figure 16.42):

1. Start from this stationary set and then add the movement. When Number 2 passes to Number 4, Number 3 slides low and Number 5 pinches. If Number 3 doesn't get the ball, he rotates to the weak side and Number 5 flashes to the ball.

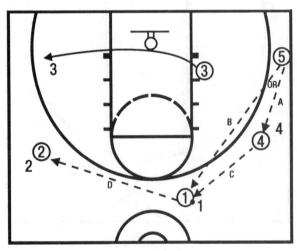

Figure 16.39

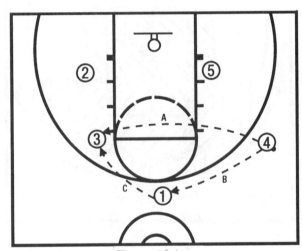

Figure 16.41

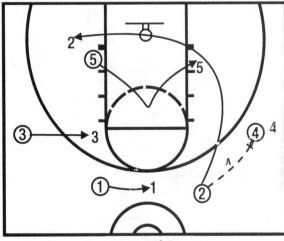

Figure 16.40

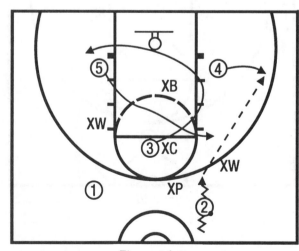

Figure 16.42

2. Against the 1-3-1 zone, try to throw as many skip passes as possible (see Figure 16.43).

Against extended zones (see Figure 16.44):

1. The defense is trying to take away the passing lanes.

2. The first thing you want to do is attack. Try not to slow down the movement of the ball. Receivers must be available. Really try to use the skip passes.

Against 3-2 zone (see Figure 16.45):

1. Try to punch the ball in, then out. If you are unable to do that, start on the side.

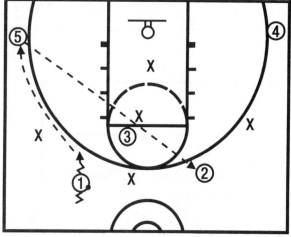

Figure 16.44

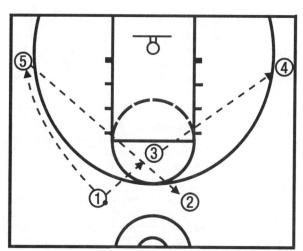

Figure 16.43

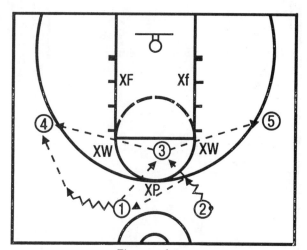

Figure 16.45

Chapter 17   **S**PECIAL **S**ITUATIONS

CONTROL GAME AND SPECIAL SITUATIONS
Morgan Wootten

One of the most important areas of basketball when it comes to X's and O's, as well as selling it to your squad, is what I call coaching special situations, like a delay situation.

I'm sure all of us can look back and think of all the games we were involved in that were 10 points or less and ask ourselves if we were really prepared. Were we really ready? Were the players really ready when push came to shove? What did you do when you were ahead by three points with a minute and a half to go? Did your team know exactly what you wanted? What about when you were down by three?

I'm a firm believer that if you take any game under 15 points, it takes a microscope to find the difference between these two teams. A microscope. Some people say 15 points is a blow-out but I think 15 points is a flip of a coin. I really believe that.

I want to show you what we call "Four to Score." I felt proud when Dean Smith sat in on one of our practices and said, "I like that – Four to Score." It's a word picture; you're still trying to score. Of course, what the time and score tells you is what kind of shot to take.

We teach our guys the Four to Score by setting them up at half court and putting them in the corners. We put the Number 5 man, who is our center, in one corner. We put the big forward, the Number 4 man, in the other corner. Our best athlete is the Number 3 man and we position him in the high post area. Any good athlete can play in that area but it's important to put one of your very best athletes there, maybe the guy after your best ballhandler. When Adrian Dantley played for us, he was the Number 5 man, but he played in the middle in the Four to Score because he was a deadly one-on-one player. So, you're not tied down to one position but you want a good athlete handling the ball.

You must come up with a Four to Score team that you want in there at the end of a game. The team might be great foul shooters and ballhandlers. You might want a pickpocket team with blazing speed if you're behind. You might want a zone team, or perhaps a rebounding team. You might want your five best scorers in there at the same time when you have to produce some points. We have a lot of special teams we know we can go to if the situation calls for it.

Our Four to Score team is very important in terms of personnel. Our big guard over in the right corner is the Number 2 man. I'll put our point guard, the Number 1 man, in the left corner (see Figure 17.1).

The rules for the Four to Score are very, very simple. Anytime the ball goes to the middle – I don't care if it's a pass, a dribble, or what – both deep corner men must go to the block (see Figure 17.2). If the ball goes back outside, Number 4 and Number 5 must immediately go back to their corners. If the ball is not in the middle, we want a receiver in every corner. Needless to say, if Number 3 gets the ball in the middle, we would like him to face the basket and be ready to play one-on-one, take his man for a ride. He might go by his man, suck up the defense, and be able to lay it off to Number 4 or Number 5.

The key is to save your dribble. Don't put the ball on the floor. That's the last thing you want to do.

Let's say Number 1 is under a lot of heat and he drives to the middle. If that happens Number 3 has to get out of there (Figure 17.3) because we never want to cross two of our men. If that happens the opponent is sure to double team us, particularly if we've got the lead or the score is tied.

They're not going to sit back and let us take the last shot in that situation. So if Number 1 has to drive hard to the middle, Number 3 has to get out of there, and Number 2 must rotate away as well.

A key thing is this – it is not an offense unless the other team is chasing you. We're looking to score, but we want to take the kind of shot we want.

Now, anytime the ball goes to the corner, maybe Number 1 goes to Number 5 – actually, one of the great passes in this set is Number 1 throwing on the diagonal all the way to Number 4 – the high post must follow in the hole on the ball side and the off corner man must be at the block. You can get a lot

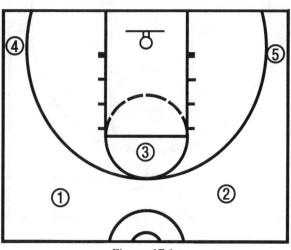

Figure 17.1

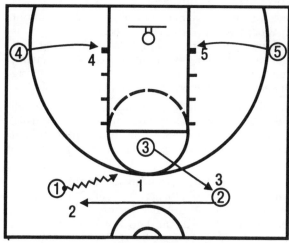

Figure 17.3

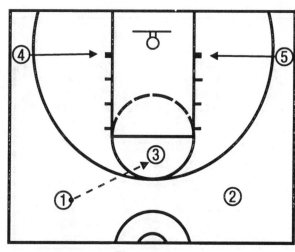

Figure 17.2

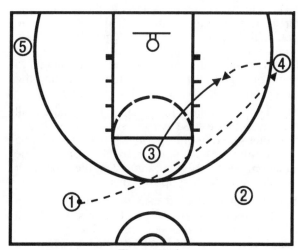

Figure 17.4

of layups out of Number 3 when Number 1 throws the ball to Number 4 on the diagonal (Figure 17.4). Generally, if Number 1 can't throw to Number 3, it means Number 3 is being fronted, so on the diagonal pass to Number 4 he can just roll on the pass and get the layup.

Every time the ball goes low, the high post has to go low, and if it comes back out, the high post must come back out with it.

Let's say Number 1 drives hard at Number 3. There's nothing that says Number 3 can't run a pressure cross and just replace Number 1 (Figure 17.5). He just has to stay far enough away so that his man can't double team Number 1. Again, as soon as the ball arrives at the high post area, Number 4 and Number 5 have to make their move toward the block. In this case, if Number 1 drives and beats his man, something good is liable to happen because Number 4 and Number 5 have moved in closer.

Special Plays

You always want to have an offense when you're in a situation to take the last-second shot.

One we have – assuming our small forward and our big guard are pretty good outside shooters – is positioning them right along the baseline with our two big men like this: Number 2 is the big guard, Number 3 the small forward, Number 4 the big forward and Number 5 the center (Figure 17.6).

The object of any offense, really, is to take the ball to the baseline because that flattens the defense. This, of course, is the 1-4 set, but instead of running it at the foul line extended you place the four down on the baseline.

So, if Number 1, the point guard, starts to take his man for a ride, our bench will stand up with 10 seconds to go. We call this "Victory." "Victory" is a very powerful word. Our bench will stand up with 10 seconds to go and we'll say "Victory." Our two smallest members available will go to the block, and our two biggest men will go to the corners, as Number 1 starts to penetrate. As he gets to the head of the circle, the big guys come in and screen for the potential jump shooters coming right off for a baby jumper at the worst. And we all know the value of a big guy coming in, screening, and then rolling and getting the guy off his back and maybe getting the dish-off from Number 1 for a layup (Figure 17.7).

That happens quite a bit. Number 1 may take it all the way, because these two screens can totally occupy the defense. So, there's not much help that's going to hit Number 1. It's going to be a one-on-one situation, because the guys guarding the other four people are really tied up with them.

Your lowest numbered man must sprint back on defense. If the man with the ball, Number 1, takes it all the way, as in this situation, Number 2 has to guard against the fast break. If Number 2 had the ball and he was driving, then Number 1 would go

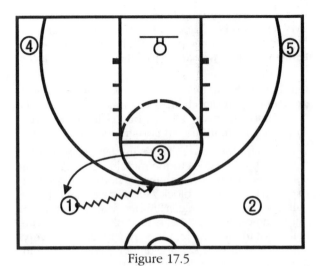

Figure 17.5

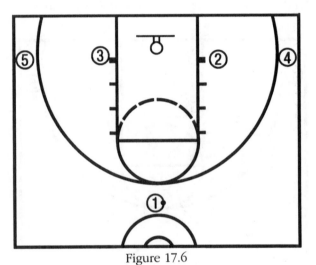

Figure 17.6

Figure 17.7

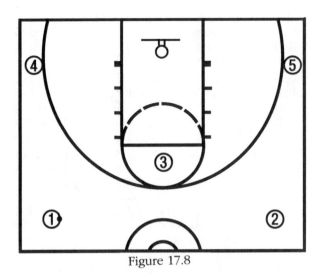

Figure 17.8

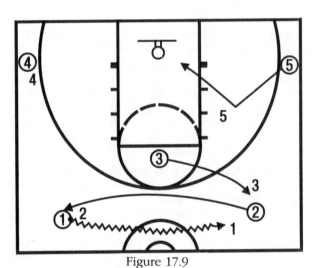

Figure 17.9

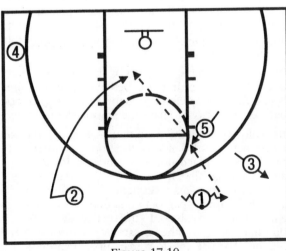

Figure 17.10

back on the defensive coverage. There's one thing for sure – you always want defensive coverage. You always have to guard against the potential fast break in this situation.

We also tell our kids one other thing. If the score is tied and we take the last shot then we settle for it. We don't go to the offensive board. If we're ahead, of course, we're not even going to take the last shot unless we have a layup. We don't go to the offensive board, and I've seen it happen so many times, they end up climbing somebody's back, the shot doesn't go, they go down to the other end and shoot one-and-one and you lose the ballgame when the worst thing that should have happened would be overtime.

Number 2, if they're already in there and they know they can get the offensive rebound, they're going to get it anyhow and stick it back in. It's just that if you tell them not to go to the board, they won't take the crazy chances where they might foul. Also, it gives our shooter tremendous confidence. We know we don't have to rebound the shot. There are some psychological aspects behind this type of thinking, as well.

We call "Victory" with 10 seconds left because Number 1's penetration will take about three seconds, so we start our move with about six seconds and the shot goes up with about four seconds left. That still leaves time for an intelligent rebound, but they're not supposed to go to the board unless they're already in position. Also, this is strictly against a man-to-man defense.

John Wooden said it was a compliment when people said his teams were easy to scout. They were easy because they executed everything so well. Execution is one of the real keys in a last-second situation. If it comes down to that last shot, you've always got to have one or two plays like this one ready to execute.

I don't like the idea of, say, with 10 seconds to go, calling time-out. I like to go right into it out of the offense you're running, like our Four to Score. Because a time-out really gives the defense every opportunity to get set, I don't like to call a time-out in those situations. Our attitude is that we're going to do these things in practice so much that they become automatic. With 10 seconds to go, I want that defense to panic a little bit while we go right into something we have worked on.

Another play we might call in a situation like this is "UCLA," because the Bruins made a living out of it with Wicks, Rowe, and those guys. We set up in our normal Four to Score offense (Figure 17.8). The team will stand up with 10 seconds left, knowing we want the last shot and we'll verbally call the play from the bench.

Number 1 will start a hard power drive toward Number 2, and Number 2 runs a guard in front move. Number 3 will immediately fly to the ball, posting up to be a super receiver. Number 5 will post up because if he's overplayed he could become a back-door receiver (see Figure 17.9).

As soon as Number 5 breaks up, Number 2 starts to move. Number 1 hits Number 5, Number 2 goes back door and I can't tell you how many layups we've shot off this play. It's a nice way to end a game when the score has been tied (see Figure 17.10).

If they play Number 5 like mad so he can't get it, we can just go over the top to Number 2 for a layup. If they sluff off of Number 5 to take care of Number 2 going through the back door, Number 5 can just play one-on-one with the ball and he should end up with a pretty good shot.

This has been a great, last-second shot for us, especially off of the Four Corners.

Just two more things to emphasize in this situation. Save your dribble and move on the pass. Those are two things we're constantly emphasizing.

WEAK-SIDE SERIES

Fred Taylor

We spend a great deal of time on our weak-side attack and I will try to give you a couple of reasons why we think it is important to us. First, any time we get into trouble offensively, we spend more of our time in practice on our weak-side play – our two-man games. Regardless of the patterns we are using, we go back to two-man games. We think it is the basis of our offensive basketball. Regardless of the pattern we're going to run, at some phase it is going to boil down to how two of our people react to defensive pressure given them in that area. We try to have rules we follow and name the types we use in these two-man games.

We don't think a good defensive team will allow us to run just straight strong-side. We've got to have some sort of weak-side attack and try to sell the players on that basis.

We also think if we concentrate on the weak-side play with two people, we can conceivably have our two best offensive men around the ball at the same time and maybe create more pressure for the defense in that particular area. I think it is a little easier to see what is going wrong when there are only two people involved.

Second, we feel that two-man play to the weak side gives us another opportunity for discipline in our offense. I know sometimes we are accused of getting that ball airborne a little too quickly, but we only average between 60 and 65 shots a game.

By coming back to the weak side, we feel we can get away from one man bouncing the ball, waving and directing traffic. In fact, we even put in another rule. If anyone on top with the ball bounces it and starts waving, we want the corner man to just stand still and wave back. That means we're not going to get into that act anymore.

We try to follow rules in our two-man play. First of all, don't try to do everything at once. We think too often we get so involved with the idea of bringing the ball back to the weak side that we actually overrun ourselves. We don't need to go quite that fast.

We spend a great deal of time on the making an angle cut to receive the basketball. We think it is pretty important. In drills we run baseline to baseline, making only angle cuts. We ask our players to work on a change of direction cut in their summer work. I think every coach has a drill where he has a player dribble up the floor, jump stop and make a reverse pivot. Typically, the body balance isn't good. We think spending time on change-of-direction drills is good for us. We think the better the competition, the more important change of direction becomes.

The same thing occurs if we are going to make the pass and follow our it. We want to make an angle cut before following our pass in which case maneuvering speed becomes a factor.

We feel that as far as our handoff is concerned on our two-man games, we want to flip the ball to the cutter. We were taught that you handed the ball to the cutter as he went past, but this presents many problems. We try now to operate much like the second baseman and shortstop in baseball when turning a close double play.

The other thing that we try to insist upon is operating on the basis that we are never going to turn away from the basketball while we are involved in two-man play. I know the big men can turn away from the ball and it sets up an excellent weak-side rebounding position, but we think if we're ever going to get the ball back it may be returned right at the time we're turning away from it.

We are not trying to get our players involved with exactly what type of defense they find on the weak side. We hope that if they meet new pressure, the cutter will veer to the outside since he ought to automatically realize that he has no opportunity to go all the way.

We try to determine our path by the amount of help needed. If you are free it is better to go a bit wider. If you find your defensive man hounding you, you had better cut close to have the advantage of a screen.

Basically we want the deep man – assuming the ball has penetrated this side of the floor – to attempt to pinch in someplace along the lane line. If we can get away with that, fine. If we can't, we try to incorporate our various two-man sequences. I suppose splits actually become a part of two-man play, even though a third man is involved. In the final analysis, there is one man who is either a sacrifice man or a "head hunter." We use the low man first, regardless. He might be a backcourt man who has gone inside off the break. We hope it gives us a rule of thumb to follow. In other words, when we hit a post man there should always be movement, not indecision as to which man is going to go first. If you want splits from out on top involving no deep men, we ask the passer to go first.

The other reason we try to send the low man first is because we feel it clears out the baseline area. We hope it is helpful to us in other patterns by complementing the action of a head-hunting screen that frees a man coming back out for a jumper.

As far as our types are concerned, I am sure you are all very much aware of all the possibilities. We give specific names to each one so we can call it out.

We identify the various games with names like outside, pick, roll, gut and gate. We don't run all of them in every ballgame. In our outside game we attempt to have the low man pinch, leaving him the opportunity to flip off or keep it for a one-on-one.

One thing we would like to do – which should be an automatic response anytime we are trying to reverse the court – is make the weak-side low man responsible for a potential back-door play. This is true even if he happened to be a clearing out guard. We used to bring our clearout man back out immediately for floor balance. The weak-side low man must always be ready to back-door. We feel this is a rule that shouldn't hurt us and we should always have it in the back of our minds.

Again, this ties in with why we need not be in such a big hurry to come back to the weak side and get something done. If, in the outside game, we cannot reverse the court and the weak-side corner defensive man is so good that we can't back-door, then we can exchange positions which includes having the man on the top screen release the low man.

In the pick game, we bring the low man all the way up. First choice, outside game, his second choice would be to slide all the way up to set a back pick, assuming the man on top had the ball. We ask him to use the lane line as his base of operations, never going on an angle to the basket. I suppose this is one of our problems – it is human nature to want to go toward the basket. If we do force a switch and cut to the basket, a smaller man may move in front and keep us from getting a return pass. By using the lane line, we feel we can keep the defensive man on our back side.

Third, if we cannot use the first two sequences, we try to have the low man come up and slide out wide. This sets up our roll game with the man on top following his pass and setting an inside screen to free the low man. Here again, he must turn with the ball to possibly receive another feed along the baseline.

The low man furthers his opportunity to drive or shoot by first faking baseline.

Once again, if the screener finds the low defensive man sagging, he must alter his course to set up a screen for a jumper. This is especially true if our low man is a guard who has cleared out from the strong side.

Next is the gut game. This is used when the defense would not allow our man on top to go outside. The defensive men may be so far to the outside that we couldn't get to the sideline, let alone get to the outside. We tried to make it an automatic response in this situation and call it the gut game. Simply take the step right down the middle, hoping this should make the defender chase us. Occasionally we could get a little inside flip pass for a basket. If nothing else we hope to sink the defender, then come back out for a jumper behind the low man.

The last game that we try to play is our gate game. We haven't had many players who executed this very well, so we have attempted to use it only for specific individuals. The deep weak-side corner man comes up high and hard for the pass from out on top. If he can execute a quick reverse pivot with the ball on his nose, he has an excellent opportunity to either hit a jumper or put the ball down once around his defender and stuff it. It is a most difficult screen for the defender to combat on top. It is a lethal yet legal screen – not like the one where you are actually turning around and handing the ball off to the cutter. You are actually turning around with the idea of doing something with the ball yourself.

SPECIAL SITUATIONS

Hubie Brown

There are special situations that occur in every basketball game which coaches must be prepared to handle. I'd like to present my theories and thoughts in these situations.

The Last Shot

First of all, you must decide who is to take the last shot. Should it be the star? We do not suggest this. Most teams will anticipate your star to be the player to take the last shot and will prepare a strong defense for this to happen. You would be better off setting up your second or third best player shooting the last shot.

After you have determined who is to shoot, the next decision is when to shoot. This, of course, will depend upon what the score is. If we are behind by one point, we will not hold the ball for one shot. We look for the first good shot and take it. We believe in our rebounding game and have confidence in our defense to retrieve the ball in case of a missed shot. As a rule, players do not want to take a shot with just a few seconds left.

However, if the score is tied and we are holding for the last shot, we will instruct our players to shoot with six seconds remaining. The reason for this is, of course, to allow us time for a rebound in the event of a miss. We instruct our players to go to the boards aggressively after second shots in these situations. As a rule, the referees will not call fouls at the end of the game. We indicate to the players on the floor when there are six seconds remaining by having our entire bench stand up at the same time. The player who has the first good shot after the signal puts up the ball.

There are other means of communicating with your team. It can be done verbally, with signs or with fingers. Whatever method you use, it's important that your means of communication be established and your team know them.

How Do You Stop the Clock When You Have No Time-outs?

There are a number of tricks you can pull to stop the clock for a short rest. Perhaps the best and most frequent used is the water or sweat on the floor, which needs wiping. The last resort would be to call an excessive time-out and suffer the penalty.

Jump Balls

Use the lineup as designated in Figure 17.11. If the opposition matches one-on-one, the jumper should tip to the open side of Number 5. Should the opposition double up on Number 5, it would create an opening at one of the wings or back to Number 1.

Free Throw Miss

When you are down by two points with only a few seconds remaining and have only one free throw left, how should you play for the miss? Figure 17.12 shows one possibility. Have Numbers 1 and 2 break

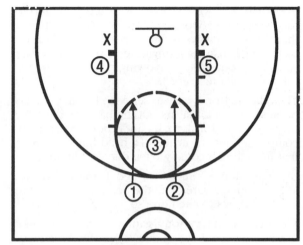

Figure 17.12

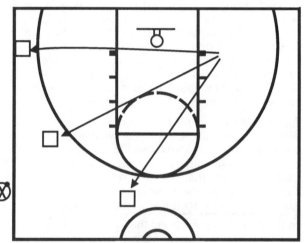

Figure 17.13

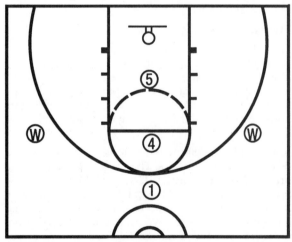

Figure 17.11

Figure 17.14

for the dotted line just as soon as the ball leaves the free thrower's hand. Statistics reveal that most rebounds will come back out to the area indicated.

Sideline Inbounding the Ball

With the ball at the 10-second line and little time remaining, chances for a makeable shot are best by breaking a man to the three areas indicated in Figure 17.13. In the majority of cases, one of the players breaking to these areas will be open.

Inbounding the Ball Against Pressure

Most of the time two defenders will go with the player making the first move. In Figure 17.14, Number 2 makes the first cut attracting two defenders. Number 1 should move in, take up the slack, and pin the third defender and hold. Inbounder Number 3 then lobs the ball over to Number 1 and a three-on-two should result.

Out-of-Bounds Against a Zone

Many times against zones it is possible to pass straight in to your shooter for the shot. Figure 17.15 illustrates this point. Lining up in a tandem and making the cuts shown can be very productive. Number 5, in cutting, can position himself underneath and pin the wing-backline defensive man in a zone and receive a pass directly from the man out of bounds.

If the middle-backline defensive man helps on this move, it creates an opening for a lob to Number 4 who is sliding down the lane.

Another possibility is shown in Figure 17.16. From the original set have Number 2 and 3 break to the 17 foot baseline areas. Then have Number 4 cut off Number 5 in tight to the basket. Number 5 reads Number 4's cut and goes opposite. Usually one of these four areas will be left open.

Figure 17.15

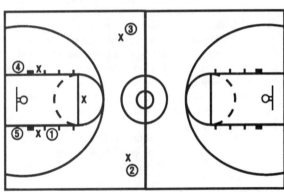

Figure 17.17

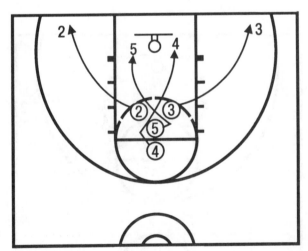

Figure 17.16

Figure 17.18

Five Seconds to Play – Opponents on Free Throw Line Must Go Length of Floor for the Shot

A play you might consider in this situation is shown in Figures 17.17 and 17.18. Number 4 will catch the ball as it goes through the net and becomes inbounder. Number 1 will block the shooter first and then go opposite Number 4 out of bounds. Number 5 will block, release, then buttonhook at the opposite "T" and look for the pass. Number 4 passes the ball to Number 1 and heads up the court along the sideline. Number 2 and 3 cut as shown in the diagram. Number 1 can now pass to Numbers 5, 3, 2, or 4. The long pass to either Numbers 3, 4, or 2 is preferred. If the ball goes to Number 5, he will look to get the ball to either Number 3, Number 2, or Number 4. In any case the nonshooters continue full speed toward the basket and become rebounders in the event of a miss.

Food for Thought

- ◆ Use alignments to cause confusion for the other team.
- ◆ In planning any type of offense when a player leaves a space, always replace him with another player.
- ◆ When a turnover is needed and your opponent has the ball out of bounds, place two men on the inbounder. Ask the referee to be alert for the inbounder moving off the spot.
- ◆ On jump balls, decide what area the jumper cannot tap the ball to and don't cover that area. Cover the other areas.
- ◆ Don't try to imitate other coaches. Be your own person with your own style and do your own thing.

TRIPLE THREAT – SHOOT THE THREE

Chip Parsley

With the addition of the three-point field goal, a team must be able to go to a set play that will afford them an opportunity for three points without calling a time-out. It should be a set call from the bench that can be utilized against a man or zone defense in the following situations: 1. To mount a comeback attempt when behind several points late in the contest. 2. To take advantage of a red-hot perimeter shooter during the normal course of the game. 3. As a last possession with time running out, no time-outs left, attempt to tie the game and send it into overtime.

We have two basic sets that we use at Tarkio College to meet the above criteria. One encompasses the concept of pick-for-the-picker while the other uses the football idea of misdirection.

In Figure 17.19 you see our basic set. Your three best long-range shooters would be in the Number 2, Number 3, and Number 4 spots, with Number 2 being your shooting guard. Number 1 is the point guard, and Number 5 your post man.

As Number 1 brings the ball past the hash mark, Number 2 down screens for Number 3. Number 2 can screen either Number 3's man, or the wing area of whatever zone the defense is in at that time. Immediately after Number 2 sets the screen, Number 4 uses the pick-for-the-picker concept and screens for Number 2, again either the low zone defensive area or Number 2's man. Number 1 can pass to Number 3 for the three pointer. Number 1 can skip pass right to Number 2 for the long-range jumper (Figure 17.20).

What is nice about this three-point set is that it has continuity (see Figure 17.21). If Number 3 or Number 2 do not have a good shot, they simply return the ball to Number 1 and the whole process starts again. Now Number 3 down picks for Number 4.

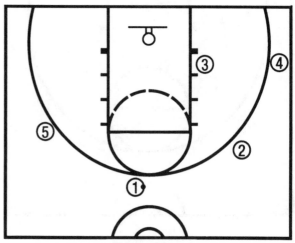

Figure 17.19

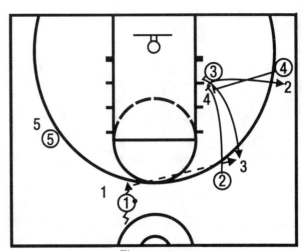

Figure 17.20

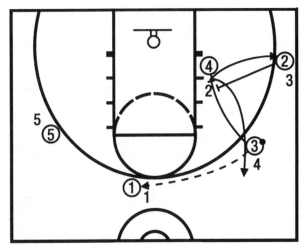

Figure 17.21

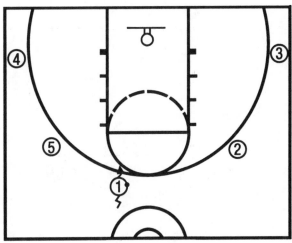

Figure 17.22

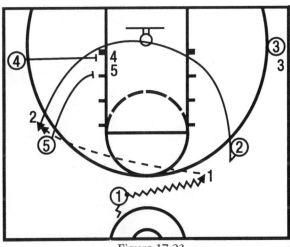

Figure 17.23

Immediately after Number 3 sets the screen, Number 2 screens for Number 3. Again we have the options of Number 1 to Number 4 for the three pointer. Number 1 can pass to Number 4, who passes to Number 3 for the three pointer. Number 1 can skip pass right to Number 3 for the long-range bomb.

This continuity action can be repeated over and over again until you get somebody open and the ball in the hands of the person you want taking the shot.

Number 1 remains out front as an outlet and Number 5 remains just outside the three-point line as a decoy. On a shot attempt Number 5 now has a running start to crash the boards. Numbers 2, 3, and 4 also go to rebound with Number 1 back for defense if necessary. Any rebounds are kicked back outside if a three pointer is dictated by the score, and the entire process starts again.

What really makes this set practical is that it can be used against man or zone defense. Numbers 2, 3, and 4 either pick someone's man or a specified area of whichever particular zone defense is being used.

The other idea we like to throw at opponents when we want a set three-point attempt is based on the concept of misdirection.

In Figure 17.22, you see our basic set.

Number 1 starts the misdirection by taking the ball on the dribble toward Number 2. Number 2 goes to the baseline and out the opposite side behind Number 4 and Number 5's double pick. Number 1 can either pass to Number 3, who in turn skip passes to Number 2 for the three pointer. Or Number 1 can fake a pass to Number 3, keep the ball himself, turn and skip pass to Number 2 for the long-range jumper. Again, Number 4 and Number 5 can either double screen Number 2's man or they can screen the weak side of the zone defense (Figure 17.23).

The key here is for Number 1 to do a good job of misdirecting the defense by making it look as though we are wanting Number 3 to take the shot.

The three-point shot has become an essential part of any offensive scheme. It should be included as part of your special situations practice time. Drill it as you would any other part of your offense, and never underestimate the triple threat.

$Part\ IV$ — TEAM DEFENSE

•••••••••••••••••••••••••••••••

I believe in simplicity and execution of
fundamental skills. Defense is one of the
most important of those skills.

— Bob Knight
Head Coach, Indiana University

Importance of Defense

Evidence suggest that winners play good defense, and good defense produces consistent winners. Teams that take pride in and have patience and determination on defense have far fewer "off" nights than teams that rely on offense-defense. Ralph Miller states that most losses in basketball games are rooted in defensive breakdowns – individual or team defense. Based on this premise, it can readily be seen that defense strongly affects game outcome.

An effective team defense is necessary for scoring from the fast break. I feel that aggressive defensive teams often generate fast-break scoring opportunities and build offensive confidence as a by-product of capitalizing on their defense.

Individually, defense can do several things for a player. It can:

♦ Build self-confidence. All players can play defense effectively if they have the determination and are willing to meet the considerable challenges of defense.

♦ Develop a reputation of aggressiveness and toughness.

♦ Assist players in attaining the best mental and physical condition possible.

♦ Earn the special pride and self-respect players get from playing at both ends of the court.

♦ Give a player the chance to make one of the biggest plays in basketball – drawing the offensive foul (worth a possible four-to-six-point turnaround for the defender's team).

One of the two primary goals of the sport is to prevent the other team from scoring – to develop a team defense that prevents the opponents from getting good shots and scoring.

WATCHDOG OF THE BASKET

Forrest C. "Phog" Allen

The guard is the bipedal watchdog of the basket. It has often erroneously been said that a good offense is the best defense. It has been my experience that a sterling defense, coupled with a better-than-average offense, will more often than not defeat a sterling offense possessed of a near-superior defense.

Many of the offensive drills are sheer fun because there is the ballhandling connected with this fundamental feature. But guarding technique is work, and hard work. A young player will practice shooting by the hour – even alone – because it is fun. Few players, however, in off moments will ever attempt to practice guarding technique to improve their defensive prowess. All players want possession of the ball so they can shoot at the basket. Therefore, a versatile coach will improvise competitive fundamental drills wherein the guard is glorified.

A good guard will hound the ball. He should always be found between his opponent and the basket. This is the first fundamental that should never be neglected.

A wily guard will never let the opposition slip in behind him. He will play the ball and not the man. A crafty guard always knows how to use his weight to advantage without fouling. All prospective guards should take boxing lessons. The boxing skills develop finished guarding technique. The guard should always be on top of the ball, and when he cannot get it, he should cover his opponent.

A versatile guard outthinks his opponent and beats him to position play. A successful guard knows his areas so well that he may intentionally leave a position apparently unguarded for the purpose of drawing his opponent into a trap.

A highly successful coach uses neither a straight man-for-man nor a strictly zone defense. He uses a combination of both because a straight man-for-man has its weaknesses, but not as many weaknesses as a zone, and a straight zone has weaknesses that are easily overcome. A man-for-man defense with the zone principle will pay splendid dividends.

Stage One – Two-on-One: When a single guard is forced to play two offensive men (Figure 18.1), he learns to play the principle of the zone defense, yet he plays the man with the ball and also keeps an eye out for the other potential scorer.

I prefer to teach my defensive fundamentals through competition. We place this primary guard seven feet under, and in front of, the basket. He can thwart any close drives to the basket, and at the same time harass his opponents should they attempt to shoot.

The two offensive players in Figure 18.1 are to locate themselves in a position they prefer before the ball is tossed to one of them by the coach. They are expected to dribble, pivot, pass and cut in, and endeavor to draw the guard out of position before shooting. They are permitted five tries. If either player illegally starts a dribble, commits a violation, or makes a foul, then one point is scored for the defense. As long as there are no fouls by either side, play continues. If the guard fouls, one point is scored against the guard.

If the guard is successful in breaking up the play of the two offensive players without a field goal being scored, the guard wins. If the offense scores two goals out of the five, the offense wins.

The players are rotated, each player on the squad taking the guard's position. This rotation also includes the offensive players until every player on the squad has had both offensive and defensive training on attack and defense. The scores of each performer's effort should be recorded. Consistently outstanding performers will invariably attract attention. There is no better method of teaching team fundamentals than through such competitive practice drills.

During the defensive drills, the coach centers on defensive pedagogy, teaching that the defensive guard is a wary performer. Never will he let either of the two forwards slip in behind him, nor will he go out too deep and leave his goal undefended. As new situations arise, he will know just when to advance or to retreat. Should the offense attempt a shot from out in front, he will constantly project his physique and his personality into both the visual and the mental paths of the shooter. Neither will he ever turn his back upon either opponent for a moment. As an aid to efficient footwork, he will interchange between the first baseman's step and the boxer's stance, as occasion demands.

The plan of teaching defense, using separate competitive scrimmage tries, conforms to recognized principles of teaching, and it is consistently carried out in each of the following setups.

Stage Two – Three-on-Two (Figure 18.2): In this situation the two defensive men are being opposed by three offensive players, according to the principle of a strata of man-to-man defense and a strata of the zone principle. The front guard is placed seven feet in front of the guard shown in Figure 18.1. This is a tandem defensive formation. The rear defensive guard has dropped back to a position about five feet directly in front of the basket and the front guard plays about seven feet in front of his teammate. The expectant

Figure 18.1

Figure 18.2

Figure 18.3

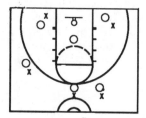

Figure 18.4

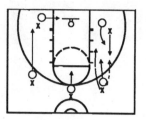

Figure 18.5

attitude of the defensive players should be stressed. This is the formation I always use against fast breaks. It will be noted that the most vulnerable point of the basket is protected, namely, directly in front, and the two defensive players shift to meet an offensive three-man thrust.

Whether the offensive attempts a shot or a pass, the defensive players will always shift the spearhead of their defense in the direction of the ball. These players will constantly be shifting positions in their endeavor to stop all offensive shots. Furthermore, both defensive players will be using every talent at their command to hurry and confuse the offensive ballhandlers. Naturally, the guards must be taught to expect the offensive players to shoot, but when a shot is made by the offense, then the defensive men are in an ideal position to recover the ball. It must be stressed that the three men are to dribble, pivot, and pass, to jockey the two defensive men out of position.

The coach handles the ball on each try, and during the interim he lectures the defensive men on teamwork, in shifting for rebounds, and strategic defensive moves.

The two guards are constantly hounding the three opponents and the ball. Their facial expressions should reveal their militant attitude. As the rear defensive guard shifts over to block a shot, the front defensive guard shifts slightly back and away as he menaces the front offensive man and discourages his idea of a return pass. When the two defensive guards are drawn out of position, they will re-form in the anterior – posterior guarding position as quickly as possible.

The weaknesses of two defensive players against three offensive players are in the corners to the right and left of the rear defensive guard. If the ball is passed from the offensive player out in front to either one of the two offensive players in the corners, the rear guard shifts toward the offensive player who is able to receive the ball in the corner, and the front guard slides back equidistant between the two guards' former positions. In using this formation as a defense against the fast break, the front man parries a thrust in front of the basket, and the rear guard underneath the basket shifts to meet the oncoming offensive player with the ball, while the third defensive player moves in on the weak side away from the ball, thereby setting up the third stage of defense with three players in a triangular position, one in front of the basket and two on either side.

Stage Three – Five-on-Three (Figure 18.3): Five offensive players are waging a scoring attack against three defenders. The defensive players are arranged in a triangular formation with the front defensive player in the apex position and the other two defensive players in their regular guarding positions. This is the defensive formation assumed, when the third player comes in from the weak side after a fast break to reinforce the two defensive players who

were in an anterior–posterior position. When more than three offensive players attack, the triangular defense is imperative. The most vulnerable positions of the basket attack are those in which these three defensive players form their triangle.

The coach handles the ball and hands it to the attacking five players who start down from the center of the floor with the defense lined up in the triangular position. Five trials are used in this competitive fundamental drill, same as in the others.

As the offensive players begin their attack by passing the ball about vigorously from one to another, the defensive players shift accordingly, ever aware of the vulnerable points. Each of the defensive players shows alertness, courage, and confidence. They all stamp their feet and menace continuously with their arms in fighting attitudes. In their desperate attempts to make their opponents muff the passes, and ultimately to recover the ball, they shift back and forth, and to the side, and stamp and yell.

The defense must know that the offensive players near the basket are creating the most perilous situation, and that it is upon these players they must concentrate. Should one of the offensive players out in the court attempt a shot, the defensive player nearest him, while feigning calmness for the moment, will be checking with himself for reassurance that he has covered all loopholes for passes, by or through his own defensive area, and to an offensive teammate under the basket.

Then, just as this offensive forward raises the ball in the act of shooting, this defensive player will feign a gigantic attempt to jump at him, at the same time emitting a starting yell that often brings the desired results. His bent arms will fly up threateningly and his feet will stomp the floor, emphatically and noisily.

As the ball leaves the offensive player's hands, the defensive player will whirl and swing toward the basket to rebound.

Stage Four – Five-on-Five (Figure 18.4): Here we have the defensive situation as it should be with five offensive players met by five defensive opponents. These drills follow all former regulations and should always follow and never precede those of the first, second, and third stages of defensive drill. The five-man defensive teams should have no trouble in stopping their five-man offense in these practice drills. Each of the defensive players specifies a certain opponent for whose movements he will be personally responsible during these regular game situations. These defensive players are taught to slide and trade and switch, so there will be no excuse for permitting an offensive opponent to score because he shook his opponent loose.

In Figure 18.5, the cut-back of the defensive forwards is emphasized. The moment the ball passes a defensive forward, this player should angle back into the area into which the ball was passed and make a one-two pass nearly impossible. You will note that the offensive guard who is handling the ball has just passed it to his own right forward, and has cut into the basket for a pass. The cut-back of the defensive forward has thwarted this and the other defensive players have shifted accordingly.

SEVEN CARDINAL DEFENSIVE PRINCIPLES

Adolph Rupp

Many – you might even say most – basketball experts contend that defense is being shamefully neglected. They point to the astronomical scores and shake their heads. "Defense," they say, "is being thrown out the window. It isn't like the old days when a coach worked just as hard on defense as he did on offense."

I don't believe this is true. On the contrary, I believe we're working harder on it today than we ever have in the past. We've got to. The modern offensive player is tremendously better equipped than the player of 30 or even 20 years ago, and coaches must work twice as hard to stop him.

To anyone who believes that modern defensive basketball is being neglected, I'd like to pose these questions:

1. How do you defense the quick, running, one-handed shot?

2. How do you instruct your players to guard against the hook shot?

3. How do you teach your players to guard the pivot man on the step-in-step-out hook shot?

4. How do you instruct a player to guard the running jump shot?

5. How do you teach a player to stop the dribble-stop jump shot?

After thinking about these things for awhile, I believe you'll come to the same conclusion that I have: Offensive techniques have simply outrun defensive techniques.

Even today, a low-scoring game doesn't necessarily indicate that good defense was employed. Far from it. What I'd want to know is:

1. How many shots were taken?

2. How long did it take a team to set up a play?

3. Was ball control permitted?

4. Was any attempt made to deliberately withhold the ball from play?

The answers to these questions may be the key to the low score.

Defensive play isn't appreciated by many spectators and coaches. Being unspectacular, good defense is often disregarded. But I believe that a check of the outstanding teams year after year will reveal that good defense has contributed greatly to their success.

Their coaches know that defense is less ephemeral than offense; that on an evening when the offense isn't clicking the game can be salvaged by that steady, consistently good defense. A team without a good defense hasn't anything to fall back on when its shooting is "off."

At Kentucky we're convinced that our defense will save us on the nights when our offense isn't working. Our players are taught to realize the importance of defense – individual as well as team play – and we spend one-third of our time on it.

I believe that good defense embodies seven cardinal principles, as follows:

1. Cut Down the Number of Shots

You've all heard the saying, "Take enough shots and the percentage will take care of itself." That may be true, so the first thing to do is cut down the number of shots you give the other team.

In going back over our shot charts for a period of five years, we've found a very reliable trend on the number of shots taken – that is to give the opponents as few shots as possible. They still must shoot to score, and if you can reduce their scoring opportunities by aggressive defense, you will eliminate the danger of a high score.

2. Cut Down the Percentage of Shots

We tell our players to be aggressive at all times. It's hard, tough work, but a lot of players like to play that kind of ball. It's a good feeling to have one of your players come up and ask to be assigned to the outstanding player on the opposing team.

Several years ago, we had such a player. He wasn't interested in how many points he scored, but he liked to take an opponent with a 20-point average and whittle him down to seven or eight. Before he left the dressing room, he'd come up and ask, "Have I got Smith Saturday night?" – Smith being the star of the opposing team.

If you can force a team to take hurried, off-balance, inaccurate shots, you'll destroy their shooting percentage. And that's the difference between aggressive defense and defense that permits a team to get good shots. When a coach comes up after a game and says, "We couldn't hit tonight," maybe there was a reason.

3. Cut Down Everything Under 18 Feet

I like to put this in, because it fits in well with the philosophy of collapsing or floating defenses. It certainly is in their favor. If you'll draw a circle 18 feet out from the basket and attempt to cut down everything in that area, getting all the rebounds, you'll have a foolproof defense. I realize this is impossible, but the fact still remains – don't give them a shot close in to the basket!

If you can imprint this upon the minds of the your players, they will get the idea and work toward this goal.

4. Cut Down the Second Shots

A good defense shouldn't permit a team to get the second and third shots at the basket. While it's often difficult to get the rebound, the first thing to do after a shot has been taken is to see that your man doesn't get the rebound.

You should block out your man and then, after you have him out of play, go for the rebound yourself. If you permit a second and possibly a third shot, one of these is apt to fall in. A good, tough rebounding team won't permit these additional shots after the initial attempt has been taken.

5. Cut Down the Cheap Baskets

How many times have you seen a good, well-played game broken up by a cheap interception, with the defender going all the way and scoring? Ever have an opponent on your own free-throw line slap a jump ball over the head of your defensive players and go all the way in to score? How many times have you had a pass-in under your defensive basket intercepted and laid in for an easy basket? How many times have you seen a ball fall aimlessly to the floor and have it picked up by an opponent and thrown up for an easy basket? How many times have you seen an opponent get an easy basket on a rebound after a missed free throw?

These are just examples of cheap baskets. Some are due to carelessness, some are due to bad judgment, but in a game between teams of equal ability, a cheap basket at a critical time often proves the deciding factor.

6. "Point" the Ball on All Long Shots

As the ball is maneuvered on the outside, the defensive man on the ball should always play tight. Two of the cardinal principles are to cut down on the number of shots and the good shots. If you'll allow good long shooters to get set unmolested, they'll ruin you. Therefore, the man with the ball should always be "pointed." This is true even in floating defenses. In strict tight man-to-man defensive play, this should always be true.

7. Prevent the Ball from Going to the Pivot

I believe that most teams feel exactly as we do – that the ball should never be allowed to go in to the pivot man. If you let the opponents do this, they can set their screens without worrying about ballhandling. We permit the ball to go to the side of the floor, but always try to prevent it from going to the pivot man.

As soon as the pivot man has the ball, you have a dangerous offensive center. He can take a hook shot, jump shot, or jump flip shot. He can fake on one side and go to the other. He can pass to a cutting teammate who has been freed by a screen.

The ball is in an extremely dangerous position when it is held by a man in the pivot. The greatest percentage of attempts at the basket are made from this position.

My objective has been to give you the benefits of our experience down through the years. On those long nights that are sure to come during the season, it might be well to check on these seven cardinal principles and see if any of them are being abused. Maybe somewhere along the way you may find your difficulty.

Even if your team is going well, you can still check. The star of your team offensively may not be a star at all. His defensive inability may be losing ball games.

Bear this in mind: I repeat it to my players thousands of times every year – your defense will save you on the nights that your offense isn't working.

HALF-COURT DEFENSE
Larry Brown

I feel all great teams have two things in common – defense and rebounding. So, we stress defense and rebounding every day as the most important aspects in the game to win. We don't want to give up second shots or layups. As a coach, I feel if you can get your players to play hard and together on the defensive end, they will automatically be unselfish at the offensive end. Also, you should be aware of two other very important aspects: 1) you must know your personnel, and 2) you must know yourself.

We tell our players several things in reference to playing defense. They are:

A. The best defenders have the best opportunity to play. Be sure your players understand this from the very beginning.

B. Every time we shoot, we think defense.

   1. We want to cover the boards.

   2. We want a chance to get fouled.

   3. We want to stop the fast break.

C. We don't want to foul.

   1. We try to teach our players not to commit more than six fouls a half.

   2. Conversely, we try to get to the bonus in the last four minutes of each half.

D. We go after every shooter.

E. All five players react when a pass or dribble is made.

F. Every time a player catches the ball, we want to make him a driver. *Pressure on the ball!*

    1. Teach your players how to guard a man who has a live dribble and how to guard a man who is dribbling.

    2. We tell our players to run instead of sliding when the man puts the ball on the floor. We want him to run and turn him as many times as possible.

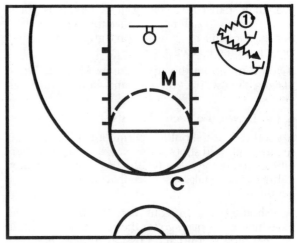

Figure 18.6

Figure 18.6 illustrates a drill to help the defensive player run and turn his man.

    1. Offense is limited to one-third of the court.

    2. We line coaches or managers up the side to cheer on the defense.

    3. Defense must do one of three things:

        a. Turn the dribbler three times before reaching midcourt
        b. Keep the offensive player in the backcourt for 10 seconds
        c. Make the man pick up his dribble.

Figure 18.7 illustrates the support and recovery drill.

    1. Point guard gets beat and forward helps on the ball.

    2. When he passes the ball, the defense must react back and cut off the baseline.

    3. The man takes the shot and you box out.

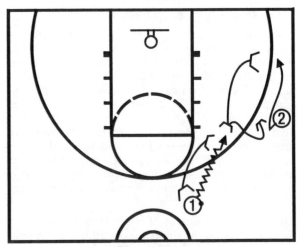

Figure 18.7

As shown in Figure 18.8:

    1. Deny one pass away.
    2. Defensive point is forcing the ball to the sideline.
    3. The forward will deny the ball to his man.
    4. The offensive forward will cut a couple of times.
    5. Then the defense allows him to have the ball; they now go one-on-one and defense box out.

As shown in Figure 18.9:

    1. Jump to the pass, defend clearout move.
    2. Point forcing ball sideline.
    3. Forward will deny the pass.
    4. The offensive forward will clear through. We shout "empty" on clears.
    5. Once the offensive man is through the lane, we shout "normal."
    6. The ball is reversed to extra player or coach and pass is made to the forward.
    7. They now go one-on-one with box out.

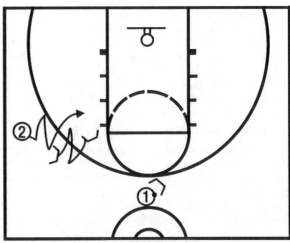

Figure 18.8

We number our defenses. Our zones are numbered: 1) for all point zones, 2) for all two-guard zones, and 3) for our scramble zone. Our man-to-man defenses, which are what I prefer to play, are numbered as follows: "20" for a man-to-man, straight up; "30" for a man-to-man but on every dribble we will double team; and "40" for a man-to-man but on every pass we will look the same. The 30 and 40 series are keyed by two different things, pass or dribble. However, every time the trap is passed out of with a "gut" pass (a pass into the scoring area), we drop all five players below the line of the ball and work our defense back out in 20 (see Figure 18.10 for gut pass).

As shown in Figure 18.10:

    1. The outlined area is considered the scoring area on any pass thrown into that area. We drop all five players below the line of the ball.

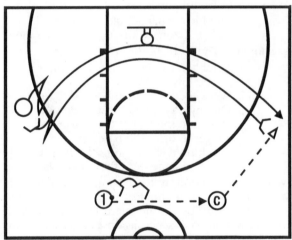

Figure 18.9

2. Defensive goals.
  a. We set a goal of only five-second shots allowed a game.
  b. We want the other team to shoot 42 percent from the field or less.
  c. Only six layups can be allowed per game.
  d. We have a goal of only .85 points per possession, so if you had the ball 50 possessions and scored 50 points, that would be one point per possession.

We have a few rules and automatics that we follow:

1. No penetrating passes.

2. Deny on the line of the ball.

3. If two passes away, see ball and man.

4. Force the ball to the sideline, except when the ball is below the foul line. Then we have two rules:

    a. If you have a man in the corner, force the ball to the corner.
    b. If no man is in the corner, force back to the middle where your help is located.

5. We try to force all cuts low-to-high away from the bucket.

6. On all traps we will have two interceptors and one protector of the basket.

7. When the ball is below the foul line and on the perimeter, we guard with our five players to opponents' three.

In Figure 18.11, notice the ball on the wing and all five defensive players playing your three. We try for this combination at all times.

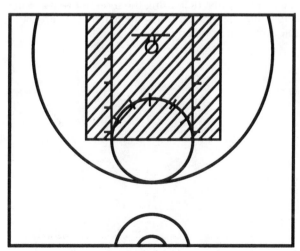

Figure 18.10

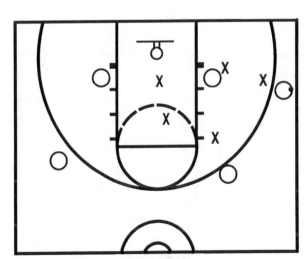

Figure 18.11

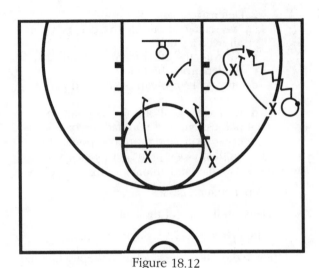

Figure 18.12

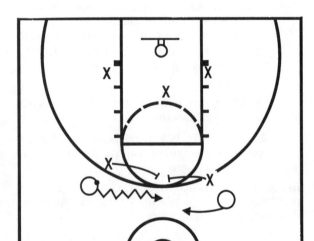

Figure 18.13

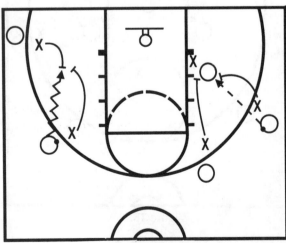

Figure 18.14

Our defenses in the numbered series are keyed by the first number. However, the area on the court where we pick up is determined by the second number. For example: 24 – pick up full-court straight man-to-man; 23 – pick up three-quarter court straight man-to-man; 22 – pick up half-court straight man-to-man. On every missed shot we go back in the 21 defense. The same principles apply to the 30 and 40 defense. Remember, all three defenses are the same, except 30 and 40 are keyed by the pass and dribble with a trap on both. Now, let's take a look at some special situations.

As shown in Figure 18.12:

    1. The baseline drive is shown where we will trap with the post, and the other three players zone.

    2. On a pass out of a trap we yell "normal" and build back in 21 defense.

As shown in Figure 18.13:

    1. Dribble exchange rule is to jump the ball and zone with our other three men.

As shown in Figure 18.14:

    1. Dribble into the scoring area and pass to the low post.

    2. We will double-team both.

    3. On any pass to the post we choke down on the ball not allowing the player to drive the baseline.

    4. On dribble into scoring, we help with trap and zone our other three players.

We use the shell drills to teach some of the concepts just mentioned. You should try to use the normal two-guard front, but a one-guard front in the shell will allow you to practice against one-guard front offenses. I have recently gone to a flex shell drill where we are defending the back-screen and the down-screen used in the flex offense. I feel if you're going to run a solid man-to-man defense, you need to introduce the passing game or motion offense. Practicing against defending the motion offense will help your players to anticipate when you are not able to see the ball and man.

Chapter 19 TRANSITION DEFENSE / PRESSES

CONVERSION/TRANSITION
Bob Knight

As coaches we talk about two things: Offense and defense. There is a third phase we neglect, which is more important. It's conversion from offense to defense and defense to offense. In converting from defense to offense, there are five things we can do:

1. Convert to midcourt.

2. Convert to primary break.

3. Convert to secondary break.

4. Convert to offense.

5. Press if basket has been made.

When converting from offense to defense, there are four things we must do:

1. Don't give up a good shot.

2. Keep the ball under pressure.

3. Don't allow team to set up offense.

4. Help out.

Basketball is a game of reaction. Conversion is the most important reaction in the game today. Anything we can do as coaches to make players quicker is very important. We probably spend less time on trying to condition a player's mind to react to different situations quickly. I think we can make players quicker by getting them to think quicker, getting them to think faster, getting them to think – period!

Drills to Improve Players' Reactions

Shooting

Time: Make five shots from the free throw line within 20 seconds. Rebound own shots.

Two-ball shooting drill. The player at the foul line takes a shot, steps, fakes, and a manager hits him with a pass. Managers rebound. Continue for 30 seconds and build up to 60 seconds.

Competition and time: Two players (see Figure 19.1). From a designated spot. The player who makes the most shots is the winner. Continue for 20 seconds. Each player rebounds his own shots.

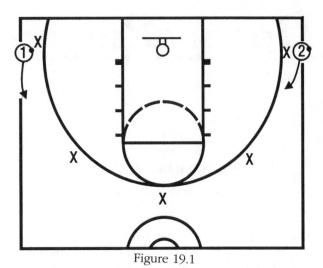

Figure 19.1

Rebounding

Two-on-one rebounding drill. Three players are in the rebounding area. The coach puts the ball on the board. All three players go after the rebound. The one who gets the ball must put it in the basket, while the other two try to stop him. We do not allow players to dribble, and we emphasize the three-point play. We tell the players not to worry about the contact. The ball is live until a basket is scored or it goes outside the lane. The coach should be inside the foul line for best control of the drill. Perform this drill for two minutes.

DEFENSIVE TRANSITION DRILLS

Bill Foster

I have become really involved in the area of transition defense in the last few years because our team has had a distinct lack of speed in comparison to other schools in our conference. Speed being a problem, we felt we had to develop a team awareness in regard to both offense and defense. That's exactly what my topic is going to be about. I'll be covering drills and ideas in developing an ability to adjust defensively as quickly as possible.

In starting on transition drills, there are a number of ways to begin them in your practice. First, we use them in place of suicide drills. We have gotten away from running simply for conditioning because I believe you should work on other areas of the game while you condition. We do run a type of suicide while working on a transition drill.

We start with six or seven players on the endline. They run forward full speed until they hear the whistle. They then turn quickly, stay low and back-pedal to the other endline. This is a simple form of turning around and going back immediately in a defensive stance. This is a start at what we're trying to teach to our players.

Most of you probably run a type of defensive zigzag drill. If I were a high school coach, this is the one drill I would make sure that every team, from junior high on up, ran every single day. I really believe in this drill. We try to run it at least four times a week and start off by pairing together players of comparable quickness (see Figure 19.2).

We have four people working at the same time and two coaches reminding the defense about proper fundamentals. I sometimes feel that I'm talking too much in practice, but when I see mistakes, I believe that is the time to correct them. We constantly try to remind and encourage our players. In Drill No. 1, the defense tries to take away a direction and give a direction. We want the defensive players to place their head and nose in front of the ball while staying

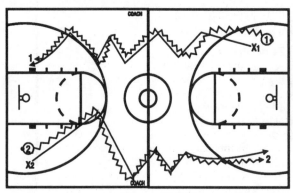

Figure 19.2

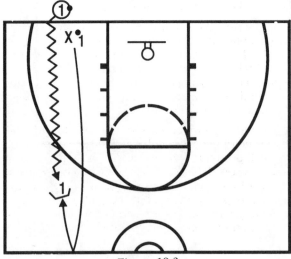

Figure 19.3

as low as possible. After we run this drill for two or three minutes we go to our "Influence Drill" (see Figure 19.3).

The defensive man hands the ball to the offense and springs back to half-court, X1 touches the line and readies himself for the man (1) coming at him. The toughest man to play in basketball is the man dribbling directly at you full speed. Defensively, we try to force the man to the outside without giving up an easy shot to the basket. After (1) shoots, X1 blocks out, retrieves the ball, and then the roles are reversed. X1 steps out of bounds and (1) plays defense. We want the defense to have a wide stance and, after forcing the man outside, cut him off at an angle.

After running this drill for a few weeks, we're able to see a tremendous amount of improvement in nearly all of our players. This is why I like to take a limited number of drills and stay with them throughout a season. We pick three or four areas that we need help in and concentrate on those areas the entire year. The way we change things up to help overcome the monotony is to rearrange our practice schedule. We'll alter practice Saturday and Sunday afternoons and then give the players a day off during the week. Occasionally we go five straight days and then give them a Monday or a Tuesday off. At least once during the pre-season I give the players both Saturday and Sunday off.

As I mentioned earlier, we work on our transition defense by talking about it at all times, checking various statistics, and working on drills. Before I cover any more drills, I want to mention a fourth method that helps in transition. This method centers around the utilization of video tape. What we do is focus on one player for four minutes when we start a scrimmage. Every four minutes we rotate to another player. At the end of practice, our manager tells each player what segment of film he's on and the player watches those minutes with one of the coaches. This gives both our staff and the players an excellent idea of what he is accomplishing on the floor.

Another drill that will help you on transition defense is a continuation of our fast break drill. We have five players block out, rebound, and outlet the ball. Our guard takes the ball into the middle and everyone else either fills the lane or becomes a trailer. After we send our cutters through, we try to continue immediately into our offense.

After a few passes and a shot, the coach under the basket grabs the ball and throws it down court. When the ball goes through the basket, those five players are now on defense. If someone catches the ball thrown by the coach before it bounces, those five are finished with the drill. If the ball bounces, they have to go again. This is a form of mentally getting ready to turn around and play defense.

The next drill that we use looks like the following: (see Figure 19.4) 1 and 2 on offense on one side of floor, and the same goes for the other side. The ball is thrown to a coach and the defense retreats. The coach throws the ball in and they go two-on-two. We involve our coaches on the sideline as indicated. In this drill we demand that the defense get back "to the line of ball" and "ball side" and be ready to play and/or keep your man from the ball. The defense is backpedaling and turning to see the ball and the man. The first week or so we don't deny the ball back from the coach. We want to concentrate on getting back to the line of the ball, being on the ball side, and seeing your man and the ball. Once the ball is returned to the offense, they then go two-on-two against the defense. The offense and defense then change positions and come back the other way. The offense is able to throw to either coach and we emphasize that the pass must be a good one. From this point we proceed to the denial of the return pass from the coach. We usually do this in a three-on-three or four-on-four format. This way we are able to work offensively on getting open and running our passing game. We want our offensive people to move without the ball, see the ball and understand how the defense is playing him. We want our players to become smarter and to continually think when they're on the floor.

I feel this is an excellent drill, offensively as well as defensively because it involves a great deal of changing direction and changing pace. These are two extremely important areas in the game of basketball regardless of size or speed, because you can improve your offensive game by working on these skills.

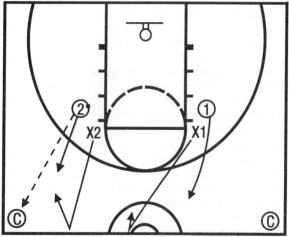

Figure 19.4

PRESSURE DEFENSE
Ralph Miller

We depend on pressure in our style of play. We use pressure tactics with our offense and defense to eliminate the rest by our opponents which occurs on exchanges of the ball. Both the offense and defense have to apply pressure to eliminate this rest. This requires instant conversion from offense to defense and vice versa. This is a simple concept to demonstrate. If both teams have the basketball 60 times during a game and neither team used a full-court defense or a fast-break offense, at least five seconds would lapse during every exchange of the basketball. Multiplication would show that approximately 10 minutes of every game are available for rest. This is one-quarter of the collegiate game. Our whole premise in our pressure style of play is to eliminate this rest and to force our opponents to play for the full 40 minutes in a game.

The purpose of defense is simply to eliminate scoring by the opposition. Pressure defense should never alter this basic premise. If a defense is good enough to use at all, it should be sound enough to use all of the time. This is an important idea, and it almost suggests that people should be conservative in their approach to defense if they are to abide by this principle. Whenever two evenly matched teams play, the winner, invariably, is going to be the team which most effectively executed its basic defense on that given occasion.

Sound pressure defenses are conservative in their operation. In evaluating the way in which ball possessions are gained during the course of a game, we find that 60 to 80 percent of the possessions are gained by rebounding and after an opponent's score. Twenty percent come from opponent's error, and only five percent of the possessions come from steals and interceptions. A study of the way ball possessions are gained makes it seem highly impractical to base a pressure defense on interceptions and steals.

Our pressure defense is based on good individual coverage and help on the ball with constant basket protection. You do not have to gamble to play pressure defense. Pressure defense uses the same principles as a so-called normal defense. Pressure defense merely extends the perimeter of the defensive coverage. By extending the perimeter of the coverage, a pressure defense elongates the distance of recovery necessary for effective basket protection.

To compensate for this extended perimeter, we have the perimeter rule: When the ball cracks the perimeter or passes the defensive floor position of any individual, all defenders, except the one defending the ball, should automatically run to the basket for protection purposes. This is the most important rule of pressure defense and it is based on the premise that once the perimeter is penetrated, pressure is eliminated and basket protection becomes the most important consideration. The weakness of many pressure defenses is that the front line does not recover when the ball passes their position. The defensive player sees his man still out on the court and doesn't sense the need to recover toward the basket. This is fatal to good pressure defense. Teams that employ this principle consistently play good pressure defense and actually make most of their interceptions, running to cover the basket area.

To simplify our usage of multiple defenses, we use a single set of rules for all our team coverage. This single set of rules applies to both our full-court and half-court defense. We believe that there is no true man-to-man or zone defense – there are only combination defenses. Man-to-man defenses feature the best pressure, and zone defenses offer the best basket protection; thus we try to combine the best of the two concepts. Our rules are quite simple: 1) the man defending the ball applies pressure and the ball-side defense plays the passing lanes. 2) the off-side players are the basket protectors. They use zone principles of coverage. By using these simple rules, you can easily change defenses. We are never faced with the problem of learning a new defense because all of our defenses are based on these simple rules of coverage. We can run a 1-2-2, 1-3-1, 2-1-2, 2-3, and 3-2 defense by applying the preceding rules. We can change defenses and vary our pressure from baseline to baseline by using our rules of coverage. Once we apply pressure, however, we slack off only when it is necessary to execute the perimeter rule.

Another rule we employ in our pressure defense is the automatic pickup rule. This rule is designed to control the fast break. We believe it is most important to stop the fast break and not only the half-court offense. Our automatic pickup rule is simply this: Guard the man who was guarding you when possession was lost. Don't run around trying to find a man, but take the man who was guarding you. Use of this rule will allow you to control the fast break at inception. It provides coverage on the rebound, the outlet pass, and as the offense attempts to fill the lanes for the fast break.

Some coaches complain that the use of the automatic pickup rule doesn't allow their best defender to guard the best offensive player. We approach this problem by telling our players they will not play until they are one of our best defenders at either a guard, wing, or post position. We will not play them until we can trust them defensively. We don't care about their offense. They are not going to play until they can handle their defensive assignment. Consequently, there is very little difference in the defensive ability of our two wings or guards. And this rule allows us to stop the fast break, which seems infinitely more important than guarding a designated man. We do this with every team we face, not just the fast-breaking teams. We have learned from experience that it is impossible for a player to play offense on one side of the court and still cut him off effectively. The automatic pickup rule has been very effective for us in overcoming this conversion problem.

We have rules to take care of many different defensive situations. However, we believe basketball is a game of reaction and not thought, and that players have to be taught to react to situations. We keep our rules few and simple for this reason.

We have a simple rule for switching. Anytime there is movement over the top of a screen, there has to be an automatic switch. If a blind pick is set on one of our defensive players, there has to be a switch. To play good pressure defense, you have to use the switch. Sometimes it does create a mismatch, but not often enough to really hurt you. The benefit of the switch is that it gives you a chance to maintain sound pressure defense more than any other method of playing screening situations.

We do not trap a great deal. Traps are overcommitments by two players for a defense on the ball. The odds are not very good when the defense sets a trap. We do not look to set traps very often. We are going to set traps only when we feel that the advantages are in favor of our defense. For instance, we trap when the offensive person can't see the player moving up for the trap. The offense may be out of control or careless, and then we set a trap. We never force the use of the trap. If you do decide to trap, everybody has to use it. The defensive players can't stand halfway toward the trap wondering about their assignment. When the trap is initiated, everybody has to go to the pass interception. If the trap does not succeed, the offense is probably going to score most of the time. That's the coach's fault and not the fault of the players. The trap is a calculated gamble which cannot be expected to produce results with dependable regularity.

In our pressure defense, the ball is the important thing. Our vision rule concentrates on the ball rather than on the man being guarded. It is impossible to have an effective offensive maneuver without the ball, but you can't learn much by watching only the man to whom you are assigned. All good defensive players keep their eye on the ball. Of course, a player should be in position to see the man involved in the play while keeping his eye on the ball. It is sometimes difficult with good player movement to see both the man and the ball, but if the defense has to make a choice, then, in our opinion, they should always watch the ball because it is the key to the game. I instruct my players that they're not going to learn anything about the game by watching their man, but that they are going to be able to provide the basket protection by watching the ball at all times.

When covering the man with the ball, the defense should be able to touch the ball with his hand. He should assume this touching position as the ball is being received. When the ball is received, the defense should discourage the pass into the post area. The hands should be kept up. Keeping the hands up reduces a tendency to foul and allows a player to move his hands quickly. Players are not able to block as many shots with their hands in this position, but they seldom will lose their balance and body position when they carry their hands up.

Keep the opposition off-balance. A lot of coaches are changing their defenses and I think that's a very good theory. Even though I believe that basic man-to-man is the best defense, playing as many as seven or eight combinations of defense during a 40-minute contest can present a real problem to an unprepared team. Many coaches have an offense for a common defense that they encounter and using several defenses during the game can keep these teams off-balance. In changing the defense, however, a coach should never forget the basic premises and rules which make for a successful pressure defense.

PRESSING PRINCIPLES

Jerry Tarkanian

I. Success Comes in Flurries

A. Don't allow your hands to get away from your body.

B. Keep your head directly over the midpoint.

C. Permit only lob or bounce passes.

D. Permit retreat or parallel passes in front rather than advance passes.

E. As soon as the ball passes your line on defense, retreat to a deeper position (line of the ball) for interception or recovery.

F. Rush the passer; pressure the ball, don't allow the passer the chance to find a receiver.

G. When there is a breakdown or transition, the help side really has to come alive.

H. Realize that by pressing there is a limit that the offense can do.

I. Always stay in the play.

II. Breakdown Drills for Pressure

A. Nose pressure build-up.

  1. Complete denial one-on-one; no lob passes (see Figure 19.5).

    a. Do on all areas of the baseline.
    b. Freeze the inbounder at first.

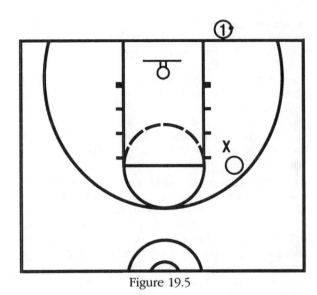

Figure 19.5

c. Allow the passer to run the baseline.
d. Emphasize recovery to defense on the ball.

2. Complete denial two-on-two; no lob passes (see Figure 19.6).

    a. Two men inbounds (screening/crossing).
    b. The inbounder can move.
    c. Pressure the passer.

3. Score; pick up three-on-three counting passer (see Figure 19.7).

    a. React to the score.
    b. Talk.
    c. Man off the ball (center field).
    d. Man on the ball.

4. Trapping the first pass (see Figure 19.8).

    a. Man off the ball (communication).
    (1) Read the step up by third defender to avoid a throwback to the inbound passer.

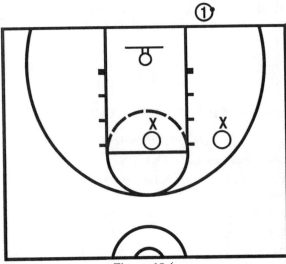

Figure 19.6

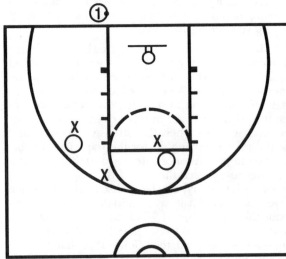

Figure 19.8

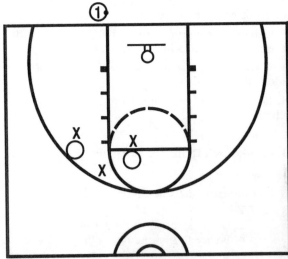

Figure 19.7

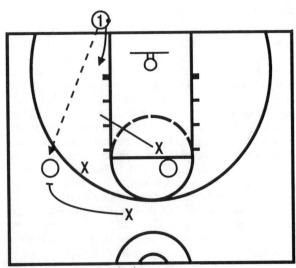

Figure 19.9

(2) Teach trapping angles (see Figure 19.9).

(3) Teach recovery to defense position once the ball penetrates.

B. Deep over play.

   1. Contest the deep pass position (see Figure 19.10).

      a. Ball side.

      b. Help side.

      c. React to the ball in the middle.

      d. Pass the ball from side to side.

        (1) Defense reacts to the ball.

      e. Stop the flash pivot but still react to the deep pass.

   2. Recovery to dribble penetration (see Figure 19.11).

      a. Talk and recognize.

      b. Recovery.

      c. Chase the dribbler.

      d. "Line of the ball."

3. Advance the ball up court (see Figure 19.12).

      a. Combine all the deep problems.

        (1) Recognize.

        (2) Talk.

        (3) Recover.

        (4) When to release.

        (5) Rotations.

4. One man back (see Figure 19.13).

      a. Recognize.

      b. Play strong on ball-side.

      c. Watch the flash pivot.

      d. Go for the deep pass.

      e. Don't remove yourself from the play.

      f. Be able to do two things at one time.

C. Deep overplay and double-up (four-on-four).

   1. Reading dribble penetration (see Figure 19.14).

      a. Force the sideline.

      b. Work on traps.

      c. Read rotations.

      d. Recovery on throwbacks (see Figure 19.15).

Figure 19.10

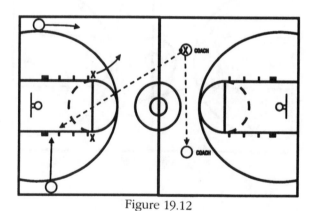

Figure 19.12

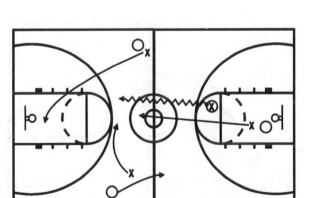

Figure 19.11

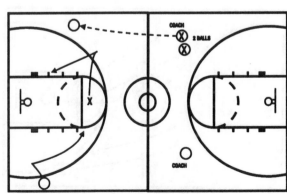

Figure 19.13

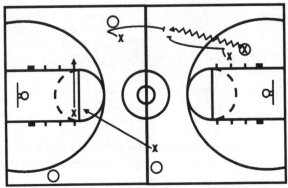

Figure 19.14

D. Recovery drills.

1. Line of the ball two-on-two (see Figure 19.16).

   a. Talk, recover.
   b. Find the ball, pick up.
   c. Stop penetration, stop penetration.
   d. The ball can be passed from side to side.
   e. Add a third and fourth man.
   f. Incorporate block out.

2. Extra man recovery (see Figure 19.17).

   a. Call a player's name and that player has to touch the baseline and recover to the ball.
   b. The other two recover to a fast-break defense.
   c. Talk.

E. Special pressure release situations to recognize.

1. Box (see Figure 19.18).

2. Back pick and release (see Figure 19.19).

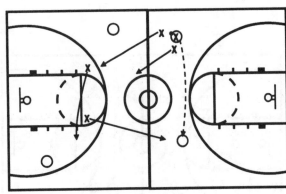

Figure 19.15

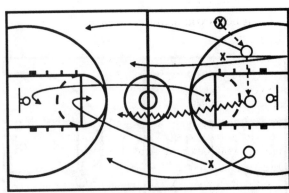

Figure 19.17

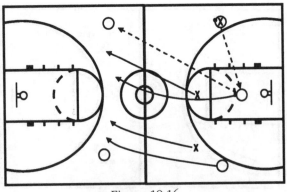

Figure 19.16

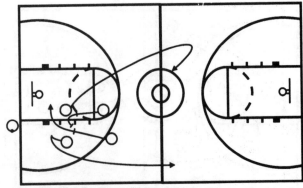

Figure 19.18

ZONE PRESSES

Denny Crum

To be a good pressing team, the press needs to be one of your major weapons. We consider it to be one of our offensive weapons and one we spend a lot of time on.

Why Press?

1. Players love it.

2. Fans love it.

3. It is a great conditioner.

4. It makes your team better prepared to run an offense against a press.

5. It creates constant pressure on both ends of the court.

6. It helps you learn to anticipate.

"It's human to error and pressure causes error."

The press is designed to make the offense do things they don't normally do. The press can make them speed up their game or slow it down, which can cause more mistakes.

Tempo is the most important single factor in the game. If you have the ability to slow people down or speed them up, you have a more rounded team and a better chance to beat all different kinds of teams.

Most teams have only one or two offenses against a press. By having four or five presses, your team will have a real edge. You take away what the offense does against the press.

Our game plan is not only to press you, but also make you do what you do not want to do. If you change your offense and our press reacts, you must change again.

We believe in spending a lot of time on changes in our press. If the offense hasn't spent time on changes, they'll have to use time-outs or rely on their players. This gives the pressing team an edge. If talent is equal, this edge will help you win.

Press Rules

1. Any time the ball gets past you, get back in front or even with the ball.

2. Don't foul (unless you want to slow the game down). You want to keep the pressure building.

Basic Press 2-2-1 (see Figure 19.20).

Personnel – Biggest and quickest laterally.

Reasons:

1. Most teams go to the right, so you want one of your best athletes there.

2. Quickness laterally helps deny the dribble to the inside.

3. The taller he is, the harder it is to pass over him to the middle.

Number 2 – Good place to hide a player (unless the offense likes to bring the ball in on the left).

Number 3 – Player with very good hands.

Number 4 – Second-best anticipator and left-hander if possible (a left-hander is good because he can more easily make a deflection).

Number 5 – Best athlete!

Trapping Spots (see Figure 19.21).

The 1 Spot – Best trapping spot because they cannot throw back across the 10-second line.

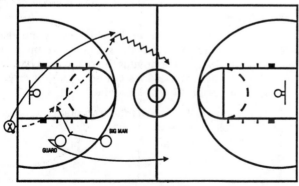

Figure 19.19

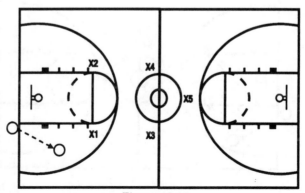

Figure 19.20

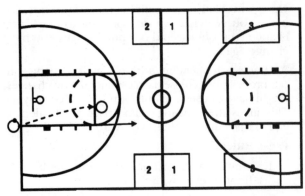

Figure 19.21

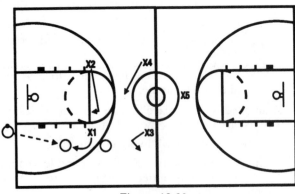

Figure 19.22

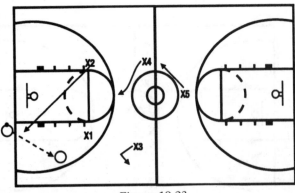

Figure 19.23

The 2 Spot – Good because the offense still must be concerned with the 10-second count. The defense can also match-up without needing to set a trap from that position.

The 3 Spot – Used if the ball is penetrated down the sideline and the Number 5 man can't intercept the pass.

2-2-1 Press ("2" Press)

We want the offense to bring the ball up the sideline and keep it out of the middle (see Figure 19.22). Number 1 and Number 2 do not deny the inbounds pass. If the pass goes in to the right, Number 1 remains a half-step in front and plays pass. Number 2 and Number 4 cheat to the middle. Number 3 bluffs at the dribble and retreats in a sideways position denying the pass to the hash mark. If the ball is farther down than that, the Number 5 man will get it. If the ball crosses the 10-second line on the dribble, Number 3 will trap.

The offense will probably try to pass to the middle or back to the inbounds passer. If Numbers 1, 2 and 4 are discouraging the middle pass, the offense will probably keep reversing the ball down the court. This will slow down the game.

Two-Up

We want to speed the game up, so if the offense likes to pass back to the inbounds passer (their best ballhandler), we will deny the pass back (see Figure 19.23). We call this "two-up." This gives us the edge because the other team will have someone handling the ball they don't want to, often a big man. Number 2 plays denial; everyone else plays zone. Number 4 takes away middle pass; Number 3 takes away sideline pass. This will invite the long pass, which results in two good things:

1. It speeds the game up.

2. It causes a turnover.

The most vulnerable area becomes the weak side. This sets up your Number 5 to anticipate the pass to the weak side. Anytime you know where the other team is going to go, you have the edge. Two-up effectively takes the offense's best ballhandler out of the play and helps dictate that the ball will go where Number 5, your best athlete and anticipator, will be.

Two-Up Man

This is a variation of two-up in which everyone else denies and plays man after the pass into the big man (see Figure 19.24). This invites the big man to handle the ball. If the offense does not pass long or cross-court, but dribbles up the sideline:

1. Numbers 1 and 3 set the trap once the ball is across the 10-second line.

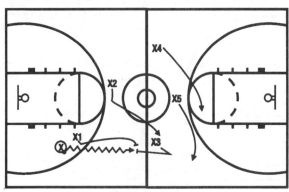

Figure 19.24

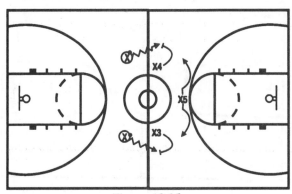

Figure 19.25

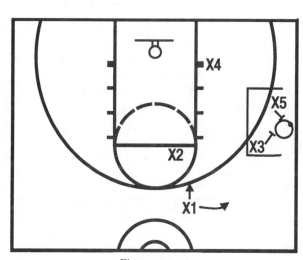

Figure 19.26

2. Number 1 must prevent penetration to the middle.

3. Number 5 rotates over to take away the sideline pass. Number 2 is physically in the gap area, but is mentally playing the pass back (where it will go 90 percent of the time). Number 4 rotates down.

Since Number 1 is tall, it is hoped that the trap will force a bounce pass or a weak lob pass. On the double team, we do not reach in, but play pass. The whole objective is not only to influence where the offense throws the ball, but how they throw it.

If the ball is in the two trap area, we do not double team. Everyone plays pass and stays matched up. The offense must now worry about getting the ball over the 10-second line.

Movement in Backline Players

If the ball is on the right side, Numbers 3 and 5 work together (see Figure 19.25). If 3 comes up, 5 goes over. If the ball is on the left side, 4 and 5 work together. If 4 comes up, 5 goes over.

If the Ball Gets to the Trap 3 Area Before Number 5 Can Intercept

Numbers 3 and 5 set the trap, with Number 5 having baseline responsibility (see Figure 19.26).

Number 4 fronts everything at the low post. Number 2 has high post and weakside responsibility. Number 1 is in the gap, but is the anticipator playing the pass.

We try to take away the easy pass and always make the offense throw through to someone or lob it.

21 Zone Press (2-1-2)

Used if the offense tries to get the ball to a big man in the middle (see Figure 19.27). This press, unlike the 2-2-1, does not have one deep protector, but initially has two protectors. The protector, once the

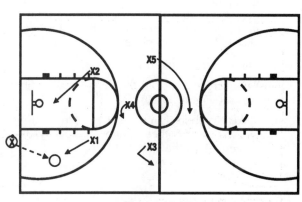

Figure 19.27

ball is inbounds, becomes the man opposite the ball deep. If the ball is inbounded to the right, Number 1 is a half-step in front. Number 3 bluffs and retreats. Number 4 takes away the middle. Number 5 protects.

Can Shift to 21-Up

This is the same as 21, but Number 2 denies the ball back to the inbounds passer. This makes the offense dribble the ball. The important point is that whatever the offense does, we have already practiced the adjustments enough that with one little command from the coach, we can change the press and make the offense do something else. The defensive changes are easy because we practice them for an hour each day. Again, we are forcing the offense to do something they do not want to do.

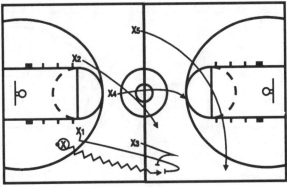

Figure 19.28

Out of 21 we can choose not to trap and just keep pressure on the offense (see Figure 19.28). Or we can change our traps from what we used in the 2-2-1. As the ball is dribbled past the 10-second line, Number 1 jumps in front to make the offense pick up their dribble or reverse dribble.

The rest of the defense follows the rule of getting back in front or even with the ball. Number 3 can sneak back and jump trap (especially on a reverse dribble). Number 5 takes away the pass down the sideline. Number 2 and Number 4 are in good intercept positions.

We have made the offense change and are still in a position to trap. There are times when you cannot trap (player out of position, etc.) but they are rare.

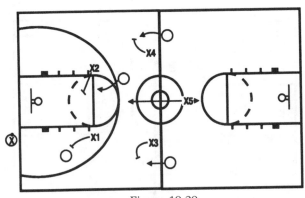

Figure 19.29

"2D" (2-2-1 Denial)

Used against an offense that likes to make the inbounds pass to their best ballhandler (see Figure 19.29). Wherever the offense lines up, the defense is to match up and deny the inbounds pass. In any denial situation, until the offense passes the ball in, the defense has them five-on-four. The defense always tries to keep one deep protector.

Most offenses try to beat the denial by:

1. Sending players up from the half-court line. It's hard to teach Number 3 and Number 4 to get up between the ball and the man, for man denial, because they always think they are going to get burned long. But Number 5 should be there to protect.

2. Using a screen and roll.

Against the screen and roll, the defense can adjust two ways (see Figure 19.30).

1. Make Numbers 1 and 2 get elbow-to-elbow, side-by-side so they cannot be split by the screen. Then they jump switch.

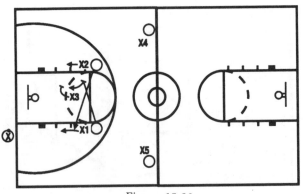

Figure 19.30

2. If the screen and roll can't be stopped, defense switches to "flop 'em." Move Number 3 or Number 4 up to double team the ball as soon as it goes inbounds. Number 5 moves to half-court to deny.

If the offensive team tries to throw the ball over the denial defense, Number 1 and Number 2 deny up front (see Figure 19.31). Numbers 3 and 5 deny at half-court. Number 4 will double team on the pass-over.

It is tough to throw over one and in front of the other. Eventually, the defense will get one of those. The pass will always be pressured. Even if the offense does throw the ball over successfully, this speeds up the game which is what we want.

"2 Bluff" or "21 Bluff"

This is used to slow the game down (see Figure 19.32). This is a 2-2-1 or 2-1-2 press in which we play head-to-head, keeping the ball out of the middle and inviting the reverse pass. This makes the offense take eight or nine seconds to get across half-court. This is especially good to use when going against a team with superior talent. I would press every time I scored. How else can you make the game short enough that you don't have to beat a team with superior players at the other end?

Another good time to slow things down might be at the end of a game when you have the lead. You don't have to trap if you're ahead.

What happens if we're in denial and they get the ball inbounds? In "21 D," if there is no offensive player in the middle, Number 4 can cheat up and play lob over pass or we can use him to double team (see Figure 19.33). We can also go "21 D-Up." Number 4 can double team with Number 1 or, if the offense likes to go back to the inbounds passer, Number 2 denies the pass back. Number 4 acts as the anticipator. Number 5 is protector at Louisville. We use "21 D-Up" a lot of times when we need a steal. Once again, this makes the offensive player who is not their best ballhandler dribble the ball.

What do we do at the end of the press once they've beaten it? How do we match up out of a zone press? We tell our players to take the man closest to them (see Figure 19.34). We're not the least bit worried about a mismatch.

Reasons:

1. If you take the first person near you, you continue to apply pressure. If you went back into a zone, you would relieve this pressure. Don't let the offense have an opportunity to set up, regroup, and get into its offense.

2. Our team is used to handling the switch as they play a switching man-to-man. Coach Wooden used a switching man-to-man and won 10 national championships in 11 years. At Louisville we use it and we have the second best winning percentage in the last 15 years. If you're a pressing team, switching man-to-man is important to you. There is someone between the ball and the basket most of the time.

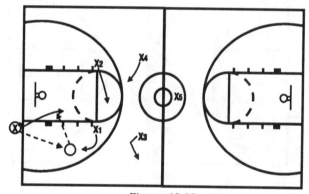

Figure 19.32

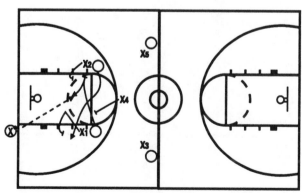

Figure 19.31

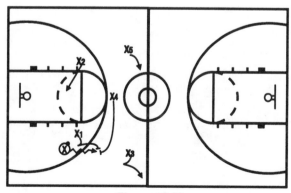

Figure 19.33

Switching Man-to-Man

To help the block, the low forward can help weak-side (see Figure 19.35). If the offense tries to screen the weakside help, the switching man is good because the players simply switch instead of fighting through. Use zone principles on double teaming on the block.

Usually Deny the Reverse Pass (Figure 19.36)

Exception to the Rule: If we are going against a good high-low offensive team and they run a flash to the high post from the weak side, the weak-side guard drops to protect the high post.

We're in an entertainment business and we want to create as much spectator interest in our program as possible. Anybody that's a pressing team is a lot more fun to watch.

Our game plan is very simple. As a pressing team, we have enough variations in our presses to make you do something differently. If we can do that, we have the edge.

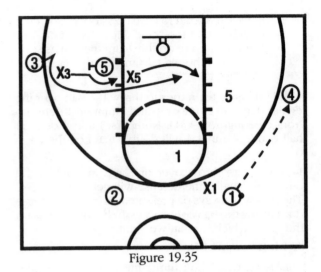

Figure 19.35

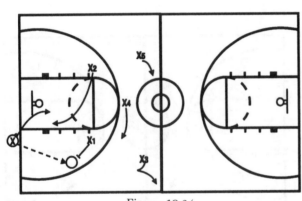

Figure 19.34

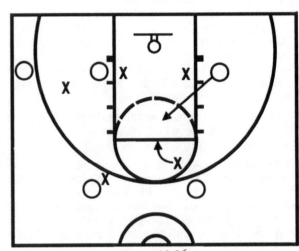

Figure 19.36

Inside Shot

WOOLPERT DEFENSE

Phil Woolpert

We have some fears of our own that have worked out primarily, I would say, because we have excellent personnel and we have the Big Guy, as he has often been termed, the "Windmill with Arms," Bill Russell, in the middle. He makes defensive situations a lot easier and thinking a lot easier, consequently it doesn't require nearly as much concentration as it would if our personnel were a little less gifted.

However, I would like to give you a few observations of some of the things we think are important, and in our own thinking those are the factors that we insist on and feel contribute to our overall team defense.

Demand Flexed Knees

First of all, relative to our individual defense, the one factor that we consider as the most single important defensive fundamental is keeping the knees flexed or bent. We insist that no player can play the game unless his knees are flexed not only on the ball but away from the ball. Any time his team reverts to the defensive situation, we want and expect him to be flexed. Period. Now, that's the ideal, of course; we don't at all approach it. We look at pictures; we look at our kids during the game; and time and again we see them straightening up, and as soon as we do, we turn seven different shades because we know probably that ball player is going to be taken at any time.

I recall a team, a very fine team from Kansas University, that came out to the coast about seven years ago and played the University of San Francisco when Pete Newell was the coach. I was very impressed with the way they kept their knees flexed continually. Pictures were taken of the game and his team came as close to approaching the ideal of flexed knees as any team I have had the pleasure of watching. To me the one thing a player cannot do without is keeping the knees flexed. And yet, as I say, in our own ball club and lots of other teams I watched, you'd find players straightening up consistently during a ball game when the other team has the ball. As far as we are concerned, those players are vulnerable and they shouldn't be on the floor unless they flex.

Loaf on Offense if Tired

We tell players, "If you want to loaf or take a breather, take it on offense." Never on defense, because the obvious answer is, on defense you don't know what the other team is going to do. On offense you should be aware of what you are supposed to be doing, and if the situation is such that you can take a rest or a breather at any time, that is the place to do it.

Stress Weight Distribution

We also place a lot of emphasis on weight distribution. Now, of course, anytime our ball players are in motion, obviously their weight must be evenly distributed. In other words, we'll shift from one foot to the other as we are in motion and consequently we insist that the center of gravity stay low. The tail stays down and we don't want any bobbing or hopping. That's a problem that we run into very often with some ball players we get from high school. They are hoppers and we find that it usually takes at least two years to break a player of that habit if he has it when he comes in from high school. If we could set up the following gadget we would do so in order to demonstrate to these fellows why they should keep the center of gravity low or not bob or weave. We would take a two-by-four and extend it across the floor and have that player move. If he is moving ideally, his head should just touch the bottom of that piece of wood and he should be able to slide across the floor laterally without having his head bump it or drop away from it. If a player is doing that, in our opinion he is then moving laterally or moving in depth. It doesn't make any difference what the term is, but he is moving ideally so far as we are concerned. Then he is a much better defensive ball player. Again it is something that we find hard to tell kids. You tell them, "Don't hop." They want to know why. What's the danger in hopping?

Hopping is Dangerous

Obviously, the danger is that every time you hop you are going into vertical motion, which is a useless waste of motion. It is necessary that you must flex again and consequently if you are up in the air in the case of an offensive man making a change of direction or making a move, you are wasting time until you can flex those knees again and move with him.

How to Guard

I'll try to show what I mean by guarding a forward. I recognize that the stance employed in playing any offensive ball player varies with different coaches. I am not saying that the stance we insist on is correct or proper, but it has suited our purpose, and for that reason I'll tell you what we insist on. For example, we'll assume now that we are assigning a defensive man to guard a right forward. The first thing we insist on is that he positions himself in what we call an open stance to the baseline. In other words, the right defensive guard would position himself with his right foot forward and his left foot to the rear.

We want the foot of the offensive man to split the crotch of the defensive man. We know and appreciate that some forwards will come out of this situation and take the ball with their out foot or side foot extended – the left foot extended. In that event we assume the left foot is then the pivot foot. In that situation, then, we insist that the defensive man station himself so that his crotch splits the right foot of the offensive man, in other words, the extended foot of that offensive man. Of course the reason we do that is because seven-out-of-ten forwards in this situation look for the baseline drive first and obviously they should because that is the short way home, but we don't want to give the other team that baseline drive if we can possibly help it.

So we overplay to the baseline, try to force the offensive man to the sideline where he either doesn't have a shot left or a jump shot is required. So that if his left foot is extended when he takes the ball, we split the right foot with the crotch. If the right foot is extended as we insist our forward accept the ball, in other words with the inside foot forward, then we assume the right foot will be the pivot foot and the offensive man will take the front turn when he faces inside. Then again we insist in this instance that the right foot of the offensive man split the crotch of the defensive man, our defensive man.

Weight on Front Foot

Now, this next situation is one which I know will immediately or very possibly arouse some controversy: The weight distribution which we insist on in a stationary position. Now, I am quite aware that the average textbook on basketball and the average coach, I am sure, insists that the weight be either on the rear foot or approximately spread between the two feet, in other words, evenly distributed. However, we insist – and again this is only our own situation, something we have found has worked to our advantage – the weight in this particular situation be carried on the front foot. There are a number of reasons for that.

First, we want our defensive players to be very aggressive. We don't want them to assume a passive role, particularly on the ball. In this illustration we assume automatically that the right forward has the ball, but we want our defensive men, as I indicated, to be aggressive. We feel and have found through experiment that the average player who places his weight on his rear foot is unconsciously in a passive or retreat situation. Consequently, we feel that mentally he is not attuned as we would like to have him attuned to playing the possibilities of the ball aggressively, to hounding the ball, to discouraging the possibility of passes to a receiving ball player.

Second, on a baseline drive in this situation we will assume now that the offensive forward was going to move baseline. In such a situation, our theory on the weight on the front foot is that the first logical step for that defensive guard to take is to the rear with his left foot. In other words, his right foot is extended, his left foot is to the rear.

With the weight on the right foot or forward foot, the left foot is released and free to slide back which is the only step of value when making a move with the offensive forward. Obviously, moving the right foot, at least in our opinion, gives you no advantage at all. You are actually not moving because it is only the rear foot that gives you any movement in depth. So in order to move the rear foot, the weight must be off the rear foot. In our opinion, if the weight is on the rear foot to begin with, then when the offensive man makes a move forward it is necessary for the defensive man to rock his weight from the rear foot to the front foot to release that rear foot so he can make the initial retreat movement. That is our number one theory relative to a weight distribution with reference to a baseline drive.

In the event the offensive forward wants to come over the top, which of course in this day of jump shooters many of them do and many of them do very effectively, again the defensive man must be in a position where he isn't vulnerable. We have found again through experiment with the weight on the front foot that it is a very simple matter for that defensive guard to pivot on the rear foot, swing that front leg in the direction of the drive of that offensive forward, and more than be in defensive position once he has started in motion. Granted, your rear foot in the case of a pivot is to protect a drive over the top; granted, the rear foot is the key foot in the situation and must be collapsed in order to effect a pivot. But we have found with the weight on the rear foot it is a simple matter to drop or collapse the rear leg and drive off or push off with the front foot, swing that leg in an arc in the direction of the drive, and obviously, in an over-the-top drive with a pivot of that nature, the amount of ground covered is such that the offensive man does not effect an advantage.

That is the type of theory we use relative to defense. Believe me, I am not at all insisting that it is right or proper. Simply because for the last couple of years we have had a pretty good defensive record doesn't indicate that we are the greatest defensive team in the world. The reason we are a good defensive team is primarily that we have the Big Guy inside. We can make mistakes out in front and he will cover up very, very well for us inside. However, the other four ball players are good defensive players. They don't make too many mistakes and one of the factors, we think, in their defensive play is this particular theory of weight distribution.

For the first two weeks of our practice, we are very insistent on the weight on the front foot theory. After two weeks, if the ball players are handling their defensive assignment in good shape we then say little or nothing further about it unless they run into additional trouble. Actually, this is our own theory. We do not care once a player is effecting a good

movement, or handling a defensive or offensive chore properly. Regardless of how he does it, if he can handle the job we don't worry about it any more. We let him do it.

Likes Phlegmatic Defensive Players

One other thing we think constitutes the best type of defensive player, and obviously you do not instruct a player to be phlegmatic; but we find that the phlegmatic individual is by far the best defensive man. I recall an AAU player, Karl Shy, who played for Universal Pictures from 1930 to 1931 and who formerly played for UCLA. He used to walk out on the court looking like a refugee from an old people's home. You wondered how he had enough strength to get the uniform on, and at any moment you expected him to lie down and curl up for a snooze. The minute the ball game started Karl would assume a defensive stance with a man on the ball and that man would fake 15 times and Karl would squat there and watch him and not move a muscle until the offensive man made the movement. Then Karl was with him.

In other words, there is too much movement on defense by too many basketball players. They want to react to each offensive movement that the ball player gives them. Obviously that is an impossibility. In the process, someplace along the line he is going to be caught out of position and then he is vulnerable. In our own situation the one reaction we want our players to make, the one reaction that we prefer if we can possibly develop it in our players, is a little reaction in depth and we want them to be very, very careful about making any lateral adjustment because the lateral adjustment is without exception the toughest in the world to handle. If a player can get along without it, we are much happier.

We also insist that any time an offensive man has the ball, we want our defensive man with one hand up. Now, very often that is of little discouragement to an offensive player. The way kids shoot the ball today you could throw a blanket up there and they'd still throw the ball in the hoop, but we want it from the simple standpoint of experience. We want that defensive man with the hand in the air whenever the ball is in the hands of the opponent and we want the other hand carried down at the side in order to deflect or discourage any bounce or lateral passage.

Center Defense

As far as we are concerned, the same theory holds very true in the center play as it does in playing either of the outside men. Namely, we definitely insist again that our defensive center carry his weight on his front foot. Obviously, the best or the only position that a defensive center should play in unless he wants to be burnt is on the basket side. In other words, if you are playing a man to the right side of the foul line, the defensive center should be overplaying behind the left foot of that offensive center. We again want his weight forward. We want him to avoid contact, but we want him overplaying to the ball side and discouraging the possibility of any passing with the hand from underneath.

Again, this does not mean that the ball won't come in and it does not mean that the offensive man won't get it, but we want the hand underneath. Whenever the player comes down with the hand not underneath, if the ball comes in your officials without exception will call a foul. A player can come underneath with a hand and hit the ball and maybe a little arm and the average official will overlook it or allow the contact to ensue. Now this again is a very ticklish situation. Obviously, when you are playing against a good post man and the wide lane has made it a little less important to get out in front, there are times when you cannot afford to allow a certain post man to get out in front. This might be a very efficient man and a good hooker, a man off whom the other team works. Obviously you can't let him have the ball, so there are times when it is necessary for you to roll your center out in front of the offensive center.

How to Play Double Pivot Men

Now, in playing a double post situation we insist that the man on the ball, the defensive center on the ball, play out in front of his man and again he rolls with the ball. We do not drop off of the other post man, but we play him very tight. Obviously, we want the weak-side defensive man on the center to play his man tight so as to reduce the effectiveness of picks. Those coaches who use double play posts and situations are more aware than I am that much of the effectiveness of the operation is one of the center picking for the other. If you have dropped off in depth, you are very vulnerable for a pick and it will result in switch situations. Consequently we insist the weak-side man play tight and we find that it is very, very difficult for the strong-side post man to pick that defensive man and we find that if there is a switch situation, it can be effected without – or at least materially reduce – the possibility of the switcher being burnt on the move.

Don't Drop Off Screeners

One important factor and something I think I have seen a great deal of this year that has hurt teams playing against screening offenses is that with the advent of the widened lane the lateral screening game has become prevalent. We have found in observing teams that many teams are getting hurt in playing screen situations because they drop too far off the screeners. For example, on lateral screens we insist the defensive man on the screener play that tight. In other words, he doesn't drop off in depth. In a situation where, for example, the left guard comes over and picks for the right guard, we insist the defensive man on that screener play very tight to his man and that he make slight contact with that offensive screener. The reason for this is that the advent of the jump shot, the tremendous facility that so many of the ball players have today to take a one-

or two-bounce dribble and go up in the air and shoot with great effectiveness, has made it imperative that you try to discourage that offensive man trying to get that quick jumper off a lateral screen. If the defensive man on the screener drops in depth or if the lateral screen is effective, the defensive man on the ballhandler is ineffective. In other words, a switch will be forced and if the defensive man has dropped off in depth on the screener then he never gets to that jumper; or he will drop off in depth and that offensive man will step over the top of the screen. The defensive man may charge him, he may fake the jumper, and as the defensive man charges, he is in the spot where he gets a good jumper inside.

Will Concede Points to the Good Big Man

I know there are a great many theories about playing the big man in defensive basketball. Frankly, with our situation we don't worry a great deal about that. I haven't worried too much about it during the last three years because we have a fairly good defensive man who is a little large. But when you are playing, for example, a team with an exceptionally efficient, good ball player, good ballhandler, we will concede that offensive center his normal output of points. Lets say he averages 25 points a game. We are ready to give him the opportunity to score his 25 points, but we don't want those other four guys coming up and breaking our backs additionally. Too often when you try to play the big man by collapsing, the only thing you are doing is possibly reducing his output by half – if you are fortunate. If he is a good man, very often you don't do it to that extent, but in the meantime the other four fellows are taking shots at the foul line or the top of the circle, 10 to 12 feet out, and breaking your back.

Force the Other Four Very Hard

Consequently, we insist when we play a team with a good big man that we push the other four players as hard as we can. We try to force them into two things. If they take a shot, it has to be a shot they have to work for and we want it to be a shot taken well out. Next, any time the offensive man is open and takes a good lead, we want the man with the ball to be so concerned about the defensive man that he has trouble hitting the post man. A good team will do it occassionaly anyway, but we think you can reduce the effectiveness of that big man hurting you by playing the four-man team, pushing them, by being aggressive rather than the collapse game. I have seen many instances of the collapse game being ineffective and beating a ball club. Granted you stopped the big man, but there are four other players on that team. If they are reduced or held to their proper amount of scoring, the big man isn't going to beat you under normal circumstances.

Half-Court Press Defense

Finally, I would like to discuss our half-court press. For the past two years we have not used the three-quarter, half-court press like we normally do. The reason we haven't is we have the big man inside and consequently we can normally allow an opponent to bring the ball over to the midline and right there put the pressure on them. To my mind the finest team I saw employ that defense is the same Kansas team in 1953, in a game played in Kansas City in which it consistently took the ball away from the opposing guards and did a tremendous job. We do the same thing normally but when we employ a three-quarter press we use one of the two things.

Force Dribblers

We either force the dribbler to the inside and play for a two-time situation or, more preferably, we find this is less vulnerable and we get hurt less. We try to force the dribbler to the outside, stop him immediately if possible over the midline in the outside corner of the frontcourt, and clamp the leads (we clamp the leads automatically). Then we either force him into a rear turn with one man or, if we think the percentage is with us for a two-time, play for the resulting pass.

Now, particularly with the five-second rule, any time you force a defensive man into a rear turn and choke the nearest lead, if the officials are conscious of the five-second rule, very, very often you come up with a jump ball on that situation. Again it is theoretically ideal – obviously any time you employ a press you leave yourself open to getting burnt and many, many times you will get burnt. If employing it throughout a situation means you might win some games you might ordinarily figure to lose, I would say it is worth the gamble.

UTEP's MAN-TO-MAN DEFENSE

Don Haskins

There are three basic principles that are necessary to have a good defensive team. They are: 1) control the tempo, 2) basket protection, 3) shot selection with good execution and patience. In controlling the tempo, it is quite necessary that your team is very capable, as far as the transition game is concerned. If you can control the 10-second line, the dribbler must be stopped at the 10-second line, and five people must get in front of the ball as quickly as possible. This is why during practice sessions we do not use half-court situations. The drills are full-court most of the time.

As far as basket protection is concerned, the frontcourt is divided into three areas (see Figure 20.1). No shots should be given up in section A, and also the shooting percentage goes down when you make your opponent shoot from sections B and C. The University of Texas at El Paso uses their shooting charts not just to tell what kind of shooting percentage they or their opponents have, but to see how many shots are taken in each of the prescribed areas.

As far as shot selection is concerned, we definitely describe a good shot for each player. The things that are necessary in this description are the game situations. By that, we're talking about things like the score, time of game, and which of your players is taking the shot. Execution of offense and having patience are very important, as far as your total defense is concerned. On many occasions, we will use a slow-down or delay-type game, especially when we are playing on the road, or when our overall talent is less than the opponent's. By using this particular offensive strategy, it will make the defense better, and also keep the score closer for possible the road victory.

Individual Defensive Rules

UTEP players do not use a square stance; they use a stride stance. They do not have hands up, but they have their hands in a position so they can move as quickly as possible. They do not do slide drills. It is our philosophy that as soon as the player moves, they go to a run rather than a slide. The reason for this is we want players to get from one position to another as quickly as possible. You do that by running. As far as closeness to the offensive player is concerned, we try to put our head and shoulders into the offensive player and watch his waist, not the ball. Another rule that is definitely stressed is that you do not fight the ball when it is being dribbled. When it comes to post defense, we do not wish to have our players lay on the post. We want to stay at least three feet away, and closer to the ball than the person we are defending. When we are playing on the off-side defense, it is important that you stay below the line between the person you are defending and the ball, and when you have your head pointed straight ahead, you can see both the man and the ball at the same time. But if you lose sight of one of them, it is imperative that you lose sight of your man, and not the ball. When defending cutters, it is our

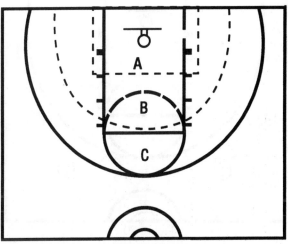

Figure 20.1

feeling that you always stay to the ball side of your man. During most of our drills, we will not switch.

Drills

1. Spot drill (see Figure 20.2). In this situation, all four players remain stationary, and each player moves as the ball is moved. Each player protects the middle, tries to instill the importance of the farthest man away from the ball, doesn't slide, but runs when the ball is moved (see Figure 20.2). Spot drill coaching points include:

   ♦ Offense must be stationary.
   ♦ Everyone moves on each pass-defense.
   ♦ Don't slide, run.
   ♦ Don't deny leads.
   ♦ Sink away from the ball.
   ♦ See the man and the ball at the same time.
   ♦ Protect the baseline.

2. Pick and help (see Figure 20.3). No switch. Go over the top most of the time, but you can go behind. The defensive man off the ball must hold up the dribbler (see Figure 20.3). Pick and help coaching points are:

   ♦ No switch.
   ♦ X1 can go over on behind the screen.
   ♦ X2 holds up the dribbler until X1 can get there.

3. Guard and cutter (four-on-four). See Figure 20.4. are as follows:

   ♦ Number 2 to Number 3, X2 must be on ball side of 2.
   ♦ X1 and X2 must move to the ball.
   ♦ This drill is for off-side help and defending the cutter.

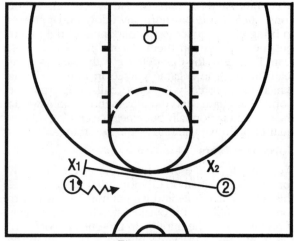

Figure 20.3

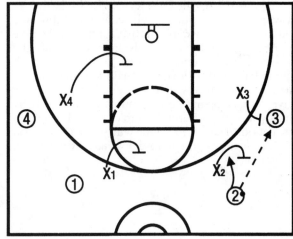

Figure 20.4

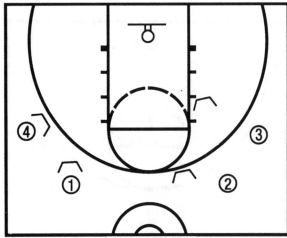

Figure 20.2

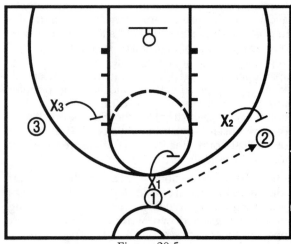

Figure 20.5

4. Three-on-three, defense (see Figure 20.5). Figure 20.5. Three-on-three – defense guidelines:

♦ Reaction: Defense reacts to the dribbler, man on the ball.
♦ Weave: No switch, X1 goes behind on ball exchange, X2 and X3 stay up.
♦ Pass and pick: No switch, X1 does not follow the screener, stays in the help position for X2 and X3.
♦ Pass and pick away: X1 stays in the middle and helps X2 or X3 avoid the screen.
♦ Pass and cut: X1 must get on the ball side as 1 passes to 2, 3 comes to the ball.

BISON BASKETBALL DEFENSE

Don Meyer

Philosophy

Our individual and team defense can only be great if we:

1. Believe in it.

2. Learn the basic rules and apply them.

3. Play aggressively.

4. Develop a defensive conscience.

The three most important factors on defense in order of importance are:

1. The ball: We must stop ball penetration to the basket.

2. Your position in relation to the ball, the basket, and your man.

3. Your man.

Why do we emphasize the ball first?

1. If the team emphasis is on the ball, we will have a maximum of help and average but aggressive players can cover better defensively because they know they have maximum help.

2. If the emphasis is placed on the man, you tend to have a minimum of help and players must be quicker and better all-around athletes to cover if they know they have only minimum help.

3. Most offenses are designed around two- and three-man plays so our emphasis on the ball and team helping out allows us to play five-on-two or five-on-three.

Our Eight Defensive Rules

1. **Transition and talk rule**. The most important thing in defensive basketball is transition. Quick, organized transition with communication by all five players keys a strong team defense. We always fast break on defense.

2. **Position rule.** Eighty percent of fouls are from poor position. Guarding a man without the ball, your position is ball, you, man. You must see the ball and your man at all times.

3. **Ball-side rule.** When a player is dribbling, passing, receiving, or shooting, hand pressure the ball to the sideline as much as possible without penetration or fouling. Pressure the sideline with your inside foot up and keep your defensive stance. Your stance keys your mental and physical balance and quickness. Start high and contest every pass one pass away from the ball, especially passes into the "power zone" or a player's "hot spots." Stay high on a back cut and open to the ball when:

   a. The ball is passed.
   b. You get to the free-throw lane.

When your man stops his dribble, he is dead. Keep your stance, cover the ball with both hands without reaching, and yell "Dead, dead, dead." This alerts your teammates to contest all passing lanes.

4. **Post defense rule.** Start high in a contesting stance and front using an arm bar. Keep a "gap" with your front arm up at all times when guarding a player in the post area. If the ball is above the free-throw line, front above the man. If the ball is below the free-throw line, front below the man. If the post catches the ball, get ball head basket position with a gap, with hands up in the umbrella position.

5. **Jump to the ball rule.** Any time the ball is passed, you must jump to the ball. Jumping to the ball allows you to be in proper position to front cutters, avoid screens, and help teammates. Any time the ball is dribbled, you should make the proper ball-side or help-side adjustment in position.

6. **Help-side rule.** The help-side defender above the free-throw line extended:

   ♦ Be close enough to help on ball penetration and recover to your man.
   ♦ Be in a direct passing lane to your man if he is one pass away.

The help-side defender below the free-throw line extended:

When you are two passes away from the ball, you are our primary helper and are extremely ball conscious.

♦ Be in line with the basket.

♦ Be in a slightly open to the ball stance; "point" to the ball and your man.

♦ Be one step off a direct passing lane to your man.

This help-side positioning allows you to do three things:

♦ You are in excellent position to help or to take the charge if the ball comes into the lane.

♦ You can stop the flash post, making the offensive man go back-door or taking the charge if he continues his cut to the ball. If he back-cuts, front him in the lane after opening to the ball.

♦ You cannot be screened as easily because you can get over the screen on either the high or low side.

7. **Help and recover rule.** We help only when a teammate is beaten. You must help stop all ball penetration and you must recover to your man as soon as the ball has been stopped either on the ball-side or the help-side. Keep vision on the ball and your man when you help. In all ball screen situations you must "show yourself" to the outside and yell, "Screen."

You must help stop ball penetration when the offense screens and you must recover to your man as soon as the ball has been stopped. We will jump switch lateral crosses by guards.

8. **Cover down rule**. When we are beat to the sideline, the nearest help-side man stops the ball penetration or takes the charge outside the lane and everyone else covers down to the baseline.

Race to the line of the ball (a line through the ball across the width of the floor) and assume defensive position or steal passes. Recover to your man when the ball is passed back out.

Conclusion

We will not expect you to learn these team defensive rules by reading them. We will execute them every day we practice. This summary can help you to understand the rules and should be used as a review and supplement of daily practice drills on the eight basic defensive rules.

When practicing the defensive rules, think about your job so you will react automatically in a game. Learn the basic rules and apply them.

THINK IN PRACTICE – REACT IN GAMES

MAN-TO-MAN PRESSURE DEFENSE

Bud Presley

I. Components of Defensive Success

A. Determination

Defense is the single most important aspect of the game. Good defense is only about 20 percent technique and 80 percent is measured by desire to succeed, which comes from great intensity and great determination. The philosophy of the coach will generally dictate the type of defense played.

B. Aggressiveness

There is no easy road for an aggressive basketball player to follow. When a team plays with winning as its ultimate goal, it will always display that extra hustle. An aggressive player is risk-taking in his play, he bleeds a little and often causes others to bleed by taking the charge, and so on.

C. Conditioning

A squad properly and thoroughly conditioned, by means of daily defensive drills, is the team whose superb stamina will win championships. Those playing aggressive pressure man-for-man defense will naturally have to hustle, scrap, and physically extend themselves more and with more intense effort than normal teams.

D. Pride

Without self-pride and desire, even players with superior physical equipment are continually beaten in pressure games. Pride is the accumulation of determination, aggressiveness, and conditioning. Pride is never felt by poorly disciplined teams.

II. Progression Drills in Building the Defense

Defensive basketball can be only as good as the drills that break down into component parts for specialized attention. During the first two weeks of the session, you should spend one hour each day on the one-on-one drills and then repeat three or four of these daily. By the end of the first week, aggressive two-on-two techniques should be taught through quick and exciting drills. With three-on-three, you should incorporate help defense, cross action, and traps by the end of the second week. Then, you start four-on-four and team defense. Keep your drills short, race from one drill to the next, then repeat them many times to prevent boredom.

A. Pressure on the Ball

1. Maintain a boxer's stance with your strong foot pointing to the ball. Your tail is kept down, your head and chest up, and 70 percent of

your body weight is over your front foot. Keep constant pressure with a bent elbow in your man's chest.

2. Jump back in the direction of the pass on all penetrating passes and chest your man on cuts to the basket and take him out of his desired cutting path.

3. Work hard on pointing the ball with an upward flicking action by the strong hand on the side of your forward foot. If he stops or steps back, belly-up on him and put him in jail.

4. Pressure the dribbler wide, take the charge, protect against the baseline drive, and wedge your lead leg and arm hard over all post and rear screens to fight over the top.

5. You must execute the proper reverse slide on all attempts against the strong lead foot – then boxer's shuffle.

6. In rebounding, if the offensive player crashes to your rear foot side, front pivot into him and reverse pivot into him when he crashes to the front foot side.

7. Communicate constantly.

B. Defense Away from the Ball

1. Deny all lead penetrating passes.

2. Maintain the flat angle of ball, you, and man with midpoint vision.

3. Beat your man to the spot when he cuts to a ball-side post position and help on the inside lob passes.

4. Help-side defense should close out hard on any cross-court passes to your man and take the charge on penetrating drives.

5. Open into the ball on back-door cuts.

6. Communicate: For example, call out "clear-right", "help-right", "screen-left."

C. Breakdown Defensive Drills

Coach Bud Presley teaches only one defense, aggressive pressure man-for-man. The following drills, which are used to teach his players to make the first move, never allow the offense the same privilege. A stopwatch is used to time every drill, play, and maneuver with a specific time requirement for each activity. In using theses drills, you must keep in mind that variations may be needed to make them applicable. In our quick moving drills, we are looking for players who will sacrifice comfort and develop pride.

1. **Cross-court one-on-one (see Figure 20.6).** The squad is spread across the sideline with the defensive player in excellent stance next to his opponent with his forearm in the upper chest as he hands the ball to him. They work back and forth for 90 seconds on reverse slides, pointing and turning the ball, looking to belly-up after the dribble or lateral fakes, maintaining great ball pressure at all times.

2. **Closeout drill (see Figure 20.7).** One defensive player and three or four offensive players stand behind the free-throw line. The defensive player under the basket tosses the ball quickly to his opponent and rushes him to assume a defensive position. With his dominant foot and hand forward and his head back like a high jumper on the plant, he reacts to the shot or drive until he gains possession of the ball. Then he quickly tosses the ball to the next player in line before rotating out, and the drill continues in this manner.

3. **Aggressive drill.** Two players start on the square under the basket with the coach rolling the ball toward the foul line or placing the ball between them on the floor. Players should be matched according to size and spread because we want them to dive through each other for the ball. The player who comes up with the ball will try to score against pressure defense. They go at it until the defensive player gains possession. Then the next two players will square off against each other.

4. **Cut and chug.** In this drill, we have three players one-on-one out front and a passer at the wing. The offensive player passes the ball to the wing and cuts to the basket. The defensive player should jump to the ball on the pass and then chest his opponent toward the basket and away from his desired cutting path. Split your squad to have equal number of players at each basket.

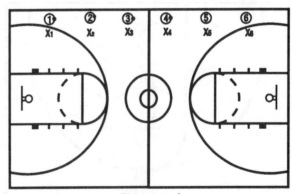

Figure 20.6

5. **Pass-cut with post screens.** Guard rub series with post screening for the guard. On the pass, jump off and chest him away and toward the basket. Defense must fight over the top on all post screens.

6. **Weak-side defense.** One man removed, be ready to help and deep recover with a quick rush on return passes. Two men removed, flat angle of *ball, you* and *man.* Responsible for all over-the-top passes to the post being fronted, all back-cuts, cross-court passes to your man, any penetration drive to the basket, and in beating your man to the spot when he cuts to a ball-side post. In this drill, allow the passes, working on midpoint vision and position. Close out to your man when he has the ball.

7. **"Z" drill.** In this drill, all four players get in the shell formation with a ball and the four defensive players either play pressure or help defense. The coach will flash his hand for the one offensive player to drive right or left, his man will pressure him on the dribble, while the other three must adjust their midpoint vision and position. Right away, the coach will signal for a different player to make his move and the defense must react to all players. The defense should work on help-side, taking the charge, jumping and recovering, and good pressure defense. If you have only 14 players, go four-on-four at one end and three-on-three on the other.

8. **Six phases drill (two-on-two).** Four players line up two-on-two for ball and opponent relationship. All players work on one side and then the other. This drill will take four minutes

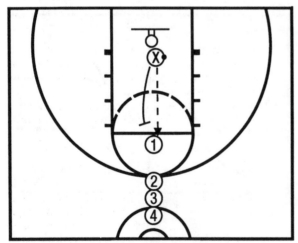

Figure 20.7

with each defensive player working four times on each side. The coach should call out the direction and then players should sprint to cover the area.

   a. Back-door-sprint back to the lane and open up to the ball.

   b. Medium post – three-quarter high side with head, chest, and arm in front but inside knee locked behind his leg.

   c. Low post – working from high to low with inside leg and arm stepping forward and driving over the top to the low post three-quarter side.

   d. Weak-side defense – take the charge, close out, and cross-court pass coverage.

   e. One-on-one – force the dribbler to pick up the ball, force down the side, help and recover, and hedging and ducktail over the post.

9. **Three-on-three drills.** Start this full-court transition game in the backcourt with the offensive players limited to passes only until they reach midcourt. Then go regular with pass-screen away, pass-cut, pass-screen the ball, etc. Defense can help and recover, flat angle on the help side, but no switching, and they might fight over screens on the inside. On the shot, both teams rebound with everyone until the defense gets ball possession. Play offense down and defense back, etc.

10. **Shell phase.** Four-on-four pressure defense 12-14 minutes per practice against the shell (see Figure 20.8).

   a. Phase 1 – Working on midpoint vision and position as four offensive players quickly move the ball around the outside.

   b. Phase 2 – Skip passes back and forth while the defense is working on the rush and flat-angle help positions.

   c. Phase 3 – Offense can empty right or left, defense must then force the ball back to the inside for help.

   d. Phase 4 – Penetration with the ball inside the shell, defense will help and recover, but the deepest outside player must rotate to the deepest weak-side baseline or basket area.

   e. Phase 5 – Cross action rotation when the offensive player penetrates the shell toward the basket.

11. **Full-court denial defense, four-on-four.** In this drill we work up to six minutes without a break. Go both ways, with great team pressure defense at all times. We fight over the screens, denial of the inbound passes, rotate to stop and recover, and fight for every rebound.

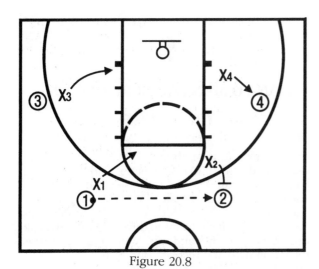

Figure 20.8

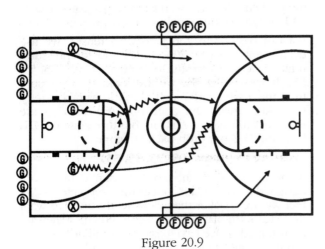

Figure 20.9

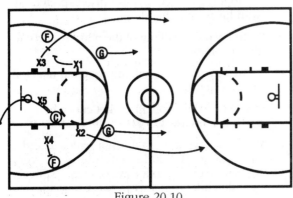

Figure 20.10

12. **Full-court transition drill (see Figure 20.9)**
In this drill, we have two lines of guards under the basket and two lines of big men on the sideline at midcourt. Start with two defensive big men and two guards at one end heading down the court. Two offensive big men will jump out from the sideline and join the two guards on a four-on-two plus-two fast break. The big men must start the break from the foul line extended on offense and the two defensive players must talk and catch their opponent. Once they go offense and defense, they drop out and back into their lines. Once the ball is turned over, the two offensive guards take the fast break to the other end with help from the sidelines. Big defensive players try to catch up to their opponents.

D. Suggestion in Stopping the Following Fast Breaks if Regular Pressure Fails

1. **Marshall fast break (see Figure 20.10).** This usually starts from a set 2-3 zone defense. They fly one guard to the one forward down the court on the shot. The middle guard will go to the outlet side while they rebound with only the post and strong forward. Looking for the long pass or outlet to the middle guard, he gets the basketball down the side quickly. Cover them by sending two guards back to front pressure the flyers, rebound tough with post and strong forward, and send your small forward to prevent the middle guard from getting the ball. Once you stop the first quick options, play them pressure man-for-man all over the court with regular rules.

2. **Speed game.** Most speed fast breaks have assigned spots to run to on the rebound or inbound pass. We scout these patterns and have the defense beat them to their spots and then play them a pressure man all over the court.

3. **Extended pressure defense.** Number the court 40, 30 and 20 with a color code for full-court, three-quarter court, and half-court defense. Blue 30 would mean three-quarter man with harassment and trap from only the blind side. Red 40 would mean full-court must pressure situations, looking to trap, smother the ball, and gambling to stop the ball.

4. **Fake zone press (see Figure 20.11).** On the made basket, post covers the passer, the left forward will take the first player in his area and, if open, the first man inside, the right forward will front the first man in his area and then look for the first open man inside or back off to guard the first man downcourt, two guards sprint to midcourt, talk, and cover the other two players. If they get the ball in play, we force them down the side with man-for-man pressure defense.

5. Four-corner defense. Force the ball down the side and don't allow the outside corner to dribble it back to the middle. If the ball goes for the basket, baseline players will jump out to smother the ball once it penetrates the lane. Outside players must race to the baseline to cover the driving corner players. For the best defense, don't get behind by playing zone.

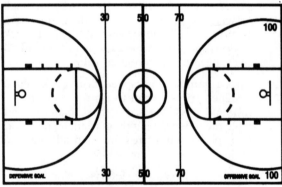

Figure 20.11

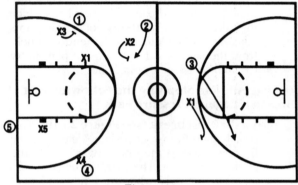

Figure 20.12

MAN-TO-MAN PRESSURE DEFENSE
Tom Penders

We play man-to-man about 90 percent of the time. Our basic defense (50) is straight up, help and recover, ball – you – man defense. Because of our quickness and desire to force an up-tempo game, we play most teams with our 99 or 55 defenses. These defenses are designed to force teams to drive, create, and break opponents' patterns and sets. While our basic 50 is reliant on help and recover, our 99 and 55 defenses are rotating and switching defenses.

Numbering System

To simplify our system and to help us move from defense to defense, we use a football field and convert the yard lines to areas on the basketball court. Figure 20.12 describes our numbering system.

For our basic help and recover defenses, we use even numbers (100, 70, 50, 30) and for pressure-rotation defenses we use odd numbers (99, 75, 55, 35). If we call for 75, we are looking to pressure from the three-quarter area on back. Numbers refer to pickup areas. Our zone pressure defenses are lettered A through D. A is full, B is three-quarter, C is half, and D is our drop-back zone trap.

Pressure Defenses (99, 75, 55, 35)

As previously mentioned, our pressure defenses are designed to force teams out of their set patterns. We feel we are quicker than most teams and we want these teams to play at a quicker tempo than they are accustomed to. We have basic rules and designs, but scouting and preparation for particular teams is essential.

Basic rules:

1. Always pressure the ball. Don't let the handler look over the defense.

2. Try to force the handler to dribble, preferably with his weaker hand.

3. Try to keep the ball out of the middle. Force to the sidelines.

4. Deny any pass that will improve the position of the offense.

5. Stay closed down on all basket cuts when you are one pass away.

6. We always want to establish a ball-side and a weak-side. Ball-side defenders are very aggressive on their offensive opponents. Weak-side defenders are always ready to rotate and switch if the ball defender gets beat.

7. Switch out on all ball screens unless scouting reports dictate otherwise.

8. Don't allow the offense to reverse the ball by passing.

9. We always want to force the drive to the baseline.

10. Post defenders must protect the baseline side of the post when the ball is at a 45-degree angle.

Defensive positions with different ball locations are shown in Figures 20.13 through 20.18.

Notes

1. If X4 gets beat, he helps Number 1 cover the post or Number 2 tries to flick from behind or he takes 0-1 if the ball penetrates along the baseline. The nearest defender rotates up and everyone else rotates either clockwise or counterclockwise. The man who gets beat zones off and looks for an open man to rotate to.

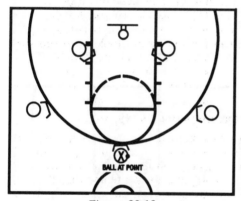

Figure 20.13

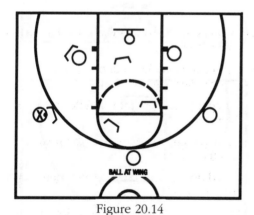

Figure 20.14

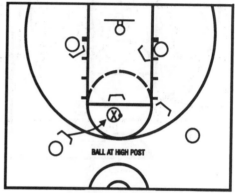

Figure 20.15

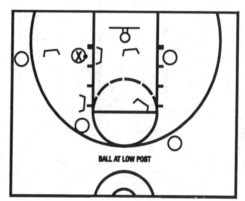

Figure 20.16

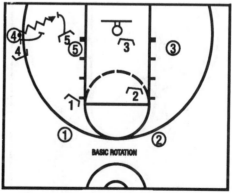

Figure 20.17

Figure 20.18

2. X3 takes driver, X2 rotates down counterclockwise, X5 stays with the high post, X1 takes 0-2, and X4 pursues the ball and zones off. X4 will take 0-1 eventually. All switches above 45-degree angle will involve only two people. (Figures 20.19 through 20.27.)

3. Force the ball up sides. Keep the ball out of the middle. If you get beat up the middle, pursue the ball and flick from behind. Full rotations occur in shaded ares only (Figure 20.28).

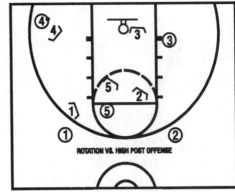

Figure 20.22

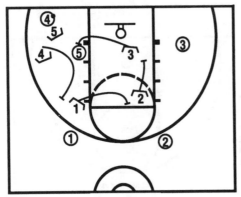

Figure 20.19

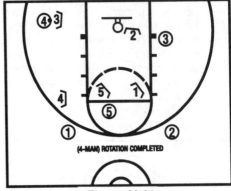

Figure 20.23

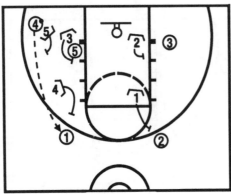

Figure 20.20

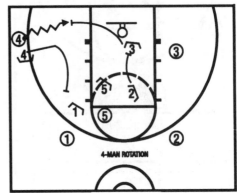

Figure 20.24

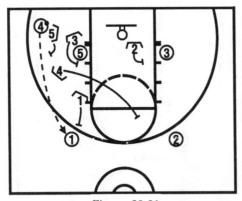

Figure 20.21

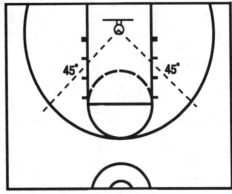

Figure 20.25

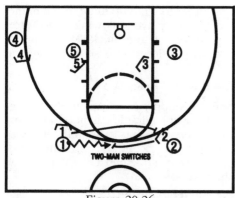

Figure 20.26

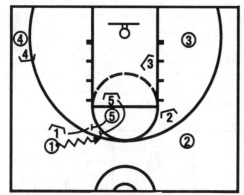

Figure 20.27

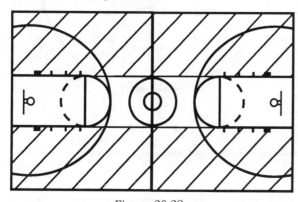

Figure 20.28

Figure 20.29. Full-court, clockwise rotation
Figure 20.30. Counterclockwise rotation
Figure 20.31. Middle penetration, no
  rotation
X1 – pursues the ball and tries to flick.
X2 – tries to get ahead of the ball.
X3 – slows down the dribbler.
X4 and X5 – zone off.

If the ball goes to the sidelines, we readjust and look to switch and rotate again.

4. We don't concern ourselves with matchups in our pressure man defenses. If you get beat, you'll get help. If you get beat, make sure it's toward the sidelines or the baseline. We might give up a few easy baskets, but it takes two or three good passes to score against our pressure. We are trying to make our opponent play our game and react to our defense rather than allow them to play at their desired pace.

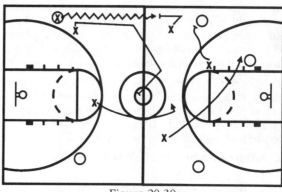

Figure 20.30

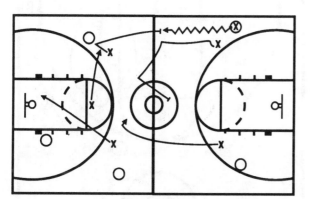

Figure 20.29

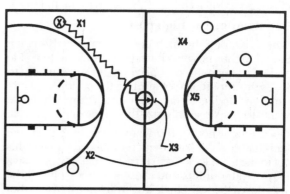

Figure 20.31

DEFENSIVE PHILOSOPHY: TEAM AND INDIVIDUAL CONCEPTS

Steve Fisber

I. Post Defense

Our philosophy of post defense rests on the premise that games are won and lost in the paint. As much as possible, we want to deny the opposing post player the ball, or at least force him to catch the ball in an area where he will be least effective.

A. Wrapping up the post player/forcing off the block

When covering the offensive post player on the low post block, we teach two basic concepts: 1) forcing the player off the block and 2) "wrapping him up." At Michigan, we've been blessed with big, strong, and physical players who we feel are well suited to this philosophy. We teach our players to "wrap" the opposing post player by extending the lead arm into the passing lane, and extending the opposite arm around the back of the offensive player. We also have our defensive players lean on the offensive player with their chest, making sure to have a good strong base with their legs for leverage.

It's important to note that we always want our post player in a 45-degree angle in relationship to the ball so he must adjust his position in relationship to the position of the ball. Additionally, we always wrap on the high side of the post player.

B. Full front when the ball is in the dead corner

We go from a wrap to a full front of the post player only when the ball goes to the dead corner. We try to teach our post player to either swing his back foot through to get to the full front position, or, if the offensive player does a good job of sealing our defense, we have our player spin around with a reverse pivot to get to the full front. Figure 20.32 illustrates a drill to practice the wrap to the full front.

C. Defending the high post

When covering the high post player, we also teach the wrap, but now we'll wrap up from the low side and try to keep the post player high. We really try to stress the importance of meeting the offensive player early and trying to take him away from where he wants to go. We emphasize this in transition as well.

Once established in the wrap at the high post, we feel that it is easier to deny the offensive player his cut to the low block. We will try to "split" the offensive player with our feet and chest, and body him all the way down the low block. This will force him to either go behind our defensive player to the low post area

(thus making it easier to wrap up there) or go in the front of our defensive player, allowing us to force him three to four feet off the block. The bump at high post to wrap position drill is shown in Figure 20.33.

D. Defending the mid-post

The same principles apply here. Again, the key is meeting the post player high, splitting him, and taking him away from where he wants to go. If he heads to the mid-post area, we want to "influence" his movement so that we can ride him a few steps out of the lane at the mid-post area.

E. Defending the flash cutter

We also work very hard at defending the flash cutter who will start on the weak side and attempt to flash to the ball. We want our defender to be at the midline in a help position when his man is two passes away from the ball. As the offensive man flashes to the ball, the defender has time to step to the cutter, bump him, and ride him out of the lane, forcing the offensive player to change direction (see Figure 20.34).

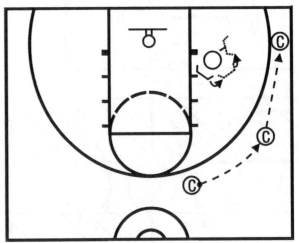

Figure 20.32

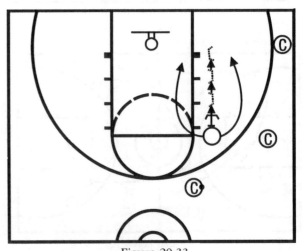

Figure 20.33

F. Defending the post player with the ball

Jump behind/leave a cushion: Everything that we've talked about so far has centered on denying the post player the ball in scoring position. Obviously, we are not always successful in this effort. It's important, therefore, that our post players be able to play individual defense on the ball.

We teach our players that when the post player receives the ball, they should jump behind the offensive player and leave a cushion so that the offensive player cannot "seal" the defense and make an easy drop-step to the basket.

G. Turn middle/post double

When the offensive player catches the ball in the low post, we want our defensive player to force him to turn to the middle, where our help is. Before a game, we will determine which of the opposing post players are scorers inside, and make a decision on which individuals we will double team once they catch the ball.

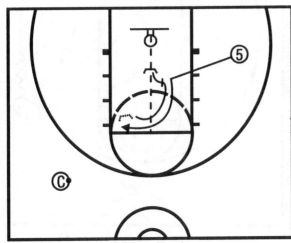

Figure 20.34

Unlike a lot of teams who drop a man off the ball for the double team, we like to double from the weak side. We like to do this for a number of reasons. First, we feel that dropping from the ball exposes us to the quick kickback for a three-pointer, and that most teams have incorporated this into their offensive attack. Second, we feel that the kickback to the opposite side is a more difficult pass for a post player to make. Finally, this allows us greater flexibility in determining where the double team will come from. This double team may come from the opposite post man or from the opposite side wing man. Before a game, based on our scouting report and individual match-ups, we may also designate a man who will be our primary "doubler." We teach our players that the double must be aggressive and that he must "chest" the offensive player so that he is not able to turn and find a teammate for the pass.

One final area to be covered regarding the post double is the need for defensive rotation by the other weak-side players. This is especially important if our post double comes from the opposite post man, as we must then receive defensive rotation to cover the opposite post man, and box him out if a shot goes up.

II. Perimeter Defense

A. Ball pressure

Our defense on the perimeter (and this includes our big men when defending on the perimeter) is predicated on intense ball pressure. We tell our players to distinguish between covering a perimeter player who does and does not have his dribble left. Obviously, the offensive player who has already used up his dribble should be pressured with the utmost intensity. The offensive player who still has a dribble remaining needs to be pressured, but in such a way that the player does not give up dribble penetration. We tell our players that when an offensive player (even one with a dribble remaining) raises the ball over his head looking to pass, that they must crowd him even more. If he lowers the ball back down, the defensive player can then retreat a half step to contain the dribble.

B. Footwork/steering to the corner

We like to steer the ballhandler to the corner and try to keep him on that side to make ball reversal difficult. We really like to stress proper footwork in this area. We like to have our players keep their feet squared to the ballhandler, rather than opening up their stance and inviting dribble penetration.

Perimeter Defense Drills

1. 1/1 steer drill (see Figure 20.35).

2. 1/1 contest/deflect/steer (see Figure 20.36).

3. 1/1 continuous (see Figure 20.37.

4. 2/2 contest/steer/off-ball help (see Figure 20.38).

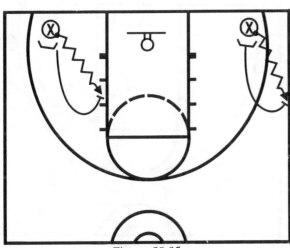

Figure 20.35

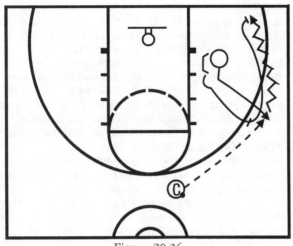

Figure 20.36

5. 3/3 contest/steer/early help (see Figure 20.39).

6. 4/4 shell drill (see Figure 20.40). We feel that the shell drill is the most important defensive drill in our system, and we work on it in practice every day. We incorporate the following concepts in our shell drill:

a. Position and technique.
b. Dribble penetration/help and recover.
c. Bump the cutter.
d. Post flash.
e. Baseline drive/rotation.
f. Post double – add a fifth player who must receive the ball in the post.
g. Six-on-four – add two offensive players in the dead corners. Their only job is to wait outside the three-point arc, and when they receive the ball, dribble as quickly as possible to the hoop looking for the layup. This forces the defense to

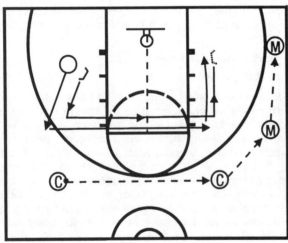

Figure 20.37

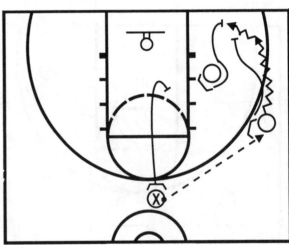

Figure 20.39

Figure 20.38

Figure 20.40

help on the ball and recover to the man. We make the rule that these additional offensive players can only shoot the layup (no pull-up jumpers) or pass to another offensive player (not the other auxiliary offensive player).

    h. Live.

III. Defensing Screens

A. Ball screens

We teach our defensive player guarding the screener to put his hand on the screener's hip, align himself parallel to the screener, and "show" himself to the ballhandler. If he feels the screener start to release to the basket, the defender merely leaves with the screener.

By defensing screens in this way, the defender covering the ball should be able to go over the top of the screen, so that we do not surrender the perimeter jump shot (see Figure 20.41).

B. Off-ball screens

We believe that there are three ways to defense off-ball screens: going ball-side, going man-side, and playing tag.

By going ball-side on a screen, we mean that the defender, who is in an "on the line, up the line" position, slides over the screen to his man, going between the ball and the screener. We find that this is effective against teams or players that like to curl screens (see Figure 20.42).

By going man-side on a screen, we mean that the player slips through the screen in between the screener and his own man. This can be done against teams that do not screen particularly well, or when guarding a player who does not use or read screens well (see Figure 20.43).

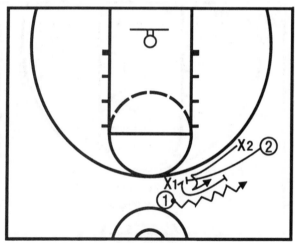

Figure 20.41

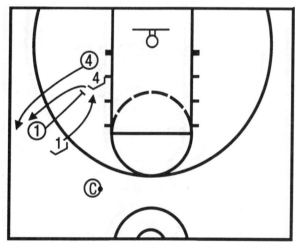

Figure 20.43

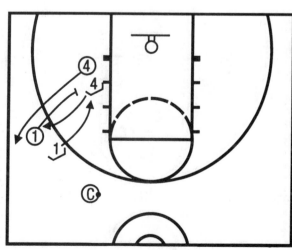

Figure 20.42

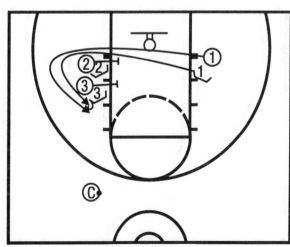

Figure 20.44

We play "tag" when covering an explosive perimeter shooter, when guarding a player coming off a double screen or staggered screen situation, or when covering a baseline runner. We tell our defender to place a hand on the hip of the offensive player and follow him through the screens. The offensive player will be unable to flair for the jump shot, and his only option is to curl the screen. We then make sure that our defender covering the screener steps out and "bumps" the cutter on the curl (see Figure 20.44).

C. Post-post screens

We have our post players switch post-post cross screens on the block when we are not worried about mismatch problems (See Figure 20.45).

A two-on-two continuous screening drill is shown in Figure 20.46.

IV. Rebounding

A. Shooter/next receiver/off-ball player

We feel that we must work on contesting the shot and boxing out the shooter, boxing out a player who is the next likely receiver, and going from a midline help position back out of the line to box out a weakside offensive rebounder.

B. Baseline rotation/post double box-out

Since our defensive philosophy involves giving help on baseline drives and doubling the post from the weak side, we feel that it is important to drill on boxing out the proper people in our defensive rotation.

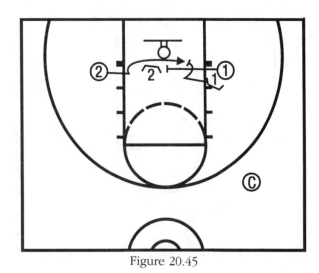

Figure 20.45

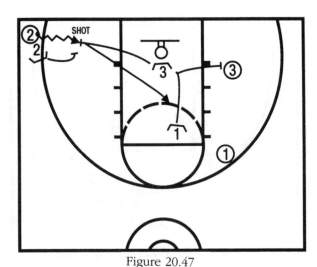

Figure 20.47

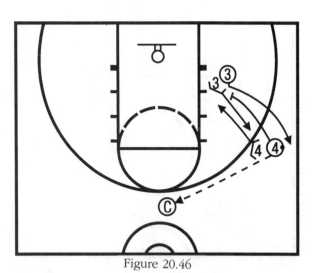

Figure 20.46

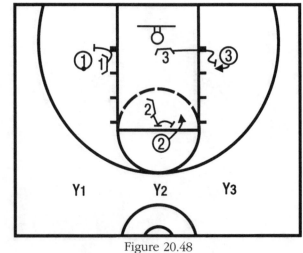

Figure 20.48

This means that quite often a guard will have to rotate down to the opposite block to box out an offensive big man, so we work on this often in practice.

We also teach our player who doubles the post that he must sprint back to the other side and attempt to lay a body on someone when the shot goes up, as we are often vulnerable to the weak-side offensive rebound when we double the post (see Figure 20.47).

C. Funnel middle

We tell our players that when moving to box out an offensive player, we want to take away their ability to slither behind us on the baseline for the offensive board, so we want to funnel everyone to the middle of the lane. This is consistent with our belief that most shots taken from the sides of the court will be rebounded on the opposite side.

D. Three-on-three rebounding game

We try to put our rebounding principles to work in a 3/3/3 rebounding game, where the defense has the opportunity to box out the shooter, next receiver, and off-ball offensive players. Three teams compete, and a team receives a point for every defensive rebound it grabs. The defensive rebounding team stays on the floor accumulating points until it surrenders an offensive rebound. The third team always enters on offense, and wins the right to play defense by getting an offensive rebound. The game is quick-paced, competitive, and our players certainly seem to enjoy it (see Figure 20.48).

V. Conclusion

Overall, our philosophy on defense and rebounding is for our team to act and force our opponents to react to what we are doing. We know that defense and rebounding win championships, and hopefully some of these drills and an explanation of our philosophy will help other teams be successful.

Chapter 21 ZONE DEFENSE

ZONE

IN DEFENSE OF A ZONE
Dr. Alvin C. Saake

Years ago I had the pleasure of hearing Dr. James Naismith speak. He said that he had gotten the idea of taking the best parts of the games that were popular in Springfield during the time (1890) and adjusting the rules to play indoors because of the severity of the winter weather in the Northeast. This idea was derived from sitting in a psychology class while an unknown Mr. Chips lectured on the topic "There is nothing new under the sun." Dr. Naismith accepted this premise and came up with the game that has thrilled millions for years. Our Founder (who is now in Heaven) said to a question from the audience that he was opposed to the zone defense because "it tends to stall a game that was devised to be constantly on the attack." Many modern day coaches agree. The professional leagues have rules to outlaw zones, but like Watergate what is a rule and what is a practice might be two different things. It is not unlike diplomacy – instead of telling a person he has a hole in his head you temper your words and indicate he has an open mind. Many of the coaching fraternity fail to have an open mind about playing zone defense. They indicate that it should be outlawed.

The success or failure of coaching the zone or of attacking the same defense is just as relative as our economy. We must work on it with the same dedication that we do with the other types of defense and offense.

One of the greatest coaches of all time, a true non-pareil and Hall of Famer, Clair Bee, said his first experience with the zone defense was in 1914. At the time, school schedules did not begin until January and the better high school players filled in on the YMCA teams that were playing Naismith's game. Around Christmas the Grafton YMCA had scheduled a game with Bee's town team – Bristol, West Virginia. Bee was a high school star and recruited to make the trip. As only Bee can tell it, the train was late, a heavy blizzard was in progress and the Bristol players had to walk two miles to the town hall where the game was to be played. A preliminary girl's game had been dragged out for over two hours to keep the sparse crowd from demanding a refund on their admission. Green pine lumber had been used in the floor construction and it was slippery as glass. Cam Henderson, who later coached with considerable success at Davis-Elkins and Marshall College in West Virginia, had his Bristol players station themselves in certain zones which they did not leave until a shot was taken. This new defense was worked out at halftime and although crude, proved effective and presented a new development in basketball.

In the many years that I have coached or lectured at various clinics I have attempted to refine the most important basic principles of a sliding-zone team defense. These assumptions make up a baker's dozen:

1. Focus of attention is primarily upon the ball.

2. Players adjust positions – not focus attention – according to positions and movements of their opponents.

3. Players shift and double-team opponents whenever possible. Always remember "Team Defense."

4. Defense is always formed from the goal first.

5. Team defense is a full-court zone defense, but as opponents get closer to our basket we compress the width of zone to eventually cover only the "half of the half" of the court where the ball is located.

6. Whenever the ball is passed behind a defensive player, move toward the goal.

7. "Windmill" hand action to reduce the normal passing lanes.

8. Always guard the most dangerous player in your area.

9. Always try for the steal if you can get a "piece of the ball." If you fail in the attempt, rotate to the least vulnerable area.

10. Always try to maintain the "three in line" principle with three defensive men between ball and basket.

11. When a shot is taken the three logical defensive players form a wide rebound triangle. The fourth player goes to foul line to cover the long rebound and the player who attempted to check the shot is free to move after screening the shooter to primary outlet area for fast break attempt.

12. Always adjust zone positions to compensate for offensive alignment.

13. Be decisive (may be in error but never in doubt), gamble with judgment, talk when it is to your advantage, anticipate offensive moves and *hustle*.

I agree with Peyton March who said "There is a wonderful, mythical law of nature that the three things we crave most in life – happiness, freedom and peace of mind – are always attained by giving them to someone else." And I don't even think he coached basketball.

FLEXING THE ZONE DEFENSE

Bill Foster

First of all, I think you can flex the man-to-man in whatever way, shape, or form you would like. I have a feeling that we get so involved with pressure defense that we believe we have to pressure all of the time. I sometimes think that when you go into a game against an opponent, you can really foul things up by running a layback defense. I think that if some people had done that to us last year, it would have caused some confusion on our part. The last month of the season we did work on what we call the "10 pickup," where we picked up at the head of the circle and just put a little pressure on the ball and clogged up the middle. This made it look like a zone. Again, I think the reason behind it is that because we were a pressure defense team, we never worked against that type of a drop-back defense. We used this defense a couple of times last year, and I think it caused some confusion. In it, we were well protected against the big man inside. We put some pressure on the ball and we were really packed in there on the ball-side. The original thought is that we do get so involved with half-court pressure defense, full-court, three-quarter, every kind of pressure, that a change from this can help you in a game.

I'd like to discuss adjusting on the zone and then our half-court trap defense. In one game in the NIT, we didn't get to half court with it. We backed it up, because we felt we could cover other areas and keep our big men underneath.

I remember using this type of thing several years ago in order to get to a double coverage type situation. This was good for us, but we couldn't do it for long periods of time. One of the problems we had with our full-court pressing defenses is that we would take it off and we had a tendency not to go back to it because a team was attacking it successfully. This made us sort of leery about staying with it. We use multiple defenses and I always try to use something early and then in the second half go back to it again. Some teams can attack one defense well but can't handle another defense. It is amazing that sometimes a defense won't hurt the offense in the first half, but it might work well in the second half.

I am not really a zone defense man because I am not sure about the rebounding situations we have from it. You have to be very careful going from pressure to the zone because your kids can become passive.

We have faced some 1-3-1 defenses that have come out a little bit, and we have done this too. We put a forward on the point, then make the ball go to one side and keep it on that side of the floor. In attacking this defense we would want the baseline man to have to cover sideline to sideline. In playing it we would try to keep the ball from going from corner to corner.

This year we used the 1-2-2 as an alternate defense and there were some basic things we did with it when we played it. These things are not new. In clinics you won't pick up entirely new concepts, but you might pick up a couple of new ideas. But I think maybe more important than that, you can pick up some reminders. Some things that we might have done a couple of years ago we have forgotten, and these clinics can remind you of those things and you can use them again. You can fit these things in with the next year's personnel. I have had players come back and ask if we are still doing a certain thing and it has reminded me that we should use certain things again.

In our 1-2-2 defense we have tried to designate responsibilities. We would prefer that we align our players in a certain way (see Figure 21.1). The rotation of the defense is simple (Figure 21.2).

The reason that we align the players as shown in Figure 21.1 is that most teams will go to the right side of the floor. This way of placing our players enables us to get our bigger players on the rebound.

Any time the ball goes out of the alley, X must move back and cover the high post area (Figure 21.2). This is a very vulnerable point in the defense and we can't let the ball get to the high post. Another very important factor in this defense is to tell the defense to protect inside out. If you turn it around, when you are on offense you want to try to go inside, so in this defense and in our man-to-man, we want to try to keep the ball from going inside as much as possible.

We break down this defense into drills. We will break it down into a drill for just X4 and X5. We want X4 and X5 to move quickly. If the ball goes to the corner, then X4 must cover (Figure 21.3). We want X5 to be able to come over and front. This prevents the pass inside, where the defense is most vulnerable. With Mike Sojourner we let him go over and play behind, but the others were to front. We felt Sojourner was a threat behind the guy and was just as effective as someone else when they fronted. So when you scouted us, you would say that one player would front when the ball went low, but Sojourner doesn't. There was a reason for that. He had the inside for rebounds on a shot and he could intimidate on a close-in shot.

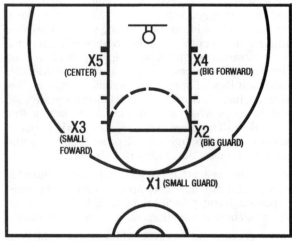
Figure 21.1

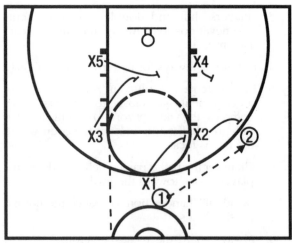
Figure 21.2

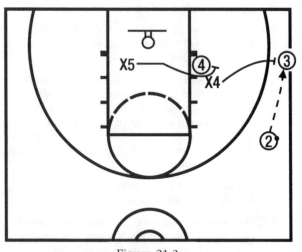
Figure 21.3

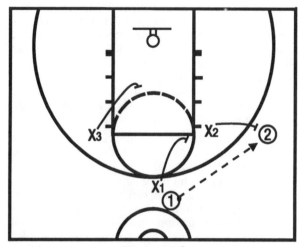

Figure 21.4

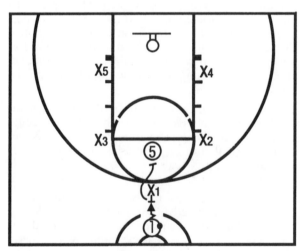

Figure 21.5

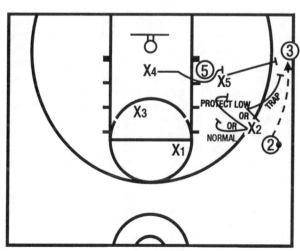

Figure 21.6

At the same time at the other end of the court, X1, X2, and X3 were working on their assignments. The thing in this phase of the defense that is important is, when the ball is on the side and is passed back to the front, X1 not only has to roar out at the ball, but just as important and perhaps more important is that X2 roars back and protects inside where X1 has left, because I think that is a vulnerable area (Figure 21.4). We attack zones with what we call a "1-4 attack high" and we feel that wing people are very lazy and don't get back to cover inside. They will protect inside out, but when the ball comes back to the point, they forget to get back to cover and take their time getting back. If you are running an offense that has a guy set up on the foul line and the ball comes back quickly, get the ball to a man before the wing gets back. This is only a small thing, but we think it is very important that we work on covering that situation. We spend a little bit of time working on this, about 10 minutes a week. We don't think one zone will improve much. It isn't our basic defense so we won't spend as much time on a secondary defense as we would on our basic defense. We only use this defense on special occasions. We use it to change or slow up our opponent.

The 2-3 zone is a zone that you probably see more of and it is easy to flex the 1-2-2 zone into a 2-3 zone. In doing this we feel it is fairly simple with a small rotation. There are two things we think we can do out of this. If they put a guy on the high post who is bothering us a lot, we try to cover him by dropping X1 back to cover him. Figure 21.5 shows X1 challenging the ball and then dropping back in front of the high post man. A lot of teams attacking a 1-2-2 will use a 2-3 set offense against it. We simply drop X1 back and cover the high post if there is no one in his area. It looks like, if you were to identify it, a 2-1-2 zone.

In our 1-2-2 we like to give several responsibilities to what we call the wing man (see Figure 21.6). This would involve X2 and X3. What we would like him to do on the ball side, on weak-side responsibility, rebounding when the ball is in the corner, is to:

1. Play normal.

2. Double in the corner; he can set a trap. This could hurt the lob to the same sideline.

3. Protect inside – we have him do this when the wing in his area is not a good shooter.

Figure 21.7 shows a move we like to make when, after a pass to the corner, the offensive wing man goes through the defense to the other side. When they use this type of attack we merely say "going through." X3 would go through with the cutter and take the opposite side of the floor as the cutter does. X1 would come to fill the gap and X3 would move up and take X1's place. This gives the appearance of being a man-to-man and will confuse the opponents. In flexing the zone in this manner, we never really

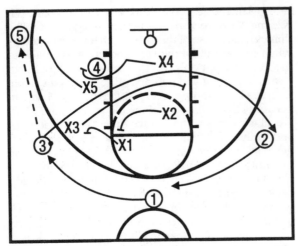

Figure 21.7

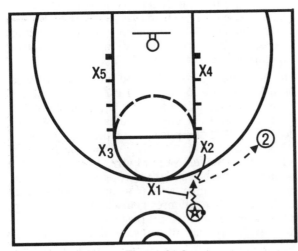

Figure 21.8

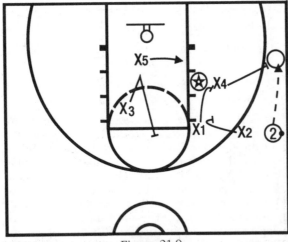

Figure 21.9

got hurt that badly. It is a weird-looking slide. You haven't changed your big guys X4 and X5, but you have changed your wing men. Your wing man and point man are usually pretty mobile people and can think. I don't want my big guys having to think out there. It is easier to change the other people around. A small move like that tends to confuse the opposing players and coach, and makes them think about changing what they are doing.

There are a couple of things that can be done out of the 1-2-2 against a good penetrating guard. Arizona had a great player by the name of Eric Money who was as good a penetrating guard as I have ever seen. In order to keep him from driving, we would go out and double team him and make him pass the ball (Figure 21.8). In flexing our zone, again you will notice that we never change X4 and X5. We think it is vital to try any way possible to keep the ball from going inside. When the ball gets inside they can hurt you too many ways.

Another idea in controlling where the ball goes is to allow or even force the ball to the corner and then keep it on one side of the floor. In order to control the reverse action, X1 needs to adjust his position and move out where the ball cannot be reversed. He protects the passing lane to the high post with his inside left hand.

In flexing the zone, it is vital to be able to adjust and slow down the offense or make the offense change what they are doing. The zone cannot be passive. You gain steals from it by closing passing lanes. If you aren't getting steals from your zone, then it is too passive a zone.

We have used the box-and-one as a defense also. I am not necessarily advocating it as a way of flexing the zone, but there is a place for it. Sometimes this is a must defense. You have to be careful what you say because you don't want to give players the impression that you are out-manned. Make every defense and every tactic sound positive.

In our basic defense and in our flexing of the zone, we give X4 and X5 basically the same rules. Really, the guy who needs to think is the weak-side wing man in the box-and-one. X4 and X5 have the same rules, but X1 is our man-to-man coverage player, and X1 fronts the man inside (Figure 21.9). In our box-and-one we are willing to concede some things. X3 is deep protector in the defense on the weak side. X1 is the man who fronts. Anyone can play that position in your box-and-one. We told that man that if the offensive player got the ball twice, he would come out. Now that's motivation. I am sure that the pressure of not allowing a player to receive the ball twice makes it a physical game.

We can do this sort of thing out of the man-to-man. We do this out of a man-to-man more than from a zone. We can alternate from a man-to-man to a zone. This can hurt the one-on-one players.

We also use the 1-3-1 some and you can flex out of the 1-3-1 zone also. To change to the 1-3-1 we move X5 into the middle and let X4 run the baseline. When we do this we try to keep the ball on one side of the floor. One good feature of the 1-3-1 is that X5 is always inside, and in this defense you can keep him there. If teams try to gap you, you can adjust or flex your zone to cover certain areas.

In our zone defenses we try to keep man-to-man principles. We are always trying to help in all of our defenses. We are help and recover oriented. This way of doing things will blend into any defense you want to run. If you are help and recover oriented it will also aid in flexing the zone.

KENTUCKY 1-3-1 ZONE TRAP

Joe B. Hall

My biggest thrill in basketball was when I put on a Kentucky jersey for the first time as a player. I've never outgrown this. After coaching at Kentucky for 12 years, my hair still stands up when the Wildcats go onto the floor. I am proud to represent Kentucky, the city of Lexington and the state.

The philosophy of the 1-3-1 zone fits in with our philosophy of basketball. The 1-3-1 is aggressive, creates action, and is exciting. Our theory for the 1-3-1 came from Chuck Noll of Virginia. We are constantly adjusting and experimenting with the zone. I like it because it also pinpoints areas of responsibility for each player.

Here are our rules for playing this defense. Number 1, the guard's ob is to keep the ball out of the middle (Figure 21.10). Push the ball to the side. How he plays a two-guard front depends on what he has to do to keep the ball out of the middle. The Number 1 man tries to push the ball to the side of our best trapper. Number 1 traps with the wing man on the strong side even with the top of the key extended to the sideline. If the ball is below him, Number 1 plays between the ball and the middle of the free-throw line.

Our players are numbered clockwise (Figure 21.11). The wing man on the left is Number 2 and his job is to play between the ball and anyone behind him on the baseline. His second rule is to stop penetration at the top of the key extended. He also traps in the corner with Number 3 from the second hash mark on down to the baseline. When the ball is away from him, he plays between the ball and the opposite corner.

Number 3 is the baseline man and his job is to cover corner-to-corner. He plays the ball in both corners. He traps with Numbers 2 and 4 in the corner. He stays in the lane until the ball is on the way to the man in the corner. He doesn't leave the baseline. Number 4's rules are the same as Number 2's. Number 5 plays between the ball and the basket wherever the ball is on the floor, fronting any man in his area.

The 1-3-1 is very difficult to play. There's no time to rest. Any time you rest, you're going to get beat. It is very hard for Number 3 to cover corner-to-corner, but we insist on it.

Let's review the rules again. Number 1 can go out as far as he wants to stop the dribble in his area. He plays the point according to his personality. A 6'5" man plays it a lot differently than someone 5'8". The shorter point man couldn't trap as easily, so he would sag off to the weak side and cut off the passing lane there. We want our point man to play according to what he does best. His solo objective is to keep the ball out of the middle. He traps with Number 2 or Number 4 on anything below the top of the key

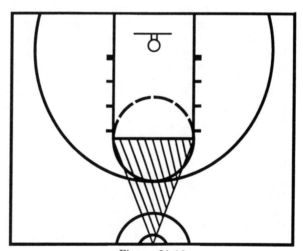

Figure 21.10

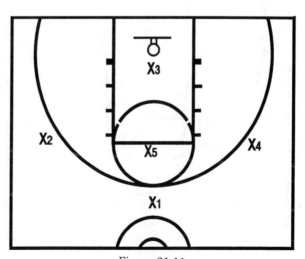

Figure 21.11

extended down to the second hash mark. If a dribbler picks up the ball above the top of the key, the point immediately falls off and plays the passing lane.

Number 2 wants the initial pass over him to be a lob pass so he can have that extra step to recover. He would take the ball man-for-man, if it is dribbled into his area. This area consists of the second hash mark to the top of the key. Then Number 2 is in a man-for-man coverage. He forces the ball to the outside. Again, these rules apply to Number 4 as well.

Number 3's area is from below the second hash mark to the baseline. He influences the ball away from the baseline to the middle. Baseline screens on the baseline are problems. He must anticipate and adjust to the screen. He has about three passes to get from corner to corner. The key is for him to leave while the first pass is in the air. If he waits until the first pass is completed, he won't cover corner-to-corner.

The Number 5 position is the simplest position to play. This player just stays between the ball and the basket adjusting to any man in his area. He must deny the ball three feet out from the sides of the lane and the middle of the free-throw lane. In adjusting to a man in his area, Number 5 doesn't move off the line between the ball and the basket farther than he can reach. His reach determines how far he can stray from the line. Number 5 stops penetration if the opponent splits Numbers 1 and 2. In the low post area, he denies the low post as long as he doesn't have to go more than three feet from the lane.

Here are some adjustments we make with our 1-3-1. We can trap only in the corner; we can trap just one guard; we can match up; we can trap one side of the floor. Adjusting the role of one player doesn't alter

the play of the other four. The biggest change we make is not trapping in the deep corner. An offense can hurt us with a diagonal pass back out (Figure 21.12). They would set a baseline pick on Number 4 and set up the baseline jumper once the ball is rotated over. We'd adjust by having Number 2 play the high post area instead of trapping in the corner. This would free Number 1 to take away the diagonal pass back out.

We've had to move our zone five feet farther out to take away a diagonal pass from a big guard to a power forward underneath (Figure 21.13). Against a team that likes to put their shooter in the dead corner, we'll put a bigger man at the Number 3 spot. Number 3 will put a lot of pressure on the shooter trying to take away the shot. The weakest areas of the 1-3-1 are the guard spots and the corner (Figure 21.14). Against a great shooting guard, we'll set up in a 1-3-1 and match up. We'll show a 1-3-1 and switch to a 2-3 by dropping Number 5 down and sliding Number 4 up to a guard (Figure 21.15). Against a spread, we match up by letting Number 2 take the ball and Number 1 drop off on the guard (Figure 21.16). Numbers 3 and 4 adjust and Number 5 sinks.

We have a move called the "panic." We want to create the panic as often as possible in a game. The panic occurs when Numbers 1 and 2 create a double-team and the man with the ball pivots away from his teammates. When this happens we immediately shoot the gap with Numbers 3 and 4 (Figure 21.17). This leaves a whole side of the court unguarded (Figure 21.18). Number 5 can often pick off the pass to the opposite guard as he comes to get the ball (Figure 21.19).

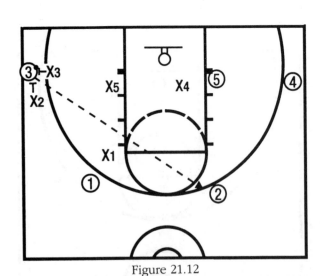

Figure 21.12

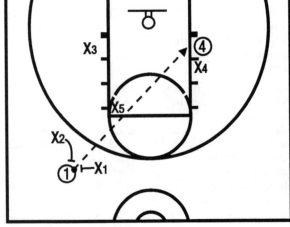

Figure 21.13

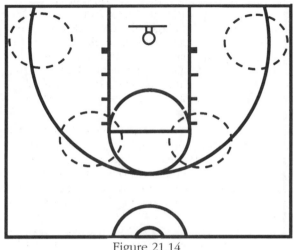

Figure 21.14

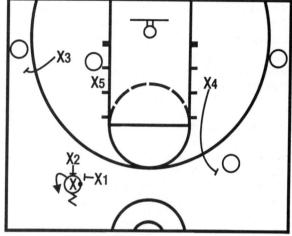

Figure 21.17

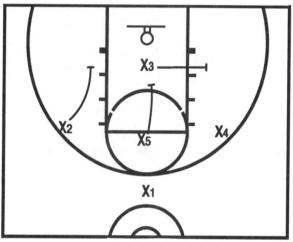

Figure 21.15

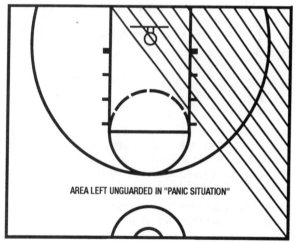

AREA LEFT UNGUARDED IN "PANIC SITUATION"

Figure 21.18

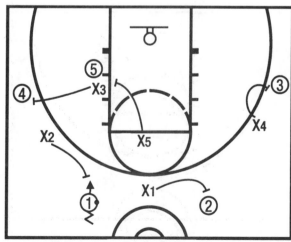

Figure 21.16

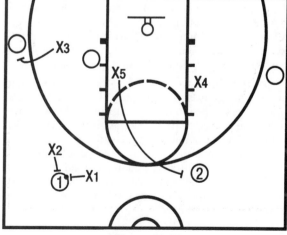

Figure 21.19

Rebounding is very difficult out of the 1-3-1 especially on shots taken from the corner and wings. We stress that all five men to crash the boards. We do send Number 1 to the opposite block and this has helped.

We spend 90 percent of our defensive practice working on man-to-man. There have been games and even seasons in which we didn't play any zone. By spending so little time on the zone, we play it better. We don't want our players to develop a dull attitude toward the 1-3-1. We work with an all-out aggressive attitude when we drill on the 1-3-1. I never start the game planning to play the 1-3-1 for the entire 40 minutes, and we use the 1-3-1 to change the tempo of the game. Again, it's a very aggressive defense that blends in well with our basketball philosophy.

Figure 21.20

ZONE DEFENSES

Marv Harshman

The primary reason we play zone defense is that we think it can change the tempo of the game. We might also play zone if we have foul trouble, if our players are fatigued, or if we are mismatched for quickness in some areas.

In our defensive play for a 2-3 zone, we want to deny the ball in the shaded area. We position our center to play the shaded area. When we have very big centers, unless the offense was in the low post area, we side play the post, rather than front.

If the ball is above the free-throw line extended, we have our guard defend that area. If the ball is below the free-throw line extended, our baseline player defends. If the high post receives the pass, we have our center come up and play man-to-man defense (Figure 21.20).

We play X1 and X2 to the inside. That is, we are protecting the middle. On a pass to the wing, X2 drop-steps first and then attacks to threaten. The best position we want to give up is the foul line extended. X2 does not run immediately toward the ball. As X2 leaves to attack, our center X4 has time to protect a pass to a possible slide by the high post (Figure 21.21).

If we are behind, we try to force the ball into certain areas. Our guards will pressure the ball more and our centers will side the post up high. We want the ball to be passed to the corner, where we will go for a trap. X5 will not come out too quickly. X2 attempts to seal O2 from above so that he can double-team. If there is another offensive guard, our off-guard will challenge him. X3, our weak side, comes to help-side low. Our rule is to deny the three closest people to the ball (Figure 21.22).

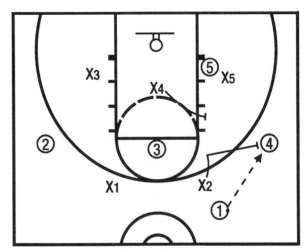

Figure 21.21

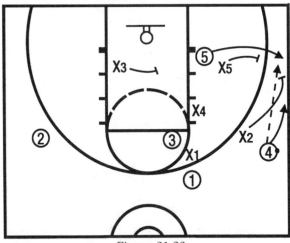

Figure 21.22

If X5 leaves, X4 must come over to protect the lane area. We are giving up a long pass to O2, hoping for a deflection or interception. Another type of zone we run is "gamble." We do not trap here. Our man plays the ball very hard. Everyone else fronts in order to invite the long pass. When we play gamble, the man who goes after the pass is then committed to go down court.

The two adjacent players closest to where the ball is going know our player is going for the pass. If he subsequently gets a hand on the pass or deflects it somehow, those two know they will probably get the ball. The deflector will be going down court for a pass and layup. We have been able to score a lot of times from this gamble defense.

The zone defenses we run are very simple and that is the way we teach. Our players know they must learn to "just adjust" by determining the position of the ball and the degree of threat of scoring.

Furthermore, rebounding position in a zone defense is difficult due to the overload. One defensive man must often rebound against two offensive players in his zone. We tell our players they must seal the gaps until we get the basketball.

3-2 DEFENSE ZONE SLIDES

Don Casey

As a rule, our 3-2 zone is a pure zone. The only time we will change is when we want to match up. This we will do on occasion when the offense shows a two-man front to combat our formations. Our basic alignment is shown in Figure 21.23.

We divide the court into areas and give definite responsibilities to our players in relation to the ball. As the ball is brought up the court, we will position the point man in line with the basket at the top of the free-throw circle. The back line men are roughly three feet up from the basket with their inside feet on the free throw lane. Basically, this is the starting position, but all five will move together with each movement of the ball. The responsibilities of each position follow.

Point man (Figure 21.24):

1. Plays the ball in his lane.

2. Covers the side high post when the ball is at the wing.

3. Double-teams high post when the ball goes there.

4. Flares opposite when ball side high post.

5. Rebounds the middle.

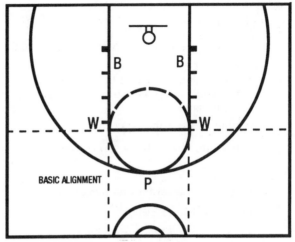

Figure 21.23

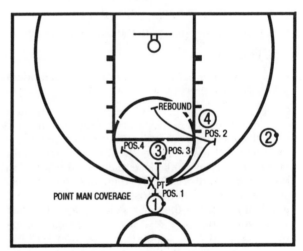

Figure 21.24

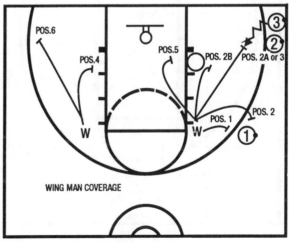

Figure 21.25

Wing man (Figure 21.25):

1. Plays the ball in his lane.

2. Blocks the pass out when the the ball is in the corner.

    a. Can double man in the corner.

    b. Blocks the pass to the post instead of the lane.

3. Doubles drive from the corner.

4. Flares when the ball goes to the high post.

5. Rebounds off side.

6. May cover the corner on emergencies.

Back line men (Figure 21.26):

1. Straddle the line, lining up as high as the defense will allow. Possibilities of the lob pass and rebounds determine exact location.

2. Assume the cheat position in anticipation of next pass or slide.

3. Cover corner man with the ball in that position.

4. Front man in the low post.

5. Cover the high post man or move to tandem defensive position.

Once we feel our players are familiar with their responsibilities and understand the individual moves, we will move into our unit drill for team defensive coordination (see Figure 21.27). We take eight offensive players and place them in the position shown in Figure 21.27. We then drill our players against all and any of the possibilities that might arise in a ball game. For the first week we do not permit any cross-court passes. After a week we might permit the cross-court pass, depending upon how well our players have mastered the various defensive slides.

COMBINATION DEFENSES

FREAK DEFENSE

Dale Brown

Back when I coached a Catholic high school of about 400 students, we had to play a lot of large public schools, and I quickly realized that we weren't going to hack it on defense.

I knew we'd have to do something different. Because of my aggressive nature, I felt the answer lay in pressure. "We'll press them the whole game," I told the squad. "We'll overplay and bump them, and when a rebound goes up we'll do this and do that and..."

It didn't work because our 5'9" guy was bumping their 6'3" guy, and by the end of the 32-minute high school game, that 6'3" guy was getting to our 5'9" guy. Plus the opponents always knew what we were doing.

And so we had to change our philosophy. The new approach would be a tough, carefully planned match-up zone. The match-up made a lot of sense and looked great on paper. But it didn't work either. The offense knew what we were going to do every time they came down the floor.

We didn't have to be Rhodes scholars to realize we had to rethink our defense. We had to come up with something that would stymie the offense – blunt some of their talent and make them wonder, "What's going on around here?"

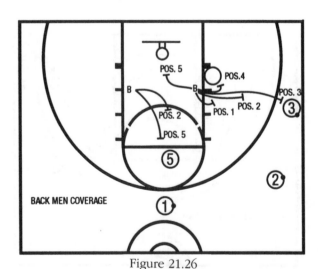

Figure 21.26

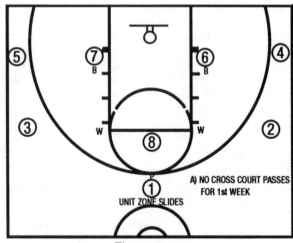

Figure 21.27

And that's when we came up with the "freak" defense – a defense that combines the best of defensive worlds: Man-to-man, straight zone, and the match-up or change-up. That, we thought, would really confuse the offense.

Actually, it was not earth-shattering. But it worked, and I think it is well worth trying, especially by high school coaches looking for an equalizer against superior talent.

We start by lining up in a 1-2-2, because that is the easiest alignment from which to shift. We feel that we can do more from it than from a 1-3-1, 2-3, 2-1-2, or any other kind of match-up (see Figure 21.28).

We are now ready to launch our "single clue" defense, which is triggered by the entry pass. Any time the entry pass is made to the right side of the court, we play our 1-2-2 zone defense (see Figure 21.29).

If the entry pass goes to the left side, we play straight man-to-man (see Figure 21.30).

If the entry pass goes down the middle of the court, we play a 1-3-1 zone (see Figure 21.31).

Now this is simple enough. Perhaps you have already done it. But the constant changing of defenses helps offset talent and nullify outstanding players.

The problem arises when you come up against a thinking coach. He's going to spot what you're doing after awhile, and he's going to say, "That guy on the other bench thinks he's smart. Every time we make a pass to the right side, he's going to play a 1-2-2 zone. When we go to the left, he's going to play man-to-man, and when we go down the middle, he's going to play 1-3-1. We want them to play us man-to-man, so let's enter on the left side every time."

Now, it's our turn to use our gray matter. We know man-to-man is not our best defense, so we have to change something. We counter with what we call

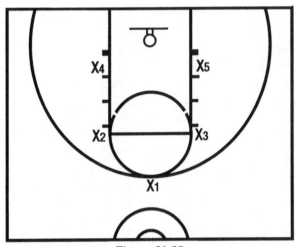

Figure 21.28

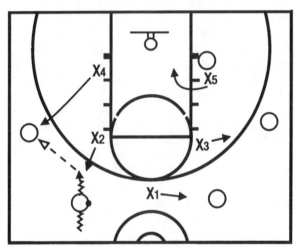

Figure 21.30

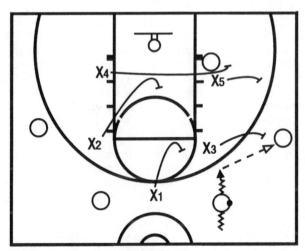

Figure 21.29

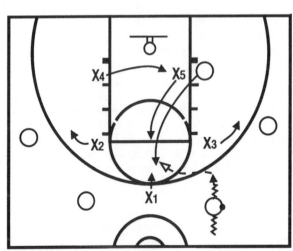

Figure 21.31

our "single clue flip-flop." First, we immediately call a time-out and tell our team that we're going to change clues: When the ball goes into the right side, we're going to play man (instead of 1-2-2 zone). When the entry pass goes down the middle, we're going to play a 1-2-2 zone (instead of 1-3-1), and when the ball goes to the left, we're going to play a 1-3-1 zone (instead of man-to-man).

In short, we flip-flop our clues (after the timeout). The defense can no longer come down and enter our left side to exploit the weakest of our three defenses (man to man). They will now find a zone awaiting them.

If you have the talent, you may seldom find it necessary to use a freak defense for special occasions: To play with the offense, fluster them at the outset, to change the momentum of the game, help out when you're in foul trouble, and so on.

I remember the first time we used it. We had played man-to-man the whole game and had piled up a good lead. Then the opponents started making a run. They cut our lead to four. I called timeout and instructed our kids to run the freak defense.

All of a sudden the opponents couldn't fast break anymore, and we scored 14 uncontested points to forge 18 points ahead. It was the sudden change in defensive style that did it.

Now, let us suppose the opponents catch on to what we're doing or we want to switch on them for some other reason. At halftime we know the opposing coach is going to replay the first half and get his team ready for our single clue freak defense.

We can flip-flop on them, if we choose. Or we can run our "double clue" at them, especially if they have two guards (Numbers 10 and 11) who are bringing the ball over the center line. The double clue can ruin all of their meticulous preparation for the second half.

We tell our team that when Number 11 dribbles the ball across, we will maintain our single clue 1-2-2 zone on entry to the right side, man-to-man on entry to the left side, and 1-3-1 zone on the left side, and 1-2-2 zone in the middle.

Sounds simple, right? It is simple, but it can be very confusing to the offense. If I were coaching in high school today and I had inferior talent, I'd use the freak defense as my primary defense. It does everything. You can fall back into a 1-2-2 zone and use it against teams that slow it up, and you can also use it with help defense and pressure defense. I think it's the greatest defensive equalizer in the game.

THE TRIANGLE AND TWO DEFENSE
Bill Jones

As a coach, what is your defensive philosophy? Are you locked into one defense? Do you play zones or man-to-man? For years coaches have heard, "Teach one defense and perfect it." When we would play a team that exploited our weakness or a team that ran a particular offense that we could not stop, I'd reconcile with "They simply had better players," when in fact I had not prepared our players for all the things they would encounter.

At our level of competition we sometimes have to recruit and coach some players who have deficiencies. Most of the time the deficiencies are in the area of man-to-man defense. We should not try to fool ourselves into believing we can turn every player into a great man-to-man defensive player. That is why we installed a combination defense known as the triangle and two.

The Advantages of the Triangle and Two

As mentioned above, not every player can be a great man-to-man defensive player. We feel as though we can "hide" two or even three below average man-to-man players when using this defense. Another advantage is that this defense causes confusion to the opponent's offense. We often will show a zone set or actually line up in a man-to-man set but really be in a triangle and two. The triangle defense is an excellent defense against a team that has two great scorers and three average players. After your man-to-man zone principles have been installed, the triangle is easy to teach. Finally, it causes your opponents to use extra practice time in order to prepare their offensive strategy.

Because the triangle and two requires the players to execute both zone and man-to-man principles, we install this defense after our man-to-man and zone defenses have been taught. Our procedure for teaching this defense involves chalkboard talks and walking through the coverages and responsibilities on the floor. This method of teaching allows us to explain and show each player what we are trying to accomplish.

The three players that form the triangle have basically the same responsibilities and coverages as they have in our zone defense. They must know their starting positions and recognize who is being guarded by our two man-to-man players. It is very important that a player in the triangle does not guard a player who is being defended by our man-to-man players. As in any defense, talking and helping out are of the utmost importance.

Responsibilities of the Number 3 Man

The Number 3 man forms the top of the triangle. This player must be an aggressive, hard-working player who takes great pride in his defensive work. He is responsible for every man above the second hash mark. If there are two players out front, then he will split them. Every time the ball goes to the corner, Number 3 must rotate and front the post. As the ball returns to the head of the circle, he must make his return slide to his original starting position just as quick as his initial slide. Number 3 cannot allow penetration at the top of the key. This is a tough position to play, so it requires a real worker (see Figure 21.32).

Responsibilities of the Number 4 and Number 5 Men

The Number 4 and Number 5 men form the baseline

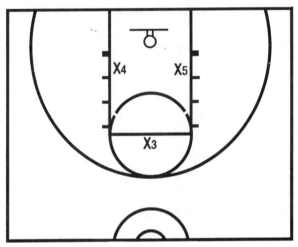

Figure 21.32

defense of the triangle. They cover the ball hard to the corner. These players allow no baseline drives or inside cuts in the post area. If the ball is away from a baseline player, he is weak-side. We teach our players to keep their butts to the basket. This allows them to help Number 3 on the high man at the free-throw line area. He helps only until Number 3 can recover. In the help-side position he will go higher than the first hash mark below the free-throw line. All return slides must be as quick as the initial slides. Again, it is very important that the players talk and help out (see Figure 21.33).

Responsibilities of the Number 1 and Number 2 Men

1. Deny: Never allow your man to handle the ball – it's bench time if he does. Face guard or any other tactics. Help: Stay one step off the lane – use man-to-man principles.

2. Allow no penetration.

3. Once your man has the ball, attack him according to the scouting report – shooting range, driver, set shooter, etc.

So you can actually play several combinations with the Number 1 and Number 2 men to alter the look of the triangle-two: Number 2 deny, Number 2 help, Number 1 deny, Number 1 help, play Number 1 deny, float Number 1.

Ideas to Help

1. Always scout your opponent.
   a. Decide who to deny, help, how to play them.
   b. When subs occur, will that change coverage?
   c. Get shooting percentages if available.

2. Use OER system – invaluable at key points in the game to change defenses.

3. Don't be afraid to use the triangle. Players love it. They love to confuse the opponent.

4. Change men being guarded by Number 1 and Number 2 if someone else starts hurting you more.

5. You can guard a larger player with Number 1 or Number 2, especially if he is a post player, because he'll always have triangle help.

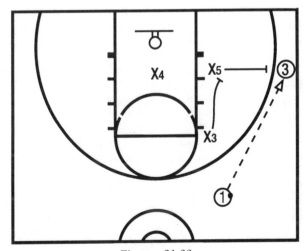

Figure 21.33

MATCH-UP DEFENSE

COMBINATION MATCH-UP DEFENSE

Clarence Gaines

I try to get the match-up over to my staff and our youngsters in my own way. I just call it "understanding." One of my most talented teams ended up with a mediocre record because there wasn't enough communication and understanding between all persons concerned.

The understanding that must be considered is between players and coaches. I think with all the broad coverage that is given basketball teams by the media, a lot of jealousies exist. If an athlete's performance merits television, radio, and newspaper coverage, or any other plaudits, then he deserves it. But it is the coach's responsibility to see that this publicity does not interfere with his program, and that ill feelings among the players or the faculty and staff do not result. We have a monumental task to perform in the development of a complete person. Opportunities only come to those who are prepared.

We have used the match-up zone very successfully for the last eight or 10 years. I call our zone "a point and something."

The first thing I try to get through to every player is that at one time or another in our defense, everybody's going to be the point man. We line up every time in 1-2-2. The players are numbered 1 through 5 (Figure 21.34). Now if anybody is dumb enough to come down without movement or to put a man in the bucket, we stay in this zone basically. We get in a basketball position; we don't do a lot of arm-waving and that sort of thing. We're always in a basketball position to try to go someplace.

If you look at this thing from a theoretical standpoint, when the ball is out front, we want Number 1 to have a man-to-man attitude, an almost pressure attitude, because we do not want him to allow the ballhandler, their one guard, to have an easy pass. Therefore, I come out with a triangle (Figure 21.35). Now, when the ball is rotated, I'm going to end up with a triangle and a square.

We're not like most coaches, who hold up cards or call out numbers to call their plays. We don't have any plays. We have four offensive sets, and we try to do what we can according to what the defense does. There's no need fighting it, no need fighting a defense at all. When the ball is rotated to Number 2's territory, or area, our players move (Figure 21.36). Let them play with it; you'll be surprised how players discover new areas where they actually should be, or learn

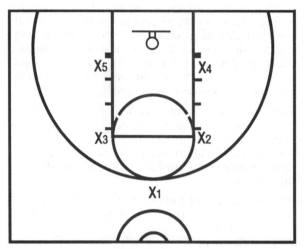

Figure 21.34

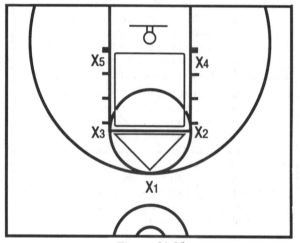

Figure 21.35

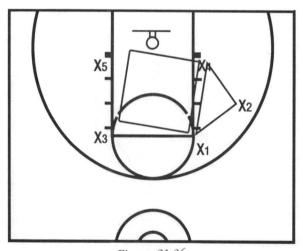

Figure 21.36

how to close off the passing lanes when you ask them to change their attitude toward it and let them do the drawing on the board.

What kinds of drills actually go with this sort of thing? The first thing we try to get our guys to understand is the conditioning process. They've got to learn to play a man full-court. For conditioning purposes, we teach the full-court defense and full-court offense before we go into any patterns and we have the guys dribble one-on-one full-court.

We have a few basic rules that we follow in the match-up. It's really not a match-up zone at all, but rather combination defenses, utilizing in some areas zone principles and man-to-man principles, and they have to be abandoned according to the situation that the offense presents.

If we get caught in a transition situation, Number 1, who is 5'11", tries to contain and hold off. During our practice sessions, everybody plays everybody else's spot so they will know exactly what their responsibilities are.

The other thing that bothers us in this setup is that we run across a lot of stack offenses. The rule that we follow is: They don't place a man in the post, they place a man on the side. Then we are in a 1-3-1 zone. We don't have a kid cover both baselines like they do in some of the zones.

We don't want them to get the ball into the middle. We're going to pressure and see that it's as hard as possible for them to do this. Ninety percent of the time when the ball gets inside, it goes to the floor and we drill against it. We have one thing we do in practice: Every time the ball goes on the floor, we clobber the guy in the middle who puts it on the floor and it is no foul. After awhile when a player gets all the bruises, he figures out that the coach wants rapid ball movement.

Another rule we have in the match-up zone is that when you turn around and get a whole bunch of movement on us, because of the shot clock we play in our league, we don't have to play defense for three or four minutes. We teach the players to go hell-for-leather for 27 seconds and you get a bad shot. All I've got to get these players to understand is that when they get the ball, they've got to shoot it in 30 seconds. I'll tell them to see if they can't bust a gut and get everybody dealing with this sort of thing, and then it's pretty easy to get the 30 seconds over with.

Another rule is that if the ball is dribbled to the corner, the moment the other team puts the ball on the floor three times our defender knows he is in man-to-man defense and follows his man (Figure 21.37). He takes the man until the series is over. When is the series over? When they take a shot.

Remember, we never plan to widen out our triangle and square too much, because we don't want the offense to find an easy way to get the ball into the middle.

MATCH-UP ZONE

Bill Green

Rules of the Match-up Zone

The basic alignment out of a 2-1-2 with players facing away for right and left direction:

X1 – the point man or man on the right side.

X2 – the takes the first man to the left of X1.

X3 – the first man to the right of X1.

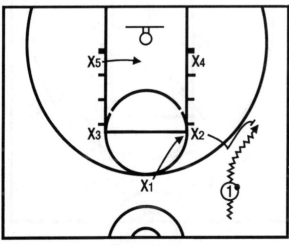

Figure 21.37

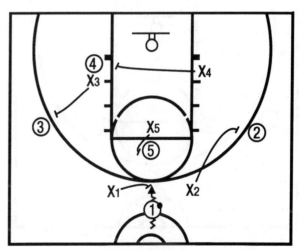

Figure 21.38

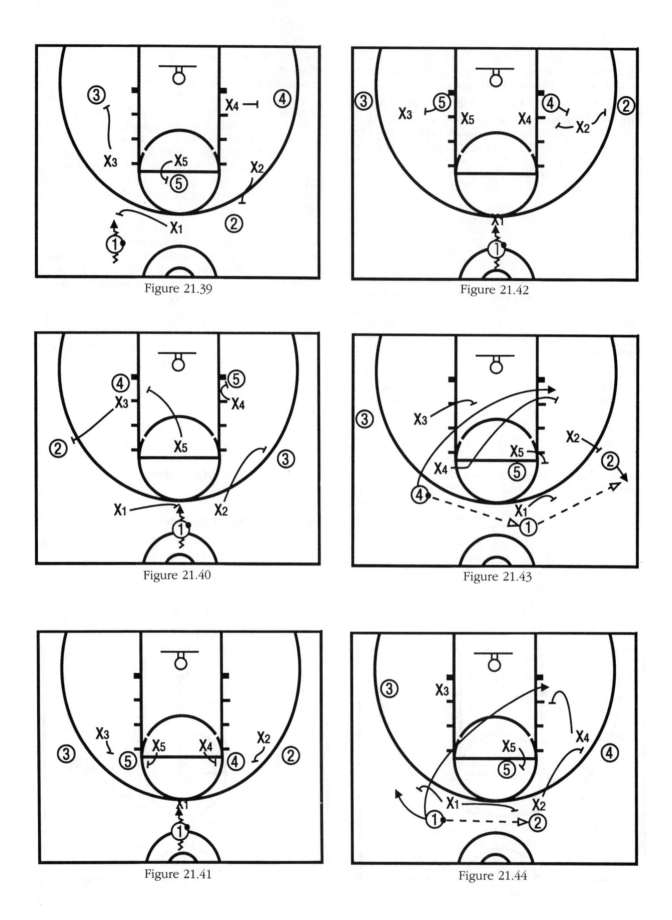

Figure 21.39

Figure 21.42

Figure 21.40

Figure 21.43

Figure 21.41

Figure 21.44

X4 – the rover, second man right or left of X1.

X5 – takes the opponent's center man-for-man. If no center, take the man on the right low in 1-2-2, and in the 1-4 pattern the man on the right high.

Figure 21.38 illustrates match-up rules from 2-1-2. Number X1 will defend the opponent's point guard and the other four players will adjust.

Figure 21.39 illustrates match-up rules from 1-3-1. Player X1's basic rule would be to guard the point guard or the man on the right side with or without the ball against the two guard front.

Figure 21.40 illustrates the match-up 1-2-2. No center from 2-1-2. X1 rotates up to take the point, X2 is the first man left, X3 the first man right. With no center, X5 will take man on right high or low. X4 exception rule, rover will take the second man to the left of X1 since X5 has the second man to the right.

Figure 21.41 illustrates the match-up 1-4 versus high 1-4 zone set. Force the first pass to the wing by bringing X2 and X3 in to prevent the pass into the middle. Then adjust with the offense into their 1-2-2 or 1-3-1 options.

Figure 21.42 illustrates the match-up zone versus low 1-4 offense. Players X2 and X3 should play up higher so that they can't be screened by the inside low post players. We don't think that we will get beat one-on-one with their point guard. Anytime that they flash a player up, we must cover them man-for-man. If the offensive players cross (with or without the ball) we simply switch.

Figure 21.43 illustrates the rover. This is adjustment against a special player who can shoot from both the outside and baseline. The rover will go with the flasher and we are right back into our regular match-up. We can do anything we want with our defense and we do not have any points of decision.

Figure 21.44 illustrates the key to teaching the match-up on teams that rotate players. Number X1 will go with the player staying outside, but if he cuts through X1 can switch to the ball, and the other four players will adjust by the matchup rules.

Reason for the Match-up Zone

This defense will dictate the offense making them play what you want them to play. Sometimes, we might be man-for-man on the ball side and zone away. Against the motion offense, the more motion they give us, the more zone offense they show us, the more active we become since we basically play one-on-one.

Our match-up started from the football umbrella defense and a monster. Instead of the monster, we play rover with all players adjusting to the X1 guard. If X1 is small, we can keep him outside.

MATCH-UP PRESS
Rick Pitino

Introduction

The objective of matching up in a full-court pressure situation is to trap the uncontrolled dribbler, thus playing the offense out of their strong areas.

The match-up press allowed Boston University to cause an average of 23 turnovers per game for a period of five years. By trapping only at opportune times, the defense stays clear of giving up high-percentage shots. Furthermore, because we only trap the uncontrolled dribbler, the trap seems to occur randomly. As a result, scouting the press may prove frustrating.

The press is designed to match man-for-man on all movement of the ball, never allowing one man to force two defenders to play him in a controlled situation.

For the press to prove effective, maximum intensity is required. In fact, even the involvement of the bench is vital. Playing nine people is the key to obtaining maximum effort. Non-athletes or weak defenders cannot discourage use of this match-up press. A mistake will not cost you a basket in the backcourt area.

The System of Bricks and Saves

The system of bricks and saves has three major objectives:

1. To help achieve maximum intensity and effort.

2. To condition and reward positive actions.

3. To condition against mistakes resulting from lack of concentration.

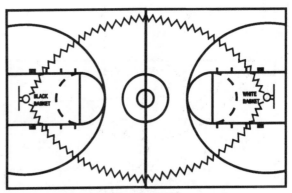

Figure 21.45

How does the system work? At any time during practice a coach may call out a "save" for a player who performs a positive action. The coach may also call out a "brick" for a player who fails to exert maximum effort or makes a mistake resulting from poor concentration. (A partial list of ways to get bricks or saves follows.) A manager keeps track of the number of bricks and saves each player accumulates. At the end of the practice the manager determines the total number of bricks and saves for each player. This is accomplished by figuring the difference between bricks and saves. If a player has more bricks than saves, his composite score is positive.

What if a player has a negative score at the end of practice? For every brick not cancelled by a save, the player must perform the task shown in Figure 21.45.

1. Start on the block at the white basket.

2. Dribble with the left hand wide to the black basket for a left-handed layup.

3. Rebound the layup and then dribble with the left hand lane wide to the white basket for a left-handed layup.

4. The player must make six layups in 35 seconds (40 seconds for centers).

    a. If the player successfully completes the task, a brick is erased.
    b. If the player fails to complete the task, the brick stays.

5. This drill may also be assigned to players from a losing team in a competitive drill or situation.

The players accumulate bricks and saves for 10 days, with the composite score of the last practice always carrying over to the next practice. At the end of the 10 days, all players with more bricks than saves keep their bricks, while players with more saves than bricks become even.

We are confident that by emphasizing points like deflections, tipping the ball from behind a dribbler, and charges, this system is an important factor in the ultimate success of our match-up press. Other

examples of ways to accumulate saves and bricks might include stealing, diving for loose balls, missing a layup, not blocking out, reaching fouls, and fouling the jump shooter.

Press Buildup

A. One-on-One (see Figure 21.46)

1. A coach or player (i.e., Number 5) takes the ball out of bounds under the black basket (offense going toward the white basket).

2. X1 3/4 denies Number 1 as Number 1 works to get open (Number 1 must get open in Area A below the foul line). Trying for the five-second count.

3. After Number 5 inbounds to Number 1, Number 1 tries to beat X1 and score at the white basket.

4. Do the same thing going from the white basket to the black basket and staying within Area C.

5. Getting open versus denial: As we build our press, we also work on offensive fundamentals. For instance, when we go one-on-one full-court, we concentrate on moves such as the following to get open:

    a. Straight slash
    b. Stationary hook
    c. Hook reverse
    d. V-cut to the ball

6. Defensive teaching points

    a. Deny the inbounds pass to get the five-second count.
    b. Once the ball is inbounded, do not force the offensive player to the sideline or middle. Hands should be above the shoulders and bent at the elbows.
    c. Ball on offensive player's right-hand side of floor – the defender should have his right foot up. Ball on offensive players' left-hand side of floor – the defender should have his left foot up.

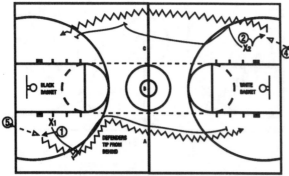

Figure 21.46

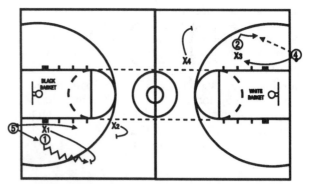

Figure 21.47

d. Defense beat:
(1) If the dribbler beats the defender toward the sideline, the defender must run and beat the man to the spot.
(2) If the dribbler beats the defender toward the middle, the defender should run behind the ball and try to tip it. Tipping the ball from behind is the key to playing the middle dribble.

7. Discourage spin dribble because:

   a. Ballhandling is a sign of weakness.
   b. It makes you vulnerable to traps and run and jumps.

B. Two-on-Two

1. Number 5 takes the ball out of bounds under the basket, with the offense going toward the white basket (Figure 21.47).

2. X1 3/4 denies Number 1 as Number 1 works to get open (in area A).

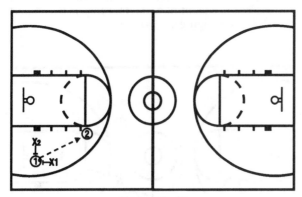

Figure 21.48

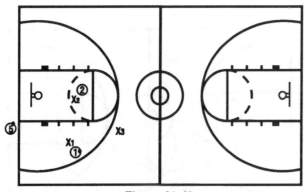

Figure 21.49

3. X2 plays center field (we strongly stress that off the ball, the defender must PLAY BALL, SEE MAN).

4. Once the ball is inbounds, we play two-on-two full-court.

   a. The defender on the ball works hard not to be beat.
   b. The defender off the ball goes back far enough to see his man, but plays ball.

5. Whenever the defender on the ball is beat and the dribbler is in an uncontrolled state, we trap the dribbler.

6. Defensive fundamentals of trapping:

   a. The two defenders should form a "T" with their feet so that the offensive player cannot step through and split the trap.
   b. As the offensive player pivots, the defenders must move to "stay on the ball."
   c. The defenders constantly work to deflect the ball.
   d. As the defenders work to deflect, they must stay in their own plane and not foul.

7. Offensive fundamentals of trapping:

   a. Try to avoid a trap by using a back dribble and then a cross-over to change direction.
   b. Avoid the spin dribble, because it will invite blind-side trapping.
   c. Pivot actively.
   d. Take on one defender or try to split the trap.
   e. Fake high to pass low. Fake low to pass high.
   f. The teammate of the player being trapped cuts to the gap that splits the trap (see Figure 21.48).

8. After the offense passes out of the trap, the two defenders immediately sprint out of the trap. Then depending on what hand the dribbler is dribbling with, one of the two defenders will try to tip from behind.

9. Clearout situation: Suppose Number 5 inbounds to Number 1 and then clears out. Our rule is that X2 must go back far enough to see his man. Therefore, if X1 is beat, X2 may be too far back to trap. In this case, X1 will tip from behind and X2 will play like a "shortstop."

C. Three-on-Three (see Figure 21.49)

1. Number 5 takes ball out of bounds under the black basket (offense going toward the white basket).

2. X1 and X2 3/4 deny. X3 plays "centerfield" (try for five-second count).

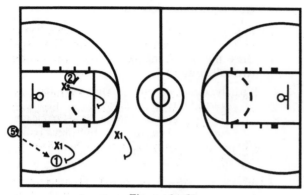

Figure 21.50

3. X1 plays ball and tries not to get beat (see Figure 21.50).

4. X2 and X3 see the man, play ball (discourage any pass, but play ball, see Figure 21.51).

Case A: Number 1 goes by X1 with uncontrolled dribble sideline.

a. Trap
   (1) X1 and X3 trap the ball (see Figure 21.52).
   (2) X2 sprints back, splits the trap, and plays ball.

b. Ball passed out of trap:
   (1) The trapper the ball is passed over or around sprints out of the trap and tries to tip from behind.
   (2) The other trapper sprints out of the trap and back toward the strong side.
   (3) The third defender sprints back toward the middle (Figure 21.53).

5. Case B: Number 1 goes by X1 with uncontrolled dribble middle. It's the same principles as in Case A except now the first trap is by X1 and X2 (see Figure 21.54).

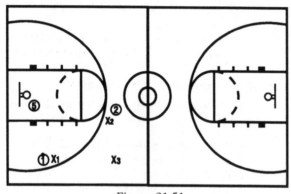

Figure 21.51

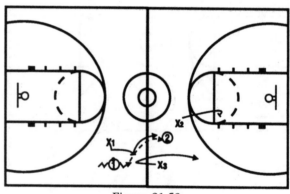

Figure 21.53

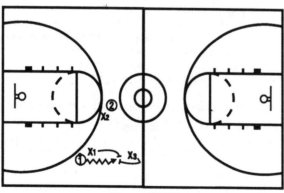

Figure 21.52

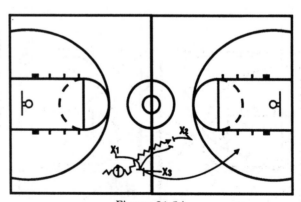

Figure 21.54

6. Special Note: The principle of the press applies at all levels of the floor.

E. Five-on-Five (see Figure 21.55)

This is a 2-2-1 press, but it is man-to-man until the ball is inbounded. Then it is 2-2-1 when the ball is on the sideline and 1-3-1 when the ball is in the middle. Example:

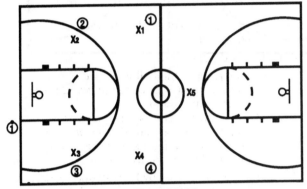

Figure 21.55

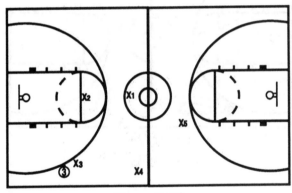

Figure 21.56

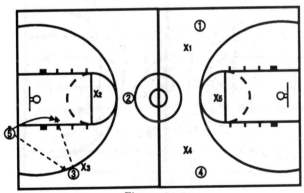

Figure 21.57

1. Try hard for a five-second count.

2. Ball inbounded toward sideline. You are playing hard man-to-man until this point. Now you get into your 2-2 alignment with the center deep (see Figure 21.56).

3. The defender on the ball has his right foot forward, his hands above his shoulders, and he is pushing back.

4. The defender on the ball is not forcing sideline or giving middle.

5. The key is to make sure the man dribbles rather than passes. So, the defensive man is up on the ball hard telling the man to dribble by him.

6. The defender off the ball backs up until he sees someone in his area. Whenever the defender sees someone, he stops. But as he backs up, he is always playing the ball.

7. Ball reversed back to the inbounder (i.e., middle man).

Most teams will come with a man in the middle, a safety valve, a man long, and a man ball-side. They are looking for the reversal (see Figure 21.57).

Four-on-Four (Figures 21.58 and 21.59)

1. General deny areas (try hard for five-second count).

2. The ball is inbounded toward the sideline – Box.

   a. The defender on the ball has his right foot forward, his hands above his shoulders with his elbows bent, and he is pushing back.

   b. The defender on the ball is not forcing sideline or giving middle.

   c. The key is to make sure that the man dribbles rather than passes, so the defender is applying pressure on the ball.

   d. The other defenders form a box. However, they back up until they see someone in their area. Therefore, depending on the spacing of the offensive players, the box is likely to be distorted.

3. The ball is reversed back to the inbounder (see Figures 21.60 and 21.61).

4. The ball is dribbled in uncontrolled state to the sideline – Trap (see Figure 21.62).

5. The ball is dribbled in uncontrolled state to the middle – Trap (see Figure 21.63).

   a. Here is where our press is different. In a normal 2-2-1 you wait and force the man sideline and have him dribble.

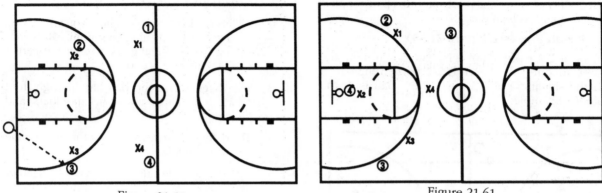

Figure 21.58

Figure 21.61

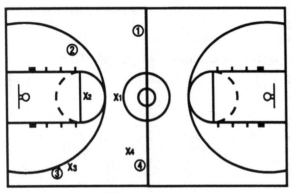

Figure 21.59

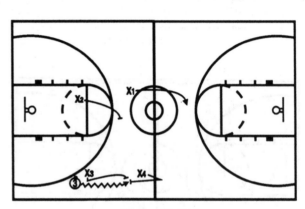

Figure 21.62

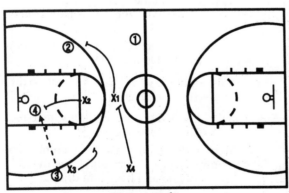

Figure 21.60

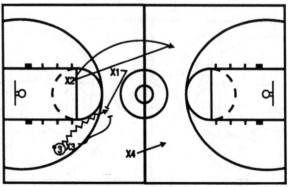

Figure 21.63

6. Because the ball is in the middle of the floor, you go from a 2-2-1 to a 1-3-1 (see Figures 21.64 and 21.65).

   a. When the ball is passed, the man who was guarding the man with the ball drops back.
   b. The man at half court on the ball side goes to the middle.
   c. The man who was opposite plays the right sideline.

7. Why did we go from a 2-2-1 to a 1-3-1 without trapping the ball?

   a. The rule of this press is that you never trap a man under control looking and dribbling.
   b. Never trap the man who catches the ball and is looking up the floor to pass.
   c. You may trap three straight times down the floor and then the next three times

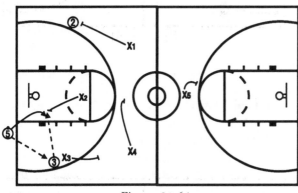

Figure 21.64

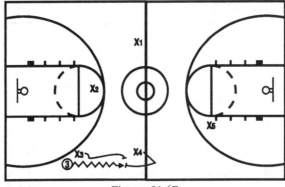

Figure 21.67

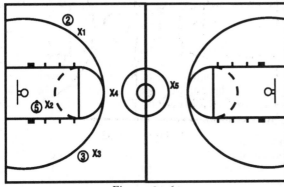

Figure 21.65

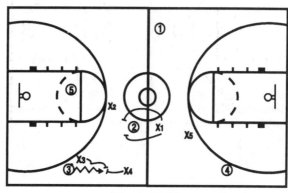

Figure 21.68

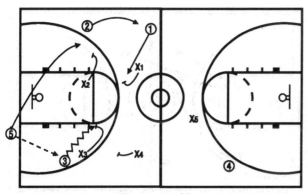

Figure 21.66

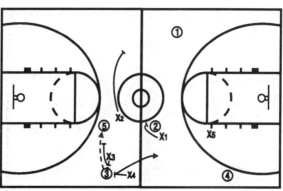

Figure 21.69

you may not trap at all. Therefore, the offense has trouble figuring out the press and getting into a routine. The offense does not get stronger as the game goes on, but gets weaker, because it cannot determine when you are trapping.

    d. The only person we trap is the uncontrolled dribbler.

8. Ball reversed to the Number 5 man. If the player taking the ball out of bounds is the Number 5 man, then after the inbounds pass the ball is reversed back to Number 5, and you stay back. Do not go at Number 5. Stay off the ball, watch the passing lanes, and make the Number 5 man dribble. When Number 5 picks up the ball, you rush him. Everyone else matches up and denies the ball. Most teams will not switch from their 2-2-1 offense even though you are in a 1-3-1.

9. The ball is dribbled to the middle (see Figure 21.66). (The ball was been inbounded and is now being dribbled toward the middle.)

    a. We are in a 2-2-1.

    b. The offense will send the inbounder away, the man opposite would come middle, and the offense would be in a 1-3-1 set against a 2-2-1. But when this happens against this press, your rule is to stay man-to-man. The other guard rotates right. The offside man comes middle and you are in your 1-3-1. (So whether it is a pass or a dribble, you go 1-3-1 when the ball is in the middle.)

Remember: Play the ball, see the man; hands above shoulders, bent elbows.

10. The ball is dribbled sideline (see Figure 21.67).

    a. Most of the time the offense will bring a man ball-side up the sideline.

    b. If X4 cannot see a man as he drops, his rule is to drop only half-court. Even if he stops at half-court, the pass will not be thrown over his head. (Remember,

X3 is on the ball hard with his hands up, not allowing the man to see.)

    c. Because we are on the ball hard, the good ballhandler is going to start to dribble by the man. Here is the rule: Do not allow the man with the ball to go by you with one dribble. He must take two dribbles before he starts to go by the defender. The second dribble is the speed dribble. That is the one where the man puts his head down and does not see the entire floor. That's when we will come up and trap the man.

    d. Here are the rules for the other people: X1 and X2 cover the middle; X5 is at the strong-side elbow, but looking sideline to steal the ball (see Figure 21.68).

11. Pass thrown to safety valve: Figures 21.69 and 21.70.

12. The dribbler beats the man to the middle.

    a. We do not want this to happen!

    b. Case A: Beat middle below the foul line – Trap.

    c. Case B: Beat middle above the foul line – Retreat into 1-3-1 (Figure 21.71).

    (1) Retreat with arms above your shoulders facing the ball.

    (2) The rule of the person who gets beat is to follow the ball and run behind the ball, not the man. As he runs behind the ball he tries to tip it to a teammate and take off in the other direction for a layup. We have the defenders ahead of the dribbler play like shortstops.

The Distortion Concept

Although we say this is a 2-2-1 press when the ball is on the sideline, and a 1-3-1 press when the ball is in the middle, it is also a match-up press. Therefore, depending on the spacing and movement of the offense, these two formations may be distorted.

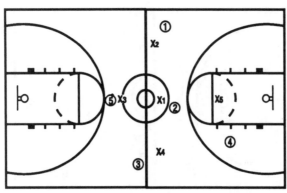

Figure 21.70

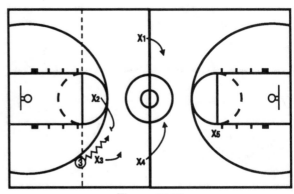

Figure 21.71

SPECIAL SITUATION DEFENSE

EQUALIZING THE STAR

Joe O'Brien

Most coaches realize that if a player is truly an All-American, or a star player on any level, it is not a matter of shutting the player out. The most you could hope for is to neutralize his talents. It is also possible to cut into his efficiency. He may get his stats by the end of the game, but it is hoped that he will have to work a little harder to get them.

Switching defenses helps to control the star player to some extent. We use switching defenses to disrupt the offensive execution. Individually we make an effort never to allow the key player to do what he does best. For example, make a good shooter put the ball on the floor or allow enough room for a great penetrator to take some uncontested jump shots. Get him out of his normal offensive tendencies.

On the offensive end of the floor, we can have an influence on the great player. By playing a running game, we could wear down this great player on the defensive end. Regardless of the type of offense that is used, it is important to make "the star" play defense. Try to run the offense at this great player. Against a great guard you might want to take him inside defensively (post him) to make him work on protecting the basket. You may even want to send the man he is guarding down the floor early on the rebound. The very fact that he is conscious of his man releasing early may hinder his effectiveness at the offensive end of the floor. In the case of a great forward or center, we have gotten the best results by attacking him. Make him play defense every time down the court. You will be amazed how much success can be achieved by making him play the basketball.

In a motion offense, every effort should be made to get the great player involved in the picking and screening action. By keeping him occupied defensively, there is a good possibility that he could become fatigued or get into foul trouble. The key is to make him work!

Against a zone defensive team, we always start the ball away from the great player. In our offensive philosophy, we like to show the defense something on one side and score from the other side. Therefore, even though the ball begins on the opposite side of the great player, the shots more than likely will be taken on the side of the great player. Once again, make him play defense aggressively and not be out there going through the motions to save himself for the offensive end.

In preparing for a season defensively, it is important to have a few defenses in your repertoire so that you are able to switch when the occasion arises. Every time you switch a defense, it should be a positive move. When you are not going well offensively, sometimes it is beneficial to switch your defenses to get the players' minds off the poor execution of your offense. In more cases than not, the team will start to play better offense because of the defensive change.

The basic defense we teach at Assumption College is man-to-man. Normally it takes about three weeks to teach this defense the way we want to play it. It is vital to our overall defensive plan that all players know the man-to-man principles before we teach them any of our other defenses.

Another defense we teach is straight 2-1-2 zone. We use the basic slides but stress certain aspects of this zone defense which will be beneficial when we use variations of this zone in conjunction with our other defenses. For example, in teaching two-and-a-triangle we may tell our back-line players to use the same technique as the back people in a 2-1-2 zone.

When we play a 2-1-2 zone, we try to attack the ball at half court. Our two guards are placed at half court in a tandem position. Our first responsibility is to stop the ball out as close to half court as we possibly can. If the ballhandler decides to dribble, the man who has gone out to pick him up stays with him and plays that side of the zone. If the ballhandler stops and makes a pass, the defensive man in the second position of the tandem follows the pass and stays to play that side of the zone. Once we are into the zone, the one thing we constantly stress is to use the inside hand to play the zone. For example, the guard on the left side of the zone would have his right hand moving and working to take away the passing lanes. This type of hand motion is used as an intimidating move to discourage the pass into the post position.

Another thing we stress in this defense is the V-move (see Figure 22.1). In attacking the 2-1-2 zone, most teams will use an odd front. The first pass will go from a point to a wing. In our 2-1-2 zone, we tell the ball-side guard he must go "through the post." Thus the guard has made his V-move by using his inside hand to the post before picking up the wing with the ball. Once the ball has gone from point to wing, with the guard making the V-move, it's the middle man's job to front the post position. In our zone, the key to success is never to allow a penetrating pass into the middle.

Most zones worry about getting caught with offensive players behind the zone. However, with our zone principles, we tell the players not to be concerned with the people behind the zone. When a player in the zone is caught in a two-on-one situation, a shooter out front and a man underneath the basket, the natural tendency is to fake at the shooter and fall back to protect the basket for a potential layup. In our zone, we tell the defensive man to attack the shooter and rely on our other defensive personnel to do their job. The players off the ball must be able to react to the situation by helping the defensive man who goes after the shooter.

In our run and jump man-to-man defense, we are able to use more players during the game. Our philosophy with this defense is never to run and jump at the weak guard, but always attack the great guard. Along these same lines, we try to double-team the great guard in this defense.

In playing against a star, we often revert to playing some type of crazy defense. If for no other reason, a crazy defense has a tendency to disrupt the offensive continuity. We never play box-and-one or diamond-and-one. These two defenses have not worked well with us because our players never adjust well to the ball when we've tried to use them. We have had the best results when we play our normal zone with someone playing the star man-to-man.

Our favorite crazy defense is two-and-a-triangle (Figure 22.2). It is most effective against a pattern team. We always play the quarterback and the best shooter. This defense is not very effective against two forwards or a forward and a center.

Never use your best two defensive players in playing the quarterback and the star man-to-man in a two-and-a-triangle defense. We use our two worst defensive players on the quarterback and the star.

In denying a guard the ball, we allow him to bring the ball up the court and try to force him to give the ball up to someone else. Once he has passed the ball, we deny the return pass. In denying a good shooting forward the ball, we attempt to frustrate him as he reaches the frontcourt. By disrupting his

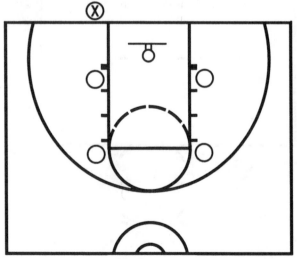

Figure 22.1

concentration through constant harassment, you might be able to take him out of his offensive game. In playing man-to-man in this defense, you never leave your man to help someone else in the triangle. Your responsibility is to play your man continually. The two players playing this man-to-man will not switch if the two offensive players start to pick for each other.

In Figure 22.2, because A and B are playing man-to-man on the quarterback and the star, we must position C, D, and E properly in the triangle. The best defensive player (C) should be used at the point. The best rebounding forward (D) and the center (E) are used in the back line. This triangle must use zone principles. Our rule is you are always somewhere heading somewhere else. Normally you are playing a man and a half.

In attacking this triangle, most offenses would attempt to split the point. We tell our point man to always match to the ball when the ball is out front. The underneath man will come to help out if the point man is being split. The weak-side man (normally your best rebounder) goes underneath to protect the basket. At this stage of the defense, we now have an inverted triangle. During this inversion the point man will always remain the point man.

If A or B should be beaten by the quarterback or the star, the people in the triangle have a right to help defend against that offensive player. You must remember the offensive team's best players (quarterback and star) are being man-to-man; therefore, the offensive team's 3, 4, and 5 players are playing against the triangle. Thus the triangle can afford to help out on the other team's two best players. It is imperative to stress that you must be beaten over the top of the triangle.

In using this crazy defense, it is best not to change to something else until you are scored on. If the offensive team has beaten this crazy defense continually, go to another defense. As a matter of fact, it is a good rule not to use the crazy defense the entire game. In more cases than not, you must be able to cheat to the great player. If at all possible, an effort should be made to camouflage the crazy defenses.

In preparing for each game, we normally prepare three types of defense: a man-to-man, some type of zone, and a crazy defense. In doing this, we are better able to adjust to what is taking place on the floor during the game. We don't like to be placed in a situation that can cost us some points and maybe the game just because we failed to do our homework.

DEFENDING THE STAR

Bob Knight

We would not do anything in regard to defending an outstanding player that we would not normally do in our defense. I've never used a box-and-one or diamond-and-one or any combination of defenses. We've always stuck with one defense with certain rules. The difference in our defense from game to game or year to year is based on where we pick up on the court. I don't believe in the press. I think you can press average or poor teams, but not the good ones.

The first thing I want to know about another team is whether or not there are any players on that team that we don't have to defend. I don't think many teams have four perimeter players that you have to guard. This can help you in guarding an exceptional player. I also want to know how we want to match up in the game. Are there switches that we can make? We switch a lot both on and off the ball. If we have two guards of equal defensive ability and they are playing against a two-guard offense, we will switch every cross. If the other team has two offensive players of the same ability, we will switch that. Movement away from the ball is easier to switch, if at all possible to do so. One of the things we might tell our player who is guarding an exceptional player is that he is not to switch or help out. He is only to be concerned with the guy he is playing. I think that to stop an offense, you must go to the heart of that offense. If it is a particular move, a screen, the break, whatever it is that they like to do and rely on, you have to work in your plans on taking that completely or as much as possible away from them. The same goes for an outstanding scorer. We tell our defensive man that he is to work only on his man, and that the rest of the team should expect no help from him.

If you're defending a good scoring guard, you want him to put the ball on the floor as much as possible. The first time down the floor, we will run somebody

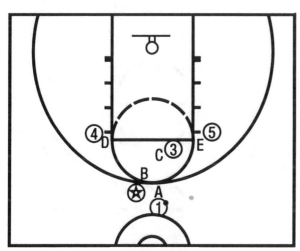

Figure 22.2

right at him and try to trap him. The second time down the floor, we'll run somebody else at him. So the first two times we're going to run a trap on a good scoring guard. We do this so he is aware that someone else is after him. We may not do it again or we might let 10 minutes go and we'll trap him again. This is to keep him off balance with the thought that he might get trapped.

If we're playing against a good scoring guard and there is a player on his team that we don't have to guard, we'll take that defender and put him at the top of the key. Now he's in a good help position and trapping position on the floor. We would essentially do the same thing with a forward. We tell our players to try to get an outstanding forward to back-cut. This moves him into congestion and we're putting him in a position where we have people to help out. The second thing we would do with a good scoring forward is to take the ball right at him. We want to direct the ball to him. We feel this is better than having our defenders getting caught in the picks set for him as he comes to the ball. We would like both the good scoring guard or forward to have the ball when we defend them rather than be without the ball. Depending on how quick our defensive player is to the guard he is guarding, that tells us where we pick up on the floor. If he's very quick or quicker, we pick up out front; a little slower, then we fall back. If the guard is really quick, we'll have our second best defensive player guard him with the idea that once he gets beat, out front, our best defensive player will be there to pick him up. The second best defensive player then falls back to guard the best defensive player's man. Another way to slow up a good scoring guard is to make him play defense inside.

When we're playing a good scoring center, we tell our team that it is not our defensive man's job to stop the center. It's the responsibility of our perimeter people to stop the ball from going inside.

One of the drills we use for this is to take the low post and allow him to move up only to the dotted line (see Figure 22.3). Next, we put three perimeter people with him (Numbers 1, 2, and 3) and defensive players on them. The ball is brought into play, and Number 5 can move anywhere up to the dotted line in the low post area in the lane. The perimeter players 1, 2, and 3 must get within 15 feet of him and make a bounce pass to him. The post has no defense on him, and the three defensive men must work extremely hard to keep the ball from going inside. They must work hard to help him out as they can trap outside, and they must keep good pressure on the ball. We try to defend against a good scoring center by putting good pressure on the perimeter.

Another drill to keep the ball out of the post is to put three perimeter men with no defense, and then put a defense on the post (see Figure 22.4). They move the ball around, every third pass must go into the post, and it is up to the defensive man to keep the ball out of there. The burden to keep the ball out of

the post is on him now. So, if we can get a combination of good perimeter pressure and good inside pressure, we can stop a high-scoring center. I honestly don't think a center should beat you.

If we have two really good defensive players, we'll alternate them on a good scoring guard or forward. I would rather have a quicker player than a strong player guard a good scoring perimeter man. It's tougher for good scoring perimeter players to score if they have to set up every time. In a free-wheeling, fast-paced game, they're going to score against you. On defense we try to force the ball to the baseline. When we're thinking about how to defend a good scoring forward, our first thoughts must be directed to how we're going to defend the ball at the top of the key. The way we force the ball determines how we play defense on the high-scoring forward.

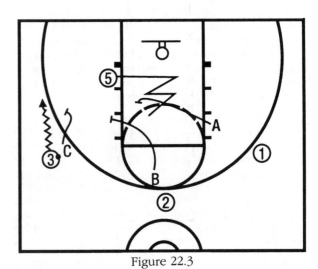

Figure 22.3

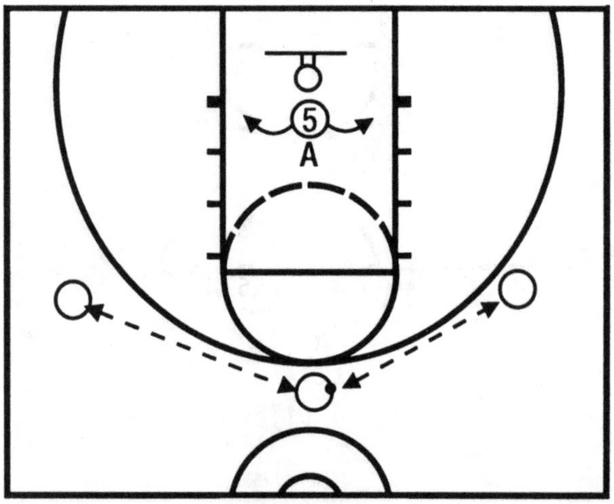

Figure 22.4

To guard a high-scoring high post, the first thing we do is to try to take away his movement to the basket or his movement to the low post area. We are not going to try to take the ball away from him. I don't think you can take everything away from a good post. If we can keep him out of the low post area, we have taken away one source of scoring from him – the boards. We play behind the high post, and we don't want to give him the angle to the basket by playing at his side. On the other hand, if the other team uses the high post as a passer in their offense, he's got to be fronted.

One of the keys to playing a good center is to find out who it is that we don't have to guard. This person then can drop to help front the post.

When a team uses a double low, with one non-scoring center screening for the scoring center, it must have its two best defensive players down there (see Figure 22.5). When the screen is set, the defender on the screener (B) plays high and about three feet off of him. The defender on the high-scoring center (A) plays low. If the center goes low, then the same defender picks him up, and if he goes high the other defender picks him up. Meanwhile, the low defender must react quickly to get back in front of the screener so he can't roll back to the ball. As soon as the ball is thrown into the post, the defensive man is to step back from him. The defender who was guarding the man who threw the pass must jump to the ball to put added pressure on the post. With off-ball help, it makes it extremely difficult for the post to turn and make a move. We would like him to put the ball on the floor.

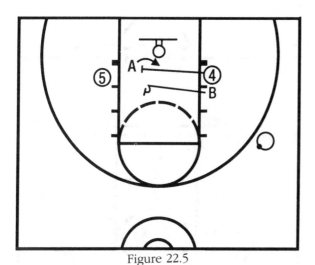

Figure 22.5

OUT-OF-BOUNDS DEFENSE
Kevin Sivils

Many coaches believe in the philosophy of keeping things as simple as possible, and for this reason play man-to-man defense exclusively. Their reasoning is that by teaching only one defense they will be able to do a better job of coaching and the players will be able to play better defense. Yet often these same coaches play zone defense against an inbounds play underneath the goal, hoping to prevent the easy score. Often the end result is an easy basket for the opponent, the very thing they were hoping to avoid.

I used to be guilty of doing the very same thing. While my teams would not give up the easy basket on the inbounds play, their ability to play zone defense was so poor that the opponent easily scored from his half-court zone offense. Switching from zone back to man-to-man assignments after the inbounds pass did not prove to be satisfactory either. For these reasons, I felt it was necessary to be able to defend inbounds situations with man-to-man defense.

After looking over old scouting reports and watching game films, I was able to identify three common alignments and some common patterns for inbounds plays. From these identifiable situations, general guidelines were developed for defending inbounds situations. In preparing for game inbounds situations, three areas of preparation are covered: the mental approach, the skill approach, and the scouting report.

The three most common inbounds formations were the box (Figure 22.6), stack (Figure 22.7), and the wall (Figure 22.8). Starting with the mental defensive approach, six steps were identified. The first step for players was to identify the formation to be defended. Second, the players then are to anticipate what we would want to do in that situation and be ready to take away any advantage. Third, we want our players to be assertive and assume positions in locations which place the offense at a potential disadvantage. Fourth, once these positions have been assumed, they are not to be relinquished. Our players are taught to believe that by playing as assertively against an inbounds situation as we do against regular half-court offense, we have an excellent opportunity to force a turnover. After all, the opponent has only five seconds to achieve its objective, inbounding the ball, and we have to deny for only five seconds. Our fifth concept involves using the court to our advantage. The inbounds defender should take away the help-side baseline pass (Figure 22.9). This effectively reduces the amount of floor we have to cover by one third because the backboard prevents passes to the shaded area of the court as shown in Figure 22.9. Our last concept covers play once the offense is in motion.

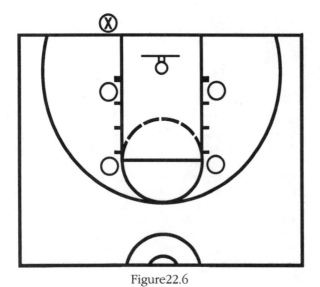

Figure22.6

Players must block everything out of their minds except preventing cutters from getting open and slipping any potential screens. The defender guarding the passer must concentrate particularly on slipping screens since many teams like to utilize a good shooter to inbounds the ball and then screen for him.

When covering the physical aspects, we stress basic positioning. The defender guarding the passer must pressure the ball yet take away the help-side baseline pass, forcing the pass to the ball-side corner. Defenders must play toward the ball on the ball and help side. We utilize on-the-line and up-the-line positioning for denying the pass for three reasons: 1) it is our normal one pass away position, 2) we want to encourage the lob pass as it can be picked off, and 3) this position makes it difficult for the offense to set screens due to the space between the defender and the offensive player. We feel we are able to do this because our players are drilled to close out on their man and to

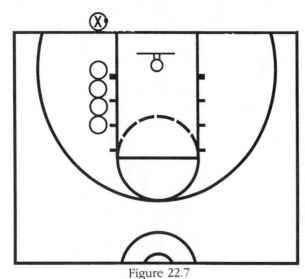

Figure 22.7

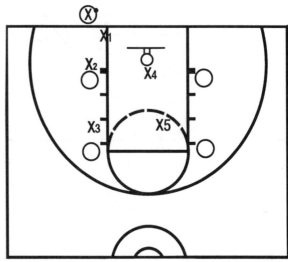

Figure 22.9

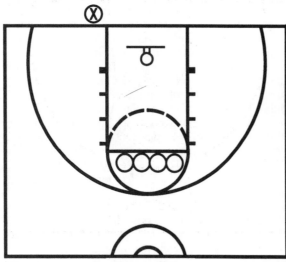

Figure 22.8

Figure 22.10

arrive there at the same time as the ball.

Figure 22.10 shows our basic positioning against the box. The help-side defenders, X4 and X5, are sagging to jam the lane and protect the basket. They are able to do so because of the backboard preventing the lob pass to the help side. X2, who is guarding the offensive player to the ball, face guards him and tries to get a five-second count. X3 plays toward the ball and is ready to slip a screen or front a cutter. X1, the inbounds pass defender, takes away the help-side baseline and tries to influence the pass to the corner.

Figure 22.11 shows our basic positioning for the stack. Because the stack usually tries to split the defense and move a player in for the easy layup, we like to insert a defender (X4) into the stack in front of the cutter. X2 and X3 play body-to-body and face guard the front two offensive players. Most stacks break the first player to the corner of the lane and the second player to the opposite spot. X2 and X3 take the player who cuts to their side and deny hard. X3 must be careful that he lines up outside the stack. This is essential or the stack can simply form a wall if all the defenders are on the lane side. This allows a shooter to step out for a short jump shot as shown in Figure 22.12. X5 plays in the lane to congest things and is responsible for closing out the lob pass to the deep outlet man.

Figure 22.13 shows our coverage for the wall. X2, X3, and X4 play on-the-line and up-the-line with their hands raised and deny or face guard their man, watching their eyes for any hint of what is about to occur. X5 slips into the wall. This prevents a shooter from stepping back behind the wall to shoot. By placing the other three defenders toward the ball, it is difficult for the offense to cut to any opening to receive a pass.

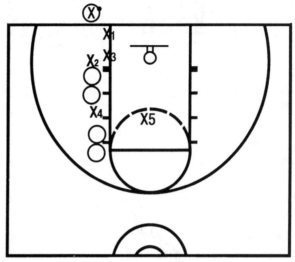

Figure 22.11

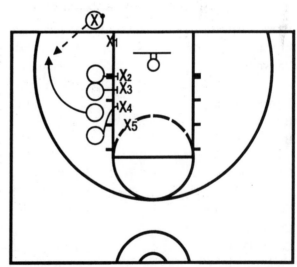

Figure 22.12

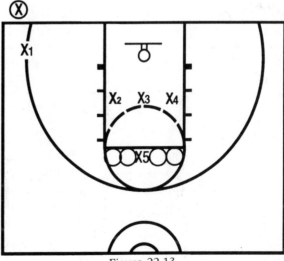

Figure 22.13

BIBLIOGRAPHY OF ARTICLES

Note: All articles originally appeared in the *NABC Basketball Bulletin* in the issues indicated unless otherwise stated.

NAME	ARTICLE	ISSUE
Allen, Forrest C.	Watchdog of the Basket	*Seal-O-San Coaches Digest*
Allen, Sonny	Sonny Allen Fast Break	Spring 78
Barrise, Tom and Mike Gentry	Strength and Conditioning	Spring 85
Bee, Clair	Teaching	1942
Beecroft, John	Off-Season Ballhandling	Winter 71
Brandenburg, Jim	Defensive Rebounding	Summer 83
	Zone Attack	Summer 87
Brennan, Steve	Progressive Footwork Drills	Winter 82
Brock, Charles	Flexibility	Spring 84
Broeg, Bob	The Basketball Man	*Saturday Evening Post*, April 1989
Brown, Dale	Motivating Your Players	Summer 80
	Freak Defense	Winter 84
Brown, Hubie	Special Situations	Spring 84
Brown, Larry	Half-Court Defense	Winter 84
Bunn, John	A Coaching Philosophy	*The Basketball Coach's Guide to Success,* Prentice-Hall, 1961
Cardinal, Bradley	Endurance	not published
Carlson, H.C.	The Bulletin's Beginnings	May 33
Carnesecca, Lou	Attacking Pressure Defenses	Fall 74
Casciano, Jim	Finding Additional Practice Time	Winter 79
Casey, Don	3-2 Defense Zone Slides	Fall 79
Cremins, Bobby	Offensive Philosophy	Winter 89
Crum, Denny	Zone Presses	Winter 89
Daly, Chuck	Organization of Practice and Season	March 75
Dean, Everett	What I'd Do Differently, the Second Time Around	Summer 79
Drake, Bruce	Compactness in Basketball	Jan. 49
Eddy, Don	Playing the Point Guard Position	Winter 83
Edwards, George	Coaches' Code	May 33
Farrar, Dave	Creating an Attitude	Fall 89
Fisher, Steve	Defensive Philosophy: Team and Individual Concepts	Fall 90
Foster, Bill	Flexing the Zone Defense	Sept. 74
	Defensive Transition Drills	Summer 76
Frank, Don	Shooting Drills	Fall 88
Gaines, Clarence	Combination Match-Up Defense	Fall 83
Green, Bill	Match-up Zone Defense	Summer 86
Halberg, Bob et al	Role of the High School Coach in Recruiting	Spring 83

Hall, Joe B.	Big-Man Drills	Winter 79
	Kentucky 1-3-1 Zone Trap	Winter 77
Harshman, Marv	Zone Defenses	Summer 78
	The 2-3: An Antidote for Pressure Defenses	Winter 76
Hartman, Jack	How to Attack Zones	Winter 82
Haskins, Don	UTEP's Man-to-Man Defense	Winter 78
Healy, Jerry	Basketball History	Fall 89
Heathcote, Jud	Zone Attacks	Fall 78
Hickey, E.S.	The History of the NABC Bulletin	Sept. 52
Hickox, Ed	The National Association of Basketball Coaches (NABC)	Sept. 52
Holman, Nat	Common Coaching Mistakes	*Holman on Basketball*, Prentice-Hall, 1941
Howell, Bailey	Offensive Rebounding	June 75
Ireland, George	Agile-Mobile-Hostile	Jan. 64
Jones, Bill	Triangle and Two Defense	Spring 87
Julian, Alvin	The 26 Magic Numbers	*Bread and Butter Basketball*, Prentice-Hall 1961
Kelly, Yvan	Evaluating a College Program	Spring 86
Kimble, John	"55 Second" Offense	Spring 89
Knight, Bob	Formulating a Game Plan	Fall 78
	Conversion/Transition	Spring 80
	Defending the Star	Summer 80
	The Screening Game	Summer 76
Krause, Jerry	Coach-Conditioning	Original Article
	Teaching-Learning Principles	not published
Krause, Jerry and Jim Conn	Chin-It	Summer 76
Krause, Jerry and Dan Hays	Score on the Throw	Winter 87
Krause, Jerry and George Sage	National Association of Basketball Coaches Code of Ethics	Fall 90
Krause, Jerry and Jim Wasem	The Sue Syndrome	Original Article
Krzyzewski, Mike	Concern for Players	Original Article
Kunstadt, Mike	Fundamentals is the Name	Summer 79
Larrabee, Harry	Flow Transition	Spring 84
Leatherman, Bill	The Rebound Game	Fall 85
Majerus, Rick	Tips on Scouting	Spring 85
Marshall, Greg	Small College Recruiting	Winter 85
Massimino, Rollie	The Running Game	Fall 77
McCracken, Branch	Passing-Catching	*Indiana Basketball*, Prentice-Hall, 1955
McGuire, Al	Thoughts on Coaching	Fall 76
McGuire, Frank	Offenses Against Full-Court Zone Press	Dec. 74
McLendon, John Jr.	Scouting	June 74
Meyer, Don	Bison Basketball Defense	Winter 80
	Playing Hard Through Team Attitude	Summer 87
Meyer, Ray	DePaul's Offensive Plan	Spring 80